PENGUIN AFRICAN LIBRARY AP 2

Edited by Ronald Segal

The Politics of Partnership

PATRICK KEATLEY

PATRICK KEATLEY

The Politics of Partnership

WITH THREE MAPS

Penguin Books
Baltimore · Maryland

Penguin Books Ltd, Harmondsworth, Middlesex
U.S.A.: Penguin Books Inc., 3300 Clipper Mill Road, Baltimore 11, Md
AUSTRALIA: Penguin Books Pty Ltd, 762 Whitehorse Road,
Mitcham, Victoria

First published 1963

Copyright © Patrick Keatley, 1963

Made and printed in Great Britain
by Cox and Wyman Ltd
London, Reading, and Fakenham
Set in Monotype Plantin

To EVE, MARK, *and* CHARLOTTE, *who helped*

Contents

N 106

Part 1: The Last Great Chance

'Those who have been once intoxicated with power,
even though but for one year, can never willingly abandon it.'
EDMUND BURKE

The Last Great Chance

The dilemma facing Britain in Central Africa is the one that has confronted mankind since Cain and Abel: how are we, as brothers, to live together? It is a dilemma that becomes infinitely more exasperating and more acute when one brother is black and the other one white. Why this should be so is a question for the psychiatrist; for the student of politics it is simply a basic and, however unpleasant, inescapable fact.

Four of the leading political figures involved in the Central African form of the dilemma have given us signposts that may have practical value in pointing a way to a solution. They are Mr Harold Macmillan, Sir Roy Welensky, Mr Reginald Maudling, and Mr Joshua Nkomo.

Mr Macmillan made his contribution when, as British Prime Minister, he had to defend the policies of his Conservative government in the House of Commons, immediately after the departure of South Africa from the Commonwealth in the spring of 1961. There were angry backbenchers on his own side of the House who regarded the loss of South Africa as a failure of the Tory high command. And there were many among the Labour Opposition who believed that the Prime Minister had, for too long, been far too tolerant of the racial policies of the Nationalist régime in Pretoria. Mr Macmillan defended himself, but he was determined to do more than that. He invited the House to move forward from a merely negative scrutiny of events now past, and take instead a positive attitude towards a problem that still lay in the future. In working out a formula for the Federation of Rhodesia and Nyasaland, he said, 'we have our last great chance in Africa'.

9

In coldly tactical terms, perhaps, one could say that Mr Macmillan was merely issuing a shrewd appeal for party unity. But in broader, historic terms his instinct was undoubtedly sound. After the calamity of South Africa, and the disastrous civil war in Algeria, the slender opportunity still remaining in British Central Africa is, indeed, the last great chance for white colonialism to rectify in the twentieth century its errors of the nineteenth. And for this task, Mr Macmillan was keenly aware, any British Prime Minister will need all the party and parliamentary unity he can muster.

He needs it all the more because at the other end of the power axis, in the Rhodesian capital of Salisbury, he is confronted by an administration of men solidly united in their determination bitterly to resist any attempt by the British government to resolve the Rhodesian problem on lines adopted in Ghana, Kenya, Tanganyika, or other parts of Africa. It is usual to call these men 'white settlers', although the term is not strictly accurate.

Take Mr Macmillan's great antagonist, for example. Sir Roy Welensky, the Rhodesian Federal Prime Minister, is the son of an immigrant Lithuanian father and a mother descended from a long line of Afrikaner forebears. He himself was born in Salisbury and knows no other home. This must have been very much in his mind when, a few months after the spring speech of Mr Macmillan, he called a special session of the Federal Assembly to consider the near-impasse in negotiations between the British and Rhodesian governments.

Sir Roy referred to the wave of violence in Northern Rhodesia, which was being contained by the security forces – including federal troops. In particular he wanted to deal with the kind of remark, increasingly made by Africans and their sympathizers during the early 1960s, that if action along such lines were to continue, the time must inevitably come when all the Europeans would be thrown out of the country. The Federal Prime Minister underlined the point with great emphasis, because he wanted to give his specific reply to it.

'There is nowhere for me to run to,' he said. 'I am as much an

African as any black African who sits in this Assembly. That is why I am anxious to produce a state of affairs in which people of all races can live side by side.'

But during that same special session of the Rhodesian parliament, Sir Roy Welensky used words which revealed another aspect of this determination to hold on to power; and revealed also the depth of the political gulf which had opened between London and Salisbury. He was referring to the moves by Britain's Colonial Office to revise the constitution of Northern Rhodesia – a revision intended to advance the political status of the Africans in that territory. He said:

One cannot predict whether changes will in fact be made, or to whose advantage they will be, though I am bound in the circumstances to be full of suspicion. I feel bound, however, to give a warning to the British Government that the patience of those who have borne the heat and burden of supporting the Federation, which the British parliament created by its own act, is not inexhaustible. If that is their conclusion [a reference to the predominately white electors of Southern Rhodesia], who can tell whether they may not feel that there is something to be said in favour of forcible resistance to changes which in their opinion might wreck everything we stand for.

This speech was as clear a hint as any British government might require that, if pressed too hard, the white settlers of Rhodesia are prepared to resort to force themselves in order to hold what they have. It was not the first time that the Federal Prime Minister had hinted how, in the last resort, the settlers were prepared to consider a declaration of independence. Although such a declaration would involve problems of military security and economic viability, it would have the merit of freeing the European citizens of the Federation at one stroke from the hated interference of Whitehall.

Sir Roy concluded this same speech on a note of defiance: 'I have lost confidence in my dealings with the British government.'

These were angry words indeed, but there was still no disposition in Whitehall to engage in a public argument. The new Colonial Secretary, who had just succeeded Mr Iain Macleod, was another of the post-war batch of young Tories of liberal outlook, Mr Reginald Maudling. Not long after Sir Roy's outburst, he faced his first full-scale African debate in the British House of Commons. And in reviewing the dilemma in Rhodesia, Mr Maudling described the clash of interests there as 'a conflict between two rights'.

The Africans, as the majority inhabitants of the country, outnumbering its white citizens 26 to 1, feel the time has come for majority rule in Rhodesia, just as it has come already in Nigeria, Tanganyika, and elsewhere. The settlers, who first held the territory by right of conquest, have since come to feel that all the trappings of a civilized state which it now possesses are the work of their hands. Echoing Cecil Rhodes they say, 'Equal rights for civilized men.' They do not say who is to judge when an African is sufficiently civilized to qualify for the vote. They do not need to; and the politically conscious Africans have their own cynical, embittered reply.

The man who emerged, in the late 1950s, as leader of Southern Rhodesia's Africans, was Mr Joshua Nkomo. As one of the founders, and later the President-General of the National Democratic Party, he began the process of airborne commuting to London so well-known to many an African nationalist leader before him.

It was on one of these journeys, when he was invited to address a public meeting in the Royal Albert Hall, that Mr Nkomo produced the phrase that summed up with a bitter irony the difference between the campaign for independence conducted by Dr Nkrumah, Dr Azikwe, and Julius Nyerere on the one hand, and that which was now confronting him.

'My African brothers were lucky,' he said. 'They had the tsetse fly and we did not.'

Like most generalizations, this is not strictly true. The white pioneers entering Mashonaland and Matabeleland, as Rhodesia was known in Victorian times, soon found that there was a tsetse belt at lower altitudes, where ranching and dairying would be impracticable. There was malaria too, which is still not altogether eradicated. Indeed, Lord Malvern, the man who was later to become the first Federal Prime Minister, when he was plain Dr

Huggins, newly out from England, did largely unrewarded medical work in the tribal areas where malaria was rampant.

But in general the significant character of Rhodesia, as the first settlers discovered, was that in contrast to the rest of the continent (with the exception of the Mediterranean seaboard and South Africa) this was a territory ideally suited to white settlement, agriculture, and industry.

In coming to grips with the dilemma of Central Africa, it may help to list the factors that have combined to bring about independence and full nationhood in other parts of the continent. For this, surely, is the pragmatic basis that will determine the course of events in the Federation.

Starting with the Sudan in 1956, the roll-call of emancipation in post-war Africa is astonishingly long and varied: Morocco, Tunisia, Ghana, Guinea, and all the states in what was formerly French Africa, Somalia, Nigeria, Sierra Leone. . . . Is there any general rule to be discerned in this political revolution that might serve as a guide for the problems of Rhodesia ? In fact there are five factors to consider, five forces which may bring such pressure upon a metropolitan colonial power as to persuade it to relinquish control. They may be characterized as the geographical factor, the economic, the internal political situation in the dependent territory, political pressures in the mother country, and, finally, international political demands.

Some, or all, of these factors have been at work in each of the countries I have listed above, to bring about a sense of nationhood and to force the metropolitan powers into granting independence. But in the Rhodesian Federation, not one of these factors has yet acquired sufficient force to bring about the transfer of power.

In the old Gold Coast colony, for instance, now Ghana, we have a classic case of the geographical factor at work in favour of African independence. Long before Dr J. B. Danquah and his associates in the Gold Coast Convention invited an unknown young man named Kwame Nkrumah to come home from London and help them organize the campaign for independence, the British government had implicitly recognized that their goal would be achieved. West Africa was 'the white man's grave' and, although much had been done to improve public hygiene and encourage modern methods of medical treatment, there were no illusions in Whitehall about the possibilities of permanent white settlement. Indeed, even before the transfer of power in 1957, the British had agreed under African pressure during the closing stages of the colonial régime to give official political recognition to this fact, and the immigration of Europeans for the purpose of permanent settlement was so rigidly restricted as to be for all practical purposes forbidden. Contrast this with the active immigration drive in Rhodesia during the post-war period where, with the encouragement of the British government as well as the federal authorities in Salisbury, immigrants from Britain have been arriving at a rate of between 5,000 and 7,000 a year, with as many again from South Africa.

The experience of the African nationalist leaders has been that (as in Algeria and Kenya) where the geographical factor favours European settlement, there the most intractable and long-drawn-out campaign for national sovereignty takes place. In South Africa, where there is the most favourable climate of all, the problem is rendered doubly complex because the 'colonial power' is not inhabiting some far-off motherland but has, indeed, given up its motherland altogether and taken up residence in the colony. There are millions of white South Africans who have 'no other home', and it must be remembered that this argument applies with equal force to many Rhodesians as well. There are families prominent in public life, like the Moffats and the Tredgolds, tracing their heritage as Southern Rhodesians back for three and four generations. The two families I have named have, in fact, a reputation for notably liberal views towards African emancipation, but they must be accounted the exception rather than the rule among the white electorate of their territory.

It may be argued that the geographical factor is, in some instances, not decisive. Most of Angola, Moçambique, and Portuguese Guinea are unsuited to permanent white settlement. But there other factors cancel this one out. With only rudimentary political organization in these territories, the African nationalists are only starting to use internal political pressure as a lever in their cause. The policy of the motherland is to regard these territories as integral provinces of Portugal, and there have been no domestic pressures in Lisbon for a liberal colonial policy comparable to those which existed in London and Paris during the post-war era. Finally, the international pressures which have so signally aided African nationalists in territories now independent, have hardly operated on Portuguese Africa till recently. The trust status of Tanganyika under the United Nations, with the obligation upon Britain to admit inspection teams and make annual reports, undoubtedly helped in accelerating progress to national sovereignty. So too did the trust status of Italian Somalia, and, when this territory became sovereign in 1960, it was able to sweep British Somaliland into orbit with it as well, to make up the new republic of Somalia.

The economic factor is hard to assess. African nationalists, with some justification, take the cynical view that, when there is a great deal of readily accessible wealth at stake, the metropolitan power will be reluctant to go. Hence, they will say, Britain makes little fuss about relinquishing its hold on relatively poor, basically agricultural economies like those of Uganda and Tanganyika, but will hold on like a bulldog to the wealth of Northern Rhodesia's copperbelt. France, equally, showed an obsession with retaining political control over the oil resources of Algeria.

Recent history, however, shows that Britain handed over power to Africans in Ghana, with all the territory's gold mines and sixty per cent of the world's output of cocoa. And, in Nigeria, a substantial new oilfield was just being brought into production with British engineering and British capital, when negotiations opened that were to lead to independence. Indeed, in terms of cold cash, the British had everything to gain by holding on to Ghana, if necessary by military force. Upon gaining political power in 1957, Dr Nkrumah and his government in Accra came into possession of gold and dollar reserves worth £240 million, the accumulation of several years of good cocoa crops at high prices. These reserves were banked in London and formed part of the backing for the pound sterling; in four years, the Ghanaian government used up two-thirds of the sum in ambitious projects that followed independence.

The economic factor therefore tends, sometimes, to work the other way in relation to African aspirations for sovereignty. Britain has hesitated to surrender power in Gambia largely because it seems impractical to conceive of nationhood yet for a tiny community of less than a third of a million people, whose budget is chronically in deficit and has to be made up by annual hand-outs from Whitehall.

Now, applying the five factors above to Rhodesia, it becomes apparent that the African nationalists there have so far failed to make very effective use of any of them as a lever for independence.

They are handicapped by their geographical factor which, as with Algeria and South Africa, has produced an indigenous white population substantial enough to resist any suggestion of African political advance with bitterness and determination. Economically, the African politicians of the Federation are just becoming aware of the very powerful pressure-group which operates in London and Salisbury to maintain the *status quo*. This may be termed the Rhodesia Lobby which, with the Katanga Lobby, is discussed in a later chapter. In terms of internal domestic pressures, the Africans of the two Rhodesias are only just beginning to learn how to organize a political machine, although Dr Hastings Banda and his colleagues in Nyasaland have made impressive headway in this direction. Finally, in seeking to marshal political pressures in their favour within Britain itself and on the international stage, the African nationalists of the Federation have succeeded in making themselves known and in winning many – some of them influential – friends, but they have been unable so far to direct this goodwill into practical forms of effective pressure on the levers of political power.

There is therefore a very real danger that if Joshua Nkomo, Kenneth Kaunda, and the other leaders of African political opinion in the Federation cannot find a way to make any one of these five vital factors effective, then they (or their successors) will be forced into the only remaining course of action. Algeria is the classic example, but the traveller in the Central African Federation today may be struck – if he talks to Africans, as so many of the local white politicians do not – by the reiterated references to Cyprus. There is a parallel of a kind, although the Africans perhaps overlook the fact that the armed forces on patrol in Rhodesia are not, as they were in Cyprus, men from a far-off motherland, with no intrinsic attachment to the country where they serve.

And here we come to a unique and complicating element in the Rhodesian dilemma. Only in Rhodesia, among all her colonial dependencies, has Britain allowed a group of colonists to form their own fighting forces. True, there have always been regiments in various African territories which, in two world wars, were pressed into service as far afield as Malaya and Indonesia. But these were regiments recruited and paid from treasuries under the ultimate control of Whitehall and the Colonial Office. None of them – not even in Kenya, despite the special 'White Highlands' – was an all-white regiment, raised and paid for by the colonists through their local government. It is a curious indictment of the fuzzy thinking in Whitehall during the last seven years, when the elements of power were skilfully being gathered up by the ambitious politicians in Salisbury, that even the French – for all their faults of muddled motives – should never have surrendered the lever of military power to the *colons* of Algeria.

It was because this vital power had not been surrendered to the settlers of Kenya that the British Colonial Secretary, Iain Macleod, was able, when it came to 'the crunch', to bang down his terms on the table at Lancaster House in 1960 and demand their acceptance by all the delegates, white, brown, and black. This is not to say that Mr Macleod ignored the arguments of the white settlers or their legitimate claims. But it prevented them from being both advocate and judge of their own cause.

It is often said, and with great truth, that there is a world of difference between the way of life in South Africa and that in Rhodesia. I myself recall the remark of my seat companion in an airliner on the run from Johannesburg to Salisbury, as we crossed the frontier at the Limpopo. 'Ah, that's a relief,' he said as we looked down upon the brown coil of the river twisting away into the distance through the green and khaki savannah. As we began the long descent to the airport, he relaxed visibly and talked far more volubly; he was, in fact, a staunch supporter of Sir Roy Welensky's conservative government. And though not much persuaded of the ability of the present generation of Africans in his own country to direct the affairs of commerce and government, he talked approvingly of 'partnership' – rather as a goal than as present policy – and at the same time made clear his personal distaste for the racially charged atmosphere of Johannesburg.

And yet, in the crudest political terms of naked military power, the blunt fact is that this civilized, urbane, and probably kindly man who sat next to me – and the many thousands of his white compatriots in the Federation – are basically closer to the Nationalists of South Africa than to any other community in Africa or indeed the world. Like the South Africans, the white Rhodesians have supreme military power within their own borders and would be answerable to no other power on earth – if it came to a show-down. This is the vital difference between Rhodesia today and all the other territories in Africa where at some time Britain has had colonial responsibilities. In those other territories, the Colonial Office was confronted by white settlers; in Rhodesia, it is confronted by white men with guns. In Kenya the settlers may have had their political machine, but it was Britain who had the army. In British Central Africa today, Whitehall has partial administrative control. The settlers have their own highly effective political machine, and they have something else as well – their own small but highly effective army and air force.

It is rare for Sir Roy Welensky or any other Rhodesian political leader to make public reference to this vital military factor, but it remains there all the same as the most powerful weapon in their political armoury. And it is always there, like another presence, when they – rather than the British colonial administrators who would be solely concerned in other dependencies – take policy decisions on the constitutional emancipation of the African. In other words, in the last resort the white Rhodesians have got the guns and they know it. They showed this during the riots of July 1960 and July 1961 in the African townships; they show it – perhaps subconsciously – by observing as their national holiday Occupation Day, belatedly renamed Pioneer Day, which simply celebrates the military defeat of the African by the white man. To the outside observer it seems an attitude incompatible with a professed policy of partnership; to the Africans, especially to the new generation of educated and politically conscious Africans, it seems like a calculated racial insult.

If Algeria is the failure of assimilation and South Africa the failure of separation, Rhodesia might be described as the failure of partnership. But this would be to indict the wrong people; the Rhodesian settlers are, after all, only behaving as one might expect any group in their position naturally to behave – given the guns. The Rhodesian Federation is, in fact, a major failure of British colonial policy, in which the chain of responsibility is clear.

It is a chain which goes directly back to the third Marquess of Salisbury, who was not only Prime Minister of Great Britain for most of the period from 1885 to 1900, but was his own Foreign Secretary as well. As such he shaped and directed Britain's Africa policy; it was he who took the decision to award the charter to Cecil Rhodes and the British South Africa Company, granting it supreme authority over much of what is Rhodesia today.

The chain of responsibility descends through successive British cabinets from Lord Salisbury to the present day. That may sound dull and wordy, the sort of 'constitutional stuff' that can miraculously empty the debating chamber of the British House of Commons and fill the Members' tea-room when complex issues involving far-off African territories come up for attention. But so was Cyprus dull and wordy, in all the inter-war and post-war years, when the Cypriots travelled hopefully to London in little delegations, holding Press conferences, submitting documents and seeking interviews with M.P.s. In 1954 they gave up

19

their delegations, their documents, their interviews, and took up guns. That is the danger in British Central Africa today.

It is a danger that used to be dismissed as wholly unrealistic a year or two ago, which is in itself extraordinary enough, seeing that it required battalions of British soldiers and a total military outlay of £70 million to deal with the Mau-Mau rebellion in Kenya.

What Rhodesia's white political leaders seem unable to appreciate is that they are not sealed off from the rest of the world. Pressures are building up all around them which should make it obvious to the myopic men of Salisbury that little time is left to white dominion. The frontiers of African nationalism have moved southward by giant strides since the present Federation was established in 1953. Today they are the frontiers of Rhodesia itself – on the north, the Congo; on the west, Angola where the amateur troops of Holden Roberto began guerrilla warfare in 1961; and to the east, Tanganyika, now fully independent. To the Africans of the Federation these are not remote events; each of the three frontiers is straddled by tribes who speak the same languages. When Dr Banda was offered air time on Rhodesian federal radio transmitters during the 1961 general election in Nyasaland, he rejected it in favour of an offer from Mr Nyerere's broadcasting system, next door in Tanganyika.

This is what makes a statement by one of Tanganyika's Cabinet Ministers potentially significant, when he referred to the flag which was raised on independence day in December 1961 on the topmost peak of Kilimanjaro, the highest mountain in Africa. The flag-raising was carried out by torchlight, a few minutes after midnight. The minister said:

The people of Tanganyika are lighting a candle on top of Mount Kilimanjaro which will shine beyond our borders and give hope where there was despair.

The speaker was not, as it happens, some visionary sentimentalist but the Minister for Home Affairs, Mr Kahama, whose responsibilities include the police and internal security. In this connexion it is perhaps also worth noting the words of an Indian

Cabinet Minister, spoken in the same month as Tanganyika became independent. The occasion was a public speech a few days after India's annexation of the former Portuguese colony of Goa, an event described as an invasion in European newspapers but as liberation by the Press of the independent states in Africa. The speaker was the Indian Minister for Home Affairs, Mr Lal Bahadur Shastri.

The terrific speed with which Asian and now African countries are achieving independence is a remarkable phenomenon of this century. It is, however, surprising that some countries have not fully realized its significance and are still sitting tight in their present position. The urge for freedom is intense, and human emotions cannot easily be suppressed. The peoples of those countries must be made masters of their own destinies. The world can not remain divided for long into two parts – part slave and part free.

Morally right or morally wrong, the Indian annexation of Goa is a fact; it may well set off a series of reactions in colonial Africa. Partly as a result of Mr Nehru's resort to force in order to achieve a political solution, and partly as a reaction to the increasing use of military power as they have seen it applied in their own country by the Federal forces, starting with the emergencies of 1959, the Africans of the Federation have begun to acclimatize themselves to think in these new terms. The London *Economist*, reviewing the new constitution offered to Northern Rhodesia after the long haggling between Britain and Sir Roy Welensky's federal administration in 1961, said this in its main editorial of the week:

Africans will ask themselves why their economically more advanced territory is constitutionally behind Nyasaland, Kenya, Uganda and Tanganyika. In Northern Rhodesia the most that can now be hoped for is that the political struggle will stay non-violent.

The tide of events is producing a mood of desperation among responsible African political leaders in the Federation, particularly among those in Southern Rhodesia, where the new constitution granted in 1961 appeared to hold out to them the prospect of permanent political subjugation. It has prompted this statement from Leopold Takawira, one of the founders of the African nationalist movement in the territory:

The African, with the aid and sympathy of the Asians and a few Europeans, is seeking ways and means of saving himself from the Sandys–Whitehead conspiracy. Some of the means chosen will, to the onlooker, seem crude and queer. But who really should morally criticize the clumsy strokes of a drowning man? The hunted African has now reached a point where he cannot advance any farther. He is faced with the problem of either sitting down to meet his death or facing the enemy in trying to escape.

Strong words from a well-read, deeply religious schoolmaster, once a pillar of that earnestly inter-racial organization, the Capricorn Africa Society, and its general secretary in Salisbury. It is this new militancy in the front ranks of African nationalism that represents the greatest danger to the Central African Federation – so long as it is denied any outlet of legitimate political aspiration. It was Abraham Lincoln, speaking of a parallel problem in race relations also involving people of European and of African extraction, who said that a nation cannot survive which is half slave and half free. The tragedy of modern Rhodesia is that it is not one nation which is seeking to survive, but two. The masters hold supreme political, financial, and military power; the slaves outnumber them 26 to 1. The aim of this present study is to examine the origins of the impasse and its possible solution.

Part 2: The Colonial Era

'Have you ever thought how lucky you are to be born an Englishman when there were so many millions who were not?'
CECIL RHODES

1 A Little Local Imperialism

'Pax Britannica is essential for the maintenance of civilized conditions of existence among one fifth of the Human Race.'
LORD MILNER

Present-day Rhodesia is the child of crisis, or – more precisely – three great political crises. The nation was born in 1890 at the height of that Imperial tension between the European powers, chiefly Britain and Germany, which had begun with the Berlin Conference and the 'Scramble for Africa'. The next crisis came in 1952–3 when, despite the gravest warnings from members of the Opposition, from distinguished academic authorities and from angry, hostile African leaders, an obstinate Conservative government in London rammed legislation through the British House of Commons which established the Federation of Rhodesia and Nyasaland. The third and present crisis may be said to date from the African uprisings of 1959. It is a crisis which has produced the sorry spectacle of white men shooting black, after more than sixty years of peace.

More than a hundred of Rhodesia's African citizens have fallen before bullets. (The official figures and the claims of the African political parties do not agree; but it *is* agreed that in the four years since the present crisis began not one member of the white security forces, either soldier or police officer, has been killed.)

The politics of partnership, then, are marked by these three great events in the growth of the nation. And much as a child's character is determined both by heredity and environment, so it is true to say that Rhodesia today is very much a creature of these events. The crisis of 1953 and that of the present day may be ascribed to environment – the earlier crisis endowing the Africans with political consciousness, and the present one producing in them a sense of national cohesion. But heredity is just as vital as environment in shaping the Rhodesia we see today; perhaps rather more important. Indeed, to understand the present crisis in Central Africa, we must peel back the layers of history and take a hard look at Britain and South Africa in Victorian times.

In a very real sense modern Rhodesia is the creature of Lord Salisbury's late-Victorian England and of the old Cape Colony whose Prime Minister in 1890 was Cecil John Rhodes. Those were the parental influences which sent the Pioneer Column, as it was called, across the frontier of civilization at Kimberley and northward into the uncharted wilds of Mashonaland and Matabeleland, where Lobengula ruled. We shall return to take a closer look at the Pioneers, after tracing the events and pressures in Imperial diplomacy which led to the decision that a group of settlers could – indeed, *must* – strike north into the plateau land of Central Africa at that precise moment in history. It is enough for the moment to note five important points about the Pioneers:

1. MILITARY: This was a military expedition of 200 picked men (more than 2,000 had applied), advancing to occupy the new country by force if necessary.

2. OUTLOOK: These were tough, resourceful, and very confident men, who felt themselves to be the superiors of their nearest rivals, the Arab slave-traders and the German and Portuguese explorers. Clearly, they regarded the Africans themselves as Stone Age savages, with whom any measure of equality was merely laughable.

3. RACE: By design, and not by accident, the Pioneer Column was composed of South Africans as well as Britons. The political aim, as frankly outlined by Rhodes, demanded a substantial number of men from Natal and the Cape, so that if things went wrong and outside help were needed, the electorate of these two colonies would join in the clamour for Britain to intervene. Again, at Rhodes's specific direction, the South Africans were 'men of both the races', so that the Afrikaners of the Cape Colony would have a stake in the new nation from the start.

4. OBJECTIVE: The object was to create a new 'white Dominion' in the heart of Africa, in a territory whose climate, mineral re-

sources and potential agricultural development were known to favour white settlement. Each man set off from Kimberley for the march (of more than 400 miles) knowing that at the end of the trail there awaited him a considerable bounty, to be given him as of right – not less than fifteen gold claims and a farm of 3,000 acres. The wandering bands of Matabele and Mashona peoples he looked upon as his potential labour force.

5. RESPONSIBILITY: It is a vital, though now forgotten fact, that the whole expedition was not a venture of Britain as an Imperial Power, but essentially a private venture undertaken through South African initiative. Rhodes was the instigator, and the man who paid the bills.

This fifth point is undoubtedly the one that is most frequently overlooked by those who survey the present problems of Rhodesia from London (or Washington, or the U.N., for that matter). Yet it is implicit in everything that has happened in the territory from its founding day, and it is the factor that every British Colonial Secretary has come up against – hard – in his dealings with the settlers. It remains of paramount significance that, in the dispatch of an expedition at once military, economic, and political, the British Government abdicated its responsibility. The initiative for the Pioneer Column came from white men in southern Africa, and, what was more, from white men who had successfully twisted the lion's tail in the very timing and financing of the expedition. It is a precedent that has led to a special political state of mind among the men who rule the Central African Federation at this present critical time in African history. And this attitude, in turn, conditions and regulates every manoeuvre in which Britain is involved with the federal government of Sir Roy Welensky or the territorial government of Sir Edgar Whitehead. Independence is not just a catch-phrase among the settlers, or a potent threat trumpeted by the Federal Prime Minister from the battlements of his capital city of Salisbury. It is, in very large measure, a political condition which the settlers of Rhodesia have enjoyed from the start. In this, as in the possession of their own superb, well-organized military machine, they are unique among the colonial dependencies of Britain.

It was in this atmosphere that the British Secretary for Commonwealth Relations, Duncan Sandys, had to hammer out a new constitution for Southern Rhodesia at the Salisbury conference of 1961. What emerged was a document which granted Africans less than a quarter of the seats in a revised legislature, provided a built-in majority for the settlers, and – without guaranteeing any further concessions to the Africans – formally relinquished any lingering, vestigial rights of political guidance or interference in the affairs of the Crown Colony by Britain. It is difficult to exonerate Mr Sandys from the charge of political surrender, but an insight into the settler mentality explains, even if it cannot excuse.

'Responsibility' is one of the dullest words in the English language; in print the eye skips it, in a sermon or a political oration men close their ears to it. Yet it is a basic fact that responsibility, and the power by which it is exercised, are the very stuff of politics. There is much to criticize in the way that Sir Roy Welensky and the men of Salisbury are exercising power and responsibility in Central Africa today. There are many political observers, by no means unsympathetic to the very real achievements and qualities of the white settlers, who are nevertheless appalled by the actions of those who rule the Federation. To many of us it is apparent that the fuse has been touched off and is hissing noisily; the only question that remains is whether the wilfully deaf and myopic men of Salisbury can be made to act before the flame reaches the dynamite.

In order to understand Central Africa today, we must look at how life is at present organized there, for black as well as for white; examine the different jobs, homes, schools, land, incomes, and amenities. Most of all, we must examine the present political structure and consider how it evolved. And that, in turn, takes us back to power and responsibility. Today in the Federation Britain lacks power and is failing in her responsibilities. The tragedy of Central Africa is that the same lack and the same failure were operative when the new state of Rhodesia was born; these twin defects of character are part of its heredity, and have been influences in its environment ever since.

It was in the spring of 1889 that Cecil Rhodes arrived in London with his plans for the formation of a chartered company that should strike northward into Zambesia, plant the Union Jack, secure the riches of what he called 'the New Rand', and form the second link in a chain of territories under British control that would stretch from the Cape Colony to Egypt. Rhodes was a millionaire whose fame had travelled in advance of him; he had wealthy friends in the City of London and titled ones near the seat of power at Westminster. For it was from the House of Lords that Britain and her Empire were ruled; the Prime Minister was the third Marquess of Salisbury, a formidable autocrat who chose to be his own Foreign Secretary as well. At the start of the building of the Empire, in the days of the first Elizabeth, it had been a Cecil who had had the ear of the Queen and had advised her. Now, with that Empire at the height of its power, another Cecil was the Queen's first minister. It is usually supposed that Lord Salisbury, as an Imperialist, was eager to extend the Empire in Africa and seized on Cecil Rhodes as a timely instrument for that purpose. Oddly, this is far from the truth.

Salisbury appears to have been suspicious of the great Empire-builder before he arrived in London, was far from enchanted by his brash personality, was publicly and witheringly scornful of the Cape-to-Cairo project even after he had given Rhodes reluctant backing in central Africa, and, though prepared to give grudging political endorsement to the Zambesia scheme, permitted not one penny of assistance from the Imperial exchequer.

Rhodes based much of his hopes on the fact that he had already won to his cause the British High Commissioner in Cape Town, Sir Hercules Robinson. But it seems that when Robinson sought to persuade the Colonial Secretary, Lord Knutsford, he ran into stiff opposition. Before Rhodes arrived in London himself, the

Colonial Secretary had sent a memorandum to the Prime Minister containing these words:

Any suggestion from Mr Rhodes (who I may advise in passing is the gentleman who presented Mr Parnell with £1,000) must be treated with some suspicion. It is supposed that Mr Rhodes is working with Mr Rudd to get very large mining concessions from Lo Bengula, and that Sir H. Robinson favours Mr Rudd as against others who are trying to get concessions in Matabeleland.

Rhodes was, in fact, twice-damned in the eyes of Lord Salisbury's Conservative administration before ever he set foot in London on his mission to secure a royal charter. Knutsford had actually underestimated his aid to the Irish Nationalists; Parnell's biographers say the correct figure was £10,000. In Salisbury's eyes, then, the ambitious colonial politician and diamond king was a man tainted by his associations with the Dublin Irish, and with the Afrikaners through his coalition government at the Cape. It is in this context perhaps that one should view Sir Roy Welensky's aspirations for Rhodesian Home Rule today.

As if he were not damned enough in the heart of the Empire, Cecil Rhodes resolved to take a hand himself in the administering of Imperial policy. Having decided that he had found a good friend for his northward expansion in Sir Hercules Robinson, he coolly sat down and wrote to the Colonial Secretary in London a wholly unsolicited letter, urging that the Imperial government should renew Robinson's term as High Commissioner.

On this score, too, as it turned out, he was equally damned. Lord Gifford, a staunch supporter of Salisbury's Tory government, had formed a syndicate for the northward exploration of minerals and had applied for a royal charter, already under consideration. Rhodes, the colonist, appeared to be contending with Gifford, an Englishman, for the mineral riches of Lobengula's kingdom. Further, there was the mounting pressure of the campaign of the humanitarian South Africa Committee, headed by Joseph Chamberlain and John Mackenzie. And these men were pressing Salisbury and his Cabinet to drop Robinson from his post at the Cape altogether, since he was deemed to have been won over to the side of these colonists, English and Afrikaner alike, who favoured a harsh policy towards the 'natives'. As luck would have it, the humanitarians had one strong political factor in their favour. Joseph Chamberlain, the Liberal Unionist, was an essential political ally, and the Tory Cabinet dared not offend him. At a Cabinet meeting on 31 January of that year, therefore, Salisbury and his Ministers unanimously decided that Robinson should not have his term renewed as High Commissioner at the Cape.

Mail packets were slow in those days, of course, but there was just time for the news to reach Cecil Rhodes as he was preparing to leave on his mission to London. Totally unflustered, the Empire's greatest optimist went ahead with his plans. The speed of the postal service being what it was, the Cabinet in London could not have known that at the end of 1888 the Great Amalgamator, as he was already known in South Africa, had neatly removed Lord Gifford as a rival by the simple process of buying up his company, as well as a number of others which were proposing to explore the unknown territories of Zambesia. Lord Gifford, as the Cabinet were shortly to learn, had in fact become one of Rhodes's most ardent backers. Furthermore, and again on account of slow communication, the Cabinet were unaware that Rhodes's agent, C. E. Rudd, had already succeeded against a group of formidable rivals and secured the concessions for mineral rights from Lobengula. The third Marquess of Salisbury and his colleagues were about to learn a few facts of power in southern Africa, facts that are still being driven home today when the Federal Prime Minister of Rhodesia comes to call in Whitehall and to visit his friends in the City.

A battle was about to begin, and one which was to end in brilliant victory for Cecil Rhodes and mute, inglorious defeat for Chamberlain, Mackenzie, and the humanitarian campaign. They too were clear about what they wanted – and what they belatedly got in Northern Rhodesia and Nyasaland – direct Imperial intervention by Her Majesty's troops and the Colonial Office, rather than indirect rule through a commercial exploitation company. Only in that way, they argued in their *Humanitarians'*

Memorial, could the African tribesmen be 'saved from Boer oppression', since a company would necessarily be able to intervene only at the cost of reduced profits. Knutsford's predecessor as Colonial Secretary, Lord Kimberley, had been confronted with this document and had rejected it in these terms:

The difficulty was, in dealing with the native question, we had not the sympathies of the white population. Either we must hold South Africa strongly by force and maintain our policy, whether the Colonists like it or not; or else we must acquiesce in a great many things being done in these Colonies of which the majority of the people in this country do not approve.

The colonists had their own way with reluctant acquiescers. Kimberley found his name perpetuated in the great diamond town that bears his name to this day. And Lord Salisbury, the reluctant ally of Cecil Rhodes, was to wake up on the morning of 12 September 1890 and find himself perpetually committed to the welfare of a new nation in the heart of Africa. When the men of the Pioneer Column hoisted the flag at Fort Salisbury that morning, their action went down in the history books as another of Britain's Imperial achievements. Salisbury was to be the capital of a new nation, and the Prime Minister of the world's richest and most powerful Empire had given it his name. It would be rather more accurate, of course, to say that its name had been taken from the Prime Minister. It was not the first time in British colonial history that the motherland had been skilfully led into acquiescing to a little local imperialism by the colonists. Nor, as Joshua Nkomo, Kenneth Kaunda, and Dr Hastings Kamuzu Banda were to learn sixty years later, was it the last.

2 The Godfathers

'Lord Salisbury and I have brought you peace – I hope with honour.' BENJAMIN DISRAELI, to the British House of Commons

'Not by speechifying and counting majorities are the great questions of the time to be solved, but by blood and iron.' BISMARCK

There is a happy breed of politicians who not only command the respect of their supporters, but also their affection, and of no one is this more true than of Sir Roy Welensky. What his African political opponents may feel about him is something else again; but for the moment that is not the point. The strength of the Federal Prime Minister with his electorate, the confidence he commanded in the 1950s, sprang from a feeling of kinship. Now this in itself is curious and worth examining closely, for Sir Roy heads an administration that is stoutly and avowedly Conservative, whereas the political leaders who generate such affection are generally men of the Left. The Americans who loved Lincoln loved him as a fellow-frontiersman, a humble man from a log cabin who had made good. The miners of Ebbw Vale who loved Nye Bevan looked on him as one of themselves, a local boy who had suffered as they suffered, who never assumed fancy airs or forgot his old friends even when he reached the seat of power.

Anyone who has seen Sir Roy Welensky stumping the constituencies in present-day Rhodesia or has been a guest at one of his famous Sunday-morning tea-drinking sessions on the *stoep* at Kabwe, his modest cottage home on the outskirts of Salisbury, cannot fail to have felt this sense of kinship and affection – provided, of course, that he is a white Rhodesian. More than any other citizen in the Federation today – any white citizen – he epitomizes Rhodesia. He is the man who was not ashamed to work with his hands, as an engine driver and union organizer, and who made good. He is no snob, he has no fancy airs about him, he is physically tough, mentally nimble, loves a good scrap, and bears no grudges. True, he does not number any Africans among his personal friends, but he has worked with them all his life, believes that he knows their ways, and proudly proclaims that most of the Africans who work for him as gardeners and house-servants have been with him for a very long time. He speaks to them in their own languages. One of them not long ago shyly asked permission to call his child 'Roy', and the Federal Prime Minister is now that child's godfather.

The fact that Roy Welensky happens to be, by parentage, half South African does not make him any less entitled to be described as the typical Rhodesian. South Africa is not just one of the influences which have shaped the present Federation; it is far and away the most potent feature, socially and politically, in its inheritance. This has emerged at every stage in the country's history, is apparent in the very accent and slang of the white Rhodesians, in their Native policy, and in their own racial origin. The official handbook of the Federation, in its breakdown of the European population, reports that thirty-one per cent are South Africans who have migrated to Rhodesia and made their homes there. It should be added that another twenty-eight per cent list their birthplace as the British Isles, while roughly ten per cent were born elsewhere. The remaining thirty per cent or so are Rhodesians by birth. These are the figures from the last census, which also indicated that about half the immigrants from South Africa spoke Afrikaans at home. There has always been a substantial Afrikaner element among white Rhodesians; as we have seen, it was Rhodes himself who ordered that they should provide part of the Pioneer Column. Today the Afrikaner heritage is visibly part of Rhodesian life; it is to be seen in the names on the shop-fronts of Salisbury and Bulawayo, in the names of many federal or territorial members of parliament, and in the many churches and missions of the Dutch Reformed Church scattered through town and country, in African communities as well as white.

It seems probable, then, that something like a third of Rhodesia's white citizens are Afrikaner by racial origin. And if we add those of English-speaking South African stock, perhaps three-quarters of the nation's electorate – those who hold the power to determine public policy – possess a South African heritage. They, or their parents, came to Rhodesia from a society of which the subjugation of the black man was an essential characteristic, where the 'native' was not only a second-class citizen but was expected to remain so for good. Seen in this light, the remarkable aspect of Rhodesia today perhaps is not that its 'Native policy' is so similar to South Africa's – which it is in many ways – but that it is in any significant respect at all different. Racial prejudice, as the experience of the Southern States in the U.S.A. has shown, is an inheritable, as well as highly infectious disease.

Certainly, there is an elusive but undeniable change of atmosphere that the northbound traveller senses as he crosses the Limpopo and leaves South Africa behind. In the Republic, the door to political equality for the black man has been closed, bolted, and nailed tight. In the Federation there is a sign informing the black Rhodesian that – at some unspecified time in the future – the door will be opened. Many white Rhodesians, and not all of them hypocrites, fervently hope that the opening ceremony will not take place within their own particular lifetime. And of course Mr Nkomo, Mr Kaunda, Dr Banda, and the other politically-conscious and 'immoderately' civilized Africans in the Federation, are understandably fed up with excuses and with waiting. They say that someone must seize the handle of the door now – it is immaterial whether it is Mr Macmillan or Sir Roy Welensky or U Thant – or the door will be smashed down and the whole structure of European society with it. It is the tragic error of the white community in Rhodesia, as elsewhere, that by their own stopped watches the day has just begun and there is still all the time in the world. Theirs is a failure to see themselves in the context of a rapidly changing continent; it is only their black 'partners' who see Africa steadily and see it whole.

Clearly if we, the outside critics of present-day Rhodesia, are to see it whole, we must look deeper than the surface which presents itself to the newspaper reader from afar, or even to the conscientious observer setting off with camera and notebook from his 'Europeans-only' hotel in the heart of Salisbury to explore the mysteries of the African townships across the railway tracks in Highfields and Harare. The political dilemma in the Federation is, more than with most countries, a problem in national psychology. One may do worse, therefore, than follow the example of the psychiatrist and start by examining the background and parentage of the patient. The parental influence, as we have seen, is markedly South African. What then of the background?

It might be said that for its godparents the new nation had an impressive trio: Lord Salisbury, the Prime Minister of Great Britain; Prince Otto von Bismarck, Chancellor of Imperial Germany; and Queen Victoria in her capacity as Empress of India.

It was the rivalry of Britain and Germany that finally persuaded Lord Salisbury, a reluctant imperialist in African affairs, to sanction the ambitious plans of Rhodes and the other Cape Colonists for a northward extension of their own little empire to the highly imagined riches of Zambesia. But over and above the mundane rivalries of the scramble for Africa, the British Prime Minister had his eye fixed upon a far richer region. India was the central jewel in the imperial crown; twenty years before, as a rising young politician and Secretary of State at the India Office, he had helped to achieve for the Queen the additional title of Empress of India. Now, in supreme power himself, he was acutely aware that Britain's position as the world's greatest commercial and military nation rested on the security of her lines of communication eastward to India. One line went by Suez, one by the Cape; between them, virtually untouched, lay the Dark Continent. Salisbury is sometimes pictured as the most avaricious of its scramblers, but this is wholly inconsistent with what we know of his character. That he was drawn into the scramble, and that he was to give his name to the capital city of an obscure new colony that he never sought nor saw, is one of the great ironies of history.

Robert Cecil, third Marquess of Salisbury, great landowner and Fellow of All Souls, was the architect and builder of Britain's foreign policy from 1885 to 1900, with the exception of a brief period when the Liberals under Gladstone held power. Yet so powerful was the policy Salisbury had constructed that, even during this interval, the Liberals found themselves building upon it. He had the strength of inner conviction; an aristocracy which would not accept the responsibility of governing, he said, was a sham. Yet for all his sophistication, even he was astonished by the gobbling-up of Africa. After centuries of neglect, Britain and her European rivals appropriated nine-tenths of a continent in the space of sixteen years. Lord Salisbury curtly observed in a public speech: 'I do not exactly know the cause of this sudden revolution; but there it is.' Doubtless, the pressures and objectives differed from one European state to the other. In Germany a great deal stemmed from the aggressive personality of one man, Bismarck. But the British Prime Minister was well aware of what it was that drove him on. America, still weak and divided after a calamitous civil war, was not yet an equal save in population. In terms of what today we would call gross national product, Britain led the world: in engineering and shipbuilding she was supreme; British money and British technology were building railways in five continents; and national income had doubled in forty years. By the time Salisbury took office it was calculated that twelve million Britons had gone overseas to settle new lands and that the nation's total investments abroad were worth £2,000 million – equivalent to perhaps £15,000 million or $45 billion today. But all this imperial power rested upon the military fulcrum of India.

Salisbury could command the services of an Indian Army that comprised 66,000 British and 130,000 Indian troops, while in the Princely States were forces totalling another 350,000 men. In addition, there were vast reserves available at short notice. As the Secretary for India observed in 1878: 'The Indian Army is not limited in numbers by an annual vote of parliament; the native portion is not even subject to the Mutiny Act.' Here was a military fire brigade, available virtually without charge, to open and protect the lines of Imperial trade. Indian troops went to China in 1839, to Burma, and to Singapore. By the end of the century, they were in Africa: Egypt 1882, Nyasaland 1893, Sudan and Uganda 1896. Two Cambridge historians, Ronald

Robinson and John Gallagher, have summed it up in these words:

Not only did the Indian taxpayer bear the cost of his own occupation, but something like half the British Army was billeted upon him. The Indian empire thus provided a uniquely self-financing army ... its revenue and manpower the rod of order, the shield of defence and the sword for further advance from Zanzibar to the Yellow Sea. At the same time, the flow of forces and trade through the Mediterranean was vulnerable to the powers of Europe.*

Disraeli's smart work in acquiring a substantial share-holding in the Suez Canal was soon to lead to military adventures in Egypt, so as to secure the route. By this time India was absorbing one fifth of Britain's export trade and providing one fifth of her raw materials. But ten years after the opening of the Canal, the Royal Commission on Colonial Defence found that sixty per cent of all Imperial cargoes were still going around the southern tip of Africa, in a trade worth £146 million annually. No wonder a Colonial Office memo described Cape Town as 'the true centre of the Empire', and the Commission itself should have advised parliament and the Cabinet that in time of war the Cape route would be vital for Imperial survival. Lord Salisbury, taking office as Prime Minister, had compelling reasons to back up his emotional attachments to India. The Royal Navy's base at Simonstown, near Cape Town, had become the queen in the Imperial chess game. Inevitably, as the German Kaiser began placing his pawns on the board and moving them forward, the British Prime Minister was compelled to challenge him. The match had begun, and the prize was Africa.

Until Lüderitz raised the red, white, and black standard of Imperial Germany on the African west coast at the bay of Angra Pequena, Britain's policy in that continent followed the lines laid down by James Stephen at the Colonial Office forty years previously:

Even if our national resources were far more potent, it would be very bad policy to employ in Africa that part of them available for coloniza-

* R. Robinson and J. Gallagher with A. Denny, *Africa and the Victorians*, Macmillan, London, 1961.

tion. In Africa we cannot colonize without coming into contact with numerous warlike tribes, and involving ourselves in their disputes. If we could acquire dominion of the whole Continent, it would be but a worthless possession.

Now that policy was about to be scrapped and replaced by what, to the outside world, appeared a ruthless British expansion in Africa directed by the arch-imperialist of them all, Robert Cecil, Marquess of Salisbury. And yet today, nearly a century later, with the Cabinet minutes available to us and the Colonial Office telegrams, not to mention all the diaries and memoirs and the benefits of hindsight, it becomes clear who the imperialists in southern Africa really were – Prince Otto von Bismarck and Cecil Rhodes. Of course Salisbury was an imperialist too, but only in respect of India and Britain's other possessions in Asia and Australasia. And though leader of the richest nation on earth, he was playing an essentially defensive game. It must have been vastly irritating to this aristocratic parliamentarian to discover, each time Bismarck moved offensively on the diplomatic chess board, that before he could make his counter-move Rhodes was at his elbow with unsolicited advice. And on occasions, such as the Jameson Raid and the staking of the British claim in Northern Zambesia and Nyasaland, it was the imperialist at the Cape who was making the moves and taking pawns or losing them.

Throughout the dozen crucial years of his rule from Downing Street, Salisbury was constantly trying to balance five factors. His first aim was to safeguard the sea-route to India by way of the Suez Canal. Secondly, because Suez would be undependable in time of war, he had to secure the route round the Cape of Good Hope. This came in practice to mean appeasing the Boers of the Bond who shared power with Rhodes in the Cape Colony, and appeasing Rhodes by sanctioning his imperial drive north to Zambesia. The third factor was the political power of the so-called Humanitarians, not only among Gladstone's Liberals but in his own party as well, men ever-alert for any surrender to the white racialists which would spell serfdom for the Africans. Fourthly, he had to counter the new challenge from Germany.

And lastly, he had to accept the fiscal limits imposed by a Victorian House of Commons, which was dedicated to the most stringent apportionment of public funds for adventures in Africa. It was this fifth factor which was to be decisive in shaping Rhodesia; it explains the mandate given to a private chartered company, with all the political consequences that were to flow from that fateful decision.

Pounds, shillings, and pence marked all the parliamentary speeches and ministerial memos. This caused a cheese-paring policy at the Colonial Office which led to most of Britain's troubles in Central Africa today. When the challenge came from the newly rich Germans, with a surplus of ready cash and no empire to spend it on, Salisbury was forced to seek priorities. The land that was to become the present-day Rhodesian Federation had to be secured at the cheapest price. Wise after the event, one may conclude that this inevitably meant the Colonial Office would abdicate its responsibilities and let race relations go hang.

By the time Salisbury took office, war as an instrument for securing the Cape route was out of the question. Parliament was fuming over the expenses already incurred for profitless purposes. A demand for a tabulation had produced this list: Sekukuni War £380,000; Griqualand Rising £222,000; Transkei War £543,000; Zulu War £5,000,000. Yet, despite such expenditure, the proud Trek Boers of Kruger's Transvaal Republic were as independent and hostile as ever; President Brand in the Orange Free State was supporting them; and the Bondsmen in Britain's Cape Colony were prepared to do the bidding of their leader Jan Hofmeyr when the time came to give the signal. It was the genius of Rhodes in forging a coalition with Hofmeyr and keeping the Cape Colony safe for the Royal Navy that made him the inevitable ally of Salisbury and secured for him a free hand in his Zambesian adventures.

For his own guidance, the Prime Minister had a Cabinet Note from a previous Colonial Secretary, Sir Robert Herbert, advocating a political confederation as the only workable solution for the clash of interests in South Africa: 'Unless and until this is done there is no prospect of avoiding the periodical recurrence of

wars carried on at great cost to this country.' Such a confederation, of course, meant some surrender to the harsh Native
policy of the Transvaal; it was Britain's decision to free the
slaves earlier in the century, and liberal policies (including voting
rights) for Africans, that had spurred the Voortrekkers north and
east to found a new republic. The Humanitarians at Westminster
pressed for stern, if expensive, measures to bring the Transvaal
into line. But as Sir Charles Dilke pointed out: 'The greatest of
our dangers in South Africa is ... the difficulty of inducing
Parliament to sanction a continuous expenditure without direct
return.' Two months after Lord Salisbury took office as Prime
Minister, the Colonial Office produced the Fairfield memorandum on southern Africa headed 'Vacillation in Policy'. It included these words:

When we find a huge bill has been run up, the advocates of retrench-
ment have their day until it is perceived that retirement and retrench-
ment have involved the abandonment of some friendly Tribe to the
mercy of the Africander. Then there is a cry for a resumption of
responsibility.

The German challenge on the coast of South-West Africa was
flung at the face of a dying Gladstone régime in 1884, just before
Salisbury's accession to power. It came at a time when the occupation of Egypt – the operation to secure the route to India at the
other end of the continent – was proving ruinously expensive for
the British taxpayer. And the French, having been outflanked by
the British in Egypt, now repudiated their standstill agreement
with Britain in West Africa and began instead to take over new
territory, directly threatening British interests at the mouth of
the Niger. Accordingly, because Britain needed Bismarck's
backing in Egypt, London could not object when the Kaiser extended a formal protectorate over the whole of that vast territory
which is today South-West Africa.

For Rhodes, now the Leader of the Opposition in the parliament of the Cape Colony, the situation looked desperate. He
dreaded a geographical link-up between the Germans on the
west coast and the iron-willed men of the Transvaal Republic on

the other side of the continent. Yet this would only be a logical consequence of the spiritual accord that had been forged in Berlin a few months before. President Kruger had toured Europe at the head of a delegation, and, at a banquet in his honour in the German capital, Bismarck had spoken of their ethnic kinship and their natural harmony of interests in Africa. He ended his speech – as had been anxiously reported in the Cape Press – with the assurance that 'we will take no steps in Africa except hand in hand with the Boer people'. Now, following the German acquisition of South-West Africa, Kruger had granted a monopoly for the building of railways in the Transvaal to a German–Dutch syndicate, and word reached Cape Town that the next move was to be a rail-link from Angra Pequena across the waist of southern Africa to Pretoria. The Imperial government in London was apparently stricken with paralysis; once the railway line was built (in fact, it never was) Britain would lose her claim to the Bechuana territory that lay between the new German colony and Kruger's republic. Sir Hercules Robinson, the British High Commissioner at the Cape, decided to act. He cabled London: 'Threatened encroachments calculated to cripple this Colony. Decisive measures should be taken.' And while awaiting such measures he hedged his bets by dispatching Cecil Rhodes to Bechuanaland as special Commissioner.

There were some cynics who thought this an odd appointment for a Leader of the Opposition; but, in the emergency of the time, there were not many to fuss over fine points of parliamentary protocol. In fact a bond of outlook between the two men had been forged, a bond which was later to result in handsome financial dividends for Sir Hercules – and some pointed criticisms in the British House of Commons. In Bechuanaland Rhodes found clumps of Boer settlers from the Transvaal already planted at two places. This was serious. These people had established themselves squarely across the so-called 'North Road' or 'Missionaries' Road' which provided the only practical access to the unclaimed northern interior. If the Germans pressed on with their railway and more settlers from the Transvaal arrived, there would be little chance for Rhodes's scheme of an all-red route from Cape to Cairo. Asserting his legal authority as Her Majesty's Commissioner for the Protectorate of Bechuanaland, Rhodes was nevertheless shrewd enough to realize that he had to offer tangible concessions in order to win the allegiance of the Boers. Unhesitatingly, therefore, he confirmed their possession of the lands they had occupied in British Bechuanaland. It was good strategy; all that he had overlooked was any negotiation with local chiefs or other representatives of the Africans. Not that the Boer settlers had done so; but it might have been presumed that the Commissioner of a British protectorate would have displayed certain scruples.

Despite Rhodes's mission, President Kruger formally proclaimed the annexation of the area in the name of the Transvaal Republic. In London the British Cabinet was at last prodded to act, and an expeditionary force of 4,000 men was dispatched to Bechuanaland under General Sir Charles Warren. Not the most tactful of men, he took with him not only Cecil Rhodes but also Rhodes's predecessor as Commissioner, the Rev. John Mackenzie, a man of diametrically opposed views on Native policy. Clearly Mackenzie must have been the winner in moral argument, because Warren, as well as asserting military authority over the territory, also took it on himself to repudiate the land-titles so liberally distributed by Rhodes and order the restitution of the land to its original African owners. It had been Rhodes's first taste of Empire-building in the North, and his first defeat. The lesson was not lost on him, and he now sought the political influence which would enable him to colour the map of Africa his imperial red; he would have to stake his claim in London. He would have to win the backing of Whitehall, either by charm or by bluff; it was a technique which Lord Malvern and Sir Roy Welensky were to employ half a century later.

Rhodes set to work. Through his influence on Sir Hercules Robinson, he was eventually able to see that General Warren was recalled; even after Warren's departure, their antipathy was displayed in a series of heated letters to *The Times*. In a private letter written about this time, Rhodes set out his aims – to thrust northward from the Cape Colony and so outflank the Germans and all other rivals, while acting as far as possible in concert with the Afrikaner:

Conduct such as Warren's is just heaping up future trouble in this country and destroying all chance of success for those who are working to cement the two nationalities on the basis of true loyalty to the British flag.

The letter was shrewdly placed; it was sent to a junior member of the British Cabinet. Rhodes had begun preparing the ground for his assault on London. And the reference to the British flag was tactful; though it hardly squared with two occasions during the crisis when he had spoken with emotion and with clearly greater candour. In the Cape parliament he had expressed his impatience with British policy:

We know that all sorts of fuel are said to be in Bechuanaland, and Imperial interference in Bechuanaland would be one source of fuel. We want to get rid of the Imperial factor in this question and to deal with it ourselves.

There, surely, speaks the authentic voice of Sir Roy Welensky. Shades of Katanga! And just as, in recent years, the Rhodesian Federal Cabinet in Salisbury has shown signs of a growing impatience with British interference and has thrown out oblique references to its own Declaration of Independence, so Rhodes in 1885 declared to the Cape Assembly: 'I came down to the House a most rabid Jingo, but I have since passed through the fire of Bechuanaland.'

The problems of South and Central Africa became the urgent concern of Lord Salisbury and his fellow Tories, when they assumed power in Whitehall during the summer of 1885. This is the most crucial – and the most ignored – period of Rhodesian history. It marks, in the notable phrase of Mr Philip Mason of the Institute of Race Relations in London, the birth of a dilemma. It is probably fair to suppose that, had the new Prime Minister not been beset by so many other problems of global complexity, he might have been able to afford the time, the troops, and the administrators that would have enabled Britain to conduct her colonial mission on orthodox lines in Central Africa. As it was, Lord Salisbury was obliged to let the colonial imperialists of South Africa conduct it for him.

In his double role as Prime Minister and Foreign Secretary, he set out to check a deteriorating situation. The Berlin Conference of 1884 had been intended to remove the points of friction between the Great Powers; in fact, what it had done was to give an air of legality to the scramble for Africa, a scramble which immediately intensified. It needed only a spark in the wrong place to set off a major war, and, to give Lord Salisbury his due, he proved to have a master-touch when it came to anticipating these sparks and stamping them out before they could start a general blaze. Through his own efforts, much more than those of his rivals, the map of Africa had been stabilized by the end of the century much along the lines we know today. (Although most of the frontiers now, of course, enclose independent African states rather than colonies.) Needless to say, Salisbury was not seeking to render dispassionate public service; he was aiming at a final settlement – a *pax Britannica* – which would provide the surest guarantee of the Imperial lifeline to India. Through yet another of those savage ironies of history, his monument was not to be the peaceful accommodation that he achieved among the European powers but the bloody colonial – partly civil – war that was to mark the end of the century in South Africa and his own tenancy at No. 10 Downing Street.

Let us look briefly, then, at those other events, many of them in Africa, which were indirectly to determine the course of development in Rhodesia, and were engaging the attention of the British Prime Minister as Cecil Rhodes began his diplomatic assault on Whitehall. The first priority was Germany. Within a month of taking office, Salisbury had broken the political log-jam between London and Berlin, through an exchange of letters with Bismarck. A judicious surrender of expendable territories in the Pacific and in East Africa brought, as the *quid pro quo*, the assurance of German support in Egypt. Now it was time to secure the other side of the Suez gate. Sir Henry Drummond Wolff was dispatched to Constantinople, and the Anglo-Turkish Convention was achieved. But this provoked France and Russia to a joint statement of opposition; the next year, while the French proceeded to retaliate by acquisitive moves in West Africa, Salisbury as Foreign Secretary was busily negotiating and signing the Mediterranean Agreement with Austria and Italy.

The problems occupying the thoughts of Rhodes and Salisbury between 1888 and 1890 were not the same. Rhodes spent his time polishing up his contacts in the City of London, enlisting powerful support for his proposed Royal Chartered Company, planning the acquisition of Nyasaland (successfully), and of Portuguese East Africa (vetoed by Salisbury because it clashed with Imperial policy towards Lisbon). In Britain, parliament and the Imperial Cabinet had neither the time nor the money for adventures in Zambesia; if Rhodes was prepared to spend his own resources – or those of the Chartered Company – so much the better for the British taxpayer.

The whole of 1888 was overshadowed, in Downing Street, by a series of naval scares. The first ominous build-up of French strength came in January and February; by April the Admiralty was reporting that 'France, the principal Naval Power with which we could be brought into conflict, has concentrated almost the whole of her Ironclad fleet in the Mediterranean.' By the summer the Royal Navy was reporting that it had barely enough ships to deal with the French fleets massed at Toulon and Brest, let alone the Franco–Russian threat at Suez. By August Lord Salisbury was reporting to Queen Victoria: 'France is, and must always remain, England's greatest danger.' That winter the Russians floated their first loan in Paris and by the following spring (as Cecil Rhodes set sail jauntily from Cape Town to squeeze the British Government into the grant of a Royal Charter) the Admiralty was reporting sinister signs of incipient action by the French and Russian squadrons. By March, Suez was considered by the Royal Navy to be indefensible in the circumstances, and the Prime Minister rushed through the House of Lords the Naval Defence Act, designed to create a Royal Navy large enough to take on all comers and defend the Suez route as well. Lucky Rhodes! By this time he was in the thick of his campaign of political pressure in Whitehall, designed to extract a charter for his company on terms that would give him the freest possible hand for territorial expansion into Zambesia. Lord Salisbury must have been acutely aware that, with the Suez route so vulnerable, the Empire's lifeline to India now depended on the Cape Colony and the naval base maintained by the Royal Navy at Simonstown. It was not a time to refuse small favours (which cost the British taxpayer nothing) to a man who was the Cape's wealthiest citizen and one of its leading politicians.

The crisis in Europe was moving to a climax, and the political empires of Salisbury and Rhodes were beginning to intersect. For the British Prime Minister it was a case of too many cooks; Cecil Rhodes was only one of a considerable list of self-appointed chefs who were threatening to spoil the Imperial broth. From their new base on the Red Sea, the Italians were preparing to advance into the hinterland of Africa. In May 1889 (Rhodes was by then in London and actively lobbying for his charter) the dismaying news reached Lord Salisbury that his opposite number in Rome, Francesco Crispi, had succeeded in persuading Ethiopia to join with Italy in the Treaty of Ucciali. Under this Rome gained access to the Blue Nile, and so, again, the Suez route to India was indirectly threatened. The British Agent in Cairo, Sir Evelyn Baring, bombarded Lord Salisbury with memoranda, variously marked 'private' and 'secret', urging swift action because in his opinion the Italians were vaultingly ambitious, would soon be at Khartoum, and were aiming at nothing less than domination of the whole Sudan. 'Whatever Power holds the Upper Nile Valley,' he wrote in one of these memos, 'must by the mere force of geography dominate Egypt.'

In that same spring of 1889, alarming dispatches from East Africa reached the Foreign Office that Carl Peters, the agent of the German Colonization Society, was on safari with a satchel full of treaty forms and a *Schutzbrief* from Bismarck giving him the backing of the Kaiser. The Foreign Office advised Salisbury that, if Britain did not act to save Uganda, the Germans would seize it and so inevitably control the Nile headwaters and Lake Victoria Nyanza. The remote regions mapped by Livingstone's explorations – the Germans were busy at Zanzibar as well – had now become interlocked with high British policy and the lifeline to India. In this emergency – the naval crisis with the French and Russians was still at its height – Cecil Rhodes and his noble backers, who now included two dukes with royal connexions, persisted with their respectable pestering. And the pressures of larger events on the international scene began to work to their advantage. At the southern tip of Africa the Boer Republics of the Transvaal and the Orange Free State entered into a formal alliance, and President Kruger was threatening to 'burst his kraal' by laying claim to Matabeleland. It began to look as if Rhodes and his friends, who asked neither for soldiers nor for money, might yet prove to be useful allies. Salisbury was well aware that no amount of shrewd diplomatic manipulation would in itself restrain the Boers of the Transvaal Republic; physical occupation of Zambesia was the only answer. But the Boers had only recently reached an *entente* with Bismarck, and it would not do to collide with the Germans head-on. The Prime Minister, who had a regular weekly audience with Queen Victoria, was only too keenly aware that the Kaiser had a ready line of access to his grandmother at Buckingham Palace.

So in that summer of 1889 Lord Salisbury methodically began to sort out the African muddle by first concluding a provisional agreement with Bismarck. This arranged the respective zones of influence for the two competing countries in the Nyasa–Tanganyika–Uganda region. The way was now almost clear for Cecil Rhodes and his chartered adventurers to trek north; only the problem of Portugal remained. Queen Victoria had personally interceded with the Prime Minister; she asked that he should not squeeze Lisbon too hard lest it bring about the fall of the Braganza dynasty. Once again Rhodes was ready with a solution, for the Chartered Company was just as apprehensive of Portuguese encroachments from the east and west coasts as of German manoeuvres. Britain, he suggested, should conclude treaties with the tribes of the interior, working north and west from the valley of the Shiré River in Nyasaland, since this would strengthen Salisbury's hand when he came to bargain with Lisbon. Since the Prime Minister was also under pressure from the Anglican missions in the west and the Scots at Lake Nyasa, who wanted to block the advance of the Portuguese Catholic missionaries, he found this plan politically attractive. It became even more attractive when Rhodes found not only the man to carry out the plan but the money as well. Within four weeks young Harry Johnston, formerly vice-consul in the Cameroons, found himself commissioned and on his way. He was Her Majesty's Consul for Portuguese East Africa, but he was being paid personally by Cecil Rhodes, who had written out a cheque for £2,000 on the spot when Salisbury wavered at the prospect of complications with the Treasury. It was all most irregular, but the Great Amalgamator must have been delighted; he was never happier than when his amalgamations included a government or two.

By late summer Johnston was able to report enough progress to indicate that the Shiré Highlands and Barotseland could be formally claimed by Britain. Things were falling into place at last. On 15 October 1889 the official gazette announced that the Queen had been pleased to grant to the British South Africa Company a Royal Charter.

Although Lord Salisbury was not to realize it at the time, he had in fact introduced another player on to the diplomatic chess board. Sooner than he expected, he was to find the newly created Rhodesian state developing a foreign policy of its own; within two years the settlers, through their powerful sponsors, were forcing the British government to settle with Portugal on rather different terms than had been planned in London. Much sooner than its British godparents had anticipated, the child of the British South Africa Company had acquired a will of its own. The lesson had been taught to Whitehall long before it was to be demonstrated for the benefit of U Thant by Sir Roy Welensky.

Lord Salisbury now proceeded to tie up the loose ends of his African diplomacy. In late December he learned that Bismarck's position was weakening, and judged the moment right to take the initiative against Berlin. In March 1890 came the impetuous decision of the Kaiser; he was 'dropping the Pilot', as *Punch* was to illustrate it in the celebrated cartoon. The British Prime

Minister moved swiftly; in the abrupt way that was characteristic of his diplomacy he handed the German ambassador a document outlining a complex and complete division of East and Central Africa. Germany was to renounce all claims in Uganda and vacate the Upper Nile altogether, but she was to get the 'Caprivi Strip' which, to this day, links South-West Africa with the Zambesi. The big plum was British renunciation of Heligoland, the North Sea Island so prized by the Kaiser and destined, in later years, to become a bombing range for the R.A.F. Salisbury also demanded territories linking northward from Lake Nyasa to Lake Victoria Nyanza, which would give Rhodes and his new Chartered Company their cherished 'all-red route'; but when the Germans jibbed at this the Prime Minister, with the security of the Nile and the Suez route to India at stake, did not hesitate to give way. Imperial interests had to take precedence over those of Rhodesia. Explaining this to the Cabinet, he described the directors of the British South Africa Company as 'a reasonable body ... quite willing to accept this solution to the problem'.

It was not to be the first time that a British Prime Minister had misjudged the determination of the Rhodesians. The Anglo-German Treaty was signed on 1 July 1890, and within a matter of days a storm of indignation was raised by Rhodes and his colleagues over the sacrifice of the Cape-to-Cairo dream and the pinching-in of Bechuanaland to make the 'wasp waist' of Caprivi. In a private memorandum still in the files of the Foreign Office, Salisbury recorded his estimation of the all-red route so strongly urged by Rhodes. 'To some minds the interior of Africa in the line of the great lakes offers the attractions of El Dorado. I do not think such anticipations grounded upon fact.' In the Lords he spoke scornfully of men whose reasoning powers were affected by too much map-reading. Such criticism as had been made in southern Africa (and was now appearing in the London papers) stemmed from what he called:

A very curious idea which has become prevalent in this country that there is some special advantage in having a stretch of territory extending all the way from Cape Town to the Nile. I can imagine no more uncomfortable position than the possession of a narrow strip of territory in the very heart of Africa, three months' distance from the coast.

There was one other quarter where the Rhodesia Lobby had been busy; through his ducal co-directors and their close links with the Prince of Wales, the founder of the British South Africa Company already stood high in the estimation of Queen Victoria. Lord Salisbury dispatched a note in his own hand to the Queen, justifying his decision to accept the Kaiser's terms and disappoint the Rhodesians:

Any indefinite postponement of a settlement in Africa would render it very difficult to maintain terms of amity with Germany, and would force us to change our system of alliance in Europe [and] must necessarily involve the early evacuation of Egypt under very unfavourable conditions.

But Lord Salisbury had been ignoring political developments in southern Africa. In July 1890 Cecil Rhodes had become Prime Minister of the Cape Colony; his relations with Downing Street would henceforth be conducted on a new level. He retained direction of British South Africa Company and, indeed, his concern in its welfare could hardly be greater than at that very moment, for the Pioneer Column – wholly financed by the Company – was in the process of pushing north to occupy Mashonaland. In the Cape parliament Rhodes made a major issue of the Anglo–German negotiations, in a motion which declared: 'That this House regrets that the government of this country was not directly represented . . . and should have a voice in any future proposed arrangement of boundaries.'

Communications being what they were in those days, Lord Salisbury was already deeply involved in negotiations with the Portuguese and was too far committed to be able to take Rhodesian views into account, even had he known them. On 20 August 1890 he initialled the Anglo–Portuguese Convention. It had the merit, as Salisbury saw it, of stabilizing a potentially dangerous situation, defining spheres of influence, delineating frontiers, securing Britain's Cape route to India, and protecting the interests of the Rhodesian settlers. But for Rhodes and his friends, it was far from satisfactory; as part of the bargain, Britain had assigned the whole of Manicaland on the east and most of Barotseland on the west to the Portuguese. The Prime Minister of the Cape dispatched a cable to his opposite number in Downing Street: 'We lose by Treaty large portions of our territories. The whole agreement is disapproved in the Colony.'

He followed this up by a formal letter to Lord Salisbury as Britain's Foreign Secretary:

I do not think I am claiming too much from your department in asking you give some consideration to my views. If you have any regard for the work I am doing, you will show it by now dropping the Anglo-Portuguese agreement.

Rhodes still had two cards in his hand and proceeded to play them. Through the nominal chairman of the British South Africa Company, the Duke of Abercorn, a devoted friend of the Prince of Wales and a loyal Tory, he let it be known that he might be driven to resign from the premiership of the Cape. All this overlapped with the arrival of the Pioneer Column in Mashonaland and the raising of the flag at the site of the designated capital on 12 September. Rhodes and his fellow directors had already charged the Pioneers with the task of formally naming the capital of the new territory Fort Salisbury, in honour of the Imperial Prime Minister, and it was tactically impossible to re-arrange things. So the naming ceremony took place as planned and is now annually celebrated as a sentimental occasion by tens of thousands of Rhodesian school-children. Lord Salisbury himself, who was nobody's fool, must have taken a certain ironic pleasure in the circumstances under which the new nation named its capital city. Barely a week later, while the protests continued to flow in from the Cape against the bargain with Portugal, one letter arrived on Salisbury's desk which had about it the unmistakable aroma of inspiration. The Duke of Abercorn, in his capacity as chairman of the British South Africa Company, pointed out that Cecil Rhodes was indispensable to the Empire, that he was 'powerful at the Cape', and that his opinions merited notice.

Meanwhile, Rhodes prepared to play his other card. It was not to be the last time that the white settlers in Africa were to deal with Whitehall by confronting their nominal masters with a *fait accompli*. Rhodes summoned two of his trusted colleagues, Dr Starr Jameson and Frederick Selous, an experienced trader and explorer, and dispatched them to Manicaland together with a small band of British South Africa Company police. They successfully won over the local chief, who ceded full jurisdiction over his territory to the Chartered Company in consideration of an annual payment of £100. The Portuguese administration at the coast replied by dispatching a small force led by one Captain Mor Goveia, a half-caste who specialized in slave-traffic and gun-running, with orders to arrest the chief and disperse the South Africans. But luck lay with Rhodes and the British South Africa Company. In the skirmish, which took place on 15 November, Dr Jameson and his Chartered police defeated the Portuguese, arrested Goveia together with one of the directors of the Portuguese syndicate which had been exploiting the territory, and promptly dispatched the two men as prisoners of war to Cape Town. The Chartered Company, and incidentally the British Crown, were now in full possession of Manicaland.

The Barotseland problem was settled by financial methods. Rhodes, on behalf of the Chartered Company, acquired from a Kimberley merchant the concession over 200,000 square miles which he had received from Lewanika, the Paramount Chief of the region. Then all at once the Portuguese parliament, faced with its own pressure-groups and problems, refused to ratify the convention. Lord Salisbury wearily observed that 'people are not reasonable, either at Lisbon or at Cape Town', and proceeded to reopen negotiations (while continuing to juggle the French, the Italians, and Suez). In the final agreement, signed on 11 June 1891, the Portuguese accepted a small salient west of the Shiré Highlands, while the whole of the Manica plateau and all of Barotseland were assigned to the British Crown, and through it, to the Chartered Company.

To conclude this account of the global diplomacy which attended the birth of Rhodesia, it is only necessary to mention that on 1 July 1890, the same day on which he signed his treaty with the Kaiser, Lord Salisbury turned his attention to the French and opened negotiations with their ambassador in London with the object of settling spheres of influence in Africa. The negotiations continued throughout the summer during which the Pioneer Column was marching into Mashonaland and, from the Cape, Rhodes and his colleagues were firing protests off to London about the settlements with Portugal and with Germany. Fortunately for Lord Salisbury's peace of mind, the Anglo-French negotiations were concerned only with Tunisia, the Sahara, and the basin of the Niger, and so had no impact upon Rhodesia. The pact was concluded in August 1890, and the British Prime Minister took the opportunity, while expounding its terms in the House of Lords, to include a little gentle mockery directed at the scramblers for Africa: 'I will not dwell upon the respective advantages of places which are utterly unknown, not only to your Lordships, but to the rest of the white human race. . . .'

Salisbury had secured French acceptance of the *status quo* in Africa and, so, a measure of protection for the lifeline to India. Only the Italian problem now remained; Baring was dispatched to Naples in September to open negotiations with Crispi. During the winter little progress was made, but, with Crispi's fall from office in the following spring, Salisbury ordered the pressure to be resumed, and on 15 April the final agreement was signed. The Italians surrendered their claims in the Nile valley, frontiers in East Africa were delineated, and the Italian threat to the Suez route was effectively removed.

The main diplomatic battle was over, although Lord Salisbury was to continue as a potent influence in African affairs until the end of the century and was – in spite of any private feelings of antagonism he might feel – to become more and more dependent on Cecil Rhodes in the conduct of Imperial policy. The godparents of Rhodesia had done their work; the new nation had been set firmly on its course. At the end of that natal year of 1890 Cecil Rhodes arrived in England for the first time in his new capacity as Prime Minister of the Cape Colony. As protocol demanded, he made his call at No. 10 Downing Street and was received with reserved correctness by Lord Salisbury. There was no love lost between them. It was Rhodesia's other godparent that Rhodes was really looking forward to meeting. Queen Victoria had invited him, as Prime Minister of the Cape, to dinner at Windsor Castle. From all accounts the occasion was a brilliant success. The Queen had taken the trouble to brief herself in very great detail on African affairs and impressed Rhodes by her clear grasp of political developments. He, for his part, gave one of his virtuoso speeches about the route from the Cape to Cairo and his great plan to paint all those empty spaces on the map in 'red – British red'.

The Queen, writing afterwards in her journal, described him as a 'tremendous strong man' and concluded the entry on that night's dinner party with these words: 'He hoped in time to see the English rule extend from the Cape to Egypt. He thought everything would be arranged and the difficulties got over.'

Like her fellow-Victorians, the Queen was an optimist.

Before we leave this tale of Victorian diplomacy and turn to the internal development of Rhodesia, it would be well to look at just one other point in Lord Salisbury's policy which was to have, in later years, profound repercussions for the new nation. For reasons which no doubt seemed cogent enough at the time, he had been forced to connive at policies of racial discrimination in the colonies of southern Africa, though these had already aroused moral doubts and widespread public anxieties in Britain. They were also to arouse a young Indian barrister-turned-politician named Mohandas K. Gandhi who would form a Congress movement and then leave his home in Africa to lead a nation to independence in Asia. This same Congress was to inspire the Africans of Rhodesia, half a century later, to found their own movements for national independence, using the Congress name. Perhaps, then, it should be said that Rhodesia had not three godparents but four, and that the fourth was Mahatma Gandhi.

3   The Treasure Chest

'Do not talk to me of Gold, the element which brings more dissension, misfortune and unexpected plagues in its trail than benefits.' PRESIDENT PAUL KRUGER

'The independence of the African primitive,' says Albert Schweitzer, 'is lost at the moment when the first white man's boat arrives with powder, rum, salt or fabrics.' The very names that the whites gave to the territories they visited – the Gold Coast and the Côte d'Ivoire – are clear enough indication of what they sought. Yet, in a paradoxical way, the airy central plateau that is today the Rhodesian Federation seemed at first something of an exception to the grim rule. The first white men (the Portuguese) arrived in 1514, but after a few bold criss-crossings of the interior, they decided that any attempt at permanent occupation would not be worth the effort and expense. They retired to the shores of the Indian Ocean where, at Beira and Lourenço Marques, they set up their trading-posts and established the colony of Moçambique, which – by virtue of military force – they hold to this day.

The Portuguese had been spurred to make their venture into the interior by tales reaching Lisbon over a period of some thirty years, ever since their bold navigator Vasco da Gama had found the sea-route to India. These were tales of a so-called Empire of Gold, a fantastic African state whose ruler was an emperor called the Monomotapa and whose people used gold to make their plates and vessels in the way that men of other nations were using clay or iron. In a strange way these stories meshed with another legend, which had reached Europe in earlier centuries, dating back to the Crusades and the Christian era in Egypt. This was one of the legends of Prester John and a great civilized kingdom in the centre of Africa; there was to be found the Land of Ophir described in the Bible, the treasure house of the Queen of Sheba, and King Solomon's Mines. It was a tale going back to Herodotus, who had written of an African kingdom where gold was so cheap and plentiful that it was even used for the shackles in the royal dungeons.

One striking discovery in Mashonaland made the whole treasure hunt seem conceivably worth while; the Monomotapa, when he was found, proved to possess a palace or fortress constructed of stone. Here was his Court and here, in a royal tomb, his ancestors were buried. The daring explorer who made this journey in 1514 was Antonio Fernandez; modern research suggests that the Monomotapa was in fact the paramount chief of a tribe called the Makaranga. Fernandez paid his respects to the Emperor and pushed on; there was the source of the fabled gold to seek. For although the African monarch was not as lavish in the use of gold at his Court as legend had promised, it was carefully noted that, when he or other chiefs wished to buy from traders at the coast, they were able to send messengers carrying quills of pure gold-dust. Modern excavations at Zimbabwe, the site of the principal royal palace, suggest that the Monomotapas had been buying jewellery and pottery from China, Persia, and India as early as A.D. 1200 and perhaps three centuries before that. Indeed, this trade continued well after the arrival of the white man as a permanent settler at the coast, though the Mashona community itself was already disintegrating and was soon to fall before the Matabele invasion from the south. One fairly recent digging has brought up a Chinese bowl that can be identified as Ming provincial pottery of around 1700. And certainly the belief in a source of gold was not altogether baseless. The first English and South African hunters in mid-Victorian times discovered evidence of pit workings as well as the easier method of 'panning' or washing. A shaft found in 1891 was 120 feet deep and had been worked by rope and bark bucket; a lateral 'stope' in a vein of gold-bearing quartz was supported by wooden pit props and looked efficient enough. But the total gold resources of the country were small, as the men of the Pioneer Column were themselves to discover at bitter cost. Not until deep-shaft operations were undertaken, forty years later and many hundreds of miles farther north on the borders of Katanga, was Rhodesia to produce the kind of mineral wealth that the early Portuguese explorers had sought. And then it was not gold, but copper.

Fernandez remains none the less important as the first white man to have seen the rich land which is Rhodesia today. He made two long journeys and passed near the sites of the present-day cities of Salisbury and Umtali. His impressions of the kingdom of the Monomotapa are recorded by the chronicler, Damião de Goes, who described the principal palace of Zimbabwe and the lesser stone forts in other parts of the country. 'These fortresses and their garrisons,' he wrote, 'were the Emperor's method of safeguarding the mines and the trading route to the coast. There are cattle, grain crops and fruit in abundance, and herds of wild elephants. About five thousand of these are killed each year, and the ivory of their tusks is another important source of the Emperor's wealth.' The chronicler noted approvingly that the people – who were called Kaffirs and had black skins – did not worship idols 'but believe in one God who is the creator of all things'.

It may seem a digression, in pursuing the politics of partnership, to reach so far back into an apparently irrelevant past. But the past, however remote, is not irrelevant to the Africans of Rhodesia. They are hungry today for history, one may even say ravenous. Call it self-defence, pride, or what you please; it is none the less a hard political fact, not only in Rhodesia but in every other part of the continent.

Admittedly this is true only of those Africans who are politically conscious, but they constitute a far larger segment of the population than the white settlers realize or admit. And, of course, this new national spirit is strongest in the younger generations who have learned to read. The *African Daily News* in Salisbury, for example, has been increasing its circulation at an annual rate of eight to ten per cent, much greater than that of the population growth. Its past editor, Nathan Shamuyarira, has told me of the marked appeal exerted by historical articles – 'flash-backs' in the national history of the Mashona or Matabele peoples, which contribute to a sense of solidarity and pride in the present day.

It is typical of the gulf in thinking which divides white from black in this schizophrenic community that the settlers consistently ignore or underrate the political consciousness of their voteless partners. Not long ago Sir Edgar Whitehead, the Prime Minister of Southern Rhodesia, told me at great length and with very evident sincerity of his efforts to persuade qualified Africans to register as voters. Teams of Civil Servants had toured the townships and Sir Edgar himself had gone along to watch and, on occasion, to persuade. The results were negligible. I myself can think of half a dozen reasons why these African citizens would choose to abstain – some of them are set out in a later chapter – but Sir Edgar told me firmly that there was only one reason: African apathy. When I mentioned this incident to one of the organizers of the African nationalist movement in the colony, he simply remarked: 'Do you suppose, if Adolf Hitler had occupied the British Isles, had drawn up a special voters' roll that gave the franchise to a selected ten per cent of the population, and then sent round Storm Troopers to whip up registrations, that Englishmen or Scotsmen would have behaved any differently from us?'

A grossly unfair parallel, perhaps; but it shows the deep currents of feeling behind apparently pliant, placid, or apathetic African faces. It also explains why, in the increasingly bitter state of tension between the races, the moderate African who chooses to cooperate with the white authorities is contemptuously described as a 'stooge' by his nationalist brother. And with this sharpening of the political edges goes the phenomenon of a new and powerful interest by the politically conscious Africans in their past. It is a phenomenon that has manifested itself in every African country: 'the search for national self-identity' – as Dr Azikiwe of Nigeria has described it. It may involve the searching out of old traditional names to replace those decreed by the European invader. The Gold Coast becomes Ghana, and in Nyasaland Dr Banda and his colleagues declare their intention to rename their country Malawi. So also with Mr Joshua Nkomo and his nationalist associates in Southern Rhodesia; in happier times, before the July shootings of 1960 and 1961 shattered the half a century old record of racial peace, they were content to call their movement the National Democratic Party. When the N.D.P. was declared an illegal organization and proscribed by the Whitehead administration, it was significant that the men who formed the new national movement chose the name Zimbabwe African People's Union. Indeed, it is now the firm intention of the men who lead the nationalist movement in Southern Rhodesia to change the name of their country on attaining independence to Zimbabwe, thus wiping out a name which now serves only to remind them of bitter military defeat in 1896–7.

Thus the stone temples and towers of Great Zimbabwe, which the ordinary white Rhodesian today regards simply as a tourist attraction, have taken on a special significance for the African nationalist movement in the territory. The official handbook prepared by the Federal government lists Zimbabwe under National Parks and Game Reserves as an 'internationally renowned site' and continues: 'Seventeen miles south-east of Fort Victoria in an amphitheatre of granite-domed hills . . . a fascinating relic of Rhodesia's hidden past . . . the origin of the ruins is still swathed in mystery and romance.'

The resources of modern research have, in fact, made Zimbabwe much less mysterious than it used to be. By means of the Carbon 14 dating process, combined with the results of two expeditions financed by the British Association, it is possible to deduce that there was a well-organized kingdom, having Zimbabwe as its royal kraal, which flourished from about A.D. 800 to 1200. Today the visitor encounters ruins with the same awesome quality as Angkor Wat, or the silent Mayan pyramids that stand in the deep Mexican jungles of Yucatan. Zimbabwe sparks the imagination and sets the mind racing. Who were these long-lost people who quarried the stone and raised these smooth, curving walls to survive the centuries? The ingenious staircases leading to long passages, the strong soaring walls, the stirring pattern in the stonework of the outer rampart – surely all these imply some earlier, grander civilization that went down to sudden and final cataclysm before the African invaders?

This, indeed, was the immediate conclusion of the early Victorian hunters and explorers who reached Mashonaland. Zimbabwe clearly implied a high degree of organization in the working force that built it and the political leaders who occupied it. Surely one could not equate it with the Mashona tribesmen now inhabiting the country, people who lived a simple existence with their wattle huts and their irregularly shaped patches of ground cultivated on the 'slash-and-burn' principle. The Victorians found, from the moment they took over political direction of the territory, just how irritating and haphazard these Africans could be as workmen – forever melting away into the bush and apparently incapable of joint organized effort over any extended period of time. Zimbabwe was surely the work of people who had learned their craft from Egypt and Babylon; Arabs, perhaps, whose dhows had been sailing down the coast to Zanzibar and beyond for a good 2,000 years. More engagingly, it might have been the Phoenicians or even one of the 'lost tribes' of Israel,

The answer, when the modern archeologists and anthropologists had done their work, was dishearteningly prosaic. The builders, organizers, and occupiers of Zimbabwe were simply the ancestors of the very same African people whom the Victorian pioneers encountered six centuries later. First there had been the Wakaranga, succeeded through conquest by the Barozwi, who in turn had been smashed by the northward drive of the Zulu regiments under their king, Mzilikazi. It was the Zulu whom the white man found in command of the country in Victorian times; he called them the Matabele, for that was as near as the European tongue could come to their tribal name, and the Victorians had a healthy respect for the Matabele as fighting men. Under Mzilikazi and later his son, King Lobengula, these tribesmen had developed their regimental formation or *impi* into a formidable fighting machine.

Just as the warlike Matabele treated the Mashona people of the veld with disdain, raiding them for cattle and women, so the Victorian explorers chose Mashonaland for their target area when they sent their Pioneer Column northwards in 1890. And it

is perhaps understandable that they found it so difficult to associate the dispirited Shonas, their tribal organization shattered,
with the towering structures of Zimbabwe. I can perhaps claim a
little insight into what the Victorians must have felt, from similar
experience in the rain forests of Guatemala and Yucatan. There
one may come upon sudden splendid Mayan temples, half-
hidden by luxuriant tropical growth, for there are so many to be
classified and investigated that the government has not yet got
round to preparing them all for display. And so, like those early
visitors to Zimbabwe a century ago, one may find oneself astonished by silent ruins, the soaring towers and the majestic
balustrades – and wonder what possible connexion there might
be between the master craftsmen who had left these monuments
behind them, and the haphazard, impoverished people of the
present-day villages near by, grubbing a simple living from their
patchy gardens in the jungle clearings. The paradox, of course, is
that they are virtually the same Mayan people, now as then,
whose once rich civilization was finally destroyed by the white
invader, although there is evidence enough that, even before the
Spanish arrived, their culture had gone into decline.

Today we know more about this phenomenon; we know that
erosion of the soil and depletion of its minerals are all bound up
in a process leading to nutritional deficiency and the abandonment of communal dwelling places. It is entirely consistent with
modern anthropological knowledge – and modern agronomy –
that the Mashona culture which built Zimbabwe should subsequently have slipped to the low point at which the Victorians
found it. We are ready today to accept that civilizations degene-
rate. But to the Victorian conquerors such an idea was unacceptable; indeed, it never occurred to them at all. Theirs was a world
of expanding horizons in science, business, and war. Carrying
Kipling in their knapsacks, they were out to conquer continents
with the rifle, the steam engine, and the telegraph line.

The people they encountered in Mashonaland, as we know
now, were the fragmented survival of several invasions; their
tribal organizations had been smashed; they were in fact not one
people, but the scattered segments of many. They occupied only

parts – agriculturally not always the best parts – of what today is Southern Rhodesia. And down upon them, irresistibly, descended the warrior Matabele from time to time, to carry off their cattle, their women, and the produce of their patchy gardens. They comprised so many different peoples that they had no generic name for themselves; it was their enemy, the Matabele, who lumped them all together and called them Mashona. And it was by this name, 'the Lost Ones' in the Matabele language, that the first Europeans came to know them. Not unnaturally, the Pioneers concluded that they themselves were entering a largely empty land from which some great and now vanished race, the builders of Zimbabwe, had departed.

In fact, the country only appeared empty; under their wasteful system of 'slash-and-burn' patch cultivation, the Africans usually occupied one piece of land for only half a dozen years or so, and then moved on because the fertility had been exhausted. They were, in fact, using much of Mashonaland as one big garden; it was the coming of the white man with his ideas of individual rather than tribal land ownership, and fenced fields instead of mobility, that was to give rise to the first and deepest clash between the two races. The quarrel over land is still the basic conflict in the politics of the Federation today; in the south, it is the paramount complaint of Mr Nkomo and his nationalist movement, the wrong above all others that they want redressed. Their fourteen-page constitution starts off with a preamble describing the Zimbabwe African People's Union as 'an association of people who have been dispossessed of their land'.

Zimbabwe, once a symbol of decline, has been rescued politically and made the symbol of African yearnings for independence and national dignity. But among the majority of white Rhodesians it is the legend that lingers, and legend more often than fact is the fuel that feeds political machines. The Victorian Pioneers felt themselves to be clearly, unquestionably superior to the Africans they found around them – first in Mashonaland and later in the territories that were to become Northern Rhodesia and Nyasaland. On this purely racial attitude, the whole political structure of present-day Rhodesia has been built, for legends have great staying power and subsequent generations have continued to build on this Pioneer premise. Sir Roy Welensky, after all, grew up in the Salisbury of the period before the First World War; it was then, too, that a young Dr Huggins arrived from England, the man who was to be Sir Roy's predecessor as first Federal Prime Minister. The Pioneers were still the dominant force in that formative era of the new nation; and their prejudices and assumptions permeate the laws and the institutions to this day. We shall look at these more closely in later chapters, but it is well to bear in mind that this whole state structure – of Urban Native Townships, of the Land Apportionment Act, of complex franchise qualifications, of a thirty-member legislature that was to remain triumphantly all-white for thirty-nine years – rests firmly upon a base that is an assumed, implicit concept of race superiority. Clearly, what matters in the politics of Rhodesian partnership is 'attitude'; and since the white partner happens to hold military, political, and economic power, it is *his* attitude which shapes the society. All the laws and institutions are only an outward manifestation of that attitude; and if this is so, then there are only two ways in which the advance to normal democracy in British Central Africa can be promoted. One is to work for a change in the attitude of those who hold the power. The other is to strip power by force from those who hold it.

The core of the Rhodesian dilemma, then, is this: are the white citizens, who wield political power and dominate the voters' rolls in Southern Rhodesia, capable of a change in attitude? A fundamental change, not just a slight shift in their rule which stops well short of democracy? Certainly, a fundamental change would seem, to a neutral observer, the logical recognition of changed circumstances in the outside world, especially in the many territories to the north where African majorities have taken over government and the responsibilities of power. It would also recognize the vast changes, educational and political, which have occurred within Rhodesia's own African community. But emotion, not logic, is the tyrant of politics. Emotionally, the white Rhodesians still find it easier to regard the Africans as backward children, to believe that they have not changed in the past seven decades since the Pioneer Column arrived on the hillside near Harare, raised the flag, and renamed the place Fort Salisbury.

So attitude matters, legend matters, Zimbabwe matters. Let us conclude our brief study of the Zimbabwe civilization by quoting again from the British authority, Philip Mason:

It is untrue to suggest that the Europeans came into an empty country. They came into a country underpopulated and with stretches fairly recently made empty, largely by Zulu incursions. The previous inhabitants could not defend it against them and thus lacked the most widely accepted of all title deeds. They were disorganized and demoralized when the Europeans came, but it is not true that they were hereditarily incapable of progress or combination. They had taken the step forward into the Iron Age, they had organized a highly centralized state; then something had gone wrong and they fell back. No one can be dogmatic as to why, but like the Neolithic people who built Stonehenge, like the Irish who led north-west Europe in civilization, like the Romans, like a score of other peoples, they fell back. Such a recession is due to many complex causes; there is no reason to suppose it is final. What men have done once they can again, and sometimes they do it better.*

Some three hundred years separate the Portuguese explorations and the return of the white man in the Victorian era – this time to stay. The last Portuguese effort at settlement was the expedition led by Francesco Barreto in 1569. He arrived in what is now Southern Rhodesia determined to quell the forces of the Monomotapa, survey the gold fields, and establish permanent mining operations, and he brought with him a well-equipped force of soldiers and miners. The expedition ended in disaster; Barreto died at Sena on the banks of the inhospitable Zambesi, and the Portuguese withdrew to the coastal strip, which they hold to this day.

They maintained trading links, of course, through their ports in Moçambique, and in the middle of the nineteenth century the English- and Dutch-speaking South Africans began to venture into the same field. The Governor of the Cape Colony concluded a treaty of friendship with Mzilikazi, king of the Matabele,

* The Birth of a Dilemma, Oxford University Press, 1958, p. 73.

which ensured trading and hunting rights. Once again tales of ivory and gold trickled from the land that the hunters called the Far Interior; and soon the English-speaking world was receiving confirmation in reports such as those of Carl Mauch and Henry Hartley after their expedition to the 'Mashona goldfields' in 1867. This coincided with the African literary fever, spread by men like Rider Haggard with his tale of King Solomon's Mines; it coincided, too, with the new crusade of the English and Scottish missionaries to drive the slave-traders out of Africa now that Britain had freed the slaves in her own dominions.

The importance of the missionary families in building what are today the three states of British Central Africa can hardly be overstated. Quite apart from the enormous legacy of education which they have bequeathed to the Africans, there has been their very direct intervention in politics – providing a warm, humanitarian, 'democratizing' influence to counter the cold rigidity of the racialists. In modern times it was a missionary-turned-politician, Garfield Todd, who profoundly altered the course of political development and, as Prime Minister of Southern Rhodesia, held the white supremacists in check until he was himself overthrown by his own party. In Northern Rhodesia during the crucial negotiations involving London, Lusaka, and Salisbury from 1960 to 1962, a vital mediating role was carried out by the multi-racial Liberal Party of the protectorate. Its leader, Sir John Moffat, and his colleagues in the legislature took up ministerial portfolios and enabled constitutional government to continue when the ministers of Sir Roy Welensky's United Federal Party withdrew from office and declared a boycott. It was another missionary-turned-politician, the Rev. Colin Morris, who left his pulpit in Chingola to help form the Liberal Party in the first place, and then, as its vice-president, played a key part in the London negotiations.

Though not a parson himself, Sir John Moffat comes of a missionary line that can quite properly be called the first white family of Rhodesia. The first John Moffat and his wife Emily established a mission at Inyati near Bulawayo in 1859, and their son, Livingstone Moffat, was the first European child to be born in the country. But the story really begins one generation before them, with John's father, Robert Moffat, who had gone out to Africa on behalf of the London Missionary Society long before the parliamentary battle in London for the freeing of the slaves had been won. On one of his trips home Robert Moffat was asked to speak at a great rally in London, organized to protest against the slave-trade. Afterwards, a young Scottish medical student attached to the Charing Cross Hospital, came up to the platform and introduced himself. He had decided to go to Africa, if he could be of any help. Moffat's reply was: 'Yes, if you are prepared to leave occupied ground and push on to the north.' The student, of course, was David Livingstone; in later years he was to marry Moffat's daughter Mary. His career, indeed, illustrates the brevity of modern political history in Central Africa. Livingstone himself may seem a far-off Victorian figure to most of us, but the present generation of political leaders in Rhodesia – the Welenskys and Whiteheads, the Nkomos and Sitholes – grew up among men of both races who had known the great missionary explorer.

'You will see the smoke of a thousand villages,' Robert Moffat told Livingstone, 'where the Gospel has never been proclaimed.' He saw that and much more in the thirty years beginning one sunny March morning when his ship docked beneath the heights of Table Mountain at Cape Town, and ending in the village of Ilala in the swamplands of Northern Rhodesia when he knelt to pray by his bedside one April evening, sick with fever and weak from loss of blood. It was his African colleagues who found him in the morning, dead, and still on his knees.

There is, obviously, a temptation to sentimentalize the role played by the missionaries in the development of Central Africa. The conservative white settlers – the tough men who pride themselves on being 'realists' – claim that things are much easier for the clergyman, jogging along on the periphery as a kind of older brother, teacher, and doctor combined. The harder task is that of the European layman, opening up a territory, creating a modern economy, and building a nation; for he must take on the responsibilities of administrator, legislator, magistrate, and employer.

Responsibilities involve discipline – rewards and punishments – and therefore a relationship in which clashes, in racial terms, must inevitably occur. Put this argument to any of today's African nationalist leaders and you will get the same, coldly logical reply: who asked the European to come into our country and set himself up as legislator, employer, and all the rest ?

I have spoken at various times to most of these men, and it is significant that they themselves draw a clear line of distinction between the missionaries and the other white men who began arriving in their country a century ago. They see the latter, even the liberals amongst them, as exploiters in varying degrees, but many men of the church as guides and associates – though of course with the normal quota of human failings. The three men who arose in the late 1950s as the recognized champions of African nationalism were sons of the Church and proud of it. It is not coincidental that Hastings Kamuzu Banda, Kenneth Kaunda, and Joshua Nkomo, should be Christians as well as fiery, nationalist reformers; their religious upbringing animates and justifies their political crusade. Dr Banda does not flaunt his faith on the public platform, but in his private life he is proud to be a member of the Church of Scotland, whose missionaries were so profound an influence in his formative years in Nyasaland. Mr Kaunda, himself a missionary's son, consciously applies in public life the principles which have ruled his private life since childhood. Mr Nkomo, a reticent man when it comes to personal affairs, is reluctant to refer to church matters on public occasions; nevertheless, when he was able to return home to Southern Rhodesia after two years of exile in England, he quietly arranged for his wife and children to go to a mission station in the country while he plunged into the hurly-burly of political life in Salisbury.

Clearly, then, today's African in the Federation is perfectly capable of distinguishing between one kind of white man and another, despite the fact that most of these more privileged citizens treat him as a political inferior, an economic helot and a cultural barbarian. For five or six generations now, individual British missionaries in Central Africa have tried to bridge the gulf between the races; it has been neither an easy nor a unanimously applauded task. In many parts of Africa today white supremacy is being matched by a dynamic black supremacy, no less ominous in its racial obsessions. That Rhodesia has so far seen few flare-ups of this new phenomenon may be substantially ascribed to the years of quiet, constructive work put in by generations of missionaries from Moffat and Livingstone onwards. In contrast to the other settlers whose aim, perhaps understandably, was to get rich as quickly as possible, these were modest men in search of modest rewards. Theirs was a most intangible investment; yet it is likely to pay far more significant dividends in the immediate political future – by the standards of the West itself – than all the activities of those hard-boiled men who prided themselves on being 'realists'.

It was the fate of the early missionaries, whether they wished it or not, to become inextricably involved in politics. The Moffats in Matabeleland, François Coillard in Barotseland, the Scotsmen on the shores of Lake Nyasa – these were people who had been settled for ten, twenty or even thirty years in their districts before the laymen who called themselves the 'first white settlers' actually arrived, to initiate politics in the modern sense of the term. It was easy enough for a settler to peg out a stretch of land; but inevitably it meant that a register had to be established as a basis for future sales and transfers. One way and another the newcomers found themselves forced to seek out the local African authority, if only to regularize the lines of demarcation. It was the missionary they turned to, because he knew the undisputed chief with authority to make a bargain on behalf of his tribe; furthermore, he could speak the tribal language and act as their interpreter. It was a delicate role, one that most missionaries accepted only with reluctance. But usually they felt bound to step in, knowing that if they did not try and safeguard African rights as far as possible, there was no one else who would. Practical Christian charity demanded no less.

This treaty-making process reached its climax at the royal kraal of Lobengula, King of the Matabele, in the year 1888; there the deal was done which was to set the pattern for all the developments in politics, business, and race relations that have followed, right through to the present day. It is worth looking at closely, and it points up once again the essentially South African parentage of what is today the Rhodesian Federation.

In the early 1800s, in what was to become known as Zululand, the chief of one of the tribes of the Nguni peoples evolved a new technique of hand-to-hand fighting. There can be little doubt that Chaka was an original military genius; he turned his ragged recruits into disciplined infantry formations, employing his new technique of spear and shield in orderly, massed formations. He combined spartan training methods with new tactics and a driving personal ambition; it was he, in fact, who welded together into one Zulu nation many widely differing Bantu peoples. The nation, in turn, produced an empire. Zulu armies under generals who had been trained by Chaka split off and marched north, reversing for the first time the general southward migration which had been moving down the length of Africa since the time of Christ. The Zulu drive to the north was like some great tidal wave, cutting across all the smaller waves and churning the more settled African communities into fragments of surf. One of Chaka's most brilliant generals was a man as impressive in physique as in intellect, Mzilikazi, who was to lead the Matabele people at the time of their first encounter with white men.

These whites were the Voortrekkers, the Afrikaner pioneers trekking north and eastwards from the Cape, in major part because they passionately opposed Britain's decision to emancipate the slaves and extend rights to men of colour. Mzilikazi knew nothing of this; he simply saw an obvious threat to his sovereignty from strangers who clearly meant to settle on his land. In the first fierce battle, sixteen members of the Erasmus-Bekker Expedition were killed. Meanwhile, other Zulu armies were harrying the Voortrekkers, and on 16 December 1838 at Blood River in Natal the main forces were smashed by the Boer army under Andries Pretorius. (The anniversary is still a national holiday in South Africa.) But Mzilikazi had not waited for the end. Recognizing that his own regiments could not match the enemy with their guns, he had shrewdly decided to cut his losses. Turning his back on the rolling grasslands of Natal which had been his home, he led his Matabele Zulus northward across the Limpopo River and on to the high, airy plateau land of what is today Southern Rhodesia. The only occupants were the scattered knots of Mashona peoples; the Matabele helped themselves to the best of the pasture lands, established their great herds of cattle on them, and made a few forays to demonstrate to the Shona tribesmen that the invaders were now in charge. But Mzilikazi did not relax discipline; on his death his son, Lobengula, inherited not only vast lands and herds of cattle, estimated to number 500,000 beasts in all, but a highly efficient military machine.

There was one other inheritance – a diplomatic problem still unresolved. In 1853 Mzilikazi had concluded a treaty with the Boers, now established in their republic of the Transvaal to the south. It amounted to a mutual agreement not to raid each other; but the situation had not really been stabilized. The new king had not long been established in the royal kraal at Bulawayo when the prospectors for gold began arriving in his territory, spurred on by the highly coloured descriptions brought back to Johannesburg by Hartley and Mauch. Perhaps more puzzling than these newcomers were the missionaries, for how were the Matabele to interpret their motives? They spoke about a King of their own, long dead, who would one day be returning. And they sought to recruit all men as His subjects. Lobengula was no fool – indeed, all the evidence suggests that, like the Princess Pocahontas who so astonished the court of King James, he had a first-class brain and may well have been in the genius class, with what today we should call an I.Q. of 150. So we may assume that it was clear enough to Lobengula himself how to assess the missionaries, their message, and their motives. Indeed, the diaries of Moffat, Coillard, and the rest give us the picture of a man who personally liked and trusted these newcomers and had a sympathetic grasp of their moral and religious teachings. But he was politician enough to know that, if he gave them *carte blanche*, he might all too soon be faced by a threat to fission within the monolithic structure of the Matabele themselves, just at a time when the nation had to brace itself for the frontal attack from another set of European invaders – the economic freebooters. The personal links with the missionaries were of long standing. Robert Moffat once said that he and Mzilikazi had been 'true friends for twenty-three years'. And the Zulu king had reciprocated. Moffat has recorded this impression of one of their meetings at the royal kraal:

I entered, he grasped my hand and drew his mantle over his face. . . . He spoke not, except to pronounce my name, again and again. He looked at me, his hand still holding mine, and he again covered his face. My heart yearned with compassion for his soul.

David Livingstone too, although he had encountered resistance among the Matabele to the Church as an institution, none the less retained a high opinion of the African ethical code – or most of it. He wrote:

The idea of the Father of all being displeased with his children for selling or killing each other at once gains their ready assent. It harmonizes so exactly with their own ideas of right and wrong.

And the French Calvinist missionary, François Coillard, wrote in his journal how he felt 'more and more drawn' to Lewanika, chief of the Barotse.

When I said we should know each other better by and by, he looked steadily at me and said: 'You speak for yourself, Moruti, but when I once saw you that was enough. I gave myself to you; it is my nature.'

It had been the strategy of Mzilikazi, confronted with the fire-power of the Boer patrols, to withdraw across the Limpopo and break contact with the white man. To his son, Lobengula, fell the task of diplomacy which the old Zulu king had neatly avoided. The new leader saw that he would have to arm himself diplomatically; and that meant acquiring an adviser who spoke the language of the invaders, but might be neutral or perhaps even partisan to the Matabele cause. His choice fell upon his father's old friend, the Rev. Robert Moffat. With his help, the new young king concluded the first of many commercial treaties. Actually, the concession of 1876 was intended to put a stop to all further pesterings by the concession hunters; Lobengula and Moffat deliberately chose the least avaricious of those petitioning at the royal kraal. He was Tom Baines, an English artist and explorer, a friend of Livingstone who had been with the Scottish missionary when he had discovered the Victoria Falls. The concession granted Baines the right to prospect for gold; but it was made clear – in words carefully chosen by Moffat – that 'I, Lobengula, reserve intact the sovereignty of my dominion'. Unfortunately for the king, Baines proved an inadequately aggressive ally for the purpose; he formed no exploitation company, and sent no expeditions. By default, the field still lay open.

It is one of the tragic ironies of this era in the history of southern Africa that Lobengula never had the satisfaction of dealing direct with the three men who, in fact, were his rivals and enemies: Bismarck, Kruger, and Rhodes. Like the gods in a Sophoclean tragedy, they remained remote, pitiless, and implacable; they had emissaries to do their bidding. Indeed, the events that followed were those of tragedy on an epic scale. Lobengula was a central figure of truly heroic stature whose ultimate, inevitable death – in pitiful but dignified circumstances – marked not just the end of his own life but the end of an era and the eclipse of a whole nation. For the Matabele people of Central Africa today, the image of their late king represents an Oedipus or Achilles, with this additional impact – that our epic heroes are remote from us in time, but theirs is a man who died within living memory. There are many thousands of black Rhodesians, now in their fifties or sixties, who as children heard eye-witness accounts of this legendary figure from their own fathers.

This is why it is not just interesting, but essential to study the Lobengula legend, which has been so deeply seared into African hearts and minds. This may sound dangerously sentimental but, as Britain's Commonwealth Secretary, Duncan Sandys, remarked on returning from his Rhodesian negotiations in 1962: 'In African politics today emotion is often more important than hard fact.' A nation which was rallied by Churchillian emotion after Dunkirk – when hard facts indicated surrender – should not find this too difficult to understand. So, although the name of this African king may sound quaint enough in British ears, it is important that they should try to see him through African eyes. To the Matabele he was, and is, their Winston Churchill. It can safely be assumed that when today's African leaders sally forth to political battle, they are consciously wearing the mantle they believe themselves to have collectively inherited from Lobengula. Mr Joshua Nkomo must have felt some of these sensations when in the spring of 1962, as leader of the African nationalist movement in his territory and President of the Zimbabwe African People's Union, he at last succeeded in his campaign to bring the problems of his people before the U.N. From the skyscraper block overlooking the East River in New York to the nameless cave in the banks of the Zambesi where Lobengula died, shuddering with fever, on a January day in 1894, still pursued by the mounted troops of Dr Starr Jameson, seems an infinity in space and time. And yet the events have two close links with each other. One is Mr Nkomo, himself a Matabele and the acknowledged leader of his people, who happens to bear a remarkable physical resemblance to Lobengula. The other is the British South Africa Company. It raised, armed, and paid the troops who pursued the king to his squalid death, and it is the British South Africa Company police – now paid by the government while retaining the old name – who patrol the African townships to this day, with armoured cars instead of horses. On the commercial side, the Chartered Company took over Lobengula's economic resources (including a handsome share in his half-million head of cattle) and has dominated the heights of the Rhodesian economy from that day to this.

The manoeuvres directed by Cecil Rhodes which led to the diplomatic defeat and military extinction of Lobengula, also laid the whole groundwork for the structure of government and commerce in the Central African Federation of today. Labour legislation, 'Native administration', the social and political colour-bar – all these aspects of Rhodesian life as they now operate – were determined by the events of a dozen stormy years. The men who defeated Lobengula took possession of a treasure chest; they were not to know that in the 1960s it would prove to be a Pandora's Box.

4 The Age of Rhodes

'Whether Cecil Rhodes is the lofty patriot multitudes believe him to be, or Satan come again, when he stands at the Cape his shadow falls to the Zambesi. He robs and slays, and enslaves the Matabele, and gets Charter-Christian applause for it.'
MARK TWAIN

One day an African Prime Minister will order a plinth to be erected in the centre of Salisbury; perhaps in the public garden that marks the spot where the men of the Pioneer Column planted their flagpole and ran up the Union Jack on a brave spring day in 1890. And on this plinth will be placed a statue of Lobengula, King of the Matabele.

But until then, the public monument dominating the Rhodesian capital will continue to be the statue of Cecil Rhodes. Larger than life size – appropriately – it shows the familiar figure of the Victorian schoolboy hero gazing out across the rich, sundrenched landscape, which was incorporated by his efforts into Her Majesty's Dominions.

For there can be no doubt about it: uniquely, at least in modern times, here is a territory conquered, colonized, and constituted as a nation through the initiative of one man. It is a staggering achievement, though not one that is inclined to provoke cries of admiration or gratitude from the territory's African citizens. 'I prefer land to niggers,' said Rhodes, in one of his not infrequent bursts of candour, when discussing his policy for the conquered domains of the Mashona and Matabele.

Whatever one's attitude to Rhodes, a study of the man's character and achievements is essential for an understanding of present-day Rhodesia. He is, indubitably, the Father of Federation, for the link-up that took place in 1953 was no more than the realization by the white settlers two generations later of Rhodes's original dream. It was he who bludgeoned a timid British Foreign Office into bringing under Imperial protection the territories north of the Zambesi that were to become Northern Rhodesia.

And it was Rhodes again, when Lord Salisbury was hesitant, who refused to watch Nyasaland fall to the Portuguese by default. At the critical moment, during one of his visits to London, he personally wrote out the cheque for £2,000 to equip young Harry Johnston for the expedition to Lake Nyasa, with a promise of £9,000 a year from the British South Africa Company if all went well. It did.

During the vital, formative years of government in all three territories, it was Rhodes's British South Africa Company which possessed supreme military and administrative power. It was the British South Africa Company police – uniformed, mounted, and so armed as to be indistinguishable from troops – who constituted the national army. British South Africa Company salaried officials set up the civil administration. British South Africa Company trading-posts were established, not only in conquered Mashonaland and Matabeleland, but north of the Zambesi to the Congo border and east to Lake Nyasa. Over these flew the proud standard of 'Chartered' – the Union Jack emblazoned with a lion grasping a tusk of ivory – 'the Dog and Bone', as some of its young employees irreverently called it.

These young men were called Assistant Collectors – a further reminder that it was the Rhodesian white settler, rather than the government of Her Britannic Majesty, who was opening up the new land. They were collectors of taxes, for it was the 'Chartered Company' and not the Colonial Office which represented civil power in this vast new territory. It was the Company which built the roads, strung the telegraph lines, and laid a railway system. It was the Company which controlled the land and the mineral rights, parcelled out acreages to farmers and claims to miners. Nyasaland soon reverted to the more normal type of British colonial rule, but it remains significant that, when European rule began, Cecil Rhodes himself took possession of all three territories and dealt with them as one. In that sense, all the later political initiatives of the white settlers – the campaign that led to federation in 1953 and the near autonomy contained in the Declaration of 1957 – was a struggle not to create some synthetic new system, but rather return to one which had existed before the turn of the century.

It was, even by the standards of the Victorian Age, a grandiose design. As Rhodes did not hesitate to point out to the Kaiser, the lion flag now flew over an area larger than France, Germany, Holland, and the British Isles all put together. Indeed, in area, the new territory exceeded its immediate parent, the land that is today the Republic of South Africa. But for Rhodes the advance was nowhere near complete. He had seized on Harry Johnston's phrase 'Cape to Cairo', and planned that the great new white dominion should be the springboard for an even greater venture. When Rhodes called on Kaiser Wilhelm in Berlin during the spring of 1899, it was to get his promise of Germany's coopera-tion in the building of the Cape-to-Cairo Railway. A London magazine had just printed an article by Colonel Prout, a technical expert on railway construction, who claimed that there had been 'nothing quite so spectacular . . . since Alexander the Great'. He had also maintained that such a line would cost at least £15 million and would be quite uneconomic, but Rhodes tactfully omitted any reference to that. The Emperor was infected by his visitor's enthusiasm, promised transit rights through German East Africa on condition that the railway would buy German steel rail and rolling stock, and spent the rest of the afternoon with Rhodes scrutinizing maps. They looked at Africa, and then at the Emperor's plan for the Berlin-to-Baghdad railway, and they talked of the civilizing task awaiting the Germanic and Anglo-Saxon peoples. Only the outbreak of the Boer War, and Rhodes's death three years later, prevented the realization of the railway project.

In retrospect it may all seem preposterous, but we must see the world with Victorian eyes if we are to understand the ideas which animated Rhodes – ideas which were firmly implanted in the minds of the first white settlers and which have remained part of the national *ethos* to this day. Every young Rhodesian grows up thinking of himself as a frontiersman, just as New York children who have never been west of Hoboken play at being Texas Rangers and millions of urban young Canadians in

Toronto and Montreal put in a spell of imaginary duty in the scarlet-and-gold of the Royal Canadian Mounted Police, bringing renegade Sioux to justice.

Present-day Rhodesia is, in many ways, still a Victorian frontier civilization. Much of the open country of the high veld has the same brilliant blue skies, broad horizons, and belting hot sunshine of the Texas plains, or Wyoming, or the Caribou country of western Canada. And as you find in such places the occasional small town with its dusty main street and Victorian false-fronted shops, so you will find the same touches of Victoriana in Rhodesia. Of course, in Salisbury there are skyscrapers and Espresso coffee bars that would do credit to London or New York, but the world of general stores and hitching-posts is never far away. It was not a cross-section of Victorian England that emigrated to Rhodesia; the intellectuals, the aristocrats, and the social reformers stayed at home.

Rhodesian society in Victorian times was not cluttered by any awkward oddities, any Bernard Shaws or Henrietta Barnetts or Beatrice Webbs. It was created by an invasion of hearty, extroverted Captain Farebrothers, reared on a healthy, simple diet of Kipling, Rider Haggard, and the *Boys' Own Paper*. All generalizations are untrue, of course, including this one; but there is enough truth in it to explain the inevitable disaster which followed the clash between these particular Victorians and a community of Iron Age people whose skins – just to complicate matters – happened to be black.

It was not so disastrous in other parts of the world where these same Captain Farebrothers were going. In India, some of them could say, with reluctant admiration, 'by the Livin' Gawd that made you, you're a better man than I am, Gunga Din!' In Canada, although apprehensive at first, they eventually lost their fear of the tiny minority of Indian tribesmen in their midst. Canadian Indians flew Spitfires in R.C.A.F. squadrons over Germany in the Second World War; today most of them have liquor licences and the right to vote, and there are men of Indian blood in the provincial legislatures and the national parliament in Ottawa. Victorian extroverts going to the Middle East created a whole mystique around Arab civilization; we not only have the Lawrence of Arabia legend; we even think it rather splendid to dress up in Arab costume.

No such glamour ever attached itself in the eyes of the Rhodesian Pioneer to the costume or custom of the black people he found awaiting the helping hand of partnership in Mashonaland. Perhaps it was in part the centuries of association between a black skin and the humiliating status of slavery. Today in Rhodesia the visitor often has quoted to him, as one of the official slogans of the partnership code, Rhodes's famous phrase about 'equal rights for all civilized men'. The suggestion, of course, is that he was prepared to consider political equality for black people – of a certain kind. But in Rhodes's career there is much more to indicate a fanatical dedication to the principle that certain races – the Anglo-Saxon and the Germanic – were inherently superior. He was able to preach equal rights for the Afrikaner with South Africans of British stock because he included his Afrikaans-speaking neighbours in his select category. The special provision of fifteen Rhodes scholarships for Germany (to be selected personally by the Kaiser) was part of this curious racialism of his. His influence was beneficial where it lay in the reconciliation between English and Afrikaner that he sought all his life. As M.P. for Barkly West in the Cape parliament, he made a special effort to explain to his constituents in 1890 what he was trying to do with his British South Africa Company. He described his 'policy of taking over the North. . . . The country to which we all belong should have as much of it as it can possibly get'. And he went on to define just who he meant by 'we'. They were 'a great people . . . an amalgamation . . . not only English but Dutch'.

Rhodes's outlook on African political rights is perhaps most clearly illustrated by his deal with Hofmeyr that very year, when arranging the coalition in the Cape parliament which made him Prime Minister. As the price of Afrikaner support, Hofmeyr listed a number of demands, including the removal of what were called 'raw natives' from the voters' rolls. Rhodes readily agreed.

He was usually discreet about committing himself to print, but there is on record his cable in 1895 to Dr Rutherford Harris, when he was pressing the Colonial Office to let the British South Africa Company take over Bechuanaland. Lobengula by this time was dead, Dr Jameson snugly installed as civil administrator, and the late king's country called Rhodesia. Three Bechuana chiefs, thoroughly alarmed, managed to reach London, alert the missionary societies, Exeter Hall, and the Liberal Press in Fleet Street, and so stimulate such an uproar that the British South Africa Company application was rejected. Rhodes exploded his fury in a cable from Cape Town: 'It is humiliating to be utterly beaten by these niggers. They think more of one Native at home than the whole of South Africa.'

An even more revealing incident had preceded this. At twenty-five Rhodes was already, if not one of the diamond kings of Kimberley, at least a prince. He had shares in De Beers and in a prosperous Natal railway, many rich diamond claims and a 3,000-acre farm in the Transvaal. His great wealth – when his *income* would touch £1 million a year – was still a dozen years away; but he decided to make a will. He had always had a weak heart and went through life convinced that he would die before his time. And although he made later wills, the mature Rhodes would never tear up this curious document; instead he treasured it and would frequently pull it out and thrust it under people's noses. It animated his political actions, his inner dreams, through all his years as Prime Minister of the Cape, founder of Rhodesia and emperor of the Chartered Company and its domains. The will left his entire estate in trust to the British Colonial Secretary, for the establishment of 'a Secret Society' whose aim was to be 'the extension of British rule throughout the world'. The Rhodes Plan called for:

. . . the occupation by British settlers of the entire continent of Africa, the Holy Land, the valley of the Euphrates, Cyprus, Candia, the whole of South America, the islands of the Pacific . . . the Malay archipelago, the seaboard of China and Japan, and the ultimate recovery of the United States.

Preposterous ? Psychotic ? Yes, perhaps the document was all these things, but it was also – of contemporary significance – the blueprint for the creation of the Federation of Rhodesia and Nyasaland. The tragedy of Central Africa is that the man who conceived the plan for this new nation, cleared the political path for it, financed it, and gave it his name, did all these things because he was spurred on by a passionate belief in white supremacy.

We may turn a blind eye to it – and a good many British colonial secretaries did just that until the departure of Mr Lennox-Boyd in 1959 – but the harsh and inescapable fact remains. Embedded in all the ingenious political progressions – the first Legislative Council of 1899, the Crown Colony annexation of 1923, the Victoria Falls conference on amalgamation in 1936, the final referendum and federation in 1953 – rests a fundamental flaw, an outlook that now in the 1960s we believe to be immoral and stupid. And until this is irrevocably discarded, until the original Rhodes Plan is finally scrapped, this unhappy nation will continue to be sapped by the moral sickness which has crippled it since its birth.

It will be said that it is easy to be wise after the event, or that the early will does not represent Rhodes's mature ideas. But the will was not the work of a schoolboy; it was drafted at the age of twenty-five, by one who had completed his studies at Oxford, had spent some years in South Africa, and was already a very rich man. And though he made later wills, Rhodes never repudiated his plan for the Anglo-Saxon domination of Africa and beyond. Nor are attacks on Rhodes the mere wisdom of hindsight. During his most vigorous years of Empire-making in Rhodesia, he was hotly and continuously criticized by such respected quarters in London as the *Investor's Review*, the *Daily News*, and, indeed, the whole of the Liberal Press, as well as some of the financial journals. From a different quarter came the total and unyielding resistance of the humanitarian forces, represented by the Aborigines Protection Society at Exeter Hall and the London Missionary Society. Seretse Khama and his countrymen in Bechuanaland today, now progressing along the well-marked path towards self-government under the umbrella of the Colonial

Office, have reason to be grateful to the 'opposition lobby' that was organized in London during the nineties to combat the tireless expansionism of Rhodes. The prospect before the Bechuana Africans is in stark contrast to the condition of their cousins just across the border. There, in Southern Rhodesia, live three million fellow-Africans who but for Rhodes, the British South Africa Company, and the accidents of history – including the political flabbiness of now-forgotten Imperial governments in London – would also be advancing to self-government on the pattern of Nigeria, Tanganyika, and the rest.

And this brings us face to face with a phenomenon of present-day Africa: that the events decisive in its political shaping cover so short a span of time. There are still people alive today who knew Rhodes; and the present Lord Salisbury is the grandson of the man who was British Prime Minister during the dozen decisive years of Rhodes's expansionism. And as for Rhodes's victims, if that is not using too strong a description of their present unfortunate condition, they still look to London for help. The Aborigines Protection Society still continues its work; Joshua Nkomo and the other African leaders in the Rhodesias call at its office when they visit London today. But usually they are on their way to the place that now offers them a better hope of unpicking the lock to their cell – the United Nations.

W. T. Stead once remarked that the history of southern Africa would have been profoundly different if Rhodes, Jameson, Beit, and Milner had been married men. Since Stead was a turn-of-the-century Imperial journalist and a trusted friend of Cecil Rhodes, it can be assumed that the remark was uttered in a spirit of friendly admiration; yet it touches on the central mystery of the man's character. Rhodes's enemies, especially after the disaster of the Jameson Raid and the failure of the British South Africa Company to pay so much as one penny in dividend, did not hesitate to drop broad hints in print and by word of mouth that he was a homosexual. It was a rumour that dogged his steps in London, Cape Town, and Rhodesia; yet not even his most rancorous enemies were ever able to produce one jot of evidence.

The truth is probably drabber; that Rhodes was simply one of Nature's neuters.

Cecil John Rhodes was the fourth son of a prosperous Hertfordshire vicar, whose three older boys had been sent to Eton or Winchester. But there could be no question of exposing this delicate, pale child to the rigours of a Victorian public school. He was shy, introverted, lonely, and intelligent; he had wispy fair hair and a high, girlish voice that inevitably made other boys rag him. But there were other traits that mattered too: an obsession with reading, especially books of Imperial history; an inner fire that every now and then blazed from him in displays of temper; and a self-confidence that some called pride but was perhaps no more than a rigid determination. Combined with these qualities was a deeply held fatalism which impelled him on, ever dreaming, ever planning, while other men paused to relax – with wine, or women, or their families. He believed that he was destined not to live out his natural life-span, as indeed proved to be true, but he did not fear that death would come a moment sooner than intended. One result was an overwhelming ambition to encompass his Imperial projects before it was too late, an ambition which became a frenzy as he approached his fiftieth – and last – year. The other result was a total insouciance in the face of danger: the flying bullets during the siege of Kimberley, the threat of Matabele ambush on his treks into Mashonaland, the unarmed advance into the Matopo Hills, where in the stronghold of the Matabele he hectored his enemies into surrender.

His parents had planned a career in the Church for him, but by the age of seventeen he was so delicate in health that tuberculosis was suspected. The specialist in London prescribed the standard treatment appropriate to a family of means in Victorian England: immediate removal to a hot, dry climate. Within weeks Cecil Rhodes was on shipboard, bound for southern Africa. In twenty years he would be a millionaire, Prime Minister of the Cape, and a world figure dealing on level terms with King and Kaiser. It is worth adding, however, that the young emigrant travelled with the useful sum of £2,000 to sustain him, a parting gift from his rich Aunt Sophy. Since in terms of present-day prices this would be worth something over £10,000, it might be said that the boy was off to a flying start.

His health rapidly improved, his energy was boundless, and in an astonishingly short space of time he sent himself back to England – now a diamond king, temporarily turned student at Oxford. Then came Kimberley again, and the rise of the De Beers empire, with Alfred Beit to help him by quietly providing the managerial stability he lacked. Soon he entered the Cape parliament and began his political manoeuvres to cut off Kruger and the Transvaal Boers from their threat to expand northwards. There was only a narrow strip, between the Kalahari desert in the west and Kruger's territory to the east, through which English-speaking South Africans could advance into the lands of the Mashona and Matabele. Until Rhodes appeared on the scene, it had been known as 'the Missionaries' Road': the route of Livingstone, Moffat, and many others. 'I shall call it the Suez Canal to the North!' he declared, in one of his moments of Imperial fervour, and the name stuck. The political parallel was clear in his mind. As an admiring student of sixteen, he had watched Disraeli's technique in snatching the canal company's shares: act first, secure Suez, and square it with parliament afterwards. Rhodes was a great believer in personal initiative of this kind; if he could just manage to deal directly – 'on the personal' was his phrase – he believed that he could win round, and he generally did, almost any man living. His strategy had little success with Kruger; but it had a great deal with the Kaiser, Lord Salisbury, Joseph Chamberlain, and an influential host of others. His other method was squaring; when he met General Gordon, he offered his unsolicited advice about how he would have solved the crisis in the Sudan. 'I would have squared the Mahdi,' he said coolly, and he probably would.

He was a man who had never known what it was to be short of money; early in life he had acquired a lot more of it; and so, paradoxically, by the time he was a millionaire he had lost interest in it. It was empire he was after: as an Oxford student he had once sat down and written a letter direct to Disraeli, offering advice on policy towards Africa. He was delighted when Disraeli coolly annexed the Transvaal Republic in 1877 – British troopers ran up the Union Jack at Pretoria on Victoria's birthday and Dizzy ceremonially presented the Boer state to his 'Faery Queene'. But now this annexation had come unstuck, and the Transvaal Boers were determined to secure their sovereignty and protect their own northern frontier by a deal with Lobengula. They might even move north themselves.

There was a standing Treaty of Friendship with the Matabele dating from 1853, and President Kruger now decided to use it in order to consolidate the position of the Transvaal. Inside Kruger's kingdom itself much was happening. The gold reef of Witwatersrand had just been discovered, British and other migrants were pouring into the goldfields, sometimes at the rate of 500 in a week, and on the London stock exchange – at that time the largest in the world – there was a speculative boom in 'Kaffirs'. Within the space of half a dozen years £57 million of British capital had poured into the mines of the Rand and from them was coming one quarter of the world's total production of gold. In ten years the white population had doubled, and so had the railway mileage. There had been nothing like it since the California gold-rush, and even the glitter of Kimberley's diamonds in the Cape paled before the golden blaze of the Rand. For all his loathing of gold and of mining magnates, President Kruger found his feet tapping to the tune of the new wealth. His little agricultural utopia had not worked out as the Voortrekkers had planned. It was falling heavily into debt, and coming under British pressure to join in a railway and tariff union on Imperial terms with the neighbouring British colonies of Natal and the Cape. That had been 1883, when the little republic enjoyed an annual income of less than £200,000 and was facing bankruptcy. Ten years later this income had multiplied *twenty times*, the Transvaal had soared out of debt, and from London the financiers and Imperial statesmen were regarding South Africa in a golden light. They had to have the Transvaal – ultimately; in the meantime they needed an instrument to block Kruger's ambitions, to prevent him from expanding eastwards to the ocean or northwards into Zambesia.

Cecil Rhodes was that instrument, by the luck that attended his actions almost all his life. His was the grand Imperial design: of a South Africa federated into one unit and part of a vast Anglo-Saxon–Germanic empire stretching northward, laminated by bands of steel, the railway from the Cape to Cairo. It was integral in Rhodes's race theories that the Boers could and should have a share in turning this dream to reality; despite their infusion of French and other blood, he pronounced them to be of Germanic–Saxon stock and therefore racially fit for the advance of his design. And practically, of course, it would make everything easier if Boer and Anglo-Saxon could combine forces in the drive to the north. In the Cape Colony he achieved it; the price of association with Hofmeyr and the Bond was acceptance of their policies towards the Africans – a price Rhodes paid without a qualm. Of course, he was genuinely fond of his valet Toni, a Cape Coloured, and in his declining years, when he had retreated to the sanctuary of Groote Schuur, his magnificent country home outside Cape Town, he opened its grounds and gardens to picnic parties regardless of race. But he expected the brown and black beneficiaries of his paternalism to know their place; when the time came for opening up Rhodesia, there was to be no nonsense about equal rights for dark-skinned people in handing out land, or gold claims, or the vote.

Unfortunately for the ancestors of Dr Banda, Joshua Nkomo, and Kenneth Kaunda, the British government during those crucial years of Rhodesia's birth was convinced it could not cross the ambitions of Cecil Rhodes. By a combination of luck and timing, the Tswana peoples to the west of Mashonaland managed to invoke the protection of the Aborigines Protection Society in far-off Exeter Hall. The Rev. John Mackenzie, that fearsome Victorian figure of righteous wrath, stormed on to the scene in the 1880s. He had instructions from his Society to save the tribesmen and their royal house, the Khamas, from the Boers who had started to trek northwards. He arrived with a cabin trunk of Union Jacks and the full backing of the Liberal government, then still in power. Gladstone saw the mission as having double merit: it satisfied the humanitarians at home, while blocking the territorial ambitions of the South African colonists, Boer and British alike. Thus the Ba-tswanas found themselves abruptly taken under the protection of the Great White Queen and their country renamed the Protectorate of Bechuanaland.

The Cape Colonists were determined that such a disaster should not be repeated. If the missionaries were to persuade Britain to act again, and declare a protectorate in Zambesia, the chance of seizing the 'Suez Canal' to the north would be gone forever. Fortunately for Rhodes, the Gladstone government fell shortly after the Bechuana intervention; the Tories who succeeded under Lord Salisbury were much less susceptible to pressure from the humanitarian societies and their obsession with rights for Africans. They were much more concerned to cut down the general expenses of overseas administration. Furthermore, such was their obsession with India and the necessity of securing the sea route as an alternative to Suez, that Salisbury and his ministers were prepared to 'keep Rhodes and his Boers sweet' by giving the Cape Colonists a free hand with their expansionist ambitions. Besides, the advance to the north would have the merit as well of keeping the Portuguese and Germans in check. By 1888–9, too, the British government was caught up in the naval race with the French and the massing of fleets in the Mediterranean. Lord Salisbury would have found it difficult to discipline the colonists; the Royal Navy had no ships to spare, even if a show of force off Cape Town had been deemed judicious. Once again Rhodes was lucky; far-off events were smoothing his path. He went through the motions of asking London's permission for the move north only because he wanted the prestige of a Royal Charter. With it, the fresh finance he would need from the City of London would flow into his hands much faster.

He was approaching his forties and was obsessed with the fear that he would die before he reached his forty-fifth birthday. He was more than ever convinced that he had been chosen for a special mission in life; he talked about himself as 'the agent of Fate'. The precedent of the Roman empire obsessed him; he was hardly ever without his copy of Gibbon's *Decline and Fall*, and it was in his pocket when he finally trekked into Mashonaland. His thoughts were running on these lines:

All the great conquests of the world came from accident. ... We have to complete with all rapidity the project before us – the project of uniting the North and the South of Africa.

There was still a schoolboy romanticist inside the adult frame. The Empire builder in the immaculate white flannel trousers, Norfolk jacket, and grey slouch hat cut an impressive figure on the veld when the time came to trek north. Yet there was the curiously high, fluty voice, remarked on by so many of his contemporaries; the sparse growth of beard; the awkwardness in the presence of women. He had an irritating trick of repeating a phrase over and over again, and at the same time appearing to wash his hands in imaginary soap and water. 'Here is where I lie and think in continents,' he told a visitor to Groote Schuur on one occasion, indicating his own bedroom with its magnificent view of Table Mountain. 'Think in continents' (rub-rub) 'in continents' (rub-rub), he repeated nervously, following up with a high, curious laugh. This was the same man who was to show a strange courage walking unarmed, with just his sjambok whip in his hand, at the head of his British South Africa Company troop as they faced the deadly dum-dum bullets of the Matabele elephant guns. And the man who would, that same evening, exhibit petty vanity about having to win at whist – a vanity often remarked on by others. Impulsive, cynical, convinced that there was no man alive who could not be 'squared', he was yet endowed as well with an undeniable magnetism – a quality that made itself felt as strongly with the Matabele chiefs as with Queen Victoria. A British nurse, working among the Africans and the white Pioneers at Umtali in the early years of the new nation, observed him. There had been sickness, grumbling, and despair; then Rhodes arrived and the gloom disappeared.

Mere personal magnetism wrought the change. Everything about the man is big – faults, virtues, projects. He is the darling of Fortune ... who does not select her favourites from the Sunday school.

Two wielders of power were to feel the full force of this magnetism: the King of the Matabele and the Prime Minister of the British Empire. It was to Lord Salisbury that he turned his attention first. To the Court of Lobengula he assigned a skilled ambassador.

Rhodes believed so fervently and urgently in his project that he regarded any means as justified. It was a process that was carried to completion only in 1953 when, again, a Tory government in Whitehall found it easier (and cheaper) to surrender to white settler pressure from southern Africa than to inquire too closely into the views of the Africans concerned. But the old rule is, of course, inexorable; the means shape the end. The rickety federal structure that finally arose in 1953 could not endure because of the means employed by Huggins and Welensky, and by their lineal predecessors, Jameson and Rhodes, sixty years previously.

The first negotiations took place in the royal kraal of Lobengula at Bulawayo. The 'buck kraal' was the particular section where the King held audience for the many concession hunters – European and half-caste – who had come to Matabeleland in the hope of securing the kind of treaty which Tom Baines had been given but had never used. Why did these strangers not simply head for the gold-fields themselves? It was what the like-minded had done on the Rand, and in California, and would soon be doing in the Yukon. There were two reasons. First, no European power had seen fit to move in and establish 'normal' government; at the moment this was an African kingdom, and, for all that anyone knew, might remain so, like Ethiopia. There were other native states – Japan, Siam, Afghanistan – where the white man had recently arrived as trader rather than conqueror; it might prove the same in Zambesia. Secondly, it was wise to apply to Lobengula because his *impis*, the well-disciplined royal regiments trained in the Zulu tradition, held supreme military power throughout Matabeleland and the gold-bearing country of the Shona peoples. It was not wise to be caught by a Matabele patrol, panning gold without a piece of paper bearing the elephant seal to signify royal approval.

The King had issued only two concessions. The first, in 1869, had gone to Sir John Swinburne, and was not of significance to Rhodes and his rivals, for it had been in the Tati area, now a part of Bechuanaland. Next, with his trusted missionary friend Robert Moffat to advise him, the King had granted the concession to Baines which was never used. Nearly twenty years had passed; the Germans, Portuguese, Boers, and British colonists were all determined to take over Zambesia and to build the railway that would tap its riches. 'The gold of fifty Rands,' Rhodes predicted confidently to his British South Africa Company shareholders, though that promise was to prove empty. Lobengula held out, in the hope that for as long as he kept his regiments in fighting trim, so long would the 'pink-faces' leave him alone. There were the treaties of friendship which had been negotiated by his father with the Cape Colony and the Transvaal; they were mutual guarantees of non-interference. Mzilikazi had kept his word; and so had his son. Lobengula had his own way of putting it: 'There is a Wall around the Word of a King.'

The King had an enormous compound which dominated the surrounding country from the crest of a hill. There were stalls for cattle, storehouses, and the huts of servants, his many wives, and his *indunas* or councillors. Oddly, in this timeless landscape, there was also a modern red-brick Victorian villa. Lobengula, not unlike other contemporary monarchs of ample means, liked to have the latest thing. He was, indeed, aware that if he was ever successfully to withstand the political offensive developing south of his borders, he would have to re-equip the royal regiments with rifles instead of spears. He had begun to do so, and welcomed traders. One of the more enterprising of these had presented him with a Cape covered wagon. Lobengula found that he preferred it to the brick villa, and the wagon became his bedroom; on state occasions the coachman's box at the front served him as a throne, and from it he could address large gatherings. Finally, there was the Treasure House, one of the huts where there hung a photograph of Queen Victoria in a heavy silver-gilt frame. Standing near by were the two famous biscuit tins which had been glimpsed on odd occasions by missionaries or traders; they were filled nearly to the brim with uncut diamonds. This was the royal exchequer, and it was kept replenished by a system of levies on the young men who went south to work in the mines. The contents of the two tins were variously valued at between £5 and £10 million, and would be worth five times that sum today.

According to contemporary accounts, Lobengula was a man of majestic proportions and great natural dignity. He stood nearly six and a half feet high and carried his 300 pounds with the grace of an athlete. He normally went shoeless, dressed only in a kind of sporran made of monkey skin, secured around his waist by a belt of blue cloth. 'I have seen many European and native potentates,' wrote the French traveller Lionel Décle, 'and with the exception of Tsar Alexander never have I seen a sovereign of more imposing presence.'

Sir Sydney Shippard, a senior representative of the Colonial Office, described the King marching at a slow pace, his long wooden staff in his right hand, looking his part to perfection. As Her Majesty's Commissioner for Bechuanaland, Sir Sydney was the official nearest to Lobengula's kingdom; when he arrived on a formal visit one sweltering day in 1888, he was careful to appear in proper dress – sun helmet, jet black frock-coat and trousers, starched white shirt, hard collar, and all. Wisely, Sir Sydney had also sent word ahead that the Queen's representative was coming and was not to be kept waiting, for it was well known that the King required from all ordinary visitors – white or African – strict adherence to Court etiquette. This normally meant waiting for hours in the hot sun at the kraal, a place reeking of acrid dung and the drying hides of cattle, where the visitor squatted on his haunches or sat on the ground. When the royal summons came for an audience, he was expected to crawl forward on his stomach. And before he and his interpreter might begin stating their business, they had to help themselves generously from a platter of half-cooked meat and consume a full calabash of lukewarm native beer. Sir Sydney wrote later:

I found that all Europeans here are accustomed to sit on the ground before Lobengula, exactly as the natives do, some actually grovelling with their hands on their knees and thus sidling up to their places in the crouching attitude of the natives who are fawning on him for boiled beef and Kaffir beer.

The frock-coated Commissioner was not going to surrender his dignity. He adds: 'I was careful to have seats carried in by my servants.' Then, politely declining refreshment and having asserted the equal status of the British royal house, he got down to business.

To understand what this particular business was, we need to look at the other negotiators already gathered in the buck kraal when Sir Sydney Shippard arrived on that crucial day in October 1888. Lobengula called them *umfagozana* – the low fellows – or if he were feeling even more forthright, 'my white dogs'. Most were hunters or traders with only modest personal capital; some were fugitives from the British colonies or Boer republics to the south. A good many were half-castes with African or Portuguese blood, and there were men of mystery like the monocled Count Pfeil, late of the Prussian guards, who arrived in the company of a man describing himself as 'the Anglican Bishop of Bloemfontein'. (He turned out to be precisely that.) But more important than all these were the syndicate men. They were the negotiators representing powerful financial groups in Johannesburg, Cape Town, or Europe, though Lobengula could only judge their power by the fact that their tents and covered wagons were obviously more sumptuous than the rest. The King was not without advisers. Robert Moffat, the missionary, was dead, but his son John had remained in Matabeleland. Lobengula called him 'Joni' and looked upon him almost as an adopted son. There was a royal decree, for example, prohibiting any white man from building his hut and bringing his woman to live in it, anywhere in Zambesia. But this rule had been waived when old Robert Moffat built his mission stations, and it was waived for 'Joni' too.

For twenty years the King had resisted the concession hunters, but now a curious sequence of events was to take place, triggered off by events in the Transvaal. The British army had been defeated at Majuba; the Gladstone government had decided that Disraeli's audacious claims could not be sustained. British forces had withdrawn; the Transvaal was once more a sovereign state and Kruger looked north. Lobengula had shown (in recorded conversations) that he had heard of this new power of the Boers and feared it. When Kruger sent an emissary, Piet Grobler, to negotiate a new 'treaty of friendship', he was well received at the kraal in Bulawayo, and the result was the Grobler Treaty of 1887. It bound the King to supply troops when asked by the President, it granted hunting and trading rights, and it would come fully into force when a permanent representative, to be known as Consul, took up residence at Lobengula's Court. There followed a swift and remarkable series of events.

The man who held the post of Her Majesty's Agent in Kruger's capital was Ralph Williams, a servant of the British government but also a close personal friend of Cecil Rhodes from Oxford days. He acted quickly, and sent a personal note to Rhodes in Cape Town. Rhodes in turn got hold of Captain Francis Newton, the private secretary to the man who as Governor and High Commissioner was Her Majesty's senior representative in southern Africa, Sir Hercules Robinson. Newton quickly arranged for Rhodes to see Robinson, who agreed that swift action was necessary to counter the Boer initiative. A British emissary had to reach Lobengula's court before Consul Grobler arrived from the Transvaal to take up residence. Once that happened, it would be too late to secure the riches of Zambesia, for occupation by colonists from the Cape would constitute an act of war with the Transvaal. Who was to be emissary for so delicate a task?

There was, in fact, no problem. The man for the job was John Moffat, who had been taken on some little time before this by Sir Sydney Shippard, to be Assistant Commissioner with not very clearly defined responsibilities for maintaining relations with the Matabele. When the King realized he was losing the services of 'Joni', he asked his help in arranging a successor, for it was essential to have an adviser always at court who spoke the language of the white man and yet would have the interests of the Matabele close to his heart. Moffat's successor was the Rev. C. D. Helm, who was to act as senior missionary to the Matabele, as well as adviser and interpreter to Lobengula.

One of the eleven syndicates encamped at the royal kraal was the team representing Cecil Rhodes, whose leader was Charles Dunell Rudd. Nine years older than Rhodes, he had a more austere and introverted nature; his background was Harrow and Cambridge. But they had worked their first diamond claim together in Kimberley, had put their first profits into a curious partnership to operate an ice-machine at Durban in 1872 (they made a good profit), had been partner-founders in setting up the mighty De Beers Syndicate, and then partners again – with founders' shares guaranteed one third of the profits – in the Amalgamated Goldfields of South Africa Ltd, now one of the biggest syndicates on the Rand. And now, Zambesia.

Rudd engaged the Rev. Mr Helm on behalf of himself and Rhodes – 'to help them a little' – with an honorarium of £200 per annum, a sum worth £1,000 in present-day purchasing power. It was a curious arrangement, perhaps, for a man to make who was the full-time salaried servant of a missionary society in London. The precise connexions of the other principal characters will never be known, for nothing has been committed to paper. But the key figure in the drama was undeniably Sir Hercules Robinson, High Commissioner at the Cape, full-time servant of the Colonial Office, who by this time had been for three years a shareholder in De Beers. In 1895 Joseph Chamberlain, as a critic of the government, was to refer to Robinson's 'close personal and financial relationship' with Rhodes. After his retirement from H.M. Colonial Service, Sir Hercules was made a director of De Beers, and Lady Robinson was the recipient of a handsome diamond necklace – also from De Beers – at a farewell party arranged by Cecil Rhodes. As the holder of supreme political power at the Cape, he was clearly a vital ally in the preparations for the advance north into Zambesia.

Two further key figures were Shippard and Newton. Shippard, as Commissioner for Bechuanaland, served directly under Sir Hercules; if as a colonial servant he had opposed the adventures in Zambesia, it would have made things difficult or impossible for Rhodes. But he did not oppose them, his mission in 1888 was distinctly helpful, and when he left H.M. Colonial Service a few years later, he emerged as Chairman of Rhodes's own creation, the British South Africa Company – at a handsome salary. This was the man who was to become known to Lobengula and the Matabele by the bitter nickname of Marana Maka – 'Father of Lies'. Later he himself had this to say about how Rhodesia was founded: 'From my first arrival in Mafeking in 1885 I was in correspondence with Lobengula with a view to ultimately securing his territory in accordance with the plan decided on between Rhodes and myself in 1878.'

Shippard's successor as Commissioner was the same Newton – now Sir Francis – who had been Rhodes's invaluable contact man at the Cape as private secretary to the High Commissioner, Robinson. After his retirement from the Colonial Service, Sir Francis too, like his predecessor, accepted a highly paid post with the British South Africa Company.

When news of the Grobler Treaty reached Cape Town, Rhodes decided on a holding action. He seems to have had little difficulty in persuading Robinson and Shippard to nominate someone – the choice fell on 'Joni' Moffat – to be H.M. Deputy Commissioner at the court of Lobengula. Not surprisingly, the King told his old friend, the ex-missionary, about his troubles with concession-hunters, Kruger, and all the rest. Moffat's advice was to avoid all entanglements and put his trust in the power of Britain, already protecting the Tswana people in the neighbouring territory of the Khamas. Lobengula affixed his elephant seal to a letter on these lines, and Moffat hastened with it to Cape Town.

Rhodes began saying repeatedly 'I must not leave a vacuum there', and persuaded his partner Charles Rudd – with all the prestige of De Beers and Amalgamated Goldfields behind him – to go himself and treat with Lobengula. But meanwhile Consul Grobler was on his way from Pretoria to the royal kraal, travelling by way of Bechuanaland – the 'missionaries' road'. An odd thing happened. The party was ambushed, Grobler was mortally wounded, and a furious President Kruger demanded an explanation. He had to be content with an apology from Sir Sydney Shippard, who said that the incident had been the work of a petty chief and that there would, of course, be a pension for Grobler's widow.

There was therefore no distracting Transvaal influence at Bulawayo when Rudd arrived in September. But the King himself was now thoroughly hostile to all concession hunters. He had been shocked by Grobler's murder and remembered John Moffat's advice to keep clear of all entanglements. Observing Helm's special position at court, Rudd made his 'arrangement' with the missionary, and at the same time sent an S.O.S. to his friends back at base. Overland communications were slow, and while Rudd waited for Shippard, there were endless parleys with the tough old monarch under his famous 'Indaba tree'. Rudd's was a formidable team. He had with him a dapper Irishman, Rochfort Maguire, who was another of Rhodes's comrades from Oxford days – athlete, double-first, formidable debater and Fellow of All Souls – who had since been called to the Bar and had resigned from the Colonial Service (a promising post in Hong Kong) to join Rhodes in southern Africa. The third member of the team was a seasoned hunter and prospector, Frank Thompson, known as 'Matabele' Thompson because of his knowledge of the language and customs of Lobengula's people. An old friend of the King, he had ready access to him and to his senior councillors – Lotje, Babyaan, and Umsheti. Lotje, the senior *induna*, was to be a key figure in what followed.

Towards the end of October 1888 the long-awaited news arrived at the royal kraal. Queen Victoria's Commissioner was on his way to Bulawayo. There were several delays, while Lobengula hesitated over allowing men to enter his dominions as visitors who might then decide to stay. Helm did what he could to calm the King's fears, pointing out that the Queen's emissary was only coming to confirm the arrangement set out in the letter which the King himself had given to 'Joni' Moffat some weeks before. That letter had gone to the High Commissioner in Cape Town, and from there by ship to England. Now the Queen was replying; not just by letter, but with even greater courtesy. She was sending her personal representative, Sir Sydney Shippard.

But still Lobengula hesitated. His scouts reported that the

Commissioner's ox-wagon was accompanied by an *impi* of the Great White Queen. (They were in fact mounted troopers of the Bechuanaland Border Police in full kit – an impressive sight.) Was this the dreaded invasion at last, the thing his father Mzilikazi had warned him to expect one day ? Again the missionaries counselled the King not to fear. If it were invasion, surely the white men at his court, those concession hunters, would have fled before this ? And, as Lotje himself argued, would it not be to Lobengula's advantage to deal directly with the English Queen ? With her consul at his court – and the Transvaal consul, whenever Grobler's successor was appointed – the King would be able to call upon outside help to keep the Germans and Portuguese at bay. For there were worrying reports that they were preparing expeditions to move inland, perhaps to belt the waist of Africa with a railway from coast to coast. If Queen Victoria were on his side, Lobengula would have as an ally the most powerful of all the white nations.

Lotje also argued that an agreement at government level with Britain would enable Lobengula to be rid of the concession hunters once and for all. Through the Queen he could formally arrange who should come and dig for gold; an agreement would be concluded at the highest level, and all the 'white dogs' pestering him could then be kicked from his kraal. Zambesia would be cleared of whites, except for the agents of the one approved concession company; the Queen would guarantee the arrangement in perpetuity; and the Matabele nation could use the income from the concession to buy wagons and firearms, to equip themselves with all the instruments that the white man used to pursue both war and peace.

Lotje was the King's senior *induna*; his counsel carried the greatest weight of all. Lobengula relented, and runners went out to tell the captains of the Matabele regiments that the Queen's *impi* might pass.

Now followed the most crucial encounter between white man and African in Rhodesia's formative years. To the present generation of white Rhodesians, perhaps, and to those holding political power in Britain today, it may seem a distant incident in a hazy history. But in the world of the 1960s, with the changed power balance at the United Nations, it is worth making the effort to see this episode as it exists in the collective race memory of the African people of the Rhodesias. To them this was the moment of sell-out, the Big Betrayal.

Sir Sydney Shippard descended with dignity from his ox-wagon and waited while his attendants carried forward the chairs he had so shrewdly decided to bring with him. He must have made a splendid figure in his frock-coat and white sun helmet. On his breast glittered the cross of the Order of St Michael and St George. The Bishop of Bloemfontein, it now appeared, had come to Bulawayo by agreement and associated himself with the royal deputation, lending to it the weight and authority of the Established Church. He it was who explained to the King that Her Britannic Majesty was head of this church, and offered at some appropriate stage to supply the King's villages with mission teachers. After this initial plenary session Sir Sydney took his leave, retiring with such dignity as was feasible across the carpet of rotting cattle dung to the sanctuary of his wagon.

There were daily interviews for a week; the calabashes of beer passed from hand to hand, Sir Sydney comported himself graciously, occasionally in cooler colonial kit, and felt encouraged to hear the King remark that Queen Victoria was apparently the only European monarch sufficiently appreciative of his rank and the importance of his people to send worthy representatives. But it was not all plain sailing. Sir Sydney reported by letter to Cape Town:

European concession hunters are becoming a source of serious anxiety to him. ... and he has a perpetual dread of an inroad of Boers. He knows all about Majuba ... how England, after the fairest promises, handed over 750,000 unwilling natives to the Boers whom they dread and detest. There's the rub. ... England has a bad name in South Africa for breaking faith with natives.

And to make his point, the King had told Helm of the chameleon and the fly – how the animal advances slowly and silently until, at last, 'he darts his tongue and the fly disappears; England is the chameleon and I am the fly'.

At length Sir Sydney departed. His precise verbal advice to Lobengula about the concession hunters is not recorded. We know that he told the King that none of them represented the Queen; only he himself had that authority. But the Commissioner must have hinted that one of the groups then at Lobengula's court was much more wealthy and important than the others, and that the Queen would look with favour on the granting of a concession to it. (As friends then, and business associates later in Rhodes's companies, Rudd and Shippard must have conferred a good deal that week at Lobengula's kraal.) In any event, Shippard's departure was followed by a royal summons to Rudd. It emerged that Lotje, whom the English had termed 'the Beaconsfield of Matabeleland', was now prepared to give his personal backing to the choice of the Rudd–Rhodes syndicate, and on 30 October 1888 the King told the Rev. Mr Helm to hand him the document. Lobengula affixed his elephant seal to it, and signed it with a cross. Helm witnessed, signing an interpreter's certificate to the effect that the document had been fully interpreted and explained to the King and his *indunas*. It was just ten years less a few months from the date when, in Shippard's own words, he had set out 'with a view . . . to securing his territory in accordance with the plan decided on between Rhodes and myself'.

The Rudd Concession, as it came to be known, is a remarkable document, consisting of one sentence some 500 words long. Its essence needs far fewer words.

I, Lo Bengula, King of Matabeleland and Mashonaland and other adjoining territories, with the consent of my Council of Indunas, do hereby grant and assign . . . complete and exclusive charge over all metals and minerals situated and contained in my kingdoms . . . and whereas I have been much molested of late by divers persons seeking to obtain concessions . . . I do hereby authorize the said grantees . . . to take all necessary and lawful steps to exclude from my kingdoms . . . all persons seeking land, metals and minerals. . . .

The chameleon had moved a step closer. The King contracted to grant no other rights to land or minerals without the consent of Rudd and his associates. For their part of the bargain, Rudd and Rhodes contracted to pay £100 a month to Lobengula and his heirs in perpetuity, and to deliver a consignment of 1,000 Martini-Henry rifles of the latest type, together with 100,000 rounds of ammunition. There was one further commitment – a steamboat on the Zambesi, 'with guns suitable for defensive purposes', which should fly the King's flag and make him impregnable to his enemies. It was a master touch contributed by Rhodes; in a letter to Rudd he instructed his partner to add this particular enticement – 'same as Stanley put on the Upper Congo' – and it may well have been what turned the trick. The King and his councillors were obsessed by reports of Portuguese activity lower down the river, and feared invasion.

The Zambesi was, in fact, not navigable, except for short stretches, within the King's territories. The gunboat never arrived. And within a half-dozen years, the concessionaires were to be relieved of the burden of monthly payments through the death of the King and the collapse of the whole African social structure.

It was a time for swift action. Rudd and Maguire left for Cape Town, where Rhodes was impatiently awaiting the news before sailing to England. They travelled so quickly that they were able to catch up with Sir Sydney and the Bishop, and tell them the good news, presumably an occasion for mutual congratulations. Even before the vital document had arrived, Rhodes, on the strength of telegraphed information, ordered an advertisement to be placed in the local Press warning off any further concession hunters from entering Matabeleland under penalty of instant arrest. It was a bluff, of course, and when the news reached London there were questions in the House from Liberal critics like Joseph Chamberlain, who asked if the government agreed that monopoly concessions were against the interests of both Britain and the African inhabitants, and likely to lead to a breach of the peace.

But Rhodes was moving too quickly for his critics or competitors. Lobengula had to wait weeks before at last a copy of the concession was delivered for him to keep and to study. Pointedly ignoring the Rev. Mr Helm, he asked two other missionaries to come to the royal kraal and translate for him. What he heard convinced the King that he had given away far more than he had intended; the unrestricted access granted to the Rhodes syndicate to dig for gold could lead to numberless white men pouring into his domains. It could end in the very thing that he had sought so long to avoid – widespread European settlement.

Lobengula decided to revoke the concession. He summoned to his kraal another Englishman from among the concession hunters, E. A. Maund – the King had known him as 'Maundy' since the days of the Warren expedition to Bechuanaland – who was agent of the Exploration Company. This was a rival syndicate to that of Rhodes and Rudd; a grouping of City men in London backed by various peers and members of parliament. The King put it plainly: if Maundy could unscramble the Rudd Concession, then the Exploration Company should have handsome compensation in exclusive mineral rights. Maund suggested a letter to Queen Victoria and the dispatch of two senior *indunas* to London. The King agreed; pointedly he by-passed Lotje, and chose Babyaan and Umsheti. With Maund as guide and interpreter, they set off.

It was undoubtedly a very great asset for Rhodes that most of his imperial manoeuvres took place beyond the reach of telegraph wires and out of range of the London papers or, indeed, observers from any Press organization at all. Shippard had the *indunas* arrested as vagrants on entering Bechuanaland, and Newton did the same at Cape Town. On both occasions it was Maund's threat to appeal direct to the Colonial Office that got them released. Rhodes had taken ship for England some weeks previously by the time that Maund and his two companions were at last free to sail.

The little delegation arrived in London at an embarrassing moment. Rhodes's campaign to secure a royal charter was well under way, and there were signs that the Tory government of Lord Salisbury was relenting from its original suspicion. But the letter from Lobengula threatened to upset all Rhodes's plans. It said in part:

Lobengula can only find out the truth by sending eyes to see whether there is a Queen. The *Indunas* are his eyes . . . . He is much troubled by white men who come into his country and ask to dig gold. A document was written, and presented to me for signature. About three months afterwards I heard from other sources that I had given the right to all the minerals in my country. . . . I have since had a meeting of my *Indunas* and they will not recognize the paper, as it contains neither my words nor the words of those who got it. . . . I write to you that you may know the truth . . . and not be deceived.

Rhodes acted at once. He denounced the letter as a forgery, and apparently had some success with his claim. But there was one trick the Great Amalgamator still had up his sleeve. He went over Maund's head and opened negotiations with the principals, George Cawston and Lord Gifford, of the Exploration Company. The result was an amalgamation of concession-holding interests in southern Africa into one great concern, the United Concession Company. Besides Rhodes, Beit, and Rudd, the Board members included Cawston and Lord Gifford. Maund found himself neatly silenced. And the poor old *indunas* – Babyaan was seventy-five and Umsheti a gouty man in his sixties – were told that all was well, that the Queen was sending a letter to their King; and they themselves went off on a skilfully conducted tour. The highlights were a visit to the Bank of England to see the Queen's many bars of gold ("if she has so much she could hardly covet more") and an excursion to Aldershot in order to witness the army man-oeuvres, where the thunder of mighty field guns and the flash of a thousand rifles served to put over a crude diplomatic point to the two astonished old Africans.

But before Maund had been silenced, he had stirred some un-easy moral reflections. At the Colonial Office, in that spring of 1889, Lord Knutsford sat down and drafted a letter for Queen Victoria to sign, in reply to the anguished appeal from Lobengula. It said in part:

The Queen has heard the words of Lo Bengula. She was glad to receive these messengers. Lo Bengula is the ruler of his country and the Queen does not interfere with the government. . . . The Queen advises not to grant hastily concessions of land or leave to dig. . . . A King gives a stranger an ox, not his whole herd of cattle. . . .

Lobengula was not to know that, by the time he received this comforting letter some three months later, the situation in London would have been dramatically reversed by the skilful diplomacy of Cecil Rhodes. The first move in this game had, in fact, been played two years before on an earlier trip to London. Rhodes had used an introduction from his partner Beit to call on the merchant banker Lord Rothschild, a man who was to describe himself later as 'a sometimes puzzled and anxious ally'. His son-in-law was Lord Rosebery, who was subsequently, as Colonial Secretary, to prove most useful to the South African diamond king.

Now in the spring of 1889 Rhodes was ready to use his connexions. For one of them he had to thank the Rev. Mr Helm. It was an introduction to Baroness Burdett-Coutts, whose house in Stratton Street, Piccadilly, was a focal point of London society. She was deeply interested in missionary work in Africa, and it did not take long for Rhodes to persuade her that his civilizing mission would also help to spread the Gospel. Was he not, after all, a vicar's son? It must have been a point persuasively argued. For it led to a supper party with the Prince of Wales as guest of honour. He, too, became infected with Rhodes's enthusiasm and agreed to do what he could to help the newly formed British South Africa Company obtain a royal charter. The Prince tactfully arranged for a close Tory friend, the Duke of Abercorn, to accept the Chairmanship of the Company, and for the Vice-Chairmanship recommended his own son-in-law, the Duke of Fife, who was a leading Liberal.

Rhodes was acquiring the noble names he would need for his Board of Directors, if he was to overcome the suspicions of the Prime Minister, Lord Salisbury. But he still faced opposition from two significant sources of influence – the humanitarians and the liberal interests in the City of London who smelled the powerful aroma of monopoly imperialism.

The South Africa Committee of Joseph Chamberlain and the Rev. John Mackenzie warned the government that the granting of a royal charter 'would have all the disadvantages . . . of shirking responsibilities'. Sympathizers among the Colonial Office staff drafted an official memorandum predicting (correctly) that one foreseeable result would be a Matabele war. (It broke out within four years.)

This prompted Rhodes to another of his master strokes. He not only won over some of the humanitarians; he actually persuaded one of the most influential to join his Board. He argued that only an extension of British rule northwards, in opposition to German, Portuguese, or Boer penetration, would guarantee the protection of the native peoples from racialist exploitation and ensure the freedom of British missionary societies to proselytize in Zambesia. Mackenzie remained unmoved by this appeal, but it proved effective with one of his hitherto staunch associates, Albert (later Lord) Grey. In July Grey was persuaded by Rhodes to accept a seat on the British South Africa Company Board and wrote to the missionary:

I should have preferred, with you, a bolder Imperial policy. But as this is evidently beyond the intentions of the present government, and as they have made up their minds to grant Rhodes a charter, I think it is desirable that one like myself who is in close sympathy with you and the South African Committee, should be upon the Board.

In the City, the opinions of the financial experts were divided. The Liberal view was put by *The Economist*, which maintained that a royal charter 'would confer a practical monopoly of Zambesia's resources upon a handful of Cape Town and London capitalists'. *The Times*, on the other hand, supported a company 'which ought to be able to draw into [its] nets most of what is worth having in Central Africa'.

Rhodes was an indefatigable believer in the power of money. With a coolness of nerve which today would seem merely implausible, he was at this time also engaged in negotiations with the poverty-stricken régime in Lisbon. His aim was simply to buy from the Portuguese, outright, the entire province of Moçambique – and he nearly succeeded. Frustrated on this score, he turned his attention to Nyasaland. Lord Salisbury had turned a deaf ear to the desperate appeals of the Scottish missions, locked in struggle with the Arab slave-traders on the lake and the Portuguese expeditions advancing from the Indian Ocean. The Prime Minister wrote in an official Foreign Office minute of the need 'to spare the taxpayers', while his Chancellor of the Exchequer, Lord Goschen, condemned what he called 'Imperial adventures north of the Zambesi' and said that the Treasury would not let itself become responsible for any more protectorates – those 'white elephants in tropical Africa'. Acting almost on hunch, Rhodes commissioned Harry Johnston, the young ex-consul who had so impressed him at a dinner party with his talk of the Cape-to-Cairo vision, to go out to Nyasaland immediately and secure British influence there. He promised him £9,000 a year from the British South Africa Company for administration costs and gave him a personal cheque for £2,000 as an advance. Freed thus from its Treasury restraints, the Foreign Office was soon drawing up fresh instructions and regularizing Johnston's position as an official of H.M. Consular Service – though the bills continued to be paid by Rhodes.

It was summer. Rhodes had been in London since the spring, organizing his contacts, getting his dukes on to the British South Africa Company Board, and mounting his campaign for the all-important charter. It had become apparent to him that the Achilles heel of the Salisbury régime was its penny-pinching policy on Africa. Lord Knutsford at the Colonial Office had received a clear order from Goschen at the Treasury: all increases in staff or expenditure were banned. Yet the Colonial Secretary had before him a series of memos from his representative at the Cape, the redoubtable Hercules Robinson. These recommended a chartered company as 'much the cheaper and altogether the most effectual mode' of resolving the Zambesia problem. The two alternatives, Sir Hercules said, were to let the territory fall to the Boers, who would soon have a successor to the late Piet Grobler installed in Bulawayo, or for Britain to annex the territory formally, a course which 'would assuredly entail on British taxpayers . . . an annual expenditure of not less than a quarter of a million sterling'.

Knutsford was by now ready to settle up with the persistent Cecil Rhodes and his new-found noble friends of the Company's boardroom, were it not for the embarrassment of public criticism. An important critic in the House of Commons was Sir John Swinburne, founder of the mining company formed to exploit the Tati concession, who now feared that his small but prospering company would be outflanked by a gigantic new rival. In parliament he complained that the Rhodes campaign in London was 'a hole-and-corner affair . . . being railroaded through the House of Commons at outrageous speed', and he issued angry warning that 'this Charter will give to a syndicate of private adventurers as much power as the old East India Company possessed'.

It was a situation not entirely novel to the Great Amalgamator. Emissaries were dispatched to make delicate overtures to Sir John Swinburne, and in due course, to the public surprise, the Tati concession and the Swinburne company were merged – at a price far above their true value – with the mighty empire of Beit, Rudd, and Rhodes.

The stage was set at last, and Lord Knutsford dispatched two ecstatic notes of commendation to his Prime Minister. Enclosing the formal application for a royal charter, he first wrote:

You may like to see the enclosed from Mr Rhodes, who with Mr Rudd got the large concession from Lo Bengula, and has now disarmed opposition by giving his opponents a share in it. I believe he has managed to win over Mr Chamberlain and Mr Labouchere. You will see he proposes to help you North of the Zambesi. He and his colleagues are well backed up in the City, and he himself is the richest man by far in South Africa.

The second memorandum, a few days later, dwelt on the advantages of a chartered company to the Imperial exchequer, citing the case of Bechuanaland next door as an example of what otherwise might happen:

Such a body may relieve Her Majesty's Government from diplomatic difficulties and heavy expenditure. . . . Nothing could be more unsatisfactory than the conditions in Bechuanaland. Every year large grants have to be obtained from Parliament . . . almost swallowed up in the maintenance of a semi-military police force.

In the same note the Colonial Secretary touched on another reason for granting the charter: Without it, he said:

... Her Majesty's Government would not be able to prevent the Company from taking its own line of policy, which might possibly result in complications with Native Chiefs and others, necessitating military expenditure and perhaps even military operations.

Why did the British government so misplace its responsibility? Fear and pride were two overwhelming motives. There was real fear in Whitehall of another Boston tea party. The American troubles had been followed by a rebellion in the Canadian colonies within living memory, and now in southern Africa another group of frontiersmen were straining at the imperial leash. Pride came into it because Salisbury and Knutsford were determined to cling to the image of imperial control at the Cape, even if they had lost the substance. They were determined to hold on to India, which in turn meant securing the coaling station at Simonstown, which in turn meant placating the Rhodes–Hofmeyr coalition, and so on through an endless chain of political dominoes extending right through into our own century. When Sir Edgar Whitehead locks up African politicians, tranquilly waiving *habeas corpus*, and Field rams Draconian decrees through his legislature in the 1960s while a remote British government twiddles its thumbs, those are dominoes falling in a line begun by Lord Salisbury in the summer of 1889. Such is the line of responsibility; and such is the source of the troubles which have beset the Rhodesias and Nyasaland up to the present day.

On 10 July Lord Knutsford told an ecstatic Cecil Rhodes that the Cabinet had met and had decided to recommend to Queen Victoria that Her Majesty should grant the British South Africa Company a royal charter. The muddled thinking on Central Africa, which continues to plague British policy to this very hour, is embedded in that original decision. Knutsford solemnly recorded in a Colonial Office minute that, in the view of Salisbury's Cabinet, there was 'a cardinal principle' which induced them to grant the Charter. This was that 'the Company which is to enjoy the profits . . . shall also discharge and bear all the responsibilities of Government'. Rhodes did not demur. As part of the price of his bargain, he offered to put up the sum of £4,000 a year for the salary and expenses of the official – tentatively styled 'the Imperial Resident' – who should move into the seat of power at Bulawayo. (Lobengula was already written off in Rhodes's balance sheet.)

Was it at all embarrassing to the high-principled Tory administration of Lord Salisbury that the first Imperial Resident should be Dr Starr Jameson, a man wholly answerable to Cecil Rhodes? A man who was to disgrace himself and Britain's reputation with the ill-conceived Jameson Raid on the territory of President Kruger in 1896?

Lord Salisbury preferred to ignore the many unpleasant details of the new territory's internal administration, provided that Imperial interests were being served. What might be called the '£sd argument' held absolute sway in Whitehall. When Rhodes, that same summer, made his gesture of underwriting Nyasaland, the Foreign Office in August altered the draft of the British South Africa Company's charter – which had limited the Company's sphere to lands south of the Zambesi – so as to leave the northern boundary indefinite. (The Company was given Northern Rhodesia by supplementary charter two years later.)

At the Cape, Sir Hercules Robinson had retired, and the new British High Commissioner, Sir Henry Loch, proved to be a tough administrator, invulnerable to the persuasive charms of Cecil Rhodes. Among other things, he began to take a dour view of Rhodes and his associates in their handling of native affairs. But this only brought down upon Loch the wrath of Whitehall. Time and again in the early 1890s the memos arrived from the Colonial Office forbidding him to interfere in the Company's affairs. Typical of these was one from Lord Knutsford:

No step should be taken practically superseding the Company's charter and relieving it of its principal obligations; that might make this country liable to have to take over at any time the government of the country.*

* C.O. minute 806/352, 10 Knutsford-Loch, 28.6.1891.

This may be shrewd economy, or even shrewd Imperialism; but it is also the language of a government which has coolly and deliberately decided to evade its responsibilities.

After his brilliant success with the British Cabinet decision of July, there was not much to keep Rhodes any longer in England. He had family business to attend to, the purchase of an estate at Dalston from a distant relative. He had the gravestones cleaned and restored in the churchyard, and augmented these with the stones of other members of the Rhodes family, acquired in villages round about. Secure in the knowledge that he now possessed a family seat – essential for one destined to be rewarded, surely, with a peerage for Imperial services – he sailed for the land that was in reality his true home. The formal proclamation of the charter, he knew, would be made in October.

Two other sons of Africa had sailed for home, just before him. They were Lobengula's 'eyes', the *indunas* Babyaan and Umsheti. They had come with high hopes, in the company of their protector 'Maundy'. They had seen Maund effectively silenced when his company was smoothly acquired in one of Rhodes's takeover deals. Now they were returning empty-handed, to tell their King that nothing could be done by the white man unless first approved by the Queen at Buckingham Palace, and to the best of their knowledge no such approval had been granted to anyone.

This was 10 August. The decision on the Company and the Charter by Salisbury and his Cabinet was already one month old, though in those days of laggardly overland posts and slow mail packets from the Cape, Lobengula could not have known of it, even had the decision been made public. The King summoned his friend, the Rev. John Moffat, to help him compose a letter and witness it with his signature to give it official status. It was addressed to Queen Victoria, though of course it would in fact be opened and dealt with in London by Lord Knutsford, the Colonial Secretary. In view of all the circumstances attending it, the letter was pitiful and ironic:

The white people are troubling me much about gold. If the Queen hears that I have given away the whole country, it is not so. I have no one in my country who knows how to write. I thank the Queen for the word my messengers gave me by mouth; not to let anyone dig for gold . . . except as my servants.

Lobengula had no choice but to forward this through the official channels, which meant the Shippard–Newton–Robinson network – already tuned to the wishes of Cecil Rhodes. The letter caused dismay when it arrived at Cape Town. Rhodes, who had arrived home again, knew that the proclamation of the Charter was not due until mid October. A copy of the letter, reaching the wrong hands, could set off a storm in the London papers and at Westminster. And so again there followed one of those strangely fortuitous occurrences: the King's letter was delayed. It did not go aboard the London packet until four days before the formal gazetting of the Charter. The normal timing for a letter from Bulawayo to the Colonial Office was seven weeks; this one took sixteen.

Before it arrived Lord Knutsford had made himself face up to a distasteful task. The Royal Charter was formally proclaimed in the *London Gazette* of 15 October, and the Colonial Secretary had now to decide how to convey the tidings to the King. Discretion, or simple cowardice, counselled an oblique approach. He would half-break the news in a letter and follow it up with a Queen's Messenger. This time there was no nonsense about giving strangers only one ox:

It is impossible for Lo Bengula to exclude white men, and therefore the wisest and safest course . . . is to agree, not with one or two separately but with one approved body. . . . The Queen therefore approves of the concession made to some white men . . . represented by Messrs Rudd, Maguire and Thompson. They are men who will fulfil their undertakings. . . . The Queen understands that Lo Bengula does not like deciding disputes among white men . . . and thinks it would be wise to entrust to that body, of whom Mr Jameson is now principal representative in Matabeleland, the duty of deciding disputes and keeping the peace among white people in his country. . . .

Kruger and his consular plan were now effectively out-manoeuvred. And it must have been clear to Lobengula, in this letter of 15 November to him, that the chameleon had taken another step forward, perhaps the decisive one. But it came as no surprise. Weeks before, soon after the return of his two *indunas* and in the long interval of waiting for word from the Queen, he had called a formal *indaba* with his councillors. Lotje, although the senior *induna* present, had been arraigned for giving the King bad, possibly fatal, advice. It had amounted to a charge of treason, and the Rev. Mr Helm records how the old African had withdrawn from the royal presence, knowing that it was for the last time. Sure enough, the royal diviners had soon scented death, and the trail had led to the kraal of Lotje. A detachment of the Mbesu Regiment had been assigned to the execution. They had killed the *induna* and every other living thing – wives, children, grandchildren, cattle, goats, chickens, and dogs – by the sword or in the fury of fire that had followed. This, for Lobengula, had been the ultimate repudiation of the Rudd Concession and the deal with Rhodes. The site of Lotje's kraal can still be found by the traveller who wants to seek it out, just north of Bulawayo. It is one of those curious, lonely hillocks rising from the Matabele plain, and to the average white Rhodesian today it either has no significance at all or else serves as a reminder of the unspeakable barbarities which were ended by the arrival of 'civilized men'. To the African nationalists, however, the hillock is a kind of symbol, a dreadful warning, and to this day they call it by its old name, 'Thabas Induna'.

A terrified witness to this execution of Lotje had been the remaining member of Rhodes's negotiating team, Frank Thompson. As a boy he had seen his father brutally murdered by Zulus; a few mornings after the Lotje affair he had seen three Matabele warriors with assegais near his hut. He hadn't waited to saddle his horse. He had ridden bareback to Bechuanaland, Shippard, and safety.

But, not for the first time, Cecil Rhodes had had one of his hunches and anticipated events. Dreading the possibility of a vacuum, he had ordered Dr Jameson to return to Lobengula's court at Bulawayo, where he had made such a brilliant impression earlier that same year. The King was plagued by gout, and by an infection of the eyelids; the doctor had treated the first with morphine and the second with antiseptic. He had also persuaded his royal patient to accept the monthly payment of one hundred gold sovereigns, despite his growing doubts over the Rudd Concession. And though the King had rejected the consignment of rifles and ammunition, he had not demurred when Dr Jameson quietly ordered the men who had brought them to erect a temporary warehouse and put them into store.

The terrified Thompson, fleeing on horseback, was intercepted at the Bechuanaland border by Jameson on his way to the royal kraal. The doctor was brimming with his invariable charm and confidence; the Charter was being gazetted in London that very week, and his commission from Rhodes was to hold the position in Bulawayo until the arrival of the actual documents. Thompson let himself be persuaded to turn round, and on their arrival at the kraal they found a much mollified King, beset by news of Portuguese penetration into the Zambesi valley of his domain. The Portuguese were building forts and giving flags to Mashona chiefs. 'Udogotele' – as he called the doctor – was ready with friendly advice, and a formal message was dispatched to the British High Commission Office at Cape Town, so that help could be summoned if needed. Meanwhile the amiable Dr Jim busied himself in curing the King's ailments, chaffing him with stories and gossip, and preparing him for the prospect that the man he called 'Ulodzi' (Rhodes) would send men into the territory to dig another Big Hole like the one in Kimberley.

At last, on a hot dusty summer's day at the end of January 1890, came the imperial gesture which Lord Knutsford had planned: a contingent of the Royal Horse Guards came toiling up the long hill to the dung-cluttered enclosure where the King awaited them. The British Army in its day has managed some paradoxical full-dress displays, from the Khyber Pass to Fort Schenectady, but none to surpass this superb theatrical set-piece in the heart of Africa on behalf of a private commercial company. The centrepiece was the heavy coach, its doors inscribed with the imperial crown and the V.R. monogram in gold, drawn by eight mules in silver-embellished harness. At some convenient place on the way, before coming in sight of the kraal, the mounted guardsmen who formed the escort must have changed from comfortable, open-necked colonial kit to full-dress uniform. Now, as insouciant as if clattering down the Mall for a Queen's Escort, they came jouncing into the royal kraal, no doubt sweating profusely beneath their scarlet uniforms, their polished silver breastplates, and their glittering white-plumed helmets.

It is recorded that Lobengula was much taken with the display and especially with the cuirasses, and so delighted with the formal sword exercise of the soldiers that it had to be repeated on various occasions. The Colonial Secretary, as it turned out, was luckier than he had dared to hope. His letter of the previous November, on behalf of the Queen, commending the Rhodes syndicate, and the firm news of the granting of the Royal Charter to the British South Africa Company had now caught up with each other and were both handed over by a captain of the Royal Horse Guards. Lobengula was sufficiently impressed by the circumstances surrounding the delivery to make no demur about the Charter, or indeed about Jameson's suggestion that the Company might make a start by 'digging a hole' in Mashonaland. Dr Jim had astutely suggested the country of the subject Shona peoples for the digging operation, reasoning correctly that the King would not fuss so much about an incursion there. But permission was granted specifically for one hole only, which makes the next action of Jameson's indefensible.

Leaving Bulawayo for the nearest telegraph station, he dispatched the message which Rhodes hastened to pass on to Sir Henry Loch, the new British High Commissioner at the Cape: 'LO BENGULA HAS SANCTIONED OUR OCCUPATION OF MASHONALAND.' This was a calculated lie. Yet it formed the basis of all that followed, and the Rhodesia of today.

Loch relayed the message to Lord Knutsford at the Colonial Office, who in turn consulted the Prime Minister. On 7 March the reply came from Salisbury: 'His Lordship considers that it would be dangerous to withhold much longer ... authority to sanction the advance of the Company's armed police force into Mashonaland.' The Colonial Secretary cabled Cape Town, and the news was relayed to Rhodes. A week later a revealing letter was on its way from the local office of the British South Africa Company to Loch. It said:

Mr Rhodes has for some time felt that to assure the position of the Chartered Company it is necessary to obtain effective possession of Mashonaland in the coming winter ... that this object could not be obtained merely by one or two prospecting parties, and that it is of the utmost importance to form ... a substantial nucleus of white population in the country.

Rhodes followed this up with a frank request for British aid; he wanted a large detachment from the Bechuanaland Police which, under Colonel H. Goold-Adams, now numbered 800 men. But here Whitehall's '£sd policy' intervened again. Rhodes was told that the British South Africa Company had to recruit and pay its own police. And military experts estimated that it would need 2,500 men. Rhodes – whose basic aim in the whole scheme was imperial, and who may have half-suspected that the gold of Zambesia would never materialize – could see the Company's initial capital of £1 million being gone in no time. Eventually, in Kimberley, he found two guides, Selous and Johnson, who considered that occupation could be undertaken by 200 men or less. Yet, even so, the bill came to £94,100 – nearly a tenth of the British South Africa Company capital committed before the expedition even departed. Rhodes issued the cheque himself; Britain's abdication of responsibility in Rhodesia, which has persisted to this day, had begun.

Sir Henry Loch did, however, attempt to recognize the traditional responsibility of the Colonial Office towards African peoples under its protection, even though ministerial decisions in London denied him the means or the money to enforce it. He had examined the Rudd Concession more carefully than Salisbury had wished or thought to do, and he wrote officially to the British South Africa Company about it:

The Concession ... does not confer such powers of government as are mentioned in clauses 3 and 4 of the Charter. Those powers will

have to be obtained whenever a proper time for approaching Lo
Bengula . . . arrives.

No such negotiations ever took place. Perhaps, in settler eyes,
and in the view of the Chartered Company, any obligation to
negotiate was obliterated by the African risings of 1893 and 1896.
By the time those were over, Rhodes's men were in firm military
control, Lobengula was dead, Loch had been removed from the
Cape and replaced by Rhodes's old friend (and fellow shareholder) Robinson, and the land of the Matabele and Mashona
had been triumphantly renamed Rhodesia.

Perhaps no one could have foreseen that in terms of pure
tactics the Colonial Office in London was going to be so brilliantly out-manoeuvred in what was, after all, *British* Central
Africa. There was a significant factor working in Rhodes's favour,
of course, and his actions on a number of key occasions show him
to have been keenly aware of it. This was the news vacuum at the
frontier and in the new lands beyond. The Zambesian assault
was taking place in an area safely distant from the critical, possibly hostile eyes of the world Press.

Just as there are no Colonial Office reports of it from observers
on the spot, so there are no newspaper accounts by eye-witnesses
either. Lobengula, and the Africans of northern Zambesia and of
Nyasaland, had only one channel of appeal, the frail line of contact through the Cape to London. And it was a line readily subject to blackout and delay, as we have seen. It is worth contrasting
this predicament with the facilities open to Rhodesian African
political leaders nowadays. We accept it as entirely normal that
the men who have inherited Lobengula's problems – Mr Nkomo,
Mr Kaunda, and their colleagues – should be able to plead their
case at the United Nations, in the language of their political
rivals. They know Whitehall and Fleet Street; they may bargain
across the desk with the men who are Knutsford's and Salisbury's
successors, and when they give a Press conference there will be
as many rows of reporters and squads of television camera crews
awaiting them as await Sir Roy Welensky or Winston Field.

But in the crucial years, when policy was being charted for
British Central Africa, the struggle was all one-sided, with every

factor favouring Cecil John Rhodes. Not only did he have access to the springs of power in Whitehall and Westminster; he was also careful to cultivate Fleet Street in the most skilled and sophisticated way. In those days before the national Press had come to occupy the position it holds now, a journal like the *Pall Mall Gazette*, referred to as 'the organ of Fate itself', commanded vast respect among M.P.s. When its editor, W. T. Stead, got into financial difficulties, Rhodes was ready to step in with a 'loan' of £2,000 (never repaid) and was rewarded with the *Gazette's* fervent support ever afterwards (though, to be fair, it should be added that Stead had already editorialized in favour of the new Zambesian initiative). Rhodes showed equal acumen with other organs of opinion. He won round one of his former critics, Sir Sidney Low, whose *St James Gazette* became one of his strongest supports. With an expenditure of charm instead of money, he gained the backing of Moberly Bell, one of the senior executives of *The Times*, and the Rev. John Verschoyle, deputy editor of the *Fortnightly Review*. Perhaps his most brilliant capture was a key figure in journalism, Flora Shaw, the Colonial Editor of *The Times*, who became convinced that his ultimate purpose was right; that only Rhodes could bring the Boer states into a federation of southern Africa under British imperial guidance. If, for this new white dominion, he deemed it necessary to gobble up Zambesia and move north towards Cairo, she would back him in that too. Soon a flow of vital correspondence issued from Flora Shaw to Rhodes at the Cape; since she had daily access to Fairfield, one of the two Permanent Under Secretaries at the Colonial Office, her information was invaluable. Her two cables in the week before the ill-starred Jameson Raid read: 'Delay dangerous. Sympathy now complete' and 'Chamberlain is sound . . . believe [he] wishes you to do it immediately.' These messages were probably decisive in persuading Rhodes to give the go-ahead to Dr Jim.

That Rhodes was sensitive to the power of the Press is shown by his swift 'squaring' of the veteran guide, Frederick Selous. This man, who was eventually to organize the march of the Pioneers, had earlier that year been threatening to send critical articles on the Company's manoeuvrings to newspapers in England. Rhodes reported to the Duke of Abercorn about 'the danger of our position if a series of articles appeared' and said that it cost him £2,000 'out of my private fund' to placate Selous, plus a contract of service with the Chartered Company at £3,000 a year.

It can hardly have been accident, therefore, that the press was not represented in the Pioneer Column, whose 184 members were picked by Selous and Johnson and individually approved by Rhodes himself. Rhodes may have abhorred vacuums as a general rule, but he saw to it that his imperial adventures in British Central Africa took place in a vacuum of news. The men of the Column, he specified, should come from every district of South Africa and – revealing phrase – from 'both the races'. Thus did these first Rhodesians, during the winter of 1890, carry north into the new country the racial virus that already infected the south. Indeed, the whole system of racial division was unconsciously transplanted, for there were some 300 auxiliaries, consisting of Cape Coloured and Bechuanas, to help with cooking and road-making.

The march itself was a notable achievement of energy and enterprise. Selous had had the forethought to find two pure-bred white bulls and have them forwarded to Lobengula as a gift. He had seen to it that each Pioneer was fitted out in smart uniform, reminiscent of the Bengal Lancers or the Royal Canadian Mounted Police, and each man was given 7s. 6d. per day, with the promise of his own 3,000-acre farm and fifteen gold claims when he reached Zambesia. Lobengula's scouts had been watching the preparations and the first stages of the advance; they reported that at night the invaders caused the sun to come out and thunder to roar. The sun was, in fact, a naval searchlight from Simonstown powered by a steam engine; the thunderstorms were dynamite charges exploded on the perimeter of the camp by means of long electrical wires. Selous had a healthy respect for the Matabele *impis*, and for 400 hard-fought miles his theatrical effects did a most effective job. Lobengula sent to the British High Commissioner at the Cape the following message:

If you have heard I have given my whole country to Rhodes, it is not my words. Rhodes wants to take my country by strength. . . . Your words were to send to you when troubled by white men. I am now in trouble.

Sir Henry Loch may have had his own uneasy feelings about events, but his reply a month later was to assure the King that 'the Queen wishes to maintain peace and friendship' and that the British South Africa Company column was simply searching for gold and would keep well clear of the Matabele kraals. Events, however, were marching beyond Sir Henry's control. In July, even while this letter was on its way to the royal kraal, Cecil Rhodes had vaulted into the premiership of the Cape Colony, just a few days after his thirty-seventh birthday. He was now his country's leading political figure, its leading industrialist, and was in the process of carving out a country which would bear his name.

In September the Union Jack was hoisted at Fort Salisbury, rifles cracked their salute, and the Pioneers declared simply: 'Possession taken of Mashonaland in the name of the Queen.' It was left to Sir Henry to find the legal means of justification after the event. The document was presented in November – empowering the Chartered Company to exercise jurisdiction over Europeans in Lobengula's territory – and the King entered into lengthy protests. His letter in January covered many points and included these words: 'Did not the Queen say I should not give all my cattle to one man? Who has the herd today?' There is no record of any reply from the Cape.

In April 1891 Her Majesty's High Commissioner at the Cape proclaimed the area to be a 'British sphere of influence'. This was followed in Whitehall by an Order-in-Council of 9 May, which asserted that the territories of the Charter were under British protection and that 'Her Majesty has power and jurisdiction in the said territories', and which ended with references to the administration of justice and the raising of revenue. Sir Henry had reported to the Colonial Office: 'There is no probability of Lo Bengula granting any concession of jurisdiction,' and he had received no message from the King to amplify or alter this. But there was no Press to pry, no United Nations team to probe; the Whitehall machine rolled smoothly and implacably on. Finally the Proclamation of 10 June gave the High Commissioner at the Cape the power to appoint commissioners, magistrates, and police inspectors. Under this proclamation Her Majesty the Queen was pleased to gazette as Chief Magistrate of Mashonaland her loyal servant, Dr Starr Jameson. The chameleon had taken the last step towards its prey. It would dart out its tongue and gobble up the royal fly whenever it pleased.

It may be said that the events chronicled here are remote and no longer important. Both conclusions would be very wrong. It is the contention of the present generation of African politicians in the Rhodesias that the initial occupation by the white man of their territory was legally and morally wrong. The point is valid, pertinent, and certainly not remote, since the whole issue is now – through African initiative – before the General Assembly of the U.N.

It is, in any event, hardly remote in time. The whole history of the Rhodesias since the coming of the white man is spanned by a single lifetime. The outstanding example is, of course, Churchill. When the Pioneers were staking out their gold claims, he was a young cavalry officer in the Sudan. When they volunteered for the South African War, he was there with them and Rhodes. When they launched their loud campaign in the 1920s for self-rule as a white dominion, the same Winston Churchill was Secretary of State for the Colonies. And when the Attlee government fell in 1951 and the incoming Conservative administration inherited a still unresolved Rhodesian problem, it was Prime Minister Churchill who gave the decisive turn to events. He appointed Oliver Lyttleton to the Colonies and issued a clear mandate to press ahead with Federation, if that was what Britain's 'kith and kin' wanted in southern Africa.

The diplomatic and, later, military defeat of Lobengula are very much a part of the political tensions in present-day Rhodesia. And the method of occupation by the Pioneers, the social attitudes they brought with them from South Africa, their way of carving up the land and recruiting the local Africans as 'native labour' – all these are more than just an interesting facet of Rhodesian history. They are the warp and woof of the country's political fabric today. They are events that white Rhodesians either neglect or else ignore. But in the politics of partnership it is becoming of prime importance to know what the African partner wants, and why. His father, or his grandfather, was sold into slavery within living memory. That is the spark that lights the fire; the present injustices only serve to feed the flames.

5 African Caledonia

'The Plan which rises up before my mind . . . is to make Africa a
blessing to Africans and Englishmen. . . . My God may in mercy
permit me to benefit both Africa and England. When He accom-
plishes His purposes, this will be a wonderful country.'
DAVID LIVINGSTONE

Modern Rhodesia is the work of not just one empire-builder but
two, and it is the second one whose achievement may yet prove
to be by far the more significant. To this very day the figure of
David Livingstone dominates the landscape of Central Africa, as
surely as if he were still on trek with his faithful companions,
Susi and Chuma, along the banks of the Zambesi, the great river
he called 'God's highway into the interior'.

Cecil Rhodes was the empire-builder in the hard political
sphere. He built with money and military power, and the empire
he had visualized, when it finally took shape long after his death
with the achievement of Federation in 1953, was a spectacular
memorial to his labour. And yet, only half a dozen years later,
that empire was already coming under the first of the blows that
must ultimately shatter it, with the riots in Nyasaland and the
emergence on to the political stage of Dr Hastings Banda. And
there was a special irony in this, for those African rebels and reformers were the spiritual heirs of the other empire-builder,
David Livingstone. They were good sons of the Church of
Scotland – Dr Banda is a leading member and proud of it – fortified by their upbringing in the mission schools of Blantyre and
Livingstonia. And it is not particularly difficult to predict which
of the two empires will last the longer, for Livingstone chose
much the sounder foundation. Not for him the clever concessions,
the diplomatic deals in London and military mastery of Matabeleland; he built his empire in the abiding allegiances of men. On
most of his journeys into the unmapped terrain of what was then
darkest Africa, Livingstone was the only white man; marching,
eating, sleeping, and working on equal terms with the two or

three dozen black companions who – significantly – provided his constant bodyguard in hostile territory. 'We soon learned', he wrote in his notebook one evening, camped by Lake Nyasa, 'to forget colour, and frequently saw countenances resembling those of white people we had known in England.' It is a familiar phenomenon to anyone who has been on trek in Africa with African companions, and with it goes the curious shock one experiences on returning to town, glancing in a mirror, and suddenly realizing that one's own face is white.

There are a number of curious parallels in the careers of Rhodes and Livingstone, and even one direct link in the person of John Moffat. For 'Joni', Lobengula's adviser and interpreter, the man who was to become a key associate of Rhodes, was also David Livingstone's brother-in-law. Moffat's own career in a way epitomizes the basic political shift that occurred in the nation's formative years, a shift brought about directly by Rhodes's initiatives. He began his career as the Rev. J. S. Moffat, missionary son of a missionary father, his life wholly devoted to African welfare. Then, he became a native commissioner in the Transvaal, and colonial magistrate in Basutoland and Bechuanaland. And with his posting to Bulawayo, he was drawn into the *realpolitik* of his day. Officially a Civil Servant, as Her Majesty's Resident at the Royal Kraal, he began – through Shippard – bending to the demands of Rhodes and the British South Africa Company, a co-worker in the team imposing white rule. Just so has many a man of God in present-day Africa, confronted with the complex politics of partnership, found himself plunging – for the best of reasons – down the same slope. Much to Moffat's credit he broke with Rhodes and, after retirement from colonial service, put on his 'dog collar' again and returned to his work among the Africans.

There is a long and honourable record of missionary work in Central Africa. Even the most embittered African politician in the Federation – and there are many today – cannot deny or ignore that, from the beginnings of white settlement, there have been white men 'on their side'. The first white settlement indeed was the mission station at Inyati, near Bulawayo, established a third of a century before the Pioneer Column came. And the first white child born in the country was the young son of John and Emily Moffat, christened Livingstone Moffat in honour of his famous uncle.

David Livingstone was the greatest foot-slogger in Africa's history, but he used every other form of transport as well. There was his favourite ox, Sinbad, on whose bony back he travelled many hundreds of miles on his first great expedition to Angola and back again, criss-crossing the whole width of what is the Federation today. He also resorted to canoe, river steamer, horseback, and Cape wagon. And at the end, weakened with dysentery and malaria, when it was apparent that he lacked the strength to fight his way across the swamps of Northern Rhodesia, his African companions made a *kitanda* – a simple palanquin of grass and blankets slung between a pair of poles – and carried him on to Ilala, the village where he died.

In his Scottish childhood he had known slavery of a kind himself. There was a cotton mill in his little village of Blantyre and there, at the age of ten, he began work as a 'piecer' on a spinning jenny. His day started with the ringing of the mill bell at half past five, and ended with night-school from eight to ten. After thirteen years of this he had saved enough to become a medical student in Glasgow and to study theology as well in preparation for mission work. It was a meeting in London, addressed by Robert Moffat, which changed the course of his life towards Africa. He arrived at Cape Town in 1841, a determined young man of twenty-eight with dark auburn hair, deep-set blue eyes, and a square-jawed face that suggested toughness and determination. His great expeditions were to come after a dozen years of practical apprenticeship among the Africans, starting in South Africa. And so we have the rough parallel with Rhodes – the religious home-life in Britain, the arrival at the Cape, and the urge to push north. But it is in the field of race relations that the paths of the two men dramatically diverge. In contrast to Rhodes, Livingstone was appalled at the attitude of the white man to his black conquests in South Africa, and was resolved to do what he could to right the balance when the time came for Europeans to make contact with the tribes of the far interior. This resolution was strengthened by what he saw of the way the Portuguese treated the Africans in their settlements on the coast, and by the tales he heard of the Arab slavers of Zanzibar.

It is often said by today's white settlers in the Federation that the overseas visitor has neither the knowledge nor the right to criticize them for what seems to be their singularly slow progress in implementing 'partnership'; that only by living there might one be able to see the problem in perspective and appreciate how much they are really doing. I think that Livingstone's own example is the simplest and shortest reply to this argument. He was in Rhodesia long before any of them – indeed, he might be called the original Rhodesian – and he lived among its black people for thirty years. He and his mission colleagues practised a practical partnership that was all but obliterated with the coming of European political and military rule. And there can be no doubt whatsoever about where David Livingstone would take his stand in the complex political battle of today, for he was never an equivocator. He would place himself on the side of the Kenneth Kaundas, Nkomos, and Bandas – as have his descendants in the mission field, men like Guy Clutton-Brock at the St Faith's Mission in Southern Rhodesia and the Rev. Andrew Doig at the Church of Scotland Mission in Nyasaland.

The way best to make contact today with David Livingstone is simply to talk to Africans. You could do this anywhere, but perhaps best in Nyasaland, his beloved land by the lake, where his influence remains most profound. And to see him – or at least his statue – you could hardly do better than to make your way to the border between the two Rhodesias at the Victoria Falls. Here is that awesome gorge of the Zambesi river, cloaked in perpetual spray, which the original residents of the area called 'the smoke that thunders'. Livingstone was the first white man to behold it. And it is little short of a miracle that the visitor today can still see it very much as he did, for the government has here at least had the imagination to place a ban on the inevitable commercial development. There is a magnificent railway bridge, but none of the souvenir shops and other trappings of twentieth-century civilization that have turned Niagara Falls into a neon wasteland.

Livingstone stands there in bronze, his right leg thrust forward in marching order, his body clothed in the baggy jacket and trousers he habitually wore. On his head is his Consul's cap, that curious Victorian contraption to which he was so attached, with its amateur burnouse tacked on at the sides to protect him from the sun.

Dr Livingstone used to give his worn clothing away, and it is thanks to this that an original coat of his can be seen now in the museum near his birthplace. It was brought to an Anglican missionary, Bishop Maples, by an old man in the Rovuma district, who explained that it had been given to him some ten years before by the white man who was their friend – 'A short man with a bushy moustache and a keen, piercing eye, whose words were always gentle and manners kind, and who knew the way to the hearts of all men.' The old African added that he had 'treated black men as brothers and his memory would be cherished all along the Rovuma Valley after we are dead and gone'.

Livingstone indeed was conscious of an existing standard to live up to, for the reputation of the British missionaries had gone before them. Travelling through Portuguese territory on his way to the then unexplored Nyasaland, he records how in one African village hostility changed to friendliness when the inhabitants realized that he was not an official from Lisbon or a Boer trader, but a British missionary. 'Ah,' they cried. 'You must be of that tribe that loves the black men.'

He gave himself no airs, was never pompous, and never underrated the ability of his African students to make excellent missionaries themselves. 'I have no hesitation in saying one or two pious native agents are equal if not superior to Europeans.'

In his journal he set out quite simply his mission as he saw it: 'To do some good for this poor Africa.' And he sketched the pattern of his daily life: 'Building, gardening, cobbling, doctoring, tinkering, carpentering, gun-mending, farriering, wagon-mending, preaching, schooling . . . besides a chair in divinity to a class of three.' All this is worth recording since this mission inheritance has also shaped the present generation of African leaders, besides the bitter heritage of Imperial exploitation. The result is everywhere, for black and white to see: physical landmarks like the extraordinary red-brick Gothic cathedral of the Church of Scotland at Blantyre, built in the jungle during the 1890s by men of the Manganja tribe who had never seen bricks until they were taught by the missionaries to make their own. And there are the spiritual landmarks: the generations of literate Africans, the mission stations and schools where, among the clergy and teachers, all but one or two are Africans. One of my most vivid memories of Nyasaland is of watching a class in arithmetic for ten-year-old boys, taught by an African teacher in a strong Scots burr, though I'm sure he had never been closer than five thousand miles to the Firth of Clyde.

The whole interior of southern Africa was one immense white, trackless space on the map when David Livingstone arrived there. And in Nyasaland, now renamed Malawi, he spent nearly three of his happiest years; of all the territories he opened up, this is the one that he made his very own. It is a land that would have special affinities for a Scotsman. One has only to travel the blue, foaming waters of Lake Nyasa in a stiff breeze, with the mountains rising sheer on the other side, to hike through the tawny jungle foothills of Dedza or the Nyika Plateau and reach the alpine uplands at six and seven thousand feet, with their pines and heather, to feel Scotland around. There are other parts of Africa that possess splendid mountains, but this is alone in its combination of lakes, peaks, and valleys.

'To make men love their country,' said Edmund Burke, 'you must first make their country lovely.' And when a land is naturally lovely you get the fierce pride, and the nostalgia away from home that is characteristic of Scotsmen and Malawians alike. This curious corner of Africa is a land of enormous evocative charm. This quality has a great deal to do with the politics of the Federation today. It was no surprise to those with a knowledge of the three member territories that trouble, when it came at last in 1959, should have broken out first in Nyasaland.

There are other similarities with Scotland as well as those of geography. The Nyasas, too, are poor. Like the Scots they inhabit a country which has nothing to sell but its scenery and its labour, and like them they have concentrated their energies on acquiring skills so as to make that labour pay more rewardingly. The Scots missionaries were men like Livingstone who knew what it was to fight for an education; they imparted to their Nyasa students an urge for self-improvement that is nowhere better exemplified than in the career of Dr Hastings Banda himself, who set out – literally – as a barefoot boy on the long road that was to lead to Edinburgh and a doctor's degree. As with the Scots, the pressure of population has led to constant emigration; even today, it is nothing unusual to see groups of Nyasas starting off on foot for the mines of the Rand, a thousand miles away. From Lusaka to Cape Town you will find the energetic, ambitious Nyasas at work as cooks, gardeners, miners, factory hands. With nearly three million people, the territory is the most populous of the three in the Federation; yet it has only one-thirteenth of the total land area. In any one year there is an outflow of anything from 100,000 to 150,000 Nyasas in search of work; a third of them go as far as the South African Republic. It is a trend that Dr Banda's administration has worked hard to reverse, from the moment that it came to power after the mid-1961 election. Yet the country still keeps its grim nickname – 'The Land of Missing Men.'

It would be difficult to exaggerate the parallels with Scotland – and their significance. It is a point which recurs time and again in Livingstone's *Journals*:

All we said to each other was 'How glorious! How magnificent! How beautiful!' The waves lifted up the canoe and made it roll beautifully. The scenery of the Firths of Forth and Clyde was brought vividly to my view.

This geographical affinity has led to the very special political and spiritual affinity which persists to this day. It must have been natural for Livingstone and his successors to impute to these African Caledonians some of those very same qualities of fierce local patriotism and spirited egalitarianism they had known at home. In how many little Nyasa mission schools of the Scottish

Kirk has the powerful political yeast of Robert Burns not set off the ferment of ideas which led to the crisis of 1959? It is no wonder that 'the man o' independent mind' rebelled in Nyasaland. The wonder is that the white settlers of Salisbury ever thought they could forcibly federate such independent men into a permanent state of political subjection.

When it comes to national struggle, the crisis of survival, men live largely by legend. Churchill showed that at the time of Dunkirk; and as it has been with the English and the Scots, so with the Nyasas – or Malawians as they would have us call them now. Among these people of the lake it is the legend that they were never conquered by force of arms, that when they came under white administration it was by choice. This is a slight oversimplification, but in essence it is true enough.

At the start of European penetration, many of the indigenous tribes around the lake were enduring a double victimization. At the southern end were the Yao, called the hunting dogs of the Arab slave-traders at the coast. Theirs was essentially an assault of self-preservation; they had been among the first victims when the Arabs had come down the coast centuries before. Their tribal structure had been shattered, they had become Moslems, and to protect themselves had shifted inland to act as agents for the slave-traders. They would raid the Nyasa villages along the lake, selecting the able-bodied men and women, and yoking them by the necks with Y-forked poles into long lines. When the Arab traders arrived with rifles, gunpowder, and cloth to exchange, each of these African prisoners would be given a tusk to carry, and the human chains would set off on the long march to the coast. Those who survived the journey would be sold, along with the ivory, to the captains of the waiting Arab dhows.

This was the oppression which Livingstone, with his Scots and English colleagues, fought and ended. But there was another, though lesser, oppression which also yielded to missionary attack – the military overlordship of the Angoni peoples in what is today the northern half of Nyasaland and the neighbouring region of Northern Rhodesia. The Angoni had arrived during the 1830s in the backwash of the Zulu peoples, withdrawing northwards before the advance of the well-armed Boer communities from the Cape into Natal and the Transvaal. They had brought with them the new regimental system of their great Zulu general, Chaka, and their code of strong social allegiances exactly comparable to the Scottish clans. They had in consequence found little difficulty in subduing the local tribes – the Manganja, the Chewa, the Tumbuka, and the rest – in exacting tribute from them, and subjecting them to regular raids.

The missionaries saw their duty clear; blessed shall be the peacemakers. And they pursued their duty though it inevitably led them into the thickets of politics – tribal at first, and inter-racial later. An early triumph was the formal treaty of peace between the Angoni and the Atonga, signed in 1887 after some skilful mission diplomacy and carefully kept thereafter. The missionaries adopted the language of the Manganja, Chi-Nyanja, as the best for general use, and made it the *lingua franca* of the land by the lake. Thus, through pacification and education, they were creating a sense of Nyasa nationalism; and, since most of them were Scots, it is permissible to wonder if this was perhaps a sub-conscious compensation for the nationhood that Scotland had lost with the Act of Union in 1707. In any event, it is clear that the missionaries gave to the Nyasas a heritage of national unity and of deep regard for learning that was to serve them well in the political battles of the 1950s and 1960s. The Nyasa political leaders who were taken away to federal prisons in the 1959 emergency showed a solidarity that was noted by their jailers. They promptly sent home for books and proceeded to organize courses of study; Dr Banda, Orton Chirwa, and Dunduza Chisiza have all spoken since of the value of this period for them and their colleagues. I can think of several men, now leading figures in Malawi politics, who have told me that during this time they read more than one hundred books on constitutional and economic subjects. In Nyasaland today the term 'P.G.' is a badge of honour among the Malawi leaders; it means simply 'Prison Graduate' and has passed into ordinary speech. It is significant as a phrase in itself, for it combines the proud defiance of the nationalist with a tenacious respect for knowledge.

Another facet of this particular characteristic was revealed in Dr Banda's ministerial appointments when he and his party swept to victory in the 1961 election. One main figure behind Dr Banda's leadership had been Kanyama Chiume: a wiry, resilient man who outranks most colleagues in actual parliamentary seniority, who had served in the old legislatures before the emergency. In those days there had been no voters' rolls in the ordinary sense, and African M.P.s had been deftly kept in a minority of five by a system of nomination and indirect election. As an exile in London, Chiume had shown he could match the experts of Voice & Vision Ltd and Welensky's party machine when it came to skilful political lobbying. Now, still a young man and tough as they come, he was clearly in a position to expect first choice of the available portfolios. And what did Dr Banda give him? The Ministry of Education. Although Mr Chiume prefers nowadays, as is the fashion, to use only his African names, I hope he will forgive me for pointing out that, as a good son of the Kirk, he was actually christened William Murray Kanyama Chiume.

I think, too, that one had to see and appreciate this deep influence of the Kirk upon the Malawi people to appreciate another of Dr Banda's actions. After his release from prison in 1960 he declared on numerous public occasions that he had complete faith in the British Colonial Secretary 'as a fine Christian gentleman'. Conceivably the circumstances of the time would have led any British Colonial Secretary to order the release; but by happy accident the man holding office was Mr Iain Macleod. Call it biased clannishness if you like, but it established a basis of trust in a strife-torn part of Central Africa at a crucial moment. It was a trust that led to the successful constitutional conference in London that summer. And again, because of it, Dr Banda was prepared to restrain his impatient followers for more than a year after that, so that electoral rolls could be drawn up and the Malawi people proceed to an orderly general election.

Clearly we are here encountering one of the wellsprings of political action in British Central Africa today. There has been deep and valuable missionary influence in many other parts of colonial Africa, of course; and there too the Biblical yeast of a brotherhood beyond colour has helped to set off a powerful ferment. But it is noteworthy how the Christian Church has been forced to assume a political role in South Africa and the Rhodesias, where in other parts of the continent it has restricted itself to its more orthodox functions of teaching and preaching. In 'black Africa' – Ghana or Nigeria, the Ivory Coast or Guinea – where the white man saw himself only as temporary governor or guardian, and not as a citizen, the missionaries avoided the platform of politics.

Significantly, however, in those parts of the continent where the white man saw himself as a permanent resident, with paramount political rights which he did not intend to surrender, the Church has been forced – often with obvious reluctance – into the political battle. The 'fighting priests' and missionary crusaders who spring most easily to mind are all associated with white man's Africa: Father Huddleston and the Community of the Resurrection defying Nationalist policy in Johannesburg; Guy Clutton-Brock at St Faith's Mission in Rhodesia, flouting the racial ethics and going to jail for it; the Roman Catholic bishops in Rhodesia issuing their defiance of such ethics from all their pulpits; the Rev. Colin Morris and his Nonconformists raising the standard of revolt on the Copperbelt with their famous signboard: 'This Church is Colour Blind.' And though their names are less familiar to us, there have been the French priests in Algeria who defied the white authorities and gave aid and comfort to the Africans of their territory, or in Portuguese Africa the American Methodists and the British Baptists as well as Mgr Mendes das Neves (the Vicar-General) in Angola – swept off into an unknown prison months ago by the P.I.D.E. political police.

It is not altogether an accident that the leaders of the African nationalist movement in southern – white man's – Africa tend to be religious men. No one can doubt that Chief Albert Luthuli, the Congress leader in South Africa, is a profoundly Christian man; his speeches when he went to Stockholm to receive the Nobel Peace Prize revealed the deep conviction that has motivated his whole political life.

And it is noteworthy that in British Central Africa the men who emerged as the leaders of the African nationalist movement in all three territories should be convinced Christians. Kenneth Kaunda in the north is a missionary's son, whose own creed has been reinforced by the Gandhian code of non-violence. Joshua Nkomo, on return from his long exile in London, automatically took his wife and children to the mission station in the country where they have made their home while he fights the political battle from Salisbury. Dr Banda is an elder of the Church of Scotland, whose whole life has been shaped and ordered by an inflexible Christian code.

This mission influence has motivated white African reformers as well as black. When, in the crisis which began with the riots of 1959, Sir Robert Tredgold resigned as Chief Justice of the Federation in protest against punitive legislation, and Sir John Moffat in the north and Robert Moffat in the south laboured to establish reform parties to help African emancipation, it was once again the yeast of missionary influence at work. Those three men are not just acting within the Livingstone tradition; they themselves are the fourth generation of the Moffat–Livingstone dynasty which had been founded in Rhodesia fifty years before Rhodes.

In a very real sense, therefore, the politics of partnership go back to that little mission station at Inyati where the first white child in Rhodesia – Livingstone Moffat – was born to John and his wife Emily. And the link goes back also to the Church of Scotland mission station at Livingstonia where David Livingstone's great disciple, Dr Robert Laws, built his church training-centre on an improbable bluff of the Nyika plateau, jutting out high above Lake Nyasa. So profoundly did Dr Laws influence his pupils that it is now the ambition of one of them, Dr Banda, to erect at the same place an independent Nyasaland's first university. (Which prompts one to ask why, if Hastings Kamuzu Banda were the racial extremist he is painted in Salisbury, he should thus wish to commemorate a non-African ?)

Livingstonia and Dr Laws have another political legacy, for this was also the training-ground of a young man of the Atonga tribe, one David Kaunda. He preached his first sermon in 1905 and later his work took him over into Northern Rhodesia where in 1924 his son, Kenneth, was born.

As a political journalist touring the Federation, I have been so struck by this mission heritage in the African nationalist movement that more than once I have felt like saying to Sir Roy Welensky or his colleagues: 'You don't know how lucky you are.' For not all parts of Africa have had such a heroic, humanitarian heritage; there have been, after all, very few Livingstones.

The answer, I suppose, is that the white community too has its legendary hero to inspire present-day actions. Certainly the aims and ideas of Cecil Rhodes are so drummed into the consciousness of the young white Rhodesian from the moment he learns to talk that the Founder, as he is called, becomes an influence just as alive and omnipresent as is Livingstone for the black man. In every town, streets and statues embody the Rhodes image; in school years the portrait looks down from the classroom walls, and his words and deeds (tactfully selected) are preached as a powerful creed. There are Founder's Day and other events to shape this sense of a special kind of nationhood; and for pilgrimage there is the tomb of the Founder in the national Valhalla, 'World's View' up in the Matopo Hills. I have yet to see so much as one publicity photograph showing a *black* pilgrim standing by Rhodes's grave.

The urgent message which the Welenskys of the Federation seem not to hear is: 'Don't push your luck.' This generation of African politicians schooled in the mission tradition must not be taken for granted. If Joshua Nkomo and Kenneth Kaunda are not going to succeed, there are far more fiery young nationalists waiting in the wings to assume the leadership. The one sure way for the white settlers of Rhodesia – now controlling their country at gun-point – to crush the African faith in the humanitarian, non-racial ideals of Livingstone is to demonstrate that those ideals do not succeed. The rules of the political pendulum are inexorable. And already the ominous signs are appearing. One of the alarming aspects of African politics in the Federation in the summer of 1962 was the appearance of breakaway movements.

In the south Mr Nkomo is now directly challenged by more ruthless nationalists who promise tougher action against 'the whites'. And in the north, after a shake-up in the Zambia high command, the 'tough boys' who are impatient with the Kaunda tactics have been temporarily rusticated. There are good reasons for believing that several of them are planning to return to Rhodesia when the time is ripe. And by mid 1962 to my certain knowledge the first batch of thirty young African graduates from Rhodesia completed the new sabotage-guerrilla warfare course, inaugurated in an independent African state with veterans of the Algerian campaign as instructors. If I could find that out through the African grapevine – and a visit to the state confirmed my information – then it seems to me that Sir Roy's Federal administration, with its considerable Intelligence services, must be aware of this development as well. The crucial point, of course, is whether the masters of Rhodesia draw the correct political conclusions.

There are many Rhodesians, white and black, alive today who were taught in mission schools by men of the Livingstone era. Dr Banda has his personal link through Dr Laws, as have others. In the 1940s and 1950s many a traveller in Nyasaland would make a point of stopping at Kota Kota by the lake for a talk with old Chief Msusa. His father was Chief when David Livingstone came. And at the station of the Universities' Mission to Central Africa they will show you in the quadrangle the 'magnificent wildfig tree with leaves ten inches long' in whose shadow, Livingstone notes in his diary, he received the Jumbe one September day in 1863.

The first boat on the lake was the four-oared gig brought in from the coast along the Shiré River by Livingstone in 1860. He learned that the Arab slave-traders were using dhows to transport their captives across the lake from Kota Kota and had shipped as many as 10,000 in one year. (There are estimated to be half a million slaves of Central African parentage in the Arab lands of the Persian Gulf today, apart from other descendants scattered in lands from Zanzibar to the West Indies.) A severely practical man, Livingstone prescribed a steamship as the answer to the problem; it had to be built in Britain, sailed out to Portuguese Africa and up the river as far as practicable. Then the plates had to be numbered and separated, the whole broken into sections, and carried up to the lake for reassembling. The little steamer s.s. *Ilala* made her maiden voyage in 1875, with the redoubtable Dr Laws in charge of the mission party and the ship under the command of Lieutenant E. D. Young, R.N.

As others were to discover afterwards, the fickle Lake Nyasa provided formidable problems. Young's diary records this:

The sea was past all conception: it is the peculiar nature of this lake to raise a sea that could only be found in the Atlantic. We got into the worst weather ... an awful combination of whirlwinds, thunderclouds and lightning that seemed to throw the lake into the wildest fury. ... We counted no less than twelve waterspouts around us and had literally to steam in and out amongst them. Of a sudden there was dead calm. Clouds of Kungu mist hung over the lake; then came the most appalling thunder and lightning.

Geographically the lake lies in the great earth fault or Rift Valley that goes right up the central plateau of Africa, through Kenya and on to the Dead Sea in Jordan. The towering mountains are split by funnel-like gashes and through this may come the sudden squally winds, the Mwera, which have played havoc with small craft. But the beauty of the place is astonishing. You get the same luminous greeny-blue water as in the lakes of the Swiss Alps or the Canadian Rockies. And the beaches of golden sand are fringed with palm trees, and the mountain winds send the rollers combing in to break in white foam.

Yet the lake has an ugly side to it. The level is subject to mysterious and erratic variations which have prevented any useful development. Over the years, since measurements were first taken in 1896, it has fluctuated through a total depth of twenty-four feet, and there appears to be no perceptible pattern. Boatyards and wharves have been set up and abandoned, farmlands have been flooded or suddenly deserted by the lake.

The scientists eventually tracked down the mystery. Growing in the shallow waters are reeds and papyrus which seem to be floating plants but actually have stems as much as fifteen feet long. When high water comes, with the run-off from the mountains in the summer, these loosen their hold and are carried off as 'sudds' – floating islands of vegetation sometimes half an acre in size. These bump on to the sandbanks around the outfall of the lake, and the vegetation proceeds to reroot itself. Sand is washed in to fill up the spaces between sudds, so that the flow-off from the lake in effect builds a kind of earth dam, thick and solid; even trees may root themselves there.

The lake is forced to find new outlets, and the Shiré River suddenly shifts its bed on the first part of its course down to the junction with the Zambesi. Eventually the dam formed by the sudds reaches precarious heights; unpredictably, depending on the size of the summer run-off from the mountains, the weight of water bursts the sudds away, and Lake Nyasa drops to a new level.

Dr Banda and his colleagues are acutely aware of the economic wastefulness in all this, as indeed are the more conscientious servants of the British colonial administration. It is, in fact, a kind of triple folly. For not only is the lake unusable; in the Shiré outrun there is a potential cumulative head of hydro-electric water power amounting to some 1,400 feet in total vertical drop, which harnessed would be of enormous value to a poor territory, at the moment forced to import all its coal. And thirdly, there is the wasted Shiré basin, where at present the river thrashes uselessly about like a violently convulsed snake. But with a system of barrages (for hydro power), controlled levels, and irrigation, this might be turned into one of the richest valleys on earth. The United States showed the way with its Tennessee Valley Administration and the Africans are convinced that they can and must have a Shiré T.V.A. It has been estimated that £3 million would build the barrages; the power stations could be started with another £5 million; and a total investment of some £100 million might be required in all. But the returns would be considerable. The experience of hydro engineers in France and California suggests that the Shiré Valley could produce rich crops of rice and other grains, sugar cane, and cotton; it would support market gardening and the raising of livestock.

For secondary industry, using the power from the hydro-electric installations, there would be a consumer market of some three million people, accessible through efficient lake transport. Stabilizing the level of Lake Nyasa would make it possible at last to build permanent wharves for deep draft vessels, and these larger ships would not be subject to the navigation hazards confronting small craft at present. Finally, with big ships it would become economically feasible to tap the coal deposits in the mountains at the northern end of the lake. There would even be a cheap water-route to railhead in Tanganyikan territory at the north end, and thus an alternative to the present supply-route through Portuguese territory – a route Dr Banda and his African administration find politically distasteful.

At present, however, nearly ten years after the start of Federation, this vast potential cascade of wealth remains a dream. The people of Nyasaland saw the Federal Assembly in Salisbury reject the Shiré and give first priority to the Kariba scheme – although many distinguished economists predicted that the rate of economic return from the Shiré would be much higher. This seems even odder when it is remembered that little Nyasaland, with its three million people, is much more densely populated than either of the Rhodesias, and lacks their mineral or industrial resources.

This, of course, is where the *realpolitik* of 'partnership' comes into play. The brutal fact is that it is not the number of people in any given territory – and especially not the number of Africans – which determines political influence; it is the number of whites.

There are approximately two and a half million Africans in each of the Rhodesias and three million in Nyasaland. But in the Federal Assembly of fifty-nine members (which resolved on Kariba and rejected the Shiré scheme), the division of seats bore no relation to these numbers. For each of the member territories, there sat five members to represent African interests (four of them are actually Africans and one is a white). The other members of the national parliament – forty-four out of fifty-nine – were all white. Southern Rhodesia (white population about 225,000) had twenty-four white M.P.s. Northern Rhodesia (75,000 whites) had fourteen. Nyasaland (nearly 10,000 whites) had six white M.P.s. Clearly the formula for the allocation of seats, and of economic and political power in the Federation, in the words of Colin Leys: 'reflects the balance of European populations and a bargain struck between the political leaders of the three European communities'.

Thus it is that a Federal Assembly, firmly proclaiming partnership and firmly founded on a secure basis of white racialism, rejected the Shiré and voted for the £110 million Kariba scheme. The final irony, of course, is that, as a result of the political troubles which have shaken the confidence of foreign investors, and the fall in world copper prices, there has been nothing like the expansion of mining in the north and industry in the south necessary to absorb the sudden abundance of power flowing from Kariba. Only part of its output is being sold, making the real cost per unit higher than anticipated whatever the sale price may be. Meanwhile the Shiré Valley scheme, whose first-stage development would have cost about a quarter of Kariba's, remains a desert of mud, scrub, and sand.

The cool self-interest of Salisbury's white traders and politicians is in sharp contrast to those white people who opened up Nyasaland. You might call it the contrast between the Rhodesians and the Livingstonians; certainly here are two clashing concepts – white supremacy in one territory, white trusteeship in the other, and Northern Rhodesia a kind of uneasy battleground where it has not been clear which would prevail. In the south they are supremacists in fact (though they loudly disclaim the description), for reasons deeply rooted in the character of Rhodes and the men who opened up the territory. Around Lake Nyasa it is again the past record of the white man which explains the temper of politics today.

Perhaps the very first action of Dr Laws and Lieutenant Young with their ship s.s. *Ilala* was symbolic of the spirit which was to prevail in Nyasaland. Young records that they set out to look for slavers and soon sighted an Arab dhow. Its slave hold was vacant, but 'guilt was writ large upon the face of its captain' and the mission ship therefore put on steam and ran rings round the dhow before leaving her. The Arabs were soon to know that a potent new influence had arrived in Nyasaland. As Livingstone wrote:

The plan which rises up before my mind is to make Africa north of Latitude 15° a blessing to Africans and Englishmen. There is room and to spare for English emigrants to settle and work the virgin soil of the still untilled land of Ham. As the African need not be torn from his country and enslaved, no more need the English poor be crowded in unwholesome dens, debarred from breathing the pure air of Heaven. There is room for all in the wide and glorious domains.

'You must give me medicine to change my heart,' said Chief Sekomi on one occasion to the great Scottish missionary. When Livingstone asked why, the answer was, simply: 'Because I want a heart like yours.'

Time and again the tireless doctor struck inland along the Zambesi, criss-crossing and mapping two-thirds of what has become the Federation today. He records how he prepared himself:

A few biscuits, a few pounds of tea and sugar, about 20 lbs. coffee. A spare shirting, trousers, shoes . . . a nautical almanac, Thomson's Logarithm Tables and a Bible . . . thermometer, compasses, a gipsy tent, a sheepskin mantle, and a horse rug as a bed.

He tells how he came upon the Victoria Falls and 'crept with awe to the verge'. And a great tropical pasture by the Zambesi he vividly described:

Hundreds of buffaloes, zebras and lordly elephants, feeding majestically. . . . It seemed like what must have been seen by Angels when megatheria fed undisturbed in primeval forests.

When Dr Livingstone died, near Lake Bangweulu, the friends who were with him were all Africans. They 'sat down and cried a great deal'. Later they wrapped the emaciated, fever-drained body in calico, sailcloth, and bark for the journey of 1,500 miles to the coast. It was a dedicated band of African friends who volunteered for the long march.

A practical combination of 'commerce and Christianity' was

Livingstone's formula for smashing the slave-trade. And so it proved, though the actual result was to come some years after his death. At first Dr Laws tried to combine the roles of merchant and missionary in himself, together with his other duties. But after reckoning that in a single year he had disposed of no less than '15 miles of calico' in undercutting the slavers, he decided to separate the commercial side of the anti-slavery campaign. He wrote to James Stevenson, a generous Glasgow merchant who sponsored the Scottish missions, and in consequence the African Lakes Company began operations in 1879. One by-product was the 'Stevenson Road', which was to open up much of Nyasaland and parts of Northern Rhodesia.

The first managers of the African Lakes Company were two Scots brothers, John and Frederick Moir – hard-headed in business, devout Christians, but handy with guns as well. Both were wounded in gunfights with the Arab slavers, in an era of unembarrassed muscular Christianity. [Bishop Mackenzie was so appalled by the barbarities of the Yao raiding parties that twice he took up arms and led the battle against them when they tried to recapture slaves who had escaped to the safety of the U.M.C.A. mission.] The white man may talk of the Lakes Company or the A.L.C., but to the African it is 'Mandala', and that word is bravely printed over the door of every A.L.C. store in Nyasaland and the Rhodesias to this day. Its literal meaning is 'reflected light', like the dazzle of the sun on a lake. John Moir, it seems, wore those old-fashioned round spectacles that gleam and flash in the light. Nyasaland's Scottish past is never very far away.

The Africans paid at the sign of the Mandala in the early days with the ivory that would otherwise have gone to the slavers. But the elephant herds were fast being reduced; ivory was a diminishing asset. The Moirs looked round for other export goods that Africans might supply. A young gardener at the Blantyre Mission, John Buchanan, sent home to Edinburgh, where he knew that they were developing hardy varieties of Arabica coffee in certain greenhouses. Three plants made the perilous journey, and two died. From the third came a crop of 1,000 beans and, from these, 400 plants that are the ancestors of all the Nyasa coffee that has followed. In time Buchanan and his associates promoted other cash crops – tea, cotton, tobacco, and the tung-oil tree – that were to become the solid base of the territory's economy, for Nyasaland lives solely by agriculture.

It would be wrong to suggest that the missionaries pacified the country unaided, although their sacrifices were considerable enough. 'We have taken possession of the country by our graves,' wrote the French Protestant missionary François Coillard at his station in Northern Rhodesia. He was to die a few days later of the fever that had killed Livingstone and Bishop Mackenzie before him. 'There was malaria in Capernaum when Christ worked there,' declared Dr Laws. 'It is enough that the servant be as his Master.' For the men of the missions, from the time they set foot on Rhodesian soil, there was a scant five years before death or invaliding home. It was customary for a new recruit to make a will, and choose a verse for his headstone, though he might be under thirty and perfectly fit. The U.M.C.A. reported at the turn of the century that, out of 200 men who had come to their missions, fifty-seven had died in service. Sir Harry Johnston, the British Consul who in many ways created Nyasa-land as an organized state, wrote of the missionaries in 1896 that 'they have done more good than armies, navies, conferences and treaties'.

Yet this ignores the hard job of sheer military subjugation which he and other civilian administrators saw through to success. The John Buchanan who introduced coffee became Acting-Consul in the days when sovereignty was uncertain, took part in much of the fighting against the Yao slavers (at one time being captured and flogged bareback by them), and proclaimed the territory a provisional British Protectorate when the Portuguese seemed bent on taking it by force. The Old Residency, with its fortress towers built by Buchanan and its grounds and gardens laid out by Johnston, can be seen today much as it was then. There are touches strongly reminiscent of the Indian Civil Service in this and everything else at Zomba, the little capital of the Protectorate. Zomba itself is a hill station in the Poona tradition: the Union Jack floats comfortably above Government House;

and beyond it are the familiar patterns of the Police Lines and the cantonment of the King's African Rifles. The old Secretariat with its cool arcaded verandas is a microcosm of Imperial India; through the trees is the cricket pitch, the golf course, and – inevitably – the Club.

Yet it was not always intended to be this way. With all the money, cunning, and energy at his command, Cecil Rhodes had tried to capture the territory for his British South Africa Company, as he had succeeded in doing with the two Rhodesias, and with the same object – to make it part of that new white dominion that was to arise in Central Africa.

Indeed, it is Nyasaland's curious distinction that its original nickname should have become that of the whole Federation. People often ask why a country so clearly a part of southern Africa should be commonly called the Central African Federation. The explanation is significant. When Consul Johnston set out on his expedition of treaty-making with the chiefs (on the staff of the Foreign Office, but paid by Rhodes and the British South Africa Company), he was doing so as a fellow-enthusiast for the All-Red Route. He it was who popularized the catchphrase 'Cape to Cairo' while home on leave from Nigeria as a young vice-consul, in that same summer of 1889 when Rhodes was doing his master job of lobbying in London for the Royal Charter. The two men met, as we have seen, over dinner at a party arranged by Verschoyle of the *Fortnightly Review*.

Rhodes heard the magic phrase for the first time that evening, and the two men went on enthusiastically to plan the new state, British Central Africa, which should stretch northward to link up with Kenya and Uganda. Beyond were the Sudan and Egypt – both securely under British suzerainty, presumably forever. Had the Rhodes–Johnston plan succeeded, there would indeed have been a long, central strip of territory, a new state running right up the spine of the continent, in British hands. It might have been a sort of onion shape, with the two Rhodesias and the Nyasa territory as the bulb at the bottom.

Thanks to Lord Salisbury, however, the onion never sprouted. The British Prime Minister preferred to sacrifice Rhodes's

Dominion of Central Africa in the diplomatic poker game, and, when he conceded German claims in Tanganyika, he blocked the northward thrust. Still, Rhodes was a salesman and a phrase-maker; there is an ironic justice in the fact that his memory was to be perpetuated, not only in the formal name but also in the nickname of the Federation established in 1953.

Today's African leaders aim, among other things, to banish the name Rhodesia from the atlases. More than one of them has quietly assured me that Salisbury is to be renamed Harare, and so on. This is understandable. Yet there is a certain wry truth in the suggestion that, but for that dinner party of Verschoyle's, the administrative language of Nyasaland today might well be Por-tuguese instead of English, and Dr Banda and his colleagues might be as far from self-government as their tribal cousins over the border in Moçambique. It was Johnston's rampant imperial-ism that saved the Nyasa country from falling as a prize to the eager Portuguese. But for this, Blantyre would doubtless bear some such name as Nova Lisboa today and the machine-guns, napalm bombs, and reconnaissance aircraft of the Portuguese colonial army would be holding down the Malawi people on the west shore of the lake as efficiently as they are holding down twice that number on the eastern side, in Moçambique.

To pile on the irony further, it was that friend and benefactor of the Africans, Frederick Moir of the Lakes Company, who mis-guidedly went to the aid of the Portuguese at a crucial point in Moçambique's colonial history and so saved the territory for Lisbon. He was returning from a trip to Scotland and learned, on landing at the port of Quelimane, that there was 'trouble' in the interior. One by one the outposts had fallen to native rebels; the last of them, still in Portuguese hands but hard besieged, was all that stood guard between the rebels and the timorous authorities at the coastal capital. A more imaginative man than Moir would have thought twice about offering his help; had he simply sat it out in Zanzibar, the Portuguese might have been driven out of East Africa for good. There would have been a quick end to the endless difficulties with which Portuguese customs and militia bedevilled all English-speaking travellers seeking transit to the interior. British and Portuguese native policies were already at loggerheads, not to mention the clash between Portuguese Catholic missionaries and the British Protestants. Lisbon's colonial officials were operating a profitable partnership with the Arab slavers and the Yao of the interior, despite the lip service they gave to the principle of ending slavery.

In Frederick Moir's direct mental reckoning, the main thing was to get through with his supplies to his African charges at Lake Nyasa. He must have been unaware that he was abetting the Portuguese in putting down the first – and nearly successful – African uprising. Putting himself at the head of a polyglot party of seventeen volunteers (none of them Portuguese) he led a successful expedition that raised the siege. He wrote in his diary: 'Peace having been re-established, I was able to resume my interrupted journey.' Professor Frank Debenham, the Cambridge geographer, has commented: 'It was by this narrow margin and by that foreign assistance that Portugal continued to hold the Zambesi.'

Clearly we have here one of those irritating 'ifs' of history. Connoisseurs of this peculiar form of torture may like to measure Moir's mistaken tactics against a further factor: Cecil Rhodes was even at that moment trying to bargain with Lisbon, to persuade the Portuguese to sell him the whole of Moçambique. Had the African rebellion been allowed to succeed there is much to suggest that Portugal would have accepted little in return for so costly a possession. The face of modern Africa would have been very different.

There had been a British consul stationed in Moçambique from 1857 onwards; the arrival of the Scottish missionaries to work in the Nyasa region meant that sooner or later the Foreign Office would be confronted with the diplomatic task of getting Lisbon to agree to a territorial frontier. Lord Salisbury set to work. But in the course of sorting things out, he found his own conduct of Britain's external affairs complicated for him by the independent imperial policies of Cecil Rhodes. There were in fact three separate episodes: the Serpa Pinto Expedition of 1889, the De Souza Affair of 1890, and the Beira Outrage of 1891.

Rhodes was mixed up in all three of them, and in two of these – in which there was a compelling aroma of stage management – the cast included that redoubtable rogue, Dr Jameson. Mid-way in the drama Rhodes became, in July 1890, Prime Minister of Cape Colony, so that we have a quite astonishing parallel with Mr Macmillan's problems in the 1960s. Just as Sir Roy Welensky conducted his own foreign policy – links with the Tshombe régime in the Congo, the refusal to accept U.N. observers on the Rhodesian frontier – leaving No. 10 Downing Street and the Foreign Office to hasten along behind him, rubber-stamping his pronouncements, so did an earlier British Prime Minister find his elbow being firmly guided by a Colonial Prime Minister in southern Africa. It is worth remembering perhaps that the policy of independent action combined with bluster is not something invented by Sir Roy Welensky; the technique was pioneered by his predecessor, the Founder.

The misgivings of many people in the Cape when Rhodes assumed the premiership were well summed up by the South African authoress, Olive Schreiner: 'I don't see how he can play the hand of the Chartered Company and the hand of the Colony at the same time.' Rhodes had no difficulty in dealing with that one. He declared: 'Within our lifetime the limits of Cape Colony will stretch as far as the Zambesi.' It was perfectly clear in his mind that the new colony he was founding in Zambesia was simply an extension of white South Africa, to be federated into it whenever convenient. Rhodes's calculation, however, was to prove wrong; in the 1922 referendum the settlers voted resoundingly against union with South Africa and in favour of 'responsible government'. What they meant – and got – was, of course, absolute independence. It was only Whitehall that kept its illusions and persisted for the next forty years in regarding Southern Rhodesia as a colony.

Though not all Rhodes's schemes succeeded, it was his strategic thinking during those three critical years, 1889–91, that brought into his orbit the territories we now know as Northern Rhodesia and Nyasaland, secured them along with the south for his British South Africa Company, and thus created the shape of the Federation as we know it today. Later the Chartered Company was to lose its hold on the territories, one by one. But it is worth considering that, when the white settlers achieved their political goal in 1953, they were not – despite much astute oratory in London and Salisbury at the time – creating something bold and new in Central Africa. They were merely re-erecting the structure of the Central African state which Rhodes and Johnston had between them produced sixty-two years before. What was new in 1953 was the public-relations campaign, the 'soft-sell' – to smooth British criticism – of racial policy, hazily defined as 'partnership' (and never defined in law). In one respect, indeed, the 1891 version of federation was superior; at least there was free movement for its peoples between member territories and not the nonsense of the 1960s which prohibited Kenneth Kaunda and Dr Banda from entry to the federal capital of their own land.

The setting up of that first tri-partite Rhodesian state, 1891 version, was a masterpiece of political gamesmanship. It might be said that in the art of settler diplomacy, Rhodes was, as in so much else, the trail-blazer. For it is a hard rule of Rhodesian politics that – being thin on the ground – the settlers have somehow to bend the power of the United Kingdom to their service. And yet there is a basic dichotomy in this, as the Rhodeses, the Welenskys, and the Whiteheads – though not the Salisburys and Macmillans – have been swift to realize. The fact is that the essential interests of the two administrations are different.

In Rhodesia, settler power is compromised by the overwhelming size of the indigenous population. In the early years, when the entire African community was living on a subsistence-agriculture basis, it constituted an economic burden on the settlers – and a kind of political albatross. In bargaining with Whitehall, the Rhodesian colonist of the 1890s was in a weaker position than his counterpart in the Thirteen Colonies a century before, measured in terms of pure political power. Cecil Rhodes had an instinct that told him precisely what to do. Whitehall possessed the power; his own strength would lie in directing it to his own objectives.

There was, of course, a considerable risk in attempting to handle such imperial high voltage: it might short-circuit. The danger lay in the liberal groups in London – the missionaries and humanitarians, some journalists, and a section of the Liberal Party – the 'negrophiles' as Rhodes and his cronies brusquely termed them. The way to by-pass them was to suggest that British national interest was threatened in Central Africa; once Whitehall threw the switch, imperial power would come pulsing down the line from London.

Rhodes considered his balance sheet: he was weak in military manpower (his British South Africa Company police), weaker in liquid cash resources than he cared to admit, but well placed for credit facilities (de Beers, Rothschilds), and far superior to Lord Salisbury in the skilled, shrewd men, with detailed knowledge of the local Rhodesian scene, behind him. He began the power game for the two northern territories during that same visit to London in the spring of 1889 when negotiating for the Company's control of Zambesia.

The atmosphere of international politics was suitably electric for Rhodes to strike patriotic sparks. The scramble for Africa was frenzied; at one end of Africa, the French and Italians were threatening British power in Egypt; at the other, the Germans and Portuguese were threatening to stop the northward thrust of Cape Colony with a double tourniquet. Verschoyle of the *Fortnightly Review* needed no convincing; he wanted Rhodes to contribute an article immediately on 'The German–Portuguese Menace'. But Rhodes turned instead to his old Oxford friend Charles Metcalfe, the eccentric engineer who wanted to build a British railway from Cairo to the Cape.

He wrote: 'It will come better from you, as I am looked on with some distrust at home.' Metcalfe's article duly appeared, warning the *Review*'s influential readers – many of them Tory M.P.s – about German ambitions in Central Africa. Soon afterwards another on similar lines appeared, by Frederick Courteney Selous, the noted South African hunter, who was to guide the Pioneer Column for Rhodes the next year. Leading Fellows of the Royal Geographical Society were much impressed and put their weight behind the campaign. France and Germany had formally accepted Portugal's claims over the whole of Zambesia; even if this was a mere paper occupation, Britain needed a representative on the spot. Already the authorities in Quelimane and the other ports of Moçambique were demanding that British travellers buy 'Resident's Permits' before proceeding to the interior.

Lord Salisbury had realized the need for a determined and energetic man to take over the Moçambique post; as British Consul he designated Harry Johnston, who had made his mark at the Foreign Office for his cool handling of a tricky situation in the Niger Delta. And so here, Rhodes decided, was a man he had to meet, in view of the British South Africa Company plans for the Nyasa territory – and his fears that Salisbury might do a deal with Portugal. (A year before the British Prime Minister had proposed a settlement which would have given Moçambique a great northward extension and cut the land bridge between Zambesia and the Nyasa missions. It came to nothing because the Portuguese decided that they could get even more of Central Africa by military conquest.)

Verschoyle arranged the famous little dinner party, and Rhodes recognized in Johnston the ideal instrument for his own imperial plans. Both men knew that Salisbury's scope in East Africa had been limited by the absolute refusal of Goschen at the Treasury – in his general memorandum of the previous 25 January – to allow so much as one extra penny or one additional Civil Servant to be added to the Africa budgets of the Foreign or Colonial Offices. But suppose someone else were to supply that deficiency . . . could not then Consul Johnston, when taking up his Moçambique post, make expeditions to the interior himself and take on the extra staff in order to negotiate treaties? The Chartered Company would pay for the clearing of the diplomatic niceties so that its men could then move in and establish the physical possession of the terrain which was what ultimately mattered.

Not since the brave days of Prince Rupert and the 'gentlemen adventurers' of the Hudson's Bay Company had there been such a cool combination of diplomacy and commerce. Who indeed but Rhodes would have supposed that a private company could take over one of Her Majesty's Consuls and his expenses of office?

Johnston must have welcomed the backing of Rhodes for his new post. He knew that there was a minute on file at the Foreign Office, written by Salisbury a few months before, in response to an appeal received from the Church of Scotland missions and the Lakes Company for aid in their struggle with the Yao and the Arab slavers. The Prime Minister (in his other role as Foreign Secretary) had told them that the best they could expect was a Consul; he could not commit Her Majesty's government to 'expensive operations'. His minute proclaimed:

To please the missionaries we send a representative of the Govt.; to spare the taxpayers we make him understand that he will in no case be supported by an armed force. The only weapon left to him is bluster.

Johnston's superior at the Foreign Office, Sir Percy Anderson, had set down in a minute of his own a similar distaste for imperial adventure. He scorned 'the impracticable idea of a British Protectorate' for the Nyasa country; and the terrain north of the Zambesi – present-day Northern Rhodesia – was 'pestilential and useless to the Empire'.

On the evening of his dinner with Verschoyle and Johnston, Rhodes acted. Taking out the cheque-book which was always in his breast pocket, he scribbled out his personal cheque for the sum of £2,000, made out to Johnston himself as payee. That, he explained, was simply a first instalment. He proposed that the Chartered Company should provide £9,000 a year for operating expenses, so enabling the young Consul to recruit and arm some kind of 'police' force. He should attempt to hold back the Portuguese on the one hand, preventing them from advancing north into the Shiré Highlands; and, on the other, to annex the whole territory north of the Zambesi as speedily as possible by a series of treaties. He was to try and reach Katanga, for its copper, ahead of King Leopold – Rhodes failed by a matter of weeks because London and Brussels had agreed on the line of the frontier while

Johnston's emissary was still footslogging across country from Lake Mweru – and to halt the southward push of the Germans in Tanganyika.

Johnston succeeded in the last objective, and the instrument he used, devised by Rhodes himself, was a characteristic combination of Rhodes's bravado and simplicity. He built and staffed two small trading-posts as far north as he dared, named them 'Abercorn' and 'Fife', and saw that the news reached the appropriate desk at the Foreign Office as speedily as possible. 'They will never dare to hand over to foreigners a place named after a member of the royal family,' said Rhodes (to Johnston, who recorded the remark with a certain laconic appreciation), thus showing a shrewd grasp of the kinds of pressures effective in Whitehall. Coincidentally, of course, the two royal dukes whose names were so neatly appropriated were also on the board of the Chartered Company. One was powerful in the Liberal Party, the other in the Tories.

Rhodes had not the faintest idea of how his £9,000 per annum 'subsidy' was going to be regularized; there were salaried constitutional experts in Whitehall who could see to that. (They did.) The panache of the whole project showed the millionaire's proper contempt for the frailty of governments. One of the less-publicized files in the Foreign Office (1893: 2/55) contains a letter written later by Johnston to Rhodes:

When the Government, though wishing to save this country from the Portuguese and the Germans, had not a penny to spend on it, you stepped forward and said: 'Make this extension of British supremacy and I will find the money. . . .' This changed the situation at once . . . and within a week new instructions were being drawn up for me at the Foreign Office.

Emboldened by success, Rhodes began to press for Chartered Company control of Northern Zambesia, a juicy plum which dropped into his lap in the form of a Supplementary Charter in 1891. But the immediate objective was to hold back the Portuguese. Rhodes had all along known of their plans for a military expedition to occupy the Nyasa region and expel the Scottish missionaries. He had been powerless to forestall them before, but now he was ready at last to play the power game – with Whitehall providing the diplomatic cannon. When Rhodes handed over that £2,000 'first instalment', he made it a condition of acceptance that the Foreign Office should speed Johnston on his way before the month was out. Johnston made it just in time.

A mixed force of 1,200 armed men under the command of Major Serpa Pinto was already moving towards the Ruo River, the frontier of what Rhodes planned should be Chartered Company territory. Johnston, doffing his British South Africa Company cap, concluded treaties with chiefs on the British side of the Ruo in the name of the Queen. That done, he coolly informed Pinto by messenger that the Shiré region north of the river had been 'placed under protection of Her Majesty'.

It was pure bluff, but Lord Salisbury did not disown his Consul. And when the hapless Major Pinto, pressed by Lisbon, massed his forces and crossed the Ruo, he found himself in a political hornet's nest. Within eleven days Johnston had got word to London, and Salisbury had cabled an ultimatum to Lisbon. Pinto and his men, who had penetrated deep into Nyasa territory, were suddenly ordered to withdraw. The main political cartoon in *Punch* that week – by Tenniel – showed a cocky Serpa Pinto dancing on the Union Jack by the bank of the Ruo, while a burly British Jack Tar growled: 'Come off that Flag!' The £2,000 had been well invested. Before Rhodes got busy, the British public had neither known nor cared about the River Ruo, and Lord Salisbury would never have wasted a twopenny stamp on Nyasaland.

The technique was now clear. Why twist the tail of the lion if you could make it jump through hoops for you instead? By the time he was ready for the next move, the Pioneer Column had raised the flag near Harare and founded Fort Salisbury, while – most valuable of all – Rhodes, now Prime Minister of the Cape, had a new advantage: his own independent military force, tactfully entitled the British South Africa Company police.

In that winter Lord Salisbury, assuming he had struck a good bargain, signed the Convention with Lisbon which kept the Portuguese out of most of Rhodes's Chartered empire – the two

Zambesias and the Nyasa–Shiré Highlands – but ceded to them most of the Barotseland on the west and the Manica country (with its supposed gold deposits) on the east. There is a classic rule for white settler Prime Ministers to follow in such a situation – fly now, pay later.

Dr Jameson, together with the invaluable Frederick Selous and a detachment of Company police, moved swiftly into what had now become the Manica province of Moçambique. The Paramount Chief succumbed to the celebrated charm of Dr Jameson (and a subsidy of £100 per annum), and the territory was formally – if unconstitutionally – ceded to the Chartered Company. When the Portuguese dispatched a force under Captain d'Andrade and Manuel de Souza to assert their rights, Jameson replied with a platoon under Major Patrick Forbes which quickly overwhelmed them. Luck was with Rhodes; the parliament in Lisbon had failed to ratify the Convention, Salisbury was spared the embarrassment of having to discipline the new imperialists now operating under the British South Africa Company flag, and the hapless Portuguese leaders were brought back in triumph as prisoners of war, significantly to Cape Town. The British public were delighted with the dash and bravado of the 'De Souza Affair'; Salisbury, much occupied with Egypt and Heligoland and the French fleet, must have heaved a well-bred sigh of relief.

The 'Beira Outrage' followed soon afterwards. Rhodes and Rothschilds had offered £1·3 million for Moçambique's best port, Beira, and its hinterland. But Lisbon suddenly withdrew from the negotiations and closed the port altogether to the Company's traffic. This was the moment to tap the imperial power line to London again, and Rhodes knew from the Pinto affair that it would be easier if British national honour were somehow involved.

He had just the man for the job: Sir John Willoughby – old Etonian, Cambridge blue, officer in the Egypt campaign, and noted horseman (he had ridden a Derby winner). Willoughby sailed his flagship into Beira harbour as if to ascend the river that led to British South Africa Company territory; the Portuguese

obligingly fired a blank shot across his bows; the flagship withdrew, and England's national daily Press erupted – surprisingly –
into headlines on the 'Beira Outrage'. Salisbury must have been
impressed when even the phlegmatic Sir Henry Loch, the British
High Commissioner at the Cape, sent a coded cable to Downing
Street urging 'action with the fleet'.

The British Prime Minister obliged with the classic gesture of
nineteenth-century power politics; and he sent not just one gunboat but two. Freedom of navigation for the Rhodesians was restored (it continues to this day), and the Chartered Company won
the right to build the railway from Beira into the interior which is
still one of the lifelines of the Central African Federation.
Manicaland was recognized as part of British – and therefore
Chartered Company – territory, and the whole deal was formally
confirmed in the Anglo-Portuguese Treaty.

From these military and diplomatic initiatives by Rhodes,
emerged the geographical outlines of the three territories in the
Federation as they are today. And equally important for the political inheritance of the new country he was creating was the code
of moral standards Rhodes himself implanted. Reinforced by
Jameson as administrator, it inevitably communicated itself to
the Pioneers and to all the other frontiersmen who constructed
the framework of the new state. It was a code that declared physical occupation and military control to be nine-tenths of the law,
that declared defiance of Whitehall and Downing Street to be
profitable and total independence for the settlers an urgent objective. And it laid down a race-relations policy which stemmed
from Rhodes's own description of 'Children just emerging from
barbarism'.

There remained a little tidying up for Rhodes to do before his
empire in Central Africa was complete. The indefinite status of
Barotseland had to be resolved in case the Portuguese to the west
in Angola should try to absorb that part of the upper Zambesi.
As emissary of the Company to Paramount Chief Lewanika went
Frank Lochner on a 1,200-mile odyssey by ox wagon and canoe.
It was known that the old monarch had, through the missionary
Coillard, who worked in his territory, written to Shippard as the

nearest representative of the Colonial Office asking to have his territory made a British Protectorate. His friends the Khamas, the royal house in Bechuanaland, had done that to forestall other, less pleasant, eventualities. This did not suit Rhodes; he wanted direct Chartered Company control, free from the fiddling interference of Whitehall. Shippard hedged when Lewanika asked to be accepted as 'child of the Great White Queen' (probably Coillard's phrase), while Lochner was advised to stress that his Company had a Royal Charter and so consisted of 'the Queen's men'. It is arguable what Lewanika thought that he had agreed to when he signed the concession which passed some 200,000 square miles into Company control. But one thing is clear. He handed over two enormous ivory tusks as a gift of gratitude to Queen Victoria. They were possibly the most splendid ever to have come out of Central Africa, a proper gift from one monarch to another.

They ended up in the board-room of the London headquarters of the Chartered Company. Settlers found this rather amusing. The London *Daily Chronicle* – a Liberal paper – described it as 'the meanest form of embezzlement, not from the Nation but from the Queen personally'.

Nothing of course embarrassed Rhodes, who smoothly proposed to the Rev. François Coillard that he might like to become Commissioner of Barotseland. The old French evangelist records that he knelt down and prayed in these words: 'O merciful God let not Thy servant become a political martyr!'

Rhodes was not yet finished with Lobengula, since he wanted land rights and the Rudd Concession had specifically been limited to mineral exploitation. Sir Henry Loch, representing the British government at the Cape, was pressing Rhodes for action. Many months had passed since the march of the Pioneers, and their occupation had still to be made legal. By this time Lobengula had disowned the Rudd Concession, had written to the Queen declaring he had been tricked, and to prove his point (and dislodge Rhodes) was announcing his readiness to make a new agreement with some other group.

John Moffat at Bulawayo was therefore astonished to receive a letter from Loch explaining that an emissary was on his way in the person of E. A. Lippert, the German financier, who would regularize the Chartered Company's dubious legal position. Could Rhodes really be so absurdly optimistic? Of course not. Lippert coolly presented himself to the Matabele King as a bitter rival of Rhodes, in pursuit of the real concession, now that Rudd had been repudiated. Once again the big bluff succeeded. To Moffat, Lippert made no bones about his double role. The ex-missionary, who had once seen Rhodes – a clergyman's son like himself – as an instrument of God and the Queen in Central Africa, was beginning to have serious doubts. He wrote to Loch:

I hope nothing will occur to bring me into any closer contact with the proceedings. If I did not feel that the Chief is quite as deceitful as those who are going to try conclusions with him, I could not sit still and let this go on.

To Rhodes himself, he wrote:

I look on the whole plan as detestable, in the light of policy or moral-ity. . . . When Lobengula finds it all out, what faith will he have in you? I am thankful that my orders do not require me to take part personally in this transaction; it is bad enough to be cognizant of it.

The deal went through; Lobengula conceded to Lippert and his syndicate 'the exclusive right for one hundred years . . . to make grants of land to Europeans'. It specifically covered Mashonaland as well as the Matabele tribal territories. Lippert hastened south with his good news, to sell out as arranged (on handsome terms) to the Chartered Company. For the King it was the final, embittering disillusionment with the Great White Queen and all her agents; he must have sensed that war was near. The Rev. John Moffat, who had proved so uncooperative, was broken, as Rhodes was to break many more before he had finished founding his new nation; the impulsive missionary found himself abruptly transferred to Bechuanaland at a reduced salary. The man who (at least nominally) gave this order was of course the same colonial administrator who had blocked Lewanika's plea for a Protectorate, winked at the disappearance of the ivory

tusks, and pleaded Rhodes's case in the stench of the royal kraal –
Sir Sydney Shippard. It would not be long before he would join
the ivory tusks in the board-room of 'Chartered'.

It seems appropriately ironic that, when the whole land issue
was long afterwards argued before the judicial committee of the
Privy Council, the resultant judgement should have declared that
the Rudd and Lippert concessions had never surrendered to the
British South Africa Company any titles to the land which for
nearly thirty years it had been busily carving up and selling.

Only in Nyasaland did Rhodes finally meet his match. And,
incredibly, he did so in the person of his former friend and ac-
complice, Harry Johnston.

For as long as it had been a simple matter of fending off the
Germans and the Portuguese, there had been no clash in their
imperial concepts. In the frontier country of the twin territories
north of the Zambesi, no man was quicker on the draw with a
loaded treaty than Harry Johnston. And when it came to a shooting war against the Yao, the Angoni, and the Bemba, the Consul
and his Sikhs proved that they could be just as resolute and ruthless as Buffalo Bill and the U.S. Cavalry – who were operating
against their indigenous tribes at much the same period.

The Afro-Arab slaver, Mlozi, was one of the wiliest and tough-
est of Johnston's opponents. The young Consul took over the
campaign from the equally youthful Captain Freddie Lugard,
who had been wounded in a brave assault on one of Mlozi's
stockaded villages. (After convalescence he was reposted to
Nigeria and ended up as that great colonial administrator, Lord
Lugard.) Johnston formed a force which, on Rhodes's advice, he
described as 'police', the euphemism which was working so well
in disarming British criticism of the Company's activities in
Zambesia. Undoubtedly Rhodes envisaged that Johnston would
form an all-white force which could be amalgamated with the
British South Africa Company police when – as he had indicated
to Lord Salisbury – the Chartered Company took over the
African Lakes Company.

But Nyasaland, even then, had a wilful way of its own, and
amalgamation was to elude the Great Amalgamator. The Moir

brothers, whose 'Mandala' company was running at a loss (because it consciously served the interests of race relations and not of commerce) incomprehensibly refused to sell out to 'Chartered'. Nor would Lord Salisbury, in deference to the Scots mission interests, abandon the Lakes Company and extend the Charter to Nyasaland. Even the 'police' plan went awry; there just weren't enough white settlers to recruit the kind of force that the Company possessed in Zambesia. Mlozi and the slave-trade would not wait; Johnston signalled the Indian Army for help, and even when the Sikhs arrived it still took two years to achieve victory. The stockaded villages were bombarded, the slaves freed, and Mlozi hanged as an awful warning to lesser slave-trade bosses. By 1898 slavery had been wiped out, the Yao chiefs and the Angoni warrior leader Mpeseni brought to terms, and the territory pacified.

The Lakes Company was receiving its £9,000 a year in subsidy from the Charter Company, but was stoutly resisting the invitation to be 'amalgamated'. Johnston, too, began to display an independence that puzzled Rhodes. He was now Commissioner in the Nyasa Highlands, and should have been on Rhodes's Company payroll, because of Goschen's economy rule against new posts. But he had managed to persuade the Treasury to pay his own salary and that of an assistant, as though they were both on the consular staff of the Foreign Office post in Moçambique. A curious moral struggle had taken place in the privacy of the Commissioner's soul; and it was resolved to Rhodes's cost. Johnston decided that the Scots missionaries were right and Rhodes was wrong; that there would be no peace in Nyasaland if the 'Chartered' view of native policy were to prevail. In the event, partition was inevitable. Rhodes and the Company got their Charter extended to Northern Rhodesia; there was no stopping them there. Johnston sat down and roughed out the frontier between the two territories along the boundary line that exists to this day, and on a trip to London got it formally recognized. In Northern Rhodesia – though Johnston was still Commissioner there – the 'Chartered' flag, the 'dog and bone', flew beside the Union Jack, and the Company was supreme.

But Nyasaland remained outside the empire of the British South Africa Company, though the Company raised its subsidy to more than £10,000 a year and Rhodes had been forced to approve overdrafts now totalling £20,000. He began to accuse Harry Johnston of 'disloyalty'. But for once he had overreached himself; this time he was not dealing with a Shippard or a Newton. He presented an ambitious plan whereby extensive tracts of land should be granted to the Company; and to his support rushed the other directors like the Duke of Abercorn, who blamed what he called 'Scotch jealousies and cussedness' for the British government's failure to grant the Company in its Nyasa operations the clear run it had had with the Pioneer Column in Zambesia.

But Johnston was already a committed man on this vital aspect of race relations. He had, in a special memorandum, proclaimed a land policy to 'protect the rights of the natives', discourage white speculators, and secure 'the rights of the Crown'. This was no way for a Chartered man to talk. The declaration, indeed, made no mention of the Company at all. Johnston had even instituted a system of 'Certificates of Claim' which apart from securing a large tract of land for the Lakes Company as help in its missionary work, would permit of no 'company development' by Chartered or anyone else.

It was the parting of the ways. The Foreign Office had, in any event, lost patience with the Chartered Company in its Nyasa operations. True, the Company was paying out handsomely and with no visible return (in lively expectation of favours yet to come). But the job – which had fallen on Johnston's shoulders – of subduing the Arab slavers and their African associates, was outpacing the subsidy; it was costing twice as much in fact. There was a bill of £9,200 from the War Office to the Nyasa administration for rifles, cannon, and ammunition; the Admiralty was presenting its claim for having built and crewed the three gunboats on Lake Nyasa which had finished off the slave dhows. Rhodes had a straight choice: to take over all the bills or withdraw altogether. When Johnston vetoed Rhodes's land-grant plan as incompatible with African rights, it was clear that he was lost to the cause of the new white dominion; he had been won over by the missionaries and their curious philosophy of trusteeship. Rhodes cut his losses.

It must have provided a bitter satisfaction to both men when Rhodes in November 1894 formally terminated the bizarre subsidy by the Chartered Company that had begun as an impulse at the Verschoyle dinner five years before. The year just ending had been particularly eventful: a rising by the Matabele in Zambesia had been efficiently crushed by the Company police; and the uneasy 'partnership' with Lobengula had ended with the King's flight and his ignominious death. The British South Africa Company was now running Zambesia by right of conquest; at a victory banquet in Cape Town the toast to the Founder was proposed by Dr Jameson, who announced the unanimous wish of the Directors that the new dominion be named 'Rhodesia' in his honour.

It was not an entirely original idea, and it must have wrung a wry smile from the now disenchanted Harry Johnston. In his eager, treaty-making days, when pegging out the Northern Zambesian frontier, he had founded a little Company post on Lake Mweru to block any southward thrust by the Belgians from the Congo. And to 'show the flag' in a way that had delighted Rhodes at the time, the young Consul had called the outpost 'Rhodesia'.

Johnston had irrevocably broken with the Company, so there had to be new arrangements made for the Northern Zambesian territory which he had opened up and administered until now. Rhodes wished to make it clear that there would be no place under the new régime for any of that chatter about African partnership – or even paramountcy – which filled official mouths in Nyasaland.

The Bemba, the Angoni, the Lunda, and other peoples in this vast, sprawling area were now – whether they wanted to be or not – inhabitants of the newly created Territory of Northern Rhodesia. In sharp contrast with Nyasaland, which had slipped from Rhodes's grasp, Northern Rhodesia was not to be permitted to become a Protectorate. The post of Queen's Commissioner, which had been held by Harry Johnston, was abolished. A new post, that of 'Company Administrator', was created, and the man chosen to fill it could hardly have differed more sharply from his predecessor in character and outlook. He was Major Patrick Forbes of the British South Africa Police, the man who had been Dr Jameson's colleague in the Manicaland invasion and the De Souza Affair, and, more recently, the leader of the main military force – the Victoria and Salisbury Columns – that had smashed and dispersed Lobengula's troops in the Matabele War.

For his territorial capital he took the Company's fort named in honour of Dr Jameson. But it is clear, from the records and letters of the period, that Rhodes and Jameson were not content. They had a further plan to realize as soon as roads and other communications had been effectively developed. The northern territory was to be amalgamated with the south and administered as one country, Rhodesia, from its national capital of Salisbury.

The significance of these earlier decisions, taken by Rhodes and Jameson, is that they set the scene for the drama that is still being played out today. They marked out the stage – the two Zambesias and the Nyasa country by the lake. It was they who determined the course of inexorable conflict, by deliberately creating the framework for a new white dominion, regardless of the basic racial facts bequeathed by Africa. And it was they who established the other conflict as well – that between London and Salisbury – which has bedevilled Anglo-Rhodesian relations from that day to this. And finally it was Cecil Rhodes and Starr Jameson who peopled this stage; into a seemingly empty but actually populous land, they brought South African white settlers – miners, farmers, merchants, and troopers. Settlers from other countries arrived as well. But it was the South Africans whose outlook was to be paramount, and was to be reflected in the laws and the whole way of life of the new land.

Part 3: The Settler Era

'Whatever happens we have got the Maxim-gun,
and they have not.'
HILAIRE BELLOC

1   The Descent of the Gods

'They that live by the Sword shall perish by the Sword.'
ST MATTHEW 26 : 52

There is something poetic, and very disarming, about the phrase used by the Africans of Matabeleland in the early days to describe the white strangers that had appeared suddenly in their midst. *'Omlimu abadla amabele'* they called them – 'the gods that eat corn'.

In these days of racial and political tension seventy years later, it is hard to visualize the African awe that was the starting-point for race relations in the pioneer period. And yet it is vital for an understanding of the political events that followed. Among the hearty extroverts pushing north under the banner of Rhodes, drawn by the twin lures of land and gold, there were very few disciplined ascetics. And when the simple local people greeted them as gods to boot, it should not surprise us that some settlers yielded to greed, lust, and arrogance.

The Rev. Ndabaningi Sithole is a dynamic young churchman and educationist who abandoned his previous 'moderation' to link up with Joshua Nkomo and the nationalist movement of Southern Rhodesia after the emergency and shootings in 1959–60, and who now leads Z.A.P.U. in exile. He has personally experienced this transition – from near worship at the first encounter to scepticism and disillusion. As a boy growing up in the Rhodesia of the 1920s, he saw a world dominated by the white men – then in their fifties – who had arrived as pioneers in the age of Rhodes. He has a vivid memory of a day when, as a seven-year-old herding cattle, he saw bearing down upon him a hut with windows, moving at enormous speed. It was his first view of a motor-car. Today this same man, still in his early forties, has university degrees and a better education than most members of

Sir Roy Welensky's Cabinet, has lectured and preached in thirty states of the U.S.A., and is equally at home in Whitehall or at the U.N. His book, *African Nationalism*,* gives a valuable insight into the state of mind of his countrymen as the era of white rule began:

The African was simply overwhelmed, overawed, perplexed, mystified and dazzled. The white man's houses that move on the water, his bird that is not like other birds, his monster that spits fire and smoke [these are all phrases from Sindabele] just amazed the African. These new white gods were conscious of the magic spell they had cast and did everything to maintain it. Mines were opened throughout the country. The dynamite that exploded the huge rocks confirmed the belief that the white man was a god . . . [possessing] all power, wealth, skills and knowledge. The African, who never argues with his gods lest their wrath visit him, adopted the same attitude to the white man . . . [who] became master in a house that was not his. And the white man saw that it was good and he smiled with deep satisfaction and said: 'Africa, the White Man's Paradise.' Any other race of human beings could have done the same thing under similar circumstances.

The phenomenon is, indeed, not unique to Rhodesia. Captain Cook and his men landing on the Sandwich Islands, were greeted as gods. So was Cook's colleague, Captain George Vancouver, on a later voyage when the Capilano Indians of the Canadian west coast greeted the 'great canoe with pale-faced gods' that had long been promised by one of their tribal legends. Montezuma, it is said, put up no resistance to Cortes because the invading Spaniards conformed to an Aztec legend of gods who would come from across the seas. Disillusion came swiftly enough to all those peoples, and so it came in pioneer Zambesia. Mr. Sithole writes in his book that the sharpest, most traumatic form of disillusion arrived when the white gods proved to have an all-too-human appetite not only for corn but for African women as well. In this he concurs with the view of anthropologists and colonial administrators who have analysed the racial clash in various parts of Africa. The white myth which at first overwhelmed his people,

* Oxford University Press, 1959.

he observes, could not persist when one of the white gods had capitulated to a black woman. And the reverse process completed their disillusionment, together with white susceptibility to bullets, during two world wars in which something like 40,000 African Rhodesians went abroad:

The street girls of London, Paris and Naples did not help the preservation of the white myth. The African soldiers saw white soldiers wounded, dying and dead. The bullet had the same effect on black and white alike. This had a very powerful psychological effect on the African. The veil between him and the white man thinned to the point of transparency. After spending four years hunting white enemy soldiers, the African never regarded them again as gods.

There is a further point to be made about the invaders who were arriving in Zambesia to found their new 'White Dominion' – that there are gods and gods. Nyasaland, in the missionaries and their dedicated colleagues of the Lakes Company, was blessed with some very good and useful men. They were not without fault, of course, but they were basically dispassionate, men who were not self-seeking and had come to serve. And in Nyasaland, too, the Colonial Office arrived – a little belatedly – in 1904, to assume its conscious burden of trusteeship.

The Africans of the Rhodesias were not so fortunate. They were caught in a commercial undertaking. True, Nigeria as well had begun as a Charter Company operation, and so had East Africa. But there shaky régimes had soon been replaced by the less predatory guardianship of Whitehall.

What made Zambesia different was the huge wealth of Cecil Rhodes himself. Where the Royal Niger Company and the Imperial British East Africa Company soon got out of their depth, either financially or diplomatically, the British South Africa Company in Rhodesia was effectively shielded on both fronts by the personal fortune of Rhodes, backed by the mighty diamond monopoly of De Beers.

His own income, as he testified on oath to the House of Commons Select Committee of Inquiry after the Jameson Raid, ranged between £1,000,000 and £1,250,000 a year. And this, of course, did not take into account the large capital gains which came his way in innumerable deals. He and Beit, for example, cleared more than a million each on the sale of the Rudd Concession. Even in the midst of the Siege of Kimberley, during the Boer War, the flow of transactions never slackened. When the British Commander denied Rhodes the use of the military heliograph, he simply had the De Beers workshops build him his own. He urgently wanted to complete a deal with a mining group whose directors lived in Cape Town; it duly went through – by heliograph – and secured at a bargain price a property which he and his partners had long wanted to acquire in order to clinch their monopoly.

Rhodes was shrewd with his money, but never mean. Wealth was merely a tool for his political purposes. He was notably generous in settling the damage claims of the Rhodesian settlers in the last months of 1896, and it is recorded that at Gwelo he noticed one local man, a Scottish blacksmith, who had entered no claim at all, though many of his neighbours were submitting well-padded accounts. 'What do I owe you?' Rhodes asked. When the Scotsman said he owed him nothing at all, Rhodes told his secretary to write out a cheque on the spot for £25 – 'for the only honest man I've met today'. It was precisely the sort of joke to which the settlers responded, and the story was recounted many times.

Literally thousands of such payments came from Cecil Rhodes's personal cheque-book. Large amounts of money from Rhodes's own fortune was the miracle that saved the B.S.A. Company from the financial shocks which eventually wrecked other chartered companies in Africa. Indeed, the Company paid not so much as one penny of dividend to its stockholders in the first thirty-four years of its existence. Only when it had disentangled itself from the costly demands of administration, with the handover to Coghlan's settler régime in the 1920s, did it become a paying concern.

The first ten years were disastrously expensive. The Company had spent a tenth of its capital on the march of the Pioneer Column alone. The cost of the police ran to more than £200,000 in the first year, and Rhodes and Jameson hastily cut the force to a quarter of its size and established the police reserve of armed volunteers which has continued through wars and uprisings to this day. Even so, Rhodes was confronted by Lord Rothschild in 1892 with the harsh news that 'Chartered' was all but insolvent. The banks in London and South Africa were no longer accepting its cheques unless they were guaranteed by De Beers or by Rhodes himself. At the second annual meeting in November of that year, Rhodes was confronted by rows of embittered investors who had seen their £1 shares sink to 12s. on the London Stock Exchange, after reaching £3 15s. the year before in the first blaze of optimism fanned by the Founder's speeches. By sheer personal magnetism, and his shrewd appeal for a project that would help 'in the suppression of the slave-trade', Rhodes won a resounding vote of confidence. He did not mention that he and his partners had tucked away some useful capital gains by selling blocks of Company stock at the peak price before the slide began.

This was of no moral concern to Rhodes. He was, in any event, pouring his personal funds into the operations in Zambesia. When he received news of the Company's threatened bankruptcy – news which never reached the public – he ordered that all cheques from De Beers and Goldfields of South Africa Ltd made out to him should be paid straight into its account. What it came to was that the investors' money, and the revenues of De Beers, and the vast flow of Rhodes's personal income were simply subsidizing his own special brand of colonial expansion in Central Africa. One man had assumed, in this particular part of Africa, the full burden that in other territories was falling on the Imperial Exchequer in London.

Rhodesia was becoming for Rhodes what yachts, mansions, and mistresses were for contemporary tycoons like Jay Gould and Rockefeller. Lonely, without wife or children, he regarded his personal colonialism as a combination of mistress, son, hobby, and luxury all rolled into one.

Such a man, when he is both rich and powerful, grows increasingly impatient of legal niceties and administrative procedure. Had the Colonial Office been in charge of the new colony, there is little likelihood that such adventures as the Jameson Raid and the military conquest of the Mashona and Matabele would have taken place. Whitehall control of army, police, and Civil Service would have seen to that. For proof, indeed, one may look next door to a sister territory, Bechuanaland, which has been spared the anguish of political battle between settler and African.

But in early Rhodesia there were no controls, no safeguards – except for the frail requirements that existed on paper, optimistically laid down by a British High Commissioner whose office was ten days' journey away by ox-wagon and slow train, a distance greater than that from London to Moscow. In the jet age, it would only be a matter of weeks, at most, before visiting journalists would learn of African grievances – or the Africans themselves would be dispatching delegates to London.

Rhodes and Jameson were not troubled by any such exasperations. The Chief Magistrate, as he was to be called, would be not only the financial controller of the Chartered Company's operations in Zambesia, selling land and collecting the royalties from gold, but also Prime Minister, Commander-in-Chief of the armed forces, Lord Chief Justice, and permanent head of the Civil Service. This is no exaggeration; he held all those roles. For a dozen years, after the débâcle of Jameson's ill-judged raid, the British government half-heartedly assumed some of these powers itself. And then there ensued a struggle between the Company and the settlers, as to which would get them back. It never entered anyone's white mind that the Africans might have a claim as well.

On the principle of impressing the British government and getting 'nothing but the best', Rhodes nominated a retired member of the Indian Civil Service, A. R. Colquhoun, to be the first Chief Magistrate. The nomination was readily approved by Sir Henry Loch, the High Commissioner at the Cape, who must have hoped that in consequence the buccaneering era would at last come to an end. Rhodes's own accession to the Premiership of Cape Colony in the same year encouraged the thought. But such hopes were soon dashed. Colquhoun, far too upright a man, quietly resigned a post which he considered highly irregular in a number of ways.

Prodded by Rhodes, the directors of the Company Board then nominated Dr Leander Starr Jameson, a choice which Loch reluctantly accepted. Marshall Hole, who served as Secretary to the Chief Magistrate in those formative years and knew at least some of his secrets, has recorded that Jameson was 'unversed in official routine, impatient of formality and always prone to take short cuts to achieve his purpose'.

Jameson changed his title to Administrator, but continued to make all appointments in the judiciary and the armed police. These two last often interlocked, so that an African might be brought before a magistrate who was also the commandant of the policemen who had arrested him. One wonders if the Africans could make the necessary subtle distinction. Nor was this the end of it. Most African offences stemmed from dissatisfaction with employment, or even outright unwillingness to be 'recruited' for service in the mines or on the farms of the white settlers. The messengers employed to recruit were Africans in the service of the Native Commissioner; by their uniforms and employment they seemed to be 'Company men' no less than the troopers or magistrates. And the Company itself seemed to take a perverse delight in enlisting as messengers, or as native constables, Africans of the former subject tribes. Not surprisingly, these men got some pleasure out of arresting their late masters, the Matabele. When the African rebellions came, in 1893 and again in 1896, it was the Matabele who led them.

Since this double revolt has proved, in retrospect, one of the basic facts of political life in Rhodesia – the fear of its recurring has inspired every punitive piece of legislation up to Whitehead's and Field's decrees – we should scrutinize the causes of the clash. They are clear enough on the African side. The expropriation of land for white farms and towns went far beyond Lobengula's original concession for the right to dig 'one big hole' – a concession that he had, in any case, now repudiated. Furthermore, there had been abruptly introduced into the territory a system of police, courts, and labour recruiters operated by the white invader and implemented without warning or consultation upon Mashona and Matabele alike. Yet these peoples in no way considered themselves subject to the new arrivals; the Pioneer Column had deliberately avoided any clash by threading its way around the native settlements so as to reach the site of Fort Salisbury without firing a shot. If a few white men went through some private mumbo-jumbo on the hill near Harare, hoisting a coloured cloth to the top of a pole, and then dispersed to look for gold-bearing rock, that was one thing. When they began, however, to direct the local inhabitants, it was another. The Africans knew well enough what had happened in the south, especially in the Boer republics; that was precisely what Mzilikazi had come north to escape.

It is on the settler side of the clash that the origins are more difficult to trace. The smokescreen of history has been kind to Rhodes and Jameson – it was partly, at least, of their own manufacture. But from the scanty documentation in Whitehall, and the reminiscences which historians assembled and published in the 1920s, four main pressures emerge:

1. LEGALITIES: Loch, the British High Commissioner, under steady pressure from Whitehall to 'regularize' the occupation of Zambesia, was in turn pressing Jameson and the British South Africa Company to produce some treaty or other formal agreement with the Africans.

2. SETTLER DISCONTENT: All through these first three years of the new colony's existence the settlers, fed up with Matabele cattle raids and African reluctance to be pressed into paid employment, were warning Jameson that the time must come soon to 'have it out with the natives'.

3. BRITISH SOUTH AFRICA COMPANY FINANCES: Rhodes had emerged successful from the angry general meeting of stockholders at the end of 1892 by the skin of his teeth. It seemed certain that the Company's capital would be exhausted before the end of 1893, and Rhodes could not meet its running costs from his personal fortune forever.

4. THE ALL-RED ROUTE: The British imperial road from Cape to Cairo, which was Rhodes's real political aim, could not be created as long as Zambesia was in ferment. The Charter Company had to be made solvent. To do that meant attracting more settlers. And that in turn meant 'pacification'.

Such pressures made an outright clash inevitable, though it is possible to suppose that events might well have taken a different course had there been a Colonial Office 'presence' in the territory, to act as referee and, when necessary, policeman. As it was, Whitehall's supervision consisted of Loch in Cape Town and a single local representative – a junior colonial officer – posted to Bulawayo as his eyes and ears but with no authority over Jameson. Loch's control was also impaired by Rhodes's double role as head of the British South Africa Company and Prime Minister of Cape Colony. The British High Commissioner might want to discipline Rhodes, the Chartered Company operator. But Whitehall wanted to keep on the best possible terms with the politician wielding supreme power at the Cape in order to secure the sea-route to India. A friendly Anglo-Saxon in the premiership was infinitely preferable to a hostile Afrikaner. Furthermore, Loch must have been aware of the exquisite pressures that Rhodes could bring to bear through the two royal dukes on his board and his friendship with the Prince of Wales.

Nevertheless, Sir Henry Loch considered that he had a duty to perform as a servant of the British government. Indeed, in choosing the man in 1890 to replace Sir Hercules Robinson, Lord Knutsford and the Tory Cabinet had selected him because of his reputation for uprightness and incorruptibility. And Sir Henry stuck out his five years, doggedly resisting all hints that he might be 'squared', with his integrity still undamaged when he sailed for home.

Lord Salisbury himself was disturbed about the hazy legal position of the Chartered Company, once it became known in London that Lobengula had disavowed the very contract upon which Queen Victoria had been induced to grant the charter. Once the Company had begun carving up the country and selling land to the settlers, the British Prime Minister wrote an anxious memo: 'It had but an imperfect right, if any right at all, to grant such titles in its field of operations.'

Loch went so far as to press the Tory Colonial Secretary, Lord Knutsford, for authority to take over all political dealings with Lobengula instead of letting Jameson as Administrator handle them direct. But the Cabinet in London were unwilling to antagonize the influential Mr Rhodes. Had Loch's advice been taken, it would have put a British governor and British troops (from Bechuanaland) into the role of supreme authority in Rhodesia. As it was, that authority remained with the Company, to pass in turn to the settlers.

Loch had issued the Order-in-Council of May 1891 – taking the territory 'under the protection of Her Majesty' – with deep misgivings, knowing that constitutionally it might be difficult to sustain in the face of criticism, should Labouchere or any other of the 'humanitarian' M.P.s at Westminster decide to challenge the basis of Rhodes's assumption of power in Zambesia. Lord Salisbury had expressed his own anxieties. When the Company proposed to introduce a hut tax, Loch turned for an opinion to W. P. Schreiner, Attorney-General in Rhodes's own Cabinet at the Cape, who read all the relevant papers and produced this opinion:

There has not yet been any grant, concession or treaty by which the ownership of land, as against the natives, has been vested in the British South Africa Company. The proposal savours of taxing the real owners of the soil for the support of a government which is in the country only by permission from the native Sovereign.

The Order-in-Council of May 1891 was the whole legal basis upon which Dr Jameson had been gazetted Administrator and the entire structure of the new state was being built. Yet Loch knew that it was imperfect in law. For the next two years he was engaged in energetically pressing Rhodes and Jameson for a treaty or concession which would regularize the whole situation. His struggle was abruptly and permanently terminated by the convenient outbreak of hostilities. In view of Dr Jameson's record for stage management in the 'Beira Outrage' and the other playlets of the years before, and his proven complicity (resulting in a jail sentence) in the Raid which followed, it is hard to suppose that the Matabele War of 1893 was not a piece of deliberate provocation; indeed, most historians have never supposed it to have been anything else.

In the months leading up to it, Loch was also engaged in a running battle with Jameson over his actual methods of administration. At least part of the trouble lay in the human resources that the Administrator had at his service. Why should any skilled colonial administrator, or even prospective recruit, have rejected the chance of a career in the Colonial Office for service with the British South Africa Company or, indeed, any other commercial company operation? The Colonial Office in those days offered a career in the largest service of its kind anywhere in the world, with the solid assurances of promotion and pension, and the attractions of global experience. The constitutional authority of the Company was being challenged by Liberal critics in the House of Commons, and it might in any event go bankrupt at any time. In due course Southern Rhodesia was to build up an orthodox Civil Service, but it is small wonder that the men who turned up at the beginning to try their hand as administrators in the unorthodox empire of Dr Jameson tended to be soldiers of fortune, or plain human misfits. Lord Randolph Churchill experienced something of the strange administration when he went to inspect the new colony a year after it had been established.

He was introduced to a certain Dr Rutherford Harris who, like Jameson, had given up medicine to enter the personal service of Rhodes. Lord Randolph had been invited to grace the opening of Fort Salisbury's first season of horse racing and was induced to sponsor one of the entries. On the day of the race his animal appeared at the course looking oddly dazed and glassy-eyed, and the plump cob belonging to Harris won at a canter. 'A good lot of money changed hands over this odd business,' Churchill remarked later. Harris himself went on to further fortune, although Jameson once described him as 'a muddling ass – on the surface a genius', and even Rhodes admitted that his new-found assistant was 'a rogue and at times a furious inebriate'. At Westminster, after his appearances in London on behalf of the Company, one M.P. described him as 'the greatest and most unashamed liar, a man without any moral sense'.

Rhodes coolly ignored all the criticisms and raised Dr Harris to the post of Secretary to the Chartered Company. At the same time – since Rhodes was heavily occupied with his other duties as Prime Minister of Cape Colony – Harris took over direction of the secretariat for Rhodes's private and political affairs and became the key figure at Groote Schuur as well as the link with Bulawayo and Salisbury. It was certainly a curious directorate that was supervising the task of founding and building a new nation. The Company was still, in every way, a South African enterprise, effectively directed from Cape Town; Dr Jameson himself was to return south in due course and succeed to Rhodes's old post as Prime Minister of the Cape. After half a dozen years of Company administration had produced two savage wars with the Africans and a little (disastrous) local imperialism in the form of the Raid – led by the Company's own Administrator and Chief Magistrate in person – the British government was at last moved to send out a strong man in the person of Milner, to crack the whip. His report, after a tour of Rhodesia, began with the basic observation that 'a lot of unfit people were allowed to exercise power, or at any rate, did exercise it, especially with regard to the natives, in a manner which cannot be defended'.

It can be argued that armed combat between the races was inevitable, if only through the Matabele custom of making regular pillaging raids upon the Mashona villages. Faced with a parallel problem in West Africa some years before, the British had been forced into full-scale war against the Ashanti warrior tribes. The Colonial Office, however, had learnt its lesson: the way to avoid such disasters was to send to the spot large numbers of first-rate administrators, with the best judges, chief constables, schoolmasters, and doctors that Whitehall could recruit. Peace was most securely maintained by strong forces of Imperial troops with no personal stake in the land, by the investment of capital in improving the lot of the African, and by the visible exercise of an impartial justice.

The under-budgeted, live-by-your-wits operation of Dr Jameson and his cadre of fortune-hunters and misfits provided a sad and squalid contrast. It was clear by the third year of what was supposed to be Occupation, that the British South Africa Company administrators and their police had utterly failed to establish peace and order in Zambesia. Lobengula's regiments roamed the countryside at will, burning the Shona villages and carrying off the cattle and women. The King had agreed to accept the 'Jameson line' – from the Shashi River to the Umniati – as the western boundary for these raiding parties. But white prospectors were crossing the line into Matabele territory, the Mashona on the other side were seizing Lobengula's royal cattle, and Lobengula himself was losing his authority – having acquired a taste for high living, and especially for the white man's champagne. He had it imported for him by the Company in wooden cases of twenty-four bottles each, and could be found most afternoons, royally fuddled and incapable of decision. It is hard to imagine any Colonial Office governor sanctioning this state of easy chaos; indeed, Colquhoun, the ex-Indian Civil Service expert, had resigned after a few weeks on learning that the Company, for financial reasons, intended paying off three-quarters of its troops and relying instead on armed volunteers. He had clearly foreseen the dangers: loose security, followed by crackdowns, with settlers acting as armed judges in their own cause.

The full story of the important Captain Lendy incidents can be found in the Colonial Office archives – Vol. 426 of the *Africa* (*South*) series. A settler called Bennett came to Jameson in Salisbury, to lay a personal complaint about thefts from his farm and accuse tribesmen in the kraal of a Chief Ngomo near by. Jameson sent Lendy, a captain in the Company police, to investigate. According to the official report, later submitted to Loch in Cape Town by the Company's Secretary, Ngomo was promised fair trial at Fort Salisbury, but refused to come and was 'very impertinent'. Lendy reported back to Jameson, who sent him out again to Ngomo's kraal with more men, a seven-pound cannon, and a Nordenfeldt-Maxim machine-gun, 'to take summary measures'. And the Company Secretary's report admits that 'some volunteers' (i.e. angry white settlers) decided to join in, although not asked – at least officially – and not given any official status.

The report spared details.

The Chief and his son, and 21 other natives were killed. All the natives in the vicinity are peaceful and thoroughly satisfied.

Loch, from the Cape, stiffly informed Jameson that 'the punishment inflicted, involving the loss of some 23 lives, appears utterly disproportionate to the original offence, the theft of some goods from a Mr Bennett'. Jameson replied at length – the whole correspondence takes up seventy-eight pages in the archives – and justified Lendy's action: 'Since these severe lessons the natives willingly submit to the decision of an officer accompanied by a couple of policemen.'

The final reproof came from Lord Knutsford himself in London. The Colonial Secretary wrote to Jameson that the shooting at Ngomo's kraal had been maintained far longer than necessary and that 'Captain Lendy acted in this matter with recklessness and undue harshness'. One would like to think that the letter had some effect when it reached the desk of the Company's Chief Magistrate and Administrator. But it seems much more likely, in the frontier shanty town that was Fort Salisbury in those days, that Dr Jameson showed it to his friend Lendy and then took him around to the nearest bar for a drink. There was only one possibility that Rhodes and Jameson feared: the appearance one day on the horizon of a long line of Imperial troopers, signifying that the British government had at last lost patience with Company–settler antics and had decided to assume direct control itself.

That possibility moved uncomfortably close in the third year of the Chartered Company's occupation, when Lord Salisbury's Tories lost the general election in Britain. The incoming Liberal administration, under Gladstone, had little patience with

Rhodes's imperial designs, and men like Lord Ripon, the new Colonial Secretary, were known to be 'soft on natives'.

Rhodes hastened to London to repair his political fences. A cheque for £5,000 to swell the Liberal Party funds must have helped, as must his connexion with Lord Rosebery, now a Cabinet Minister, whose father-in-law was Rhodes's banker Lord Rothschild. But nothing could save the Company's monopoly if the British public, and the M.P.s at Westminster, took it into their heads to believe that matters in Zambesia were being mishandled. An angry report had reached the Colonial Office from the Barotse chief, Lewanika, which indicated that Jameson's administration had not been able to stop Lobengula's raiding parties from crossing the whole width of Zambesia and invading the Lozi country on the other side:

They scoured Batoka for three months, destroying property and killing many of my people in the most revolting manner. Women were ripped open and impaled, men and children made targets of, and roasted alive like meat. Not a dog escaped where they passed.

Such events turned public sentiment against Lobengula, making it less politically imprudent for Jameson and his troopers to crack down on the Matabele in particular and all Africans in general. On the other hand, it indicated a state of Wild West lawlessness which could only result, if it continued, in Gladstone's at last losing patience, and ordering in the Imperial troops to make Zambesia an orthodox colony under Colonial Office rule. Skilfully, Rhodes sketched for Harcourt, the new Chancellor of the Exchequer, a horrifying picture of the burden that this would load on to the backs of the British taxpayers. It was an article of Liberal faith to escape the costly imperial adventures which had been inflicted upon the nation by the Tories, and as a makeshift the argument proved effective.

But time, nevertheless, was short, if Rhodes and Jameson were to secure permanent control of Zambesia. Everything pointed to one effective method – all-out war and an end to the 'native problem' for good. That would stop Loch and Schreiner at the Cape from forever demanding a proper treaty. It would present

Gladstone and the negrophiles of Exeter Hall with a *fait accompli*; which would escape serious criticism if it could only be shown that the lives of British mothers and children had been at stake. It would stop the slide of the Company's share prices on the London Stock Exchange. And there was the prospect of a tantalizing bonus. Tucked away in Lobengula's kraal was the wattle hut which served as a royal treasure house. In it were those two ridiculous, rusted biscuit tins. And in them were uncut diamonds equal in value perhaps to ten times the issued share capital of the British South Africa Company.

It seemed only a matter of time before Lobengula would present Jameson with the excuse he wanted. The hot-blooded Captain Lendy had been posted by Dr Jameson to Fort Victoria in the double capacity of Magistrate and Commandant of the Company's police detachment. Trouble began when 500 yards of the main telegraph line near by were cut. It was the work of a Mashona group led by a headman called Gomalla, who admitted their guilt (they had disposed of the wire by barter) and paid a collective fine to the Company in the form of cattle.

Unfortunately, these had not been Shona animals at all, but belonged to the royal state herd of the Matabele. Jameson said he would discipline Gomalla, but Lobengula did not consider that he had granted to the white man anything more than 'the right to dig'. He was still the King and, indeed, if he did not act like one, his *indunas* would soon enough depose him. (Joshua Nkomo and the other African leaders experience similar pressures today.) Through his missionary interpreter Lobengula drafted a letter, on 29 June 1893, for the attention of Captain Lendy in Fort Victoria, explaining that two *impis* or regiments, consisting of some 2,500 men, would be carrying out the forthcoming expedition against the cattle thieves, and adding: 'The *impi* will probably come across white men, who are asked to understand it has nothing to do with them.'

Lobengula's regiments swept down on the offending Mashona with terrible effect. Columns of smoke rose from the Shona villages, and as some of the abandoned cattle wandered on to settler farmland, angry Matabele warriors extended their plundering,

convinced that the settlers were in league with the Mashona.
Their conviction hardened when they found that scores of terrified Shona refugees had fled for sanctuary to Fort Victoria. The
Matabele commander, Manyao, entered the town and sought out
Captain Lendy, demanding that the refugees be surrendered to
him. The youthful magistrate gave 'the only reply which it was
possible for an officer to give' – in the words of the Company's
testimony to the parliamentary inquiry that followed later in
London. The angry Matabele now turned to plundering the
deserted settler farms in vengeance; Jameson, arriving three days
later, found the town virtually in a state of armed siege.

On 17 July he gave Manyao a two-hour ultimatum, pointing
to the sun and demanding that by sundown the whole Matabele
force should be moving out of Mashonaland. As the deadline
expired, he dispatched Captain Lendy at the head of thirty-eight
mounted troopers to see that the order was being obeyed.
Manyao and the main force seem to have been on their way home,
as ordered, and had already crossed the Tokwe River, which was
the accepted frontier. But Umgandan, a tall aristocratic young
chief who was deputy commander of the *impi*, argued with his
leader that Jameson had no authority to issue such an order at all.
(Legally he was right, as Loch must have known.) Umgandan and
300 of his men camped for the night on the bank of the Tokwe
which the settlers considered to be their own side of the river.
There was no evidence that they were being deliberately defiant
or planning an ambush; they were quietly cooking their evening
meal by their campfires when Lendy and his men came upon
them. It is not disputed that the Company's troops were the first
to fire; that evidence was given to parliament later by Rhodes's
great friend, Francis Newton, who was eventually to become head
of the Company. Umgandan and two dozen others were killed on
the spot.

For all practical purposes, this was accepted by both sides as a
declaration of war, though Loch spent the ensuing eight weeks
in a last-ditch effort to effect a truce. When the next Company
messenger arrived in Bulawayo with the monthly payment of a
hundred gold sovereigns, the King refused to accept it, calling it

blood money, and returned the 1,000 rifles and all the ammunition which had been given him after the signing of the Rudd Concession. It was a proud gesture, but tactically unsound.

Rhodes at the Cape – not, of course, in his capacity as Prime Minister – had sent a laconic telegram to Jameson: 'Read Luke XIV: 31.' When Dr Jameson consulted his Bible, he found the verse about the King 'going to make war against another King ... that cometh against him with twenty thousand'. This message is now part of Rhodesian folklore, and is frequently repeated for the benefit of visitors to the country today, as an example of Rhodes's splendid audacity and his neat way of circumventing the meddlers of Whitehall.

On 14 August Jameson and Lendy enlisted 672 volunteers for the impending war, handing to each man a signed copy of a secret document. It was to cause a sensation when the British government eventually learned of its existence many years later, in 1913. The material of the document was usual enough; in southern Africa, a commando expected a share of the spoils. What was unusual was that the promise of plunder should have been committed to cold print, and it may suggest that a certain impatient mistrust was already developing between the settlers, who had come for gold and found very little, and the Company. For Jameson himself, who was already planning his raid on Pretoria, there were few greater attractions than a covert conspiracy.

The Victoria Agreement was a pledge, in the name of the Company, to give each volunteer a £9,000 farm in Matabeleland, once it had been conquered, and the selection of twenty gold claims apiece. Further, Paragraph 7 of this contract between civilized men dealt with the disposition of Lobengula's vast herd of cattle, estimated at anything up to 500,000 head.

The loot shall be divided half to the British South Africa Company and the remainder to officers and men in equal shares.

These cool preparations by the white forces contrasted sharply with a certain naïve confusion at the royal kraal. The King seems to have accepted Loch's role as peace-maker (though it was ignored in Salisbury) and issued a series of pathetic messages. To Dr Harris, now Secretary of the Company, he wrote:

I thought you came to dig gold but it seems you have come . . . to rob me of my people and country as well. You are like a child playing with edged tools. Captain Lendy is like some of my own young men; he has no holes in his ears and cannot hear. He is young, and all he thinks of is a row. But you had better caution him or he will cause serious trouble between us.

Lobengula wrote as well to his friend John Moffat, now in disgrace with Rhodes and back at his old post in Bechuanaland, asking him to appeal to Sir Henry Loch. The King said he was 'not aware that a boundary exists between Dr Jameson and myself'. And he went on:

Who gave him the boundary lines? Let him come forward and show me the man that pointed out to him these boundaries.

He made a final appeal to Queen Victoria herself:

Your Majesty, what I want to know from you is: Why do your people kill me?

Loch in Cape Town transmitted the Queen's reply:

You can tell the King from me I have no intention of invading his country or of dragging him into war.

And the High Commissioner invited Lobengula to send a delegation to Cape Town to work out the terms of a long-term peace settlement. He was uncomfortably aware of the mass meetings of settlers in Victoria and Salisbury, demanding action either by the British South Africa Company or by British Imperial troops to prevent what they were sure would be an annual recurrence of Matabele raids. From London the Liberal Colonial Secretary, Lord Ripon, cabled to Loch that Jameson and the Company police commandants should be told: 'Their duty must be limited to defending their occupied territory and Her Majesty's government cannot support them in any aggressive action.'

Lobengula chose his half-brother and two other *indunas* as his envoys, dictated a letter for them to take to Loch at the Cape, and sent them on their way with Dawson, his trader friend, as their escort. In Bechuanaland, stopping for the night at one of the Imperial garrisons, Dawson was taken to eat with the officers, while the three black envoys were shown into the compound with the other 'boys'. An officer heard that there were three Matabele in the camp, presumed that they were spies, and ordered their arrest. In the scuffle that followed, two were shot, and only the King's half-brother survived, to return home with a bitter tale of what must have seemed like the white people's treachery. Dawson abandoned the mission, but cabled Lobengula's letter to Loch. It was a straight accusation that Jameson and the settlers were planning full-scale war, and concluded: 'When you have made up your mind to do a thing it is not right to blame it on my people.'

In fact, there was a basic difference of view between white and black which Loch could not have resolved, even had the *indunas* reached him. Jameson and the Company asserted that there was a well-defined frontier between the King's zone and the settlers' zone, splitting Zambesia in two. But Lobengula maintained that he had never agreed to cede half his kingdom to anyone, that the Rudd Concession empowered the white men only to dig for gold. In 1918, long after his death, the judicial committee of the Privy Council was to declare that the King had been right.

As Loch himself saw, and observed in a secret dispatch to Lord Ripon after the fighting had begun, the only thing that could have headed off a war would have been a full-scale Colonial Office operation in Zambesia, with governor, troops, budget, and all the rest. But neither Gladstone's Liberals nor Salisbury's Conservatives would pay the price then. Instead, Britain and the black man are paying a different price today.

On 5 October Loch received messages that Matabele with rifles had fired on the Bechuanaland border patrol and that another party had fired on Company troopers near the Shashi River. It would take a Devlin Commission at least to sort out what really happened, and who sent whom what messages. Undeniable is that Jameson cabled Loch on the 7th to say that his forces would move to press back the Matabele. That done, he placed himself as Commander-in-Chief at the head of his army, the Company's police, and the settler volunteers, and, in a long-planned pincer movement, launched an all-out assault on the King's capital of Bulawayo itself. His forces had seven-pounder cannon, Maxims and other machine-guns, and of course the 1,000 Martini-Henry rifles which Lobengula had so obligingly returned. Using these weapons against Matabele armed only with spears was like running a hot knife through butter. At the Shangani River, 5,000 of Lobengula's finest men advanced in Zulu crescent formation, chanting their war songs and falling like ripe corn under the scythe of the Maxims. At the next big battle, again in open country near a river, the Mbesu and Ingubu regiments were wiped out, almost to a man. As a campaign, it was embarrassingly easy; by the time that Jameson and his victorious troops swept into the smouldering ruins of Bulawayo on 4 November, the total casualties on the settler side amounted to no more than five dead and a dozen wounded. The African losses on each count were a thousand times larger. It hardly qualified as a Waterloo.

Indeed, since smallpox was raging among the Matabele (Jameson had prudently seen to it that all his men were vaccinated some weeks before), it became apparent that victory had been won by fit men, with vastly superior arms, against primitive, inadequately armed men, who were sick into the bargain. There had been a kind of heroic grandeur, too, in the King's destruction of his own capital, especially when contrasted with the actions and motives of his pursuers. The Victoria and Salisbury columns had joined for the advance on Bulawayo; soon after passing Thabas Induna, they heard the prolonged rumble of a vast explosion and saw an umbrella of black smoke filling the summer sky.

The hilltop, when they reached it, was a smoking desolation. The royal kraal had been fired first; then sticks of dynamite had finished off the brick house and anything else remaining. The King's bodyguard, Bosungwana, with a dozen warriors of the household regiment, had loaded the royal treasure on to the big ox-wagon, and Lobengula with his family and retainers had struck out for the north. Waiting to greet the victors as they stormed unopposed into Bulawayo were the traders Fairbairn and Dawson, alive and unhurt. Lobengula had said that no white man who came in peace to Matabeleland would be in danger, and he did not go back on this promise during the one-month Jameson War. Some traders had chosen to go, and been escorted in safety to the frontier. The two who remained were treated with scrupulous correctness to the last. Lobengula had meant it when he said that there was a wall around the word of a King.

Attacked by smallpox, and shivering with a recurrence of his old malarial fever, the King was now north of the Shangani River on his way to the Zambesi. For the main force of settler troops, there was a respite, time to look for disappointing scraps of 'loot', and the hollow triumph of the ceremony at the old Indaba Tree. Here, where Jameson had once cajoled Lobengula with his smooth promises, the Company banner – the 'dog and bone' – was now pompously hoisted. But amid these excitements, Dr Jameson had not forgotten the biscuit tins. A scout column under Major Forbes was hot on their trail.

Fate still had one more ironic twist in store for Lobengula. Realizing that he was beaten at last, he decided to parley. His Commander-in-Chief, Mjan, was instructed to fill a bag with 1,000 of the gold sovereigns which had been received in the monthly payments from the Company, and to dispatch them to Jameson or Rhodes, with a request for a council of peace. But Mjan's messengers chanced only upon two stray troopers, from Forbes's main column, who kept the gold and said nothing. (They confessed and were prosecuted a year later.) On the afternoon of 3 December the pursuers reached the point on the Shangani where the King and 3,000 of his men had just forded across. Forbes sent over a mounted patrol under Major Allan Wilson, with orders to reconnoitre and return, preparatory to an attack the next day. But when he came across three of the King's abandoned wagons, Wilson decided to disobey orders and give immediate chase, meanwhile sending messengers back to inform Forbes of his decision.

The Shangani Patrol came close to the main Matabele party

and sighted what they believed to be the royal wagon, but in sharp fighting they were driven back. When Mjan realized that the main force of white men – and the Maxims – were still on the other side of the river, he ordered an attack, though his men were undoubtedly as weary as Wilson's after twelve days of forced march. The thirty-three troopers found, as Forbes had anticipated, that the rising river had cut off their retreat. They formed their horses in a ring, inflicted heavy losses on the vastly superior African force, and died – pointlessly – but with the greatest gallantry.

Since the incident has become so politically important, a foundation stone of the settler mystique in present-day Rhodesia, most historians have made a point of retelling it in detail. There is a legendary account, familiar to all white Rhodesian schoolboys, of how, when only seven of the troopers remained alive behind the barricade of dead horses, these men who were doomed to die sprang to attention and sang one verse of 'God Save the Queen'. The last man left alive, Jack Robertson, is said to have gathered up the weapons of his dead companions and continued firing while Mjan's men closed in upon him. Robertson fell, pistol in hand, with an assegai through the heart. Rhodes later arranged for the bodies of Wilson and his men to be reinterred at World's View, the national Valhalla in the Matopo Hills, and for life-size bas-reliefs in bronze to be sculpted by Tweed – who later designed the grave for Rhodes himself, at the same spot. The significance of the affair has been well summarized by Philip Mason:

This tale of high courage and some folly is necessary to an understanding of Rhodesia. It has become a legend, perhaps an inspiration, certainly a symbol. Walk into any public building and the odds are you will see a painting of the last stand of the Shangani Patrol, the dead horses serving as cover, the piles of bodies, the charging savage stopped with a revolver shot. You will see the same picture in many private houses too, and the name of Allan Wilson is remembered in medals, in prizes, and in sermons.

It was the necessary blood sacrifice in a war that, up till then, had been won too cheaply and not very honourably.

After the loss of the Shangani Patrol, Forbes and his men abandoned pursuit and retired southwards for fresh supplies of food and ammunition. Four months later Mjan and his commanders surrendered. But in the meantime, somewhere along the banks of the Zambesi, Lobengula had quietly died one January day in 1894. There is a legend that he was buried in a cave in the river bank, but no one has ever been able to find it. And what of the royal treasure, those two biscuit tins full of diamonds? The only man who knew was the bodyguard, Bosungwana, and the secret went with him to his grave a few weeks later. To this day the treasure of Lobengula has eluded each generation of Rhodesians, just as it eluded Rhodes and Jameson.

In June 1894 Dr Jameson formally declared that 'The King being dead, the white government has taken his place', and the sentence is duly preserved in the Colonial archives (Vol. 461). Rhodes had put it more simply. Speaking to the troops and volunteers assembled in the dead King's capital, he had said:

You will be the first entitled to select land. . . . It is your right, for you have conquered the country. . . . The reason you came was that you knew your property in Mashonaland was worthless unless the Matabele were crushed.

Loch at the Cape, aware that he could get no backing for a takeover by Whitehall, accepted the inevitable. The territory of the Matabele and the Mashona was to be treated 'as one country under the administration of the Company, with such safeguards as may be necessary for the security of Imperial and native interests'. But even this was not sufficient concession for the victorious Rhodes:

I claim that people here have beaten the Matabele. . . . The Company never asked the British government for any assistance. We have paid expenses and I claim we should have settlement of the terms of peace.

The details of the argument that followed hardly matter since, as Jameson well knew, the power lay with the administering authority, regardless of what any document might say. The 1894

Agreement, promulgated as an Order-in-Council that May, established the basic framework of a settler rule which has persisted to this day. But it is clear that Loch granted no authority to the Company or to the settlers which would justify the vast panoply of legislation which covers the African today from the cradle to the grave. Clause 23 stated specifically that 'Natives shall not be subjected to any exceptional legislation', and then listed the only four categories where this rule would not apply: (1) Liquor; (2) Arms and ammunition; (3) Title to land; (4) Hut tax.

Rhodes and Jameson now had a legal basis for the full Company rule which had hitherto eluded them, but the territory was not in actual fact as 'pacified' as they and the settlers believed. Resentment smouldered over the allocation of land, and the disposal of the King's herd of cattle. Burning in African hearts was the sense of deep injustice that would blaze into full-scale rebellion three years later.

Colin Harding, who served himself as trooper and officer in the British South Africa Company police, recalls in his book of reminiscences, *Far Bugles*, how 'it was very widely said . . . that the Native rebellion had, as one of its causes, the treatment of the Native young women by white men, and also by Native police'.

The Rev. John White, a Methodist missionary of the day, reported to his headquarters in London after the rebellion that, if he suggested there had been any cruel treatment of Africans, he would be curtly told by the settlers that this was 'a cowardly and wicked lie'. Yet, said White, a well-known official of the Company had been found guilty of using threats to compel a chief to give him his own daughter for immoral purposes. The man left the colony, but: 'So trivial seemed the offence that within nine months he was back and held an official position in the force raised to punish the rebels.'

Locusts and drought had coincided with the arrival of the Pioneers. This was chance, but then rinderpest broke out towards the end of 1895, killing off the cattle that were meat, milk, and transport for the Africans, and the Company officials shot other animals to prevent the spread of the disease. Such animals were infected, of course, but the Africans were not always to know that.

It was clumsy of Dr Jameson to choose such a moment for his ill-starred raid into the Boer Republic of the Transvaal, in the crude display of local imperialism which he and Rhodes had planned in hopes of toppling President Kruger. The Company's resources were lavishly poured into this manoeuvre. Troopers were recruited as volunteers for the uniformed force of 512 men which was to invade the Boer Republic in late December. The British government had refused to grant Rhodes sovereignty over Bechuanaland, so that he could incorporate it into Rhodesia. So Rhodes manoeuvred instead to get approval for a special 'railway strip', pleading that this was needed for the rail link which the Company was to construct under the terms of the Charter.

He was lucky. At the Cape, the vigilant Loch had retired, to be succeeded – at Rhodes's insistence – by his old friend Hercules Robinson, miraculously brought back from retirement. This was possible because the Liberals had lost office in London, and Lord Salisbury was now back in power with Joseph Chamberlain as his Colonial Secretary. Chamberlain was puzzled by Rhodes's sudden need for the 'railway strip', but gave his approval. Within a week Jameson had moved his volunteers on to the strip, with Rhodes's raid specialist, Sir John Willoughby, in charge of training.

Finally, the Chief Magistrate and Administrator of the British South Africa Company turned over his duties in Salisbury to a deputy, and arrived at the training-camp in Pitsani. He placed himself at the head of his heavily armed irregular force and, on the fateful morning, led the invasion into Kruger's republic.

Rhodes received a curt note from the Colonial Secretary, asking for the resignations of Beit and himself from the Board of the British South Africa Company. He complied, resigning at the same time as Prime Minister of the Cape. Jameson, after his ignominious capture and some embarrassed diplomatic manoeuvring by Britain, was released from Kruger's custody, to be taken by British warship to London and trial. Convicted on a charge of having 'unlawfully fitted out a military expedition . . . against a friendly state', he was sentenced in June 1896 to fifteen months' hard labour and imprisoned in Wormwood Scrubs. It is a significant reflection on politics in the formative early period of Rhodesia that, some years later, the irrepressible Dr Jameson was back again in the Company, holding an even higher post than the one he had vacated: nothing less than the Presidency itself.

For Rhodes himself, rehabilitation was even swifter. In less than three years he was triumphantly back in office as Managing Director of the Chartered Company. It was the shareholders who re-elected him; Chamberlain at the Colonial Office reluctantly confirmed the appointment. The whole tangled tale of the Jameson Raid would require a book in itself, though it intimately concerns the British South Africa Company and the ultimate political control of Rhodesia. Through it all runs the mystery of the 'missing telegrams' which were said to implicate Chamberlain himself; at the parliamentary inquiry in the House of Commons, Rhodes steadfastly refused to produce them and Chamberlain ignored the subject.

In the dispatch box of Jameson's aide-de-camp on the Raid – an ex-Guards officer called Major the Hon. Robert White – the Boers found a naïve jumble of incriminating letters, instructions from Rhodes and Jameson in opulent detail (containing references to Chamberlain), and even the key necessary to unlock the coded texts.

Lord Salisbury and Queen Victoria herself had gone on record after the Raid with firm denials of any connexion that could implicate the British government or any individual member of the Cabinet. Rhodes did not have to worry about saving himself; Chamberlain would do it for him, and did so in his famous speech on the Colonial Estimates of 26 July. This, however, did not prevent the Chancellor of the Exchequer, Lord Harcourt, from expressing the opinion of Rhodes and the Company's operation in Rhodesia which was then current in the City. He talked about 'a squalid and sordid picture of stock-jobbing . . . these unscrupulous men who have deceived everybody, who have ruined the character of the British nation for honesty and fair dealing'.

As for Rhodes himself, Harcourt called him 'that arch liar', and declared that 'the mendacity of the man is sickening'. The *Investor's Review* was moved to call him a freebooter and braggart who disgusted all honourable men. And the *Daily News*, for the Liberals, did some research into the stock-unloading operation which had been conducted quietly on the side by Rhodes and Beit. The Company's shares, having recovered after the Matabele War, had rocketed to £8 each. But the drought and the economic turn-down in the colony, combined with the Jameson fiasco, brought them tumbling once more. The *Daily News* and other papers estimated that, by selling off at the top, the Rhodes–Beit group had made a net capital gain of just over £3 million.

The political repercussions of the Raid upon Rhodesia itself are most important. But the military repercussion came first. Even today one finds most settlers baffled by any suggestion of a connexion between the Raid and the African uprising which followed. But to the Africans at the time it was real enough. Jameson's humiliating defeat and capture at Doornkop transformed him overnight in their eyes. Perhaps the 'gods that eat corn' were not infallible after all. For here was their chief god, the victor of Bulawayo, now a prisoner behind bars. From a granite cave in the Matopos, there came a divine message from the spirit of harvests and fertility known as the Mlimo. Lobengula had always consulted him as a kind of oracle. Now the Mlimo told his people that Lobengula had not really died; that he was returning to lead them; and that they would never escape the evils of the land – the drought, the locusts, the rinderpest, and all – until the white man had been driven from the soil of Zambesia.

The Africans reacted as did the Britons summoned by Boadicea and many nations have since. They rose with the full moon on the night of 23 March 1896. Within a week 130 settlers had been killed, among them five women and three children. Within a fortnight the only Europeans left alive in Matabeleland were those who had managed to reach the towns – Bulawayo and Gwelo – or one of the four or five big farms where the settlers had improvised some sort of laager and were holding out with diminishing supplies of food and bullets. Companies of volunteers were swiftly raised by men like Selous, Napier, Gifford, Spreckley, and George Grey, who had fought against Lobengula. Relief parties rode out to rescue the besieged settlers, and the hair-raising tales of their heroism and often severe losses are still part of Rhodesian folklore today.

'They came like flies over the hills', wrote Otto Hoffmann in his diary, during the siege of Bulawayo. Mostly it was the Maxims, chattering out their deadly defence, that cut down the swarming attackers. And meanwhile the townspeople fought shoulder to shoulder with the Company's troopers and the armed volunteers. They had stormed the government stores demanding rifles and ammunition, and no one had been in a mood to deny them. By the end of the first month no fewer than twenty-five Bulawayo women were listed as 'killed in action'.

Notably absent, of course, was Dr Jameson, whose fate it was at this crucial moment in Rhodesia's history to be on trial in the High Court in England. And such is the logic of human nature that even this was held to be an example of Whitehall's mischievous meddling. The settlers felt that their leader had been taken from them at the very time he was needed. It did not strike them that it might have been Jameson's bad administration, his plunder of the Africans, his long record of slippery dealings, and his totally illegal adventure into the Transvaal that had brought their calamity upon them.

In his place there had arrived from England a new Administrator in the person of Lord Grey, one of Rhodes's original recruits when he had created his Board in the summer he applied for the Royal Charter. It was a curious appointment considering the storm that had broken in the House of Commons with the Jameson Raid; many Opposition M.P.s had said that it was high time to cancel the Charter outright and establish normal Colonial Office rule in Rhodesia. Chamberlain had answered by declaring that the Imperial exchequer could simply not afford this at a time when enormous sums were being poured into controlling Egypt. (Gladstone had groaned the previous year: 'we are the government of Egypt as well'.)

Rhodes, turning his back upon his critics, sailed from England in a small German steamer direct for Beira, leaving his good friend Dr Jameson to battle it out in the High Court on his own. He no longer held any position in the British South Africa Company or Rhodesia, but he still had his cheque-book. And he was still a close personal friend of Lord Grey, whom he named in his last will as a trustee of his estate. Perhaps in Westminster the optimists thought that a peer, like Lord Grey, would transform the post of Administrator in Salisbury into the equivalent of governor in a normal colony; it is doubtful if Rhodes entertained any such illusions. In any event, luck was on his side; in the crisis of the uprising, the arrival of the Founder seemed just what was needed to bolster settler morale. Grey ignored protocol and pressed him into service.

Rhodes was reluctant to accept help from Imperial forces; partly because he would have to pay and feed the troops, but also for fear of political interference afterwards. But events forced his hand; Bulawayo was surrounded by 15,000 of Lobengula's veterans, one-time members of the élite regiments now thirsting for revenge. At the Cape the Assistant Military Secretary, Colonel Plumer, was ordered to raise an Imperial volunteer force, and 800 men were soon on their way to the north. In Salisbury the settlers organized the Mashonaland Column, which set off from Bulawayo. In June Britain offered the use of 1,000 Imperial soldiers stationed in South Africa, and General Sir Frederick Carrington, an Imperial officer, assumed overall command.

The leaders of the African forces were three Chiefs named Mgwati, Kagube, and Nyanda. In the history books they are invariably described as witch doctors or 'priests of Mlimo', since the only written histories are based on settler accounts. But by present-day Africans, the three are regarded in much the same light as we would regard the leaders of the Norwegian underground or the French Maquis in the Second World War. In the end, Mgwati was killed in the successful bombing of rebel headquarters, while Kagube and Nyanda were captured and executed.

Rhodes was tortured by the thought that the war, already costing £4,000 a day, would drag on indefinitely; for in June the

Mashona, too, rose in a single night, to kill 119 settlers within the week. The Salisbury town jail was buttressed to make it into a laager, and 250 women and children crowded into safety within. But slowly the military tide began to turn, as the vastly superior firepower of the white forces began to take effect. By the end of the year the Imperial troops had been sent home, since the Company's troopers and a few bands of volunteers were all that was needed for mopping-up operations. The Matabele had retreated to their redoubt in the Matopo Hills, and it was there, after a seven-week siege, that their flag of truce appeared. Rhodes had been able to trace Lobengula's former adviser, old Babyaan, and to persuade him to act as intermediary. Now, by arrangement, the final parley began, with Rhodes and five companions riding unarmed for five miles into rebel country and up into the hills. After eight weeks of intermittent negotiations peace was concluded. Rhodes scribbled out two cables for urgent dispatch to London: one contained the good news; the other was prudently directed to his stockbroker – and was sent first.

With the final conquest of the African tribesmen, the era of modern Rhodesia began, one which has persisted, politically, without interruption right through to the settler administration of today. It has been an era of prosperous economic development: railway building, copper mining, the laying out of great cattle ranches on an almost-Texan scale. By the 1960s, the settlers had created a sophisticated industrial civilization with – for white people at least – the Civil Service, the schooling, and the technical resources of commerce and finance that are the norm in Europe and North America, but have long been the exception in Africa itself. Indeed it is often claimed by settlers, as their case for keeping political direction indefinitely in their hands, that there is some *mystique* in the operation of a modern industrial society that places Rhodesia and South Africa permanently beyond African capabilities.

The visitor who is told this, by industrialists or Cabinet Ministers in Salisbury, must remind himself firmly that this argument is just another aspect of settler myopia. It was something that may have *appeared* to be true, up to that avalanche of political liberation that transformed the map of Africa from 1957 onwards. To dismiss this settler myth as silly today one has only to spend a week in Lagos, for example, or Dakar or Mogadishu, and see how effectively the Nigerians, the Senegalese, and the Somalis are running government and industries.

In pioneer Rhodesia, of course, there was no thought of permitting African participation in legislature or Civil Service; though at that very time the process had begun in India and the Gold Coast. There was not even the customary official genuflection towards such an objective, as there might have been, had Rhodesia itself been an ordinary colony, with a governor and direct supervision from Whitehall. But the incendiary antics of Rhodes and Jameson did at least result in a certain timid Imperial intrusion, though with their usual luck the two did not lose the precious Royal Charter that made the British South Africa Company politically sovereign in Zambesia.

After the first shock of the Jameson Raid, Chamberlain at the Colonial Office realized that there would have to be some kind of 'British presence' in Salisbury – the point that had been made time after time by Loch in unheeded memos from the Cape. While the Chartered Company was replacing Jameson with Lord Grey, the Colonial Office created the post of Resident Commissioner in Salisbury and sent Sir Richard Martin, a colonial servant in the 'trustee' tradition, to fill it. To the Cape itself, as British High Commissioner, came Sir Alfred Milner, a new force in the politics of southern Africa. Such was the aroma of intrigue and freebooting, arising from the parliamentary inquiry then in progress at Westminster, that Milner was able to ram through a further stipulation to safeguard Imperial (and so, in the settler context, African) interests. Control of the Company's armed police had been taken away from the Administrator, to prevent any future Jameson Raids, and given to the new British Resident Commissioner. Now, in the Order-in-Council of 1898, Milner decreed that the Resident Commission should become a purely political post, with its military or security function attached to another office. Both the Company and the settlers were determined that this office should be theirs, but Milner was firm. He said that henceforth the Imperial government would itself appoint a 'Commandant General', who would have final control over the Company's police and any other military forces that might be raised from time to time. This supreme commander would be an Imperial army officer, chosen by the Colonial Office, and paid by the British government.

Britain threw this power away in the handover from Company to settler rule in 1923, when the white Rhodesians themselves assumed full control over their own police and armed forces. British dependence upon white Rhodesian goodwill in the Boer War and the First World War had weakened the Imperial line of control to vanishing-point. And, in any event, the British Treasury had been unwilling to pay the true price of responsibility, which would have been the stationing of British troops in Rhodesia just as they were stationed in all other colonies. It is hard to visualize Iain Macleod, as Colonial Secretary in 1960, successfully imposing his tough but realistic African majority constitution on Kenya if he – and the settlers – had not been aware of Britain's ultimate sanction in the form of the Guards regiment at Kahawa, just outside Nairobi.

The Milner Constitution of 1898 shifted the safeguards of the 1894 Agreement a notch further in favour of the African. It no longer conceded the right to pass special laws about African land. Section 80 clearly stated that there should be 'no conditions, disabilities or restrictions . . . imposed upon natives by Ordinance which do not equally apply to persons of European descent'. The only exceptions to this rule were to be laws concerning firearms and liquor; land was specifically dropped from the list.

Milner had taken a hard look at what the settlers and the Company had done with government in the first four years, and he declared that it had been either 'rather harum-scarum' or 'exceedingly drastic'. Now he introduced a legislature of five M.P.s nominated by the Company and four elected by the settlers. The common roll and franchise system were borrowed from the Cape, which meant that a few exceptional Africans with private wealth or highly paid jobs – in the white economy but not in the African areas – might have the vote. When an inquiry was made in 1914, it was found that fifty-one Africans had managed to qualify. All of them, significantly, were 'colonials', which meant that they had immigrated from South Africa, usually with their white employers. The legislature at that time agreed to leave the franchise law as it was but to make no provision for Rhodesian Africans to get the vote, since 'they could be represented by the Secretary for Native Affairs'.

Under the Milner constitution, the Company Administrator was to preside over the legislature and over his own small Executive Council, or Cabinet, consisting of four M.P.s of his choice. This is what a governor would have done, had it been a normal colony, but he would have represented Britain's Imperial interests as well. Milner tried to overcome this difference by making his Resident Commissioner a kind of observer-M.P., attending all meetings of the tiny parliament and Executive Council. He could speak, but not vote. This proved, however, an unhappy arrangement from the start. In the early debates, the settler M.P.s time and again begged the British Resident Commissioner to show his hand, to express an opinion on the laws being drafted, rather than have them wait until stern criticism emanated from the Cape, to show that their observer-colleague had secretly disapproved of their acts. The Company's nominee M.P.s were equally suspicious, too, and at times the Hansard reports show them as 'ganging up' with the settlers in trying to pull their alien colleague around to their view.

The first British official to hold this uncomfortable post, Sir Richard Martin, proved difficult – for the settlers. He was a careful guardian of African interests. One of his reports to Milner at the Cape described the labour recruitment system employed by the Chartered Company, the mines, and individual farmers, as 'compulsory labour . . . a system synonymous with slavery'. The very existence of this British spy-M.P. in the settler midst increased the friction which was bound to develop between Rhodesia and Britain in any event, since the settlers had one view of native problems and Whitehall another. Perhaps, lacking Treasury support to intervene more effectively, Milner thought that it was the best he could do. But the settlers heaved a sigh of satisfied relief when the whole clumsy arrangement came to an end and full control passed to them and their own Cabinet with the end of Company rule in 1923.

In three respects the intervention of Whitehall came too late to protect the Africans. Hut tax and land apportionment had been formally recognized in the 1894 Agreement, and a system of passes introduced in 1895. All three forms of control had been initiated by Jameson in the gold-rush era, when Britain was looking the other way and he had a free hand. All three have continued to this day and have become explosive political issues between black and white. They strike at the fundamental liberties for which Englishmen have fought over the centuries. The hut or poll tax is simply taxation without representation, since it is a racial measure imposed on black people by whites who do not impose it on themselves. In the very year that it had been introduced into Rhodesia, the Company's officials had calculated that it would take a 'native' two to three months to earn the necessary cash – and that to do so he would have to enter the money economy, work for the white man and thus provide a constant flow of labour. Equally, passes had been imposed on the black man by the white who had not imposed them on himself, while the land had been carved up by arbitrary white initiative. The settlers had successfully laid down the terms on which the African could survive in the society of their dominion: where he could live, how he could earn his living, the taxes he must pay, and (through the pass system) the limits on his freedom of movement. By the time that Milner and Martin arrived on the scene, they were a good half-dozen years too late. Jameson and the settlers had beaten them to it.

The settler philosophy in Rhodesia had been clearly declared by Jameson after the death of Lobengula: 'The King being dead, the white government has taken his place.' Three years later, despite the Raid and Jameson's disgrace, Rhodes was busily establishing the other basic precept of Rhodesian life – settler independence of Whitehall. Sir Roy Welensky made it his declared aim for the 1960 constitutional review conference in

London; when it eluded him then, he returned to the attack in the autumn of 1962, warning Mr Macmillan that a 'final settlement' could not be much longer delayed.

Generally speaking the Rhodes game is to get rid of Imperial control in the B.S.A. Co.'s territory. He hates it, as he hates all control.

So Sir Alfred Milner had reported to London soon after taking up his post in 1897. A few months later he had found himself faced with a skilfully directed pressure campaign from the settlers, demanding a legislature of their own. Just before ordering the 1898 constitution, he had warned the Colonial Secretary in London of the ultimate objective that lay behind the settler campaign.

Rhodes is going for it hot and strong, avowedly with the object of strengthening his own position in any differences with the Imperial government. . . . They may bully the Company, he says frankly, but they won't dare to bully a representative Council. . . . It should make us careful not to give the Council the control of anything – armed forces for instance – which for reasons of Imperial policy it is not safe to put absolutely into the hands of one strong-willed and hasty man.

In the legislature the racial issue quickly asserted itself as the dominant concern of white Rhodesians. Hut tax and labour recruitment recurred as the main subjects in debate after debate, and the settlers grew increasingly exasperated by the intervention of Whitehall on behalf of the African – weak and remote though this intervention was. Colonel Napier, one of the leaders in the military campaigns that had crushed the Matabele regiments back in 1897, turned up again ten years later in the legislature, still a Company man but now, of course, an M.P. He asked the Native Commissioners to use coercion upon 'the subject races', and he added: 'They are like children and must be treated as such. A little parental persuasion in the shape of a caning might have a good effect.'

By 1900 the legislature was demanding that the hut tax be changed to a poll tax, and doubled to £2 a man; the Administrator accepted the demand and forwarded a formal request to

Whitehall for approval. It was rejected. One year later, Chamberlain asked Milner to investigate what seemed to him to be 'a form of compulsory labour' in the way that Africans were being coerced to leave their village life for work on white farms or in the mines. The Salisbury–Whitehall tug of war had begun. And, logically, the settlers set about the task of gaining control over the local legislature as a first step towards cutting the link with London altogether.

Rhodes was able to make one useful contribution to this campaign by seeing that the Administrator at least was on their side. When Lord Grey gave up the post and returned to England, Rhodes shrewdly arranged that the man who had been his own secretariat head at the Cape, Sir William Milton, should succeed. And so, for the best part of two decades, there was a man at the helm who had the southern Africa settler viewpoint rather than that of the Whitehall 'trustee'. This was, inevitably, a vital factor in Rhodesia's formative years, for Milton combined in his office the roles of governor, head of the Civil Service, and, of course, general manager of the Chartered Company's monopoly commercial operations. The influence of South Africa – especially on Native policy – was accordingly imprinted on Rhodesia, for Milton drew heavily on the institutions at the Cape. Its system of Roman–Dutch law became Rhodesia's, as did its Civil Service, the school system, and, above all, its structure of Native administration. Not surprisingly this meant a northward flow of lawyers, and judges, teachers, and recruits for the Civil Service, which has persisted in Southern Rhodesia to this day.

Meanwhile economic factors were at work which were to accelerate the campaign for independence from Whitehall. Spurred on by the need for effective military control of the territory, Rhodes had ordered a big speed-up in the railway construction programme after the 1896 uprisings and the gangs were soon pushing the line of steel forward at the rate of one mile a day. A few weeks after his successful *indaba* with the surrendering Matabele chiefs in the Matopo Hills, Rhodes saw the first train steaming into Bulawayo, with the proud banner 'Advance Rhodesia' fluttering across the boiler. Five years later, the line from Beira, in Portuguese territory on the Indian Ocean, reached Salisbury, and the two rail networks were linked. The risk of a new African rebellion had been significantly diminished. And there was a further political consequence. Once again the penny-wise policy of Whitehall had sown the seeds of future problems. Because of the expensive adventures in Egypt, followed by the vast outpourings on the profitless Boer War, successive British Chancellors had refused to advance the loans for railway construction that the settler legislature had requested. Thrown back on their own resources, the settlers saw Rhodes and the Chartered Company provide the money to finance the various railway companies – which became Chartered subsidiaries – and drew their own conclusions over where to find friends when in need. Imperial advice on African rights could be securely ignored.

Railway construction was a calculated risk, for the value of various potential mining sites could not be realistically appraised until heavy rock-crushing machinery had been brought in and used. Rhodes himself had promised the Company's shareholders the wealth of 'fifty Rands'. But there proved to be very few of the alluvial deposits that had made millionaires of lucky men in California and the Klondike. Nor were there any signs of the rich Transvaal type of reef, where the gold occurs equally diffused throughout a stratum of rock. The Rhodesian pioneers found themselves instead up against all the vagaries of quartz-reef mining. The 'shoot' of gold might be rich for some yards, then peter out, perhaps to reappear farther on, perhaps not. It proved economically safer to leave mining to the 'smallworker', using a minimum of capital and equipment. Most mines were too small to justify the formal flotation of a commercial company.

In the first four years after the march of the Pioneers, some 68,000 claims had been recorded and nearly 200 companies and syndicates registered. Settlers poured in, basing their hopes on the bonanza to come; by 1898 their numbers had grown to 13,000 from the 1,500, mostly men, in the first year of occupation. Yet aggregate gold production over those same eight years only reached £20,000. Then the newly completed railways began to do their job. The very next year saw gold production soar to

£126,000; but any boom was cut short by the Boer War. After some years of uncertainty, production reached the £1 million mark in 1905, touched £2 million two years later, and levelled out at £3 million by 1914. In the 1920s it declined, then revived during the next decade, and moved to a peak of £6·9 million in 1940. After another war and further uncertainties, gold production settled down in the 1960s to an annual figure of £6 million. As such it is surpassed by the high-quality asbestos from the mines of Shabani and Mashaba, which is worth about £9 million a year. And for many years now the production of tobacco in Southern Rhodesia has far outranked gold as a money-earner, bringing in some £20 million each year.

The pioneers found some very useful deposits of chrome ore at Selukwe, which were exploited in the First World War, and have again been mined in increasing tonnages lately. Tin has been found and may soon be worked in sufficient quantities to supply southern Africa. Lithium came into demand for the construction of nuclear reactors in the 1950s, and Southern Rhodesia now rivals America for first place in world production. The territory also has some high-grade deposits of iron ore, and a modern industrial complex, directed by the Rhodesian Iron and Steel Commission, is now taking shape at Que Que. What makes this all practical is the availability of good-quality coal from the Wankie fields, that have already been worked for half a century. The collieries provide a valuable source of income for the Chartered Company, which operates them through a subsidiary concern. The reserves are estimated at 700 million tons, and production now touches five million tons a year, for the coal lies in a rich seam about forty feet thick, close to the surface, which can be worked cheaply. There is a valuable export trade in it to Katanga and other near-by territories.

Today all this underground wealth, with the export earnings of tobacco, beef, and other farm products, forms the base for a manufacturing industry which stretches from tinned foods and paints, to electronics, a tyre factory, and huge assembly plants for cars and trucks. And, thanks to Federation, there is the vast copper production of Northern Rhodesia, now worth between

£70 and £85 million a year according to fluctuations in the world price of the metal, to buttress this southern economy. From the north, too, comes the lead and zinc of the Broken Hill mining complex, worth £3 million a year – enough to supply all the needs of the Rhodesians, from car batteries to builder's hardware, and still leave plenty over for export. It is a rich economy; and the new £110 million hydro-electric development at Kariba can provide cheap power for a further upward boost. Small wonder that the Rhodesians – or, rather, the white ones – should have so high a standard of living and, with it, the firm conviction that, if Britain and the people they call 'unrepresentative African extremists' will only leave them alone, they might have an even higher one in the next decade. Along with the white South Africans, these are incomparably the richest people in Africa.

But this is not how the picture looked half a century ago, as southern Africa was emerging from the economic depression which followed the Boer War. Rhodes had died in 1902, still convinced that somewhere in the land that now bore his name a new Witwatersrand would be found. Indeed, he had been so confident that he had consistently refused to accept the bleak estimates of the geologists, and the British South Africa Company's Board in London had been obliged to commission a full report without his knowledge. The bleak truth, it soon became obvious, was that, in gold production, Rhodesia would never be fifty Rands but only a mere fiftieth. True, there was other mineral wealth in the south, and the richness of the Copperbelt in the north, but these resources would only be exploited in the 1920s and 1930s. A quarter of a century before that, the directors of the Company were forced to face the fact that gold was a failure, that the railways were losing money for lack of ore tonnages that never materialized. The flow of immigrants had diminished to a trickle, disgruntled miners were leaving the country, and those who had turned to farming, fruit growing, or cattle ranching were finding it increasingly difficult to get the labour that they needed from the sullen ranks of defeated African tribesmen. There was even an attempt by the Company to recruit indentured workers from India, but this was vetoed by the Indian administration of the day. Even then Rhodesia's reputation for racial politics was stirring hostility abroad. The Indian Office replied: 'The pioneers of colonial enterprise are . . . masterful men, not very squeamish or tender-hearted.'

And the memo maintained that the terms of discipline, of segregated township or compound life, and discrimination in civil rights would be unacceptable. Efforts to get Chinese, Arabs, Somalis, and West Indians all failed for the same reason.

Lacking the resources of an external imperial government, the Company administration in Salisbury had to resort to ingenious improvisation. And, in practice, this meant deferring to settler wishes in all things, especially Native policy. Gold-mining royalties were cut from a fifty per cent rate to thirty per cent, then finally reduced to a scale which began at seven and a half per cent and slid down to nil. Permission to negotiate a governmental loan was refused by the Colonial Office, which replied that a commercial company could not contract a public debt. This left only one manifest asset – the land. The directors increased the Company's capital to £6 million; then they borrowed £3 million more. But the Charter itself was due to expire in 1914, and selling off blocks of land, with the necessary encouragement of immigration, would be a slow process requiring many years. It became vital, in order to recoup their enormous capital outlay, for the Company directors to get the backing of the settlers in applying to the British government for an extension of the Charter. And that in turn meant conciliation, if not outright appeasement.

The Company acceded to settler wishes that the franchise, in its very restricted form, should remain frozen for Africans. In 1907 it agreed to give settlers an elected majority over Company M.P.s in the legislature, in the ratio of 7:5. And this was formally ratified in 1911 by an Imperial government anxious to conciliate Boer opinion across the border and keep the whole of southern Africa friendly. Germany's expansion and rearmament might mean war, and Britain needed to secure the Cape route to her main reservoir of troops – in India.

Thus Chartered Company policy and British Imperial strategy coincided in 1911 to drop political power, like a ripe plum, into settler hands. The event passed relatively unnoticed, but it was and remains decisive, for it marked the surrender by Britain of final effective control over Southern Rhodesia. By 1914, since there was nothing more to lose by allowing the settlers their head, the number of elected, or settler, M.P.s had risen to twelve, against the Company's five nominees. A convention was formally established that the British High Commissioner at the Cape and his local representative, the Resident Commissioner, would interfere only when the Rhodesian parliament considered Orders-in-Council affecting constitutional precedent. The settler-legislators accordingly resorted to Ordinances, as a convenient way of avoiding Imperial intrusion; and this gave them pretty well a free hand in all matters, especially the most vital of all – the administration of Africans.

By the outbreak of the First World War, therefore, the British South Africa Company was only in apparent command of Southern Rhodesia; real power had in fact passed to the settlers. They had already assigned forty-five per cent of their African peoples to Native Reserves – comprising in all a mere twenty-two per cent of the territory's total land surface. And contemporary reports, some even by Company men themselves (like Marshall Hole), make it clear that the African land was the less productive, the leftover, the second-rate. It would be astonishing if it had been otherwise; the Company's financial position, the need to please the settler-dominated legislature, the constant demand for cheap African labour, all ensured that the choice tracts of land would be kept available for immigrants. Why else should immigrants come? And how else could the Company make Rhodesia pay?

In the north the Company had extended the line of rail to the Congo border. The Copperbelt did not yet exist; where the great sextet of mines now belch out fourteen per cent of the world's copper supplies, only two nomadic sub-tribes, the Lala and the Lamba, hunted in the scrublands among the gaunt ant-hills. Along the railway, land was aggressively sold to white men for farming and large-scale ranching. Africans had managed to get their complaints heard by the Colonial Office; they objected to the poll tax, the ubiquitous colour-bar, and the selling of their tribal lands to white men on the shaky legal basis of treaties negotiated with one particular King, Lewanika, whose jurisdiction most of them did not recognize. (Mr Kaunda and his nationalists still plan to challenge the British South Africa Company on the land issue when more immediate political problems are settled.)

Britain proposed classifying Northern Rhodesia as a 'tropical dependency', so recognizing that African rule would ultimately have to come, as in Nigeria or Uganda. But when the Company's directors resisted this, the British government backed down, and the Africans – with their more vocal friends, the missionaries – had to content themselves with the declaration that the territory was now a Protectorate.

In the south the final collapse of the Imperial façade was being prepared. With the outbreak of the First World War, some 7,000 of Rhodesia's 25,000 whites volunteered to fight for Britain – first in the African campaigns for the capture of the German colonies, then in France and Flanders. When the Company's application for a supplemental charter was granted early in 1915, it had the support of eleven out of the twelve settler M.P.s. But settler support for an extension was conditional on the grant of 'responsible government' as soon as possible. The leader of the settlers was Sir Charles Coghlan, the flamboyant South African lawyer who had emigrated to Salisbury. He was an 'Empire man', as he reminded the post-war Colonial Secretary, Winston Churchill, and Rhodesia had sent to the war a higher proportion of her manhood than any other British territory.

But an Empire man could be a Rhodesian first. The settlers resented having to pay, through the Company in Salisbury, fat fees to absentee landlords in Britain who probably knew little and cared less about Rhodesia. They challenged the Company on land ownership in an action before the judicial committee of the Privy Council which lasted until 1918.

The Company based its claim on the Lippert Concession and

the 'right of conquest'. A counter-claim on behalf of the Africans was financed by liberal philanthropists in England. (How the Rhodesian settlers hate liberals!) This held that the land in Zambesia had been communally owned by the Africans, and that the death of one King, Lobengula, could not alienate it. But there was a third claimant still, the Crown, and when the judges at last reached their verdict, it was the Crown that won. The Company, they ruled, was entitled to act as no more than an agent for the rightful owner of the land – the Crown. Only for as long as it continued to be the administering authority in the territory, should it have the receipts from land sales to help cover the costs of government.

In recent years the few Africans of the Federation who have managed to qualify as lawyers have found a certain wry fascination in the legal concept that the British Crown had owned land for twenty-five years in a territory which it had never formally annexed.

This was now belatedly rectified, though it became immediately apparent that Britain, once again, was unwilling to bear the costs of running Southern Rhodesia as a normal colony. The Duke of Devonshire, who had taken over the Colonial Office, believed in the 'trustee' concept, but he could not persuade his Chancellor of the Exchequer to accept the implications for Rhodesia. If the white settlers of Southern Rhodesia wanted their freedom from the Company, they should pay for it. And pay they did, to the tune of £2 million. In terms of the 'Devonshire Agreement', as it was called, the Chartered Company received a cash payment of £3·75 million. But the British Treasury made it a political condition of the deal that the settlers should provide £2 million of the total, with only the balance found by Britain herself.

What was to be the status of the territory now? Churchill had tried unsuccessfully to persuade Coghlan and his colleagues to enter the South African Union as its fifth member state. The settlers, who saw themselves about to shake off the Company's control – such as it was – as well as the last vestiges of Whitehall rule, were unwilling to accept a new domination. Smuts had used troops to smash a strike by European miners in Johannesburg; Rhodesians in an affiliated union feared that he favoured the substitution of cheap black for skilled white labour. In the referendum of October 1922, the white Rhodesians voted by 8,774 to 5,989 in favour of 'responsible government' – authority over their own affairs and absolute control of a million Africans. There remained the proviso that any law passed by the new, all-white parliament of thirty members might be amended or vetoed by the British government, and this was to constitute the safeguard of African rights. But in all the thirty-nine years from then until the new Sandys–Whitehead constitution of 1961, that right was never exercised, though at the time of the township riots and shootings in mid 1960 Garfield Todd and Joshua Nkomo made a dramatic joint appeal to Lord Home in London to intervene. They called – but were not received – at the Commonwealth Relations Office, and left their typewritten message for Home, who ignored it.

For the bargain price of £2 million, the white settlers of Southern Rhodesia gained in effect the same freedom of action that the white South Africans had acquired a dozen years before. Officially the money was payable to Britain (to be passed on to the Company), in return for ownership by the Southern Rhodesian government of all 'unalienated' land in the colony. In practice, there were seventeen million acres of good land that were later put up for sale to Europeans; and another twenty-four million acres, most of it not very good, that could be earmarked for Africans. At least 6·8 million acres of this were reckoned to be saleable – at a lower price than the white land – in the form of Native Purchase Areas.

As a real-estate deal alone, the Devonshire Agreement was no mean bargain. The new settler government led by Coghlan had only to realize an average price of 1s. 8d. per acre on the land that they decided to put up for sale, in order to recoup the £2 million that they had paid to the British Exchequer. But the political bargain was even better. The post of British 'Commandant General' disappeared; the Company's police, as well as the small Rhodesian Militia (or army), fell under the direct control of the colony's

Prime Minister. The British Resident Commission was abolished. The post of Governor was created, but without the powers enjoyed by the governor of any other colony; he became simply a head of state (and is nowadays a Rhodesian). No terms were imposed by Britain to broaden the franchise, or admit Africans to the all-white parliament. In everything but name, and certain aspects of external affairs, Southern Rhodesia became a Dominion. And if any proof were needed, Coghlan was promptly invited to the next Commonwealth Prime Ministers' Conference (then known as the Imperial Conference), along with Canada, Australia, and the rest. The territory would henceforth be known as a 'Self-Governing Colony', that term which has recently so puzzled the United Nations General Assembly and its Committee of seventeen.

It was specified in the 1923 deal, in order to safeguard 'Native interests', that legislation affecting Africans should be reserved for the Secretary of State. But, in practice, no subsequent Tory administration in London, nor any of the three Labour governments, ever blocked the will of Southern Rhodesia's all-white legislature. By custom, therefore, the veto became obsolete, and indeed, when Duncan Sandys went to negotiate the 1961 constitution with Sir Edgar Whitehead, his constitutional lawyers advised him that, in a test case, it could probably be established that the right of veto had lapsed. The Africans were thus, by British unwillingness to 'make a fuss with our kith and kin', stripped of their constitutional armour. Yet this supposed safeguard was, ironically, the 'price' that Coghlan had paid to achieve independence in all other fields.

Secondly, the establishment of the Dominions Office in 1925 brought the Tory administration face to face with its true intentions towards Southern Rhodesia. The late L. S. Amery was the Cabinet Minister responsible, and he did not hesitate. Southern Rhodesia would be dealt with through the Dominions Office, or what today is the C.R.O. Thus, by the decision of one man – an 'Empire man' of the old school – the final link was snapped and the guardianship of the Colonial Office removed from the Africans of Southern Rhodesia forever. It had never amounted to much, thanks to the ingenuity of Rhodes and the British South Africa Company rule.

Relieved of its administrative burdens, the Chartered Company promptly began to show a profit and paid a dividend – the first in the thirty-four years of its history – in 1924. There was an even greater bonanza to come, from the copper ores which lay underground and unsuspected in the belt of scrubland adjoining the Katanga border. Fortunately for the Africans of Northern Rhodesia, this was not discovered until the American copper magnate, Chester Beatty, teamed up with Sir Ernest Oppenheimer of the Anglo–American Corporation in South Africa, and others, to launch a vast aerial survey in the mid 1920s. Today we know that there are in excess of 712 million tons of proven ore bodies, from which twenty-five million tons of pure copper can be recovered. It is the largest copper lode in the Commonwealth, and in 1953 – the year in which the Federation of Rhodesia and Nyasaland was formed – Northern Rhodesia emerged as one of the greatest copper-producing territories in the world. The co-incidence of the date is noteworthy, for it was the copper revenues of Northern Rhodesia, providing export earnings which reached a peak of £121 million in 1956 and have now steadied at around £80 million, that largely paid for the task of building the Federation. In the first seven years, it has been calculated, some £70 million of tax revenue from the north went to develop the infrastructure of government in the other two territories – through the agency of the Federal government in Salisbury. Most of this £70 million was taken by Southern Rhodesia, and it is the complaint of the Africans – which almost every dispassionate study seems to support – that this tax money was directed by settler governments in Salisbury in such a way as to benefit the white community most and the black majority least.

It was the glittering wealth of the Copperbelt that, among other factors, led the southern settlers to launch their Federation campaign immediately after the Second World War ended. But in the Chartered Company era things had looked very different. To the settlers of Salisbury and Bulawayo the scrublands of the north were a tropical slum, with an African problem slightly worse than their own in terms of numbers. Rhodes had wanted to link the two territories as part of his 'All-Red Route' across the continent. Jameson had tried to achieve this as well when he became President of the Company in 1913 – partly because he believed in Rhodes's political vision of Empire, and partly because it was obvious that amalgamation would save the Company money on administration. But the settlers had determined to get rid of the Charter Company's ball-and-chain and were unwilling to put themselves back into shackles again, even for 'Dr Jim'. Having gained their own sovereignty in 1923, they lost interest in the north until the 1940s. Only then did they begin to desire it for its copper wealth and as a buffer state against the southward advance of black African nationalism.

In Northern Rhodesia itself there were, in 1920, only 3,634 whites, outnumbered by a million Africans in the ratio of 270:1. And not all whites were settlers, for in that tiny community there had to be a good number of Chartered Company administrators, while many more were nomadic prospectors, gold panners, and the usual assortment of 'rolling stones' to be found in a frontier land. Missionaries, too, were there, in proportionately far greater numbers than in the south. Working among the Africans, they assumed the roles of political guardians, to constitute a liberal white element that was to become an important factor in the constitutional battles of the 1960s.

Rhodes had pushed Lord Salisbury into extending the Charter so as to take in the north. But, after the Jameson Raid, the Colonial Office in London grew wary. It vetoed the Company's proposal to extend South African systems of administration, such as establishment of Native Reserves and the introduction of Roman–Dutch law, to the north. The Company police, which had become a settler-directed national army in the south, were made to function as a police force and no more; later they were replaced by the Northern Rhodesia police, a mixed force with a large number of African constables who might – as in Nigeria – aspire to senior rank along with the white members. By 1924, when the Company withdrew from administration entirely, as it had done in the south the previous year, there was no settler lobby strong enough to make Britain endorse the hypocrisy of a 'Self-Governing Colony'. The territory was clearly defined as a Protectorate of the normal kind. It was now in a parallel situation to Nyasaland: it had its own police, it was under Colonial Office rule, the governor held effective power – and there was no settler Prime Minister. Most important of all, the militia in both of the northern protectorates was not a home-based, home-paid army, as in the south. It consisted of mixed regiments only, such as the King's African Rifles, white-officered – by Rhodesians or Britons – but under the direct control of Whitehall, paid by the Imperial exchequer, and subject to the immediate command of the British governor.

This is the trump card that a Tory government in London threw away in 1953. Churchill as Prime Minister and Lord Chandos, then his Colonial Secretary, agreed to the amalgamation of these units into the Federal Rhodesian Army, paid and directed by a settler government in Salisbury. The only security force under the sole control of each governor in the two northern protectorates remained the police.

Northern Rhodesia is still linked to London today because the settlers in 1920 found that they had to turn to London to free them from Company rule. In that year the British South Africa Company proposed to introduce a system of income tax; there was no question of getting 'the consent of the governed', since there was no legislature, although a faint-hearted 'advisory council' had been running for three years. The northern settlers dispatched a petition, with 175 signatures to King George V. And, in view of the sensational Privy Council decision of two years before over the ownership of land in Southern Rhodesia, they seized the chance to raise this issue, with that of mineral rights, as well. 'The people', said the petition, meaning of course the white people, 'claim that both these belong to the Crown.' No African signed the petition, nor was any asked to.

Lord Milner had by this time become Colonial Secretary, and he passed the problem to a committee, the Buxton Commission, which recommended the establishment of a legislature and the testing of the Company's land and mineral rights by submission to the Privy Council. By this time the Presidency of the Chartered Company had fallen to Lobengula's old antagonist from the days of the dung-carpeted royal kraal, Rochfort Maguire, the Irish-Oxonian barrister.

Maguire scented the unpleasant aroma of a long and possibly unsuccessful piece of litigation. He settled instead for a straight political bargain – horse-trading would be a not inappropriate word – and so left behind him the great constitutional argument which, to this day, remains unresolved. What would the Privy Council have ruled? There were standing claims from the War Office against the Company for £2 million expended in the East Africa campaign against the Germans. The Company was counterclaiming for £1·7 million of accumulated deficits on the costs of government. In the settlement, the Company retained the right to half the proceeds of land sales in north-western Rhodesia, and the outright ownership of three estates acquired from the African Lakes Company amounting to 2,500,000 acres. Mineral rights remained in the possession of the British South Africa Company; they had brought in a mere £13,000 the previous year and might well dwindle to nothing. The prospectors had learned to their sorrow that the copper-oxide ores they encountered were of poor grade and unprofitable, quite unlike the rich surface ores of Katanga just twenty miles away across the border. What no one could suspect was that, by the 1960s, the value of these mineral royalties would have risen from £13,000 to an amount varying between £10 and £12 million a year.

With the end of Company rule, Northern Rhodesia acquired a legislature of fourteen members – nine Colonial Office men and five settler M.P.s. With the qualitative franchise set securely high, no one expected any African voters to take part for a good many years – and none did. The first two African M.P.s would not take their seats in the legislature before another twenty-four years had passed. But – in contrast to the south – the possibility was accepted.

In 1902 a Rhodesian hunter named Collier shot an antelope by a river bank in the Lamba country of the northern frontier. As he picked it up, he noticed that its head lay against a rocky stratum whose tell-tale green banding meant copper. The mighty Roan Antelope mine, with its gracious perimeter of white miners' suburbs and neat African township, stands there today. But the surface oxide ores proved disappointing and it was not until the advent of cheaper methods of deep test-boring that these low-grade oxides were found to be just a covering for something far richer. About a thousand feet below lay the valuable copper sulphide ores, easier to work and occurring in vast quantity.

The discovery coincided with the advent of the popular motoring age: the bull-nosed Morris, the Baby Austin, and the Model-T in their millions would want the copper of Rhodesia, as would electrical companies, especially those in the expanding field of radio. The boom began, and after reaching one peak during the Second World War, it reached another ten years later. The number of white settlers, less than 4,000 when the Colonial Office assumed control, swelled to 37,000 by 1951 and is today approaching the 80,000 mark. The Africans remain far ahead, since there are nearly three million of them. But ratio is not all. In absolute terms, the existence of a sizeable, prosperous, confident white community was enough to ensure that the demand for self-government would not be long delayed. Furthermore, the natural source of skilled white recruits for the mines was South Africa, and at times more than half the annual northbound immigrant flow consisted of men whose mother tongue was Afrikaans and whose outlook on 'native policy' was far removed from that of the Colonial Office. The old missionary attitude of guardianship survived on the farms and in the bush country, but on the Copperbelt itself racial discrimination was soon as sharp and bitter as in Salisbury.

The same forces which had operated a quarter of a century before in the south now came into play in the protectorate.

A trade-union leader named Roy Welensky entered politics in 1938 and sprang into prominence during the years of the Second World War. Battling for the rights of his own European Railwaymen's Union, he grew increasingly resentful of Colonial Office control. When he campaigned for election to the legislature a second time, in 1941, he sought amalgamation with Southern

Rhodesia, so that the meddling hand of Whitehall could be removed from the territory forever. Settler control of 'native policy' was, of course, a powerful stimulus. Welensky believed, like his neighbours and fellow white trade unionists, that the 'man on the spot' knew best how to handle this problem, and that the intervention of remote Colonial Office theorists was, at the very least, unrealistic and unfortunate. He and the four colleagues who stood with him on a Labour ticket were easily elected and Welensky took this – with reason – as a mandate from the settler voters to press his demand for political union with the colony to the south.

The war years brought prosperity to Rhodesia, and a new confidence to the settlers of the north, who now began passionately to claim that they were entitled to the same control over their own affairs as their fellow white Rhodesians had enjoyed, for so long, south of the Zambesi.

Even in Nyasaland the white community no longer thought of itself as an island in an ocean of blacks; its numbers had doubled since before the war, to a total of 2,000, and they doubled again from 1945–50. (By 1958 the community would number nearly 9,000.) The Nyasaland legislature was constituted by a system of nomination and indirect election; the three million Africans in the territory were still without a direct vote in the 1955 reshuffle of their constitution, and their representatives were chosen through three Provincial Councils. The five African M.P.s seemed unimportant; the six settler M.P.s felt that the next stage in constitutional change would merely whittle down the number of Civil Servants, then holding eleven seats. Two of the settler M.P.s had already been invited to join the governor's Executive Council. All in all, the white community was satisfied with the course of events. Nyasaland's tobacco industry boomed in the post-war period, as a consequence of Britain's dollar shortage and the switching of purchases to sterling sources of supply. It was reasonable to suppose that the flow of white immigration would continue, and that any African takeover could be indefinitely postponed.

This post-war settler confidence reached a peak in Southern Rhodesia, where national income doubled to £75 million by 1949 and in the next three years proceeded to double again. Men who had fought in their own (white) Rhodesian contingents, or as the white officers of African regiments, grew impatient with the continuing status of Southern Rhodesia as a 'Colony', 'Self-Governing' or not. The powerful settler party of Sir Godfrey Huggins reasserted its dominance in the 1948 elections by winning twenty-four of the thirty seats in the legislature. Huggins's cocky self-assurance showed itself in other ways: in the campaign to boost white immigration, which was to cost £200 million (though most of that sum would be recoverable in instalments); in the outright purchase of the railway companies, the price of which was to be largely recouped by the upswing in freight tonnages; in the calling of a conference at Victoria Falls in 1949 to plan a Federation.

The success of the Federation campaign, and the racial crisis which was to be its bitter harvest six years later, is the material of another chapter. Ironically, its open clashes between black and white would halt economic expansion, threaten a flight of capital, reduce white immigration to a trickle, and then to a reverse flow, eroding the very prosperity which had encouraged the settlers to launch their audacious campaign. The Federation of Rhodesia and Nyasaland came into existence in October 1953. In the riots, shootings, and emergencies which were to follow, some 3,000 Africans would be imprisoned, and 200 would lose their lives. But African nationalism would take coherent political form. And nine years later, almost to the week, the process of unpicking Federation would begin, directed by Britain's Deputy Prime Minister.

Part 4: The Smash-up

'The greatest of faults is to be conscious of none in oneself.'
THOMAS CARLYLE

1 The New Bourbons

'The settler and the pioneer have at bottom had justice on their side; a great continent could not have been kept as nothing but a game preserve for squalid savages.' PRESIDENT THEODORE ROOSEVELT

The white settlers who hold political and military power in Rhodesia today are the Bourbons of Africa; they have learned nothing and they have forgotten nothing.

Like their precursors in Europe, they are a governing minority who cannot see that the world around them is in a state of accelerating change. Like them too, they are rich and privileged themselves and have acquired a convenient blindness when confronted with people who are not.

'I know my Africans,' says Sir Edgar Whitehead, 'and they are not interested in politics.' He used just these words on a recent visit to London, when chatting with a group of political correspondents who had all visited Central Africa on various occasions. I asked him to expand his remark, since it did not accord with my own observations and conversations in Rhodesia.

'They are interested only in things of immediate practical concern,' Sir Edgar explained blandly, 'schools for their children, the improvement of their land, raising their standard of living, and things of that kind.'

It was a staggering statement; 'things of that kind' are the stuff of politics in any country. Yet in our subsequent questioning of him, it was evident that the Prime Minister either would not or (as I think myself) could not see it. It is a mistake to conclude that the white settlers are crafty hypocrites, for they are not. They are sincere; blindly, tragically perhaps, but sincere none the less. It is their greatest strength.

I think it is important to stress this, because there comes a moment for every visitor to Rhodesia when it dawns upon him suddenly that his white host is not an insidious hypocrite, but a man who passionately believes in the current political order. Since most of us rate sincerity as a virtue, the effect is to disarm criticism and persuade the visitor that there is 'really something in it' when the white Rhodesian talks of preserving civilized values for the foreseeable future. Perhaps it is our legacy of Dickens as well as the films we see which serve to confuse our judgement; those working for evil ends are shown as consciously scheming and insincere, while those whose countenances radiate a deep sincerity are on the side of Right. The last war ought to have put a stop to that one; Hitler was sincere enough in his obsessions. Southern Africa offers a similar lesson in the hard realities; one's Rhodesian host may well be a man whose every action radiates sincerity, yet his political creed may be leading his country inexorably into chaos as brutal and tragic as that which blasted the *quartiers* of Oran before Algeria achieved self-determination.

'Believe me, Mr Keatley, the troubles of this country of ours are not political, they are economic.' This was the judgement of Sir Roy Welensky, the Federal Prime Minister, when I first went to visit him at his home in a pleasant suburb of Salisbury. Sir Roy typifies the outlook of most white Rhodesians; that is why they keep returning him to office, and why it is important to study his judgements.

The Federal Prime Minister is in no confusion over the problems confronting his administration and the way to resolve them. He wants independence for his country now; full dominion status and the removal of the last vestiges of British government intervention. That would put an end to the interminable trafficking with Whitehall, the constant fussing of Fleet Street, and the actions of certain British M.P.s who take it upon themselves to be watchdogs of Rhodesian affairs. Sir Roy genuinely feels that the politically conscious Africans constitute a small minority; and, of those, the only civilized ones have joined his own United Federal Party. By this thesis, the way to advance lies through an economic expansion which could make the country boom as North America boomed in the last century. That would pay for the schooling, the rehousing, the industrial and agricultural development which would turn millions of primitive Africans into modern men and women, equipped for the responsibilities of helping to run a civilized state. But to achieve all this, the settlers must be free to plan and direct their affairs, free from the interference of Whitehall. Sir Roy accepts, he has told me more than once, that the Federal Prime Minister may, in time, be a black man. He has made the point in speeches and Press conferences (for British rather than white Rhodesian audiences). But he has been equally clear in maintaining that full democracy, the programme of one man one vote, cannot be useful or applicable in the present circumstances of Central Africa. Ghana is for him the terrible symbol of what he and the settlers want to avoid in Rhodesia, and he refers to it again and again.

Sir Roy's list of priorities for African advance is the same as Sir Edgar Whitehead's. Both men reveal the identical blind spot. What they have ignored is precisely that which Africans rate as their top priority – the achievement of human dignity. Two examples should suffice.

The African National Congress of Southern Rhodesia, which was banned in the 1959 emergency and succeeded by the Z.A.P.U. movement under much the same leaders, placed 'the attainment of human dignity' as first on the list of its objectives. All the other demands – land, schools, economic development, and the 'things of that kind' which Sir Edgar Whitehead describes as 'non-political' – were given a deliberately lower priority on the list. The significance is clear; the African's demand for the achievement of human dignity will not wait.

The second piece of evidence in support of this comes from one who may be described as the father of African nationalism – at least in West Africa. Dr Nnamdi Azikiwe, who became Nigeria's Governor-General after the achievement of independence in 1960, was the man who helped get young Kwame Nkrumah his fare to go to the United States to study; recently (through one of his newspapers, the *West African Pilot*) he has criticized Dr Nkrumah for infringements of democratic liberties in Ghana. Twelve years before the battle for independence had been won, when Africans still constituted a minority in British colonial legislatures, when nationalist leaders were in prison or organizing resistance to imperial rule, and there were dozens of specific reforms which Africans in each territory were demanding, Dr Azikiwe began a speech: 'My country groans . . .' One might have expected to hear some catalogue of wrongs – the inadequate schooling and hospitals, the loaded votes, the low wages and high taxes. But the Nigerian nationalists were fired with fury against something even more outrageous. 'My country groans', said Dr Azikiwe, 'under a system which makes it impossible for us to develop our personalities to the full.'

What a curious mouthful of words to use as a political battle-cry for people who – if Sir Edgar and Sir Roy are right – were much more concerned with poor food and leaky roofs than with abstruse concepts of individual dignity and national identity.

Miss Margery Perham, the distinguished Oxford historian, cited Dr Azikiwe's statement when she was trying to explain the dynamics of African nationalism to a nation-wide audience on the B.B.C. 'It is difficult to exaggerate the state almost of possession felt by African leaders during their struggles,' she added. 'Above all, they are on fire with indignation at their individual and racial status.'

It is this total inability – or refusal – to understand this basic surge in the blood of their own African peoples that is the tragic and terrifying characteristic of the white settlers in Rhodesia today. It seems to me the key to the whole Rhodesian crisis. For, in practice, this gulf between the thinking of the two races, and their two sets of political leaders means that the white settler politicians take their day-to-day decisions on the basis of ignorance and illusion.

It is one of the special ironies, in a land which has more than its due share, that the Europeans should so completely misjudge the attitudes and aspirations of their African neighbours as to ascribe to them an obsession with purely physical possessions. A Freudian psychologist, no doubt, could sound the deep currents that lie beneath that error. For it is the European settler himself who displays this obsession, while the African (despite the visions of

Sir Edgar Whitehead) rates liberty and political rights higher than any simpler, more tangible gains.

And surely – to those for whom democracy is a prize beyond any purchase – this African aspiration should not appear quixotic or irrational. Benjamin Franklin was a young man learning the printing business in London who could have had, physically, a far more comfortable life if he had stayed out of politics; but he went home to Philadelphia. Patrick Matimba, two centuries later, was a young man in the same trade and the same quandary; he went home to Salisbury. (Or, more accurately, the segregated African suburb of Harare.) Joshua Nkomo, Kenneth Kaunda, and Kanyama Chiume, to name but three, are former teachers who, if they rated possessions and income as highly as white people in those three territories, would long ago have chosen a quieter, more comfortable life.

To achieve a working racial compatibility in Central Africa, it seems to me, it is the whites who should adjust their attitudes and aspirations, rather than the blacks. If these new Bourbons claim that their way of life demonstrates 'civilized standards', then I would only reply that someone has the values of civilization curiously muddled, and that it is not the African. I leave to those more competent the delicate task of deciding whether Jesus Christ would approve the race policies of the two settler régimes – of Welensky and Winston Field. To the plain visitor from abroad, there are simple figures available requiring a less complex judgement.

There are some 8,500,000 people in the three territories composing the Federation; the ones with white skins come to just over 300,000, and are outnumbered by the Africans in the ratio of 26:1. (This was the position in 1962, before Nyasa secession.)

The register of voters, however, provides a topsy-turvy reflection of these figures. Of the 91,767 voters listed on the Federal roll, only 1,164 are Africans. They are outnumbered in the ratio of 79:1.

In the Federal Assembly of fifty-nine seats, the voting and constituency arrangements are such as to reserve forty-four of them absolutely for men with white skins, not only now but 'for the foreseeable future'. The phrase is Lord Malvern's. He was formerly Sir Godfrey Huggins and was the first man to hold the office of Federal Prime Minister after the establishment of Federation in 1953. In May 1956, defending these electoral entrenchments of white minority privilege, he said:

We want to indicate to the Africans that provision is made for them to have a place in the sun, as things go along. But we have not the slightest intention of letting them control things until they have proved themselves, and perhaps not even then. That will depend on our grand-children.

He then expressed the sentiment which was reverently preserved in that organ of settler opinion – the country's largest and wealthiest newspaper – the *Rhodesia Herald*: 'Political control must remain in the hands of civilized people, which for the foreseeable future means the Europeans.'

The bewildered visitor, anxious to be fair to the white settler, might feel obliged to refer to the Preamble to the Federal Constitution, which assures a policy of partnership between the races. But here again the laconic candour of Huggins cuts through any optimism with the edge of reality.

'That was forced on us,' he later declared to members of his white electorate. Huggins did not disguise his own interpretation of partnership. He called it the relationship between rider and horse. Here, then, is the picture up to the end of 1962:

The visitor, seeking to plumb the mysteries of white settler politics, may perhaps recall having heard or read somewhere that the territorial régime of Sir Edgar Whitehead represents a more liberal school of thought than Sir Roy Welensky's Federal government. In Salisbury, which is the capital of Southern Rhodesia as well as of the whole Federation, the two parliament buildings stand conveniently back to back. It is easy enough for the visitor who has taken his first look at the baffling spectacle of Federal politics to walk round to the other street and inspect the territorial legislature.

As he enters, he may recall that the territory has over three million inhabitants, of whom only 225,000 are white. Yet, as he looks down from the strangers' gallery, he sees that there are thirty members of parliament, and that all thirty are white! Outside is Africa – and, in Southern Rhodesia itself, almost three million African people, whose schools, taxes, jobs, and futures are all decided in that cool stone building. But along its seats of power, there is not so much as one black figure visible. That was the astonishing scene one saw in the years 1923–62; it might have been a Swiss cantonal assembly or a borough council in Surrey. In the election of December 1962 the voters (more than 90 per cent white) swung right; Winston Field's Rhodesian Front won control of the new House in which 14 seats out of 65 went to Africans.

Sir Godfrey Huggins once summed it up by saying that 'the Europeans in this country can be likened to an island of white in a sea of black'.

In reality, however, it is not an accurate description because those fifty-one white faces in the Southern Rhodesian Assembly are not European at all, except in the sense of their ethnic origin. In political as well as social and economic terms, they are the faces of White Africans. It is an important distinction.

These men are not just 5,000 miles and fifty years away from Britain – or whatever was their European country of origin. They are infinitely distant in terms of land, labour, housing, political and racial tensions, the whole way of life. They are a new breed developed by the special environment of settler Africa. In Kenya they gained and enjoyed political power for a few years and then, in the Macleod Constitution of 1960 and the Maudling Plan of 1962 that followed, were decisively toppled. Only 65,000 of them lived in Kenya, outnumbered by the Africans in a ratio of almost exactly 100:1. Was that their fatal weakness? That question haunts the mind of every white M.P. on the floor of the Southern Rhodesian parliament. In the Federation as a whole, the ratio was 26:1. In Nyasaland, a formidable 330:1. It is better in Northern Rhodesia: there it used to be 40:1 only ten years ago, but the high wages paid to white miners on the Copperbelt have enticed many immigrants, and now it is 31:1. The immigration drive has done wonders in the south, as well. In the years before the war the ratio was 25:1, but now it is down to the much more manageable figure of 12:1.

There must be few white settlers in Southern Rhodesia who do not consider those figures, frequently and anxiously. The model, of course, is the Republic of South Africa, where the race ratio seems relatively safe, both in political and military terms. There a good solid community, of more than three million whites, is outnumbered by the Rest in the ratio of only 4 to 1. Even in Rhodesia – at least in the south – the military commanders and the British South Africa Police visibly assure the politicians of their ability to secure control. The main forces might have to be withdrawn south of the Zambesi: Nyasaland is going; if necessary, the North with its Copperbelt may go as well. Whatever else is lost, the Whites intend to hold the south, and their defence chiefs are confident that they can do it. I have watched their soldiers and police on manoeuvre, with their impressive squadrons of armoured cars and light automatic weapons – ideal for 'mopping-up' operations, or cordoning off a township, or high-speed action on the open veld – and I am convinced that Rhodesia's defence chiefs could contain any open unaided African insurrection.

It is, the visitor to Central Africa soon realizes, absurd and even dangerous to regard the white minority rulers of Rhodesia as fellow-Europeans. They are no more European than the Texans, whom they resemble in so many different ways. We would not expect a Liverpool docker – who has voted Labour at every opportunity, while grumbling at the moderation of his leaders, who wants to see far more nationalization and enjoys watching football more than most things – to have much in common with a Texas rancher who likes the straight Republican ticket, Sen. Barry Goldwater, and the late Joe McCarthy, fears 'creeping socialism' and pilots his private plane up to Canada on fishing holidays. Conceivably the two might bear the same surname and be descendants of the same Scottish clansman. You might send their sons to Eton and from there to the Brigade of Guards, and end up with similar products of the Establishment.

But in immediate, pragmatic, political terms, it is the current circumstances and attitudes that differentiate and matter.

The white Africans of Rhodesia dislike the word 'settler', because it implies that they are merely ex-immigrants (statistically, most white Rhodesians are). They have chosen to call themselves 'Europeans', because the word 'white' seems improperly crude, and 'British' would imply subservience to the political direction of Downing Street (which, of course, for the Federation as a whole, is nominally the case). Like most of us, the white Rhodesians want it both ways: their whole political campaign, culminating in Federation, has been aimed at throwing off the last restraints of Whitehall; yet Sir Roy Welensky and his followers never tire of declaring their Britishness. Most have great regard for knighthoods – the first Prime Minister not to have accepted one was Mr Garfield Todd – and Sir Roy has said more than once, when speaking in London, that the 'Federation will be the last place where you will see the Union Jack still flying in Africa'.

One thing has eluded these privileged people of the high veld. Lacking the distinction of a separate language, like their Boer neighbours to the south, they have no convenient and distinctive word by which to describe themselves, comparable to 'Afrikaner'. Yet, by sheer pressure of personality and public relations, they have given a special meaning to the word 'Rhodesian'. If someone in London says to a neighbour, 'I've got a Rhodesian friend coming to see me this afternoon,' the neighbour will probably expect to see a person with a white skin coming up the garden path. But if the same Londoner were to talk about 'a Congolese friend', a Tanganyikan or a Sudanese, the neighbour would normally expect to see somebody black.

It is a considerable achievement for a tiny white community in the middle of Africa; the 'public image' that springs to mind – or the British mind at least – at the mention of the word Rhodesian is not one of the eight million black citizens of this huge territory the size of Western Europe. Instead, it is the image that has been implanted by two wars, by the (white) Rhodesian contingents in five Coronation processions, by films and books, and by brave tales of settler deeds in childhood magazines. It is the image of a white-skinned man in a broad-brimmed 'wideawake' hat, with a tanned face and eyes searching the far horizon. In the background there may be a horse, and perhaps a faithful coloured man of indeterminate tribe, and somewhere in the picture is a gun that the Rhodesian knows how to use. Dismiss this as romanticism, if you like, but it is the image in the mind of many a British Cabinet Minister as he climbs into his aeroplane seat at London Airport, impressing him and intimidating a little. It is an image, in other words, that is politically profitable.

Now it is fascinating to track down who precisely this prototype Rhodesian can be. He is certainly not Sir Roy Welensky, a burly man whose political career stems from engine-driving on the railways and trade-union organization. He is not Sir Edgar Whitehead, the semi-recluse whose public life represents a triumph of will-power over poor hearing and failing eyesight; he has a large farm near Umtali, but the library or the council chamber is his natural habitat. No, the answer is to be found two generations away. The 'Rhodesian', in fact, is that redoubtable African, Cecil Rhodes. His was the canny mind that sensed the importance of giving the country a distinctively Anglo-Saxon name, so blotting out older descriptions like 'Mashonaland' and 'Zambesia'. Rhodes had an instinctive flair for public relations and image-making, for exploiting the emotional advantages of the British connexion while minimizing its political restraints.

The settlers have learned from him the trick of plastering the word 'British' on institutions – like the British South Africa Police – while keeping the realities of power firmly in white Rhodesian hands. The British South Africa Police is a mounted, armoured, para-military gendarmerie, altogether free of any Whitehall control. The British flag flies bravely outside the palatial mansion in one of Salisbury's all-white suburbs where the Governor-General, a British peer, resides. But woe betide him if he seeks to intervene in the realities of Rhodesian political power, as did one of his predecessors in 1957. That fearless man sent a fourteen-page memorandum to Lord Home at the Commonwealth Relations Office, detailing what he considered to be wrong with Sir Roy Welensky's proposals for constitutional change. He got no reply from Lord Home at all, and he was curtly informed by Sir Roy that he was 'not to report on political matters'. Any suggestion that the Governor-General's assent might be withheld from legislation was brutally dismissed, and the Governor-General himself was subsequently replaced.

Such are the realities of power. Let the visitor, then, make his little tour of the Federation to see how and where this settler power is based. His first surprise is to learn that the white Rhodesian today (like the ranchers of Calgary and Houston) is not a frontiersman at all. As far back as 1930, the shift to the towns had brought the urban portion of the total settler population to a point just above the half-way mark. By 1951, this had crept to sixty-five per cent, and the latest census figures show that the fraction is now approaching eighty per cent.

The white Rhodesian today is a townsman, and in a way this emphasizes his seldom spoken yet always present race neurosis. Far fewer of these privileged white people have the degree of day-to-day social contact with the African that was typical and normal in the real frontier days. And from this there follows the familiar human phenomenon: they fear what they do not know.

Correspondents from Europe and America who hurried by jet plane to Johannesburg after the Sharpeville shootings in March 1960 were unfailingly struck by one aspect of prosperous South Africa. It is perfectly possible to live in a comfortable white suburb, drive to work by super highway to one's office in town, lunch in a white man's restaurant – which restaurants are not ? – and return home having scarcely exchanged words with a black man. Indeed, one may even gain the subconscious impression that it is the white race which constitutes the majority. And so it is in the urbanized Rhodesia of today, though not of course as convincing as below the Limpopo. There is something enormously reassuring to the white Rhodesian, as he drives to his office in central Salisbury, to see soaring skyscrapers lining the boulevards, reaching up fifteen and twenty storeys in shimmering vertical lines of steel and glass, just as they do in Texas and California, in Calgary and Salt Lake City. The visitor bowling in from the airport is bound to be impressed, whether he likes it or not. The message is stunningly clear: this, say the skyscrapers, is White Man's Country; we have made the wealth here, we pay our way – and we pay for the health and welfare of the Native too. We run the country, and what we have we hold.

Until a couple of years ago, before the Whitehead administration's belated assaults on the social colour-bar, it was possible for the urban settler of Salisbury to visit any restaurant in town at lunchtime, knowing that no Africans would be there to disturb his susceptibilities. Now several of the large hotels are officially multi-racial, and you will see black men here and there – very much a minority, of course, because the economic barrier is highly effective. The visitor may ask his host if there is any simple way to get a comparison of the respective spending power of the two races. I myself was lunching with a man who is enmeshed in liberal politics and has a healthy respect for facts, and he referred me to the latest issue of the Annual Economic Report, published by the government printer. This revealed the average annual income of all white Rhodesian wage-earners as £1,209. For black Rhodesians, it was given as £87.

My first reaction was to assume, with irritation, that the £87 was a misprint. But then I remembered encountering this extraordinary wage-gap before, in annual reports or just in conversation with people. The proud foreman on the tobacco company's housing estate in Nyasaland had told me that he was the most senior African employee – and the highest paid. He had a house of his own at a subsidized rental, and a salary of £16 a month, far above the level of the apprentice Africans in the factory, 'just out of the bush', who earned between £4 and £5. I remembered having cross-questioned my informant on that occasion before I could be sure that I had heard him correctly; yes, it was £4 or £5 a month. And the Africans were not, despite the settlers' description, just out of the bush or down from the trees; they were just out of mission school.

The great income gap between the races in Rhodesia is partly excused by whites through the supposed need of 'inducement'. The white officials at that tobacco factory in Nyasaland were making between fifty and a hundred per cent more than they would ever have earned for doing the same job in Britain. 'Got to pay inducement to get them out here,' was the laconic comment of the white manager. And the same excuse echoes along the Copperbelt of Northern Rhodesia.

Moses Chona, let us call him, has been in the copper mines for a dozen years, sweating it out with the drill in humid, choking dust underground, and gradually working his way through a series of jobs to the highest-paid surface worker's category – for Africans. He will earn £720 this year, and that puts him into a pretty exclusive club, for among the three million African people of Northern Rhodesia, not one in ten thousand achieves that level of income.

Jacobus van der Merwe – the name is fictitious, of course – is, like fifty-five per cent of Northern Rhodesia's white copper miners, a South African. Let us say that Jacobus is not, unhappily, one of Mother Nature's most gifted creatures, and that because of his limited intelligence (lower than that of Moses Chona) he has been assigned the simplest sort of job and has never been promoted. For a dozen years now, he has been a concentrator crusher operator. He will earn £1,898 this year.

It is often said in excuse that Chona's wages, and those of Africans who are paid much less, should be seen only in company with the subsidized housing, medical services, and other benefits of real cash value which are added. But the same is true for van der Merwe, whose larger house in a better-serviced part of town has a beautiful green lawn, and whose gleaming car compares favourably with Chona's motor-cycle.

You do not have to be an inquisitive liberal to formulate the next question, for it is asked by thousands of ordinary Africans on the Copperbelt. Suppose that an African government directed policy in the capital, would this cruel – and costly – system of social and economic discrimination be allowed to continue? Not long ago the question, asked as it was – if only in silence – by tens of thousands of Africans, had no real answer; it was hopelessly hypothetical.

That was before the independence procession had begun. But it is hypothetical no longer. Today there *are* African governments in Nigeria, in Ghana, in Tanganyika, in Sierra Leone – to name only four English-speaking territories. And the Northern Rhodesian with a black skin has only to look across the border, to what was once the Belgian Congo, where, long before independence, Africans were driving trains, operating complex mining machinery, and performing dozens of sophisticated industrial jobs which are still blocked and barred to them in this 'British' territory, through the 'job classification' negotiated by the white Mine Workers' Union. Now, on the other side of a mere line drawn across a map, the black Northern Rhodesian knows that men of his own skin colour – indeed, perhaps of his very own tribe – are in political control of their affairs.

One knows with what disgust these black Rhodesians regard the manoeuvres of Sir Roy Welensky and the other white politicians in Salisbury. One wonders also what their feelings are when they pass any one of a hundred public buildings from Chingola to Lusaka where that banner of freedom, the Union Jack, floats comfortingly against the African sky. Symbols are just as good or just as bad as people make them. If the African in the Federation today has lost all faith in the Union Jack – and it is the recurrent subject of bitter comment to visitors like myself – then it is not the fault of the flag but of purblind timid politicians in London who have failed to stand up to Sir Roy Welensky, or Sir Edgar Whitehead, or Winston Field or their settler predecessors.

If the visitor wants to know what Africans are thinking, it seems likely that the white settler may be wondering too. And this is indeed what he does, perpetually. Behind the prosperous, sun-tanned countenance that greets the visitor's eye is a neurotic struggling to escape. Go to a Sunday-morning cocktail party in the safe white citadel of suburban Greendale, just outside Salisbury, and you will see how, fight as they will to resist it, the new Bourbons surrender themselves to The Topic. Race relations. Black versus white. 'What are They thinking?' 'I give it another fifteen years before the balloon goes up.' 'Good old Roy.' It is dull, interminable, and exhausting.

For as long as I have been concerned with African affairs, this has been The Topic among the political rulers of Rhodesia. It seems a tragic waste of brains and energy – and time. It has only one parallel: the same ceaseless subject dominates the club bars, the living-rooms, the stoeps, the kitchens – even the bedrooms – of the richest nation on the continent, South Africa. To me it is the symptom of a sick civilization, and instinct tells me that therefore it cannot last; though one has but to look at the Royal Rhodesian Regiment and the airborne commandos on manoeuvre to wonder if the latter-day Bourbons will not pull down the temple with them as they go. There is something tragically barren about this neurotic, ubiquitous debate that – in white Rhodesia today – is never adjourned. Go to one of the newly independent African states, and you will hear no echo of it: in Lagos the talk is of the new £700 million development plan; in Dar-es-Salaam it's the new university college, and a dozen other projects (including assistance to the liberation movements in neighbouring territories of southern Africa). In nearly all the emergent capitals there is a fresh, outward-looking vitality – the 'surge of new effort', as the Indian Ministry of Finance described it. (Mr Desai has estimated that it adds five or six per cent to national productivity.)

What a wretched contrast greets the visitor to Salisbury. And again I recall the Sunday-morning drinks in Greendale, for there in the room with me were two of Welensky's Federal Ministers, several leading members of his United Federal Party, some senior Civil Servants, (solidly U.F.P., of course), and local businessmen who supported the present régime. They were frontiersmen all, and bundles of nerves from my own observation. The talk was negative, inward-looking, and centred wholly on the one, never-ending subject that in my own mind I now call The Topic.

It seems to me that this purely personal, qualitative assessment – based not on just that one party in Greendale, but on a dozen gatherings of settlers like it elsewhere – more closely reflects the mood of white Rhodesia today than all the statistics I can marshal on the printed page. And I had confirmation of this not long ago from a source I regard as impeccable: one of Her Majesty's Ministers, whom I should not identify, perhaps, any further than to describe him as a loyal Tory.

I have a feeling [he told me] that those politicians in Salisbury have wasted three good years since the troubles broke out in Nyasaland and they started their big crack-down in Southern Rhodesia. Instead of developing a positive policy of their own, they've put most of their energy and a great deal of legalities and mathematics into trying to block us from making any changes in the northern protectorates. They've poured money into trips to London and fees to Voice & Vision trying to hobble us by getting at the back-benchers in my party. But the really wise thing would have been for them to do a little positive, long-range thinking. Sooner or later they've got to come to that anyhow.

The most positive piece of planning, in terms of race relations, that is visible to the visitor today, is the impressive build-up in the military forces of the Federation. I can remember when in 1955 the defence budget was £3·5 million, and I was not especially conscious of troops or air-force contingents. But by 1962 this figure had more than doubled, to £8 million, with the promise of further increases to come. 'We may have to restrict the expansion of our social services in the interests of national security,' said Sir Roy Welensky in 1962, preparing the white minority for the next stage in this process. And to the eye of today's visitor, there is an unhealthy devotion to accumulating arms that can only be directed against citizens of the Federation itself, since no visible enemies are threatening the borders. In the bar of Meikle's and the Ambassador and the other fashionable settler hotels, the talk is of the special air regiment – all white, of course – and the light aircraft that will be needed for 'spotter' work, as well as the jets and the armoured cars to be ordered.

Bar gossip, as every political correspondent knows, provides a valuable account of the political mood in any country – but one notoriously subject to rumour and exaggeration. Very well, then, what are the facts?

In 1955 the total expenditure by the federal and territorial governments on defence, justice, and police came to £7·6 million, while the budget for health services was £5·3 million. Five years later, the expenditure on health was £7·4 million, while the security budget had soared to £15·6 million – an increase of 102 per cent. This was a rate of increase far in excess of anything comparably achieved by the United States, the Soviet Union, or, indeed, most of Rhodesia's neighbours on the African continent. It had only one parallel, and that, needless to say, was on the other side of the Limpopo. South Africa possesses the melancholy distinction of having boosted its military budget by a slightly higher percentage during the same period. White Rhodesians, seriously and defensively, quote this comparison to show that they are 'moderate' politically.

What really matters in the overall picture is how a nation allocates its house-keeping money. And in the case of Rhodesia the 'sickness' of political thinking can be proved by a very simple tabulation. Total security costs in the Federation five years ago, and total expenditure on public health services, were given about equal priority. The former took 8·8 per cent of total revenues, the latter 6·2 per cent. In 1959 came the blow-up in Nyasaland, the bannings and imprisonments in all three territories, and in 1960 the armed police actions in Southern Rhodesia when, for the first time in more than sixty years, the security forces shot and killed Africans. In that year, health declined to 5·9 per cent of total expenditure, while security soared to 12·4 per cent. No independent African politician had any part in the decision to establish this new scale of priorities – a decision which made security twice as important as health, and left education trailing far behind. And Africans in the Federation – who have never been stupid people and are today better-informed than their white masters are willing to believe – cannot help but compare this topsy-turvy state of affairs with conditions in Tanganyika next door. There, too, is an African country of eight million people. But there the white minority is far smaller. It is a country governed by its African majority. And there health and education have their proper place as two of the top-priority items in the budget; expenditure on security – as is only sensible – trails far behind.

The Salisbury settlers might be morally justified in determining public expenditure in the way that they do if it were only their own funds and their own standard of living that they were manipulating. But the truth is that they are distorting the economy of not just their own 312,000 people, but of eight million Africans as well. The Annual Economic Report reveals the total cash income for the respective communities. Lumping the Asians with the Europeans, as the Report does, (they are still largely neutral in the political battle), it appears that the total of their personal incomes is £195 million; that of the Africans is just under £100 million. On an average, therefore, the individual African during the course of the year earns one fiftieth the income of his more privileged neighbours. In fairness it should be noted that the Africans outside the cash economy altogether have their own little patches of ground for food-cultivation. This 'subsistence farming' produces crops worth perhaps £40 million – another £5 per head – each year.

The white settlers can claim – and do – that when it comes to personal income tax, it is they who 'foot the bill'. This is a half-truth. Most Africans are so meagrely paid that they do not reach the lowest income bracket subject to tax. For the few who do, there is a curious government policy of 'leniency', which means that the law is not enforced. But on this point it is worth examining the comment of a distinguished Canadian constitutional lawyer, Dr Thomas Franck, who has recently conducted an exhaustive survey of the Federation, with the help of the American university where he teaches, the Ford Foundation, and the Canadian Institute of International Affairs. The results are printed in his book *Race and Nationalism*,* and on the aspect of African income tax he has this to say:

The 'leniency' has, however, been used as justification for the imposition and enforcement of other, special taxes. ... These are grossly discriminatory since they are paid by persons who, but for their colour, would on the basis of their incomes be paying no taxes at

* Allen & Unwin, London, 1960.

all. Chief among them is the head tax or hut tax: in Northern Rhodesia £1 per year paid by every male over 18, in Nyasaland 30s., and in Southern Rhodesia £2. Although these impositions do not appear particularly large, they constitute a major source of revenue to the territorial governments.

Professor Franck notes that this African tax produces for Southern Rhodesia nearly £1·5 million a year, or about one sixth of the total collected from the income and profits taxes levied on all white settlers and business corporations.

Not all Africans are permanent wage earners with cash incomes; it is just the fortunate minority who have ready cash to meet this charge. Yet the head tax is meticulously and strictly enforced; it has been, since the 'Company days', the white man's device for driving the black man from his village into the labour market, to work for the settler. This is not a personal opinion or biased deduction; it was the stated purpose of the levy when originally introduced. The effect is certainly impressive, if not particularly humane. Everywhere in the Federation you find African men making the necessary arrangements to leave their farm, their family, or their village and find work to 'earn the tax money'.

Flat-rate taxes like the head tax are notoriously unfair. But in most countries where they exist, at least rich and poor alike are caught by them. Not so in British Central Africa. There the head tax hits only the poor (for whom it sometimes represents ten per cent of income); it is levied solely on a basis of skin colour, and paid only by Africans. It is taxation levied by a white minority holding full political power on a black majority holding none. It is, to drag up a hoary phrase from a half-forgotten past, 'taxation without representation' in a territory proclaiming itself 'British' and flying the Union Jack. The whole crass business is a source of never-failing astonishment to the visitor, and of embarrassment to settler administrations which are professedly determined to remove the 'pinpricks' of race discrimination. Indeed, the Whitehead régime in Southern Rhodesia attempted a couple of years ago to appease African resentment and disarm a little of the overseas criticism by introducing a poll-tax of £5 a head on the white settlers. The angry uproar from Southern Rhodesia's outraged Bourbons was so great that the measure had to be withdrawn.

English and American history is signposted by disputes over taxes which pointed the way to great political upheavals. And although this does not seem to have registered yet with the Bourbons in their curious isolation, there have already been tax riots in all three constituent territories of the Federation. But in a nation that has only half a dozen daily newspapers, all but one of them settler-owned and with monopoly positions in their various areas, this simple and basic point does not seem to have been accepted or recorded. It can be confirmed readily enough by talking to the political leaders of the African nationalist parties. It can even be confirmed by some British colonial Civil Servants, if they could only be persuaded frankly to review the causes of disturbances in the recent past. The white masters in Salisbury are unaware, of course, that there have been tax riots – though they would agree that there have been disturbances on the dates in question, incited by 'extremist agitators'. It is the Bourbon instinct, when there is a rumbling outside, to order someone to close the shutters.

Indeed, sheer ignorance of the disgraceful *facts* of racial discrimination is a typical characteristic of these cheery and apparently relaxed white people one meets as a visitor to Rhodesia. Let us suppose that your host is, like two-thirds of present-day white Rhodesians, a man born in some other country who arrived here not so long ago to settle. (He is, in fact, a white settler, even though the term was ruled to be 'unparliamentary' and out of order during a recent debate in the legislature.) Mr Smith, we'll say, is twenty-nine years old, and has three young children; before he left his home in Birmingham, he had been an office worker. He had earned £1,200 a year, or slightly less than his older brother, an office worker as well.

Now, within a few months, life has been transformed for him. There was the magic of the overnight flight itself; from grey skies and drizzle on a Thursday evening to the hot blue cloudless sky of Africa the next day. There was his first sight of the fruit stalls heaped with bananas, grapes, oranges, and fresh ripe pine-apples, all at half the price they had been in Birmingham. Men and women were doing their shopping in modern and luxurious stores. And their clothes were so informal: the men in casual open-necked sports shirts; the women in summery fashions. The children looked sun-tanned and healthy. And parked in solid phalanxes, up the length of one street and down every other were cars, cars, cars – cars gleaming in the exotic colours of Hollywood musicals, lots of estate cars, cars on the lavish ratio of one at least for every white family – proportionately three times as many as there were in England.

Mr Smith soon finds that there are a good many two-car families; in quite ordinary white households, the husband has bought a little 'mini' as a runabout for his wife. Purchase tax at brutal U.K. rates is unknown – the tax simply doesn't exist. Of course, there is transport and excise to pay, but cars are still cheap. There is a lot of talk locally about the big new pipeline to be built, to bring the 'crude' up from the Indian Ocean to the new refinery.

And speaking of the Indian Ocean, the Smiths cannot help noticing those gay travel posters in the windows of the numerous travel bureaux, with their pictures of other white people swim-ming from golden beaches lined with coconut palms. Is it far? Is it expensive? No, to both questions. 'Everyone goes down to Beira,' they are told. (Not, perhaps, Moses Chona, but we're not talking about him or even really thinking about him at the moment.)

But there is also a recreation wonderland awaiting the Smiths in Rhodesia itself. And – within the white community – there are no class-barriers to close any part of it off; the Hurlinghams and the Cowdray Parks of Central Africa are open to all, one man's money is as good as another's, and there is no 'accent problem'. So the Smiths learn that they can join a sailing club or a polo club, whenever they like. If they prefer golf, they can choose the local club or motor up some time to Nchanga, rated by Bobby Locke as the finest course in southern Africa. For trout fishing, there are streams in the Inyanga highlands that are just waiting for the fly – as rich as the Test or Wetherall, but without 'restrictions' and a lot easier on the pocketbook.

There is cricket summer and winter; there are mountain holidays in the Chimanimani Range, where the white-painted hotels with their broad terraces make you think of Lucerne in high summer; and there is a two-week safari with guides, up in Northern Rhodesia, available every year from July to October and not just for film stars. Rhodesians and South Africans (white, of course) turn out in force, and they are people with quite ordinary incomes. And, finally, there are the Victoria Falls, and the mysterious ruins of Zimbabwe, and the many National Parks where the Smiths may see and photograph lions, zebra, elephants, giraffes, and so on – in colour, of course.

Mr Smith has a pleasant surprise awaiting him at the office on Monday. For doing the same work, at the same seniority, in a commercial operation precisely like the one he left behind in Birmingham three days before (but in a more modern office), he will now be earning an annual income of £1,733. More than £1,200 of that is tax-free, and there would be only a modest levy on the remainder – of £40 or so – if Mr Smith were not to claim any exemptions. But in view of his new earning power, he decides to set aside £100 a year for a medical aid society and to save £100 a year through the pension fund operated by his firm. The personnel office works out the figures and brings Mr Smith the happy result: on his salary of £1,733, his total annual income tax will be precisely £0 0s. 0d. The exemptions to which he is entitled have made his income wholly tax-free. (This is, in fact, a specific example cited in the Rhodesian parliament by the Federal Minister of Finance.)

There is only one cloud in this new Central African sky: the 'gearing-up' programme for the police and military forces may mean a few pounds on the tax bill next year. Mr Smith is vaguely aware of this; he learns, too, that like all men of European racial stock, he is liable for call-up in the Federal forces. Someone at the office may ask him if he has thought of volunteering as a 'Special' – the British South Africa police maintains a reserve force of 11,000 special constables, all white, of course, for 'emergencies' – or of joining the Territorials, nine battalions of infantry and two of artillery.

The next week-end the Smiths go to their first 'sundowner' at the cosy home of white neighbours in all-white Greendale. Drinks are served by a semi-invisible black man, addressed as 'boy', though in fact himself the father of three children just like Mr Smith. He has had two years of primary schooling and is regarded by those present as semi-civilized. Doubtless, in an English-speaking context, he is. Equally, of course, these white people would probably not quite fit in if Peter took them home to his Bemba village. Peter sends a shilling a month to his branch of Mr Kaunda's African nationalist party, and is quietly determined that before he dies he will go at least once into a polling booth and vote for the politician of his choice. He has a cousin, now working in Tanganyika, who first voted two years ago.

It comes as rather an effort for Mr Smith to sit down and write a letter 'home'. Birmingham now seems very small, very grey, and far away. He is now earning much more than his older brother (whose salary is heavily depleted by P.A.Y.E.) and wouldn't consider trading jobs with him. He can already see himself, in a year or two, flying 'home' like other Anglo-Rhodesians (with interesting detours via Nairobi, Athens, or Cairo) for a summer visit, perhaps in time for the Test match at Edgbaston. He will stay in the best hotels, of course. But home is now really Rhodesia. It has become so with remarkable speed. And Mr Smith is already experiencing another Rhodesian phenomenon: the rationalization process.

He came out to Salisbury knowing perfectly well that there was some kind of race problem – though nothing was said about it, just as no population figures were given, in the forty-eight-page coloured brochure that he received from Rhodesia House in the Strand. But since his arrival (and this could apply equally well to Bulawayo or Ndola or a dozen other white communities), he has seen strangely little of any Africans. He is unlikely see any more of them unless some business trip takes him down past the Native bus station and the ranks of '2nd Class Taxis', and then – literally – across to the other side of the tracks. On his way towards the railway freight yards, he may catch a glimpse of the dust, mud huts, pavementless filth, and apparently happy squalor of Harare. If he were an experienced anthropologist, he might know that protein-deficient, bilharzia-ridden, landless peasants in many countries do not inevitably wander around with long and tragic faces.

But by now, in his second week, Mr Smith will almost certainly have experienced the 'cheek' of some irritated, half-educated, black Rhodesian. Mrs Smith, at home in sunny Greendale, has learned that on their tax-free £1,733 they can easily afford a houseboy and a gardener, as well as a nanny or a cook when necessary. And this in turn has brought its problems. She finds – as ten thousand settler wives have learned before her – that 'Africans have no sense of time', that spoons disappear, that nanny fails to arrive (no phone call, no explanation) when she was counting on her so as to leave the children and go out to a tea party. She needs no further convincing that the blacks are irresponsible.

The rationalization process is predictable. The Smiths, not inexplicably, want to keep what they have; they don't want to go back to Birmingham, high taxes, lower salary, less glamour, and no savings account. They find that they have joined a fortress community; although the moat is invisible, it is real enough, and eight million sullen people are massed on its other bank. Among the 312,000 defenders in the citadel of Easy Living, the rule of mutual survival is 'Thou Shalt Conform'. (It has been said by one Cambridge historian that fifty years of settler politics have failed to create a two-party system in Rhodesia; government consists of the one-party machine plus a row of critics whose viewpoint has always been the same – that the government is surrendering to the Natives and to Whitehall and is failing to stand up for Settlers' Rights.)

Like most people in most communities anywhere, the Smiths don't enjoy being badgered with politics and public affairs for twenty-four hours a day. And yet, unless they adopt a simple, pat formula, that is precisely what the race problem becomes for them. 'A dripping tap. Drive you mad if you go on thinking about it all the time, old chap. Leave it to Roy and Edgar. Leave it to those who've been here a bit longer; they *know* the African.'

And, after all, only a small percentage of people in the average community feel any positive urge to go exploring in a two-culture world. Studying Rhodesia's central, unresolved political problem takes time and effort; you can't deal with it on paper, you can't write a cheque to settle it by post. It means discovering Harare or New Highfield, it means meeting Africans whose first language is not your own, it means *effort* – an effort which is simply beyond most people in Rhodesia's settler community, as indeed it would be for most people in Reading, or Bristol, or Dagenham, communities of similar size. This, understandably, is why Rhodesia's little band of liberal reformers consists of people who are almost always highly educated and above the intellectual average – doctors, lawyers, students, professors, clergymen – people who feel the prick of conscience, who are self-confident and secure, who are not afraid to be different from their neighbours, who read books, who will make the effort after working hours to go out and meet African neighbours (across the tracks) instead of relaxing, with feet up, before the tiny TV screen.

The Attitude Survey carried out with Ford Foundation funds under the initiative of Dr Franck sustains this contention. It also indicates that five years is the maximum period for most new settlers to retain any liberal ideas on the race question. After that, they join the other Bourbons in their gold-plated citadel. It is all very understandable, depressing, and explosive. And it is, of course, the present state of play on the white side of the moat, in the dangerous game we call the politics of partnership.

2 Sex and Settlers

'The conqueror considered . . . that one of the fruits of victory was the women of the conquered race.' MAX BUCHAN, Rhodesian M.P.

Fear, lust, and greed play an important role in shaping the conduct of public affairs in any society. But in the racially-polarized politics of Rhodesia, these familiar sins have constituted an outstandingly important factor.

Sex, especially, has been such a potent force in settler politics that it becomes more and more astonishing to discover how slight are the references to it when Rhodesian affairs are discussed – in print, in parliament, and in private conversations. Perhaps this is the normal operation of a deeply implanted Puritan inheritance. All the same, the more one examines the origins of the race battle now raging in the Rhodesias, the more one wonders whether sex lusts and sex fears may not be the origin of it all.

It is not considered good taste to raise the matter in a House of Lords debate, and you will find scant reference to the subject in all the millions of words that have been spoken there about Central Africa's partnership problems over the last twenty years. The standard works of reference, and the recent spate of topical books about Rhodesia, are notably reticent. And yet, if one turns to that lowest common denominator, the daily newspaper, one finds that what is raging between the races is in some senses a sex war.

'Would you want your daughter to marry an African?' is the standard phrase that appears in letters to the editor, when the racial debate hits rock bottom. That is the polite, modern phrase for it. When you leaf back through the yellowing files of pre-war newspapers, and those before the First World War when the original pioneers were still settling in, you find the lust-fear psychosis raging in cruder terms. You learn that 'the carnal desires of the Munt are well known', and you encounter oblique references to the wild stories that circulated at the time of the Mashona and Matabele risings – folk legends that are still passed down in hushed kitchen conversations, tending to dwell on the killing of women and their daughters, and the violation – before or after death – of their bodies.

The modern, civilized state of Rhodesia has a past of particularly brutal racial clash. It is worth bearing in mind. The Americans have their Civil War to recollect, but the Southern planters cannot cite any widespread slaughter in which they were the intended victims of black people. Yet that, specifically, is what happened in Central Africa, and there are some still alive today who can remember it. More importantly, it was the very people who survived their intended slaughter who were to assume political control a few years later. It is not surprising, therefore, that they should have packed the statute book with punitive legislation. Even before they had achieved majority control, they produced the Masters and Servants Ordinance and the notorious Immorality and Indecency Suppression Act of 1903. It is only fair to note that there was some protection for black as well as white in the first of these; but the second law constituted a staggering display of racial bias. It provided for a sentence of up to five years hard labour for a 'Native' convicted of illicit sexual relations with a white woman. But on the reverse situation – a white man found having intercourse with an African woman – the law was silent. There was good reason for this – as the pioneer legislators well knew, the practice was already widespread.

Disinterested observers of the Rhodesian political scene are not numerous; often they are English patricians of title, education, and wealth who do not feel the passionate sense of 'commitment' that compels settler solidarity. Such an observer was Colonel Sir Aubrey Woolls-Sampson, who made a leisurely and attentive tour of the Rhodesias before the First World War and a few years after the passing of the Immorality Act. In Salisbury, he summed up his impressions in a public speech.

I am convinced that the crimes of the Native against white women are largely influenced by the infamous behaviour of a considerable class of white men in their relations with Kaffir women. In Northern Rhodesia I found a great many of the white men living with Kaffir women. . . . In Matabeleland the number living with Native women is positively appalling.

Sir Aubrey referred to the *lobola* system practised by the Africans for several hundred years, but now coming under pressure from the white man. (The *lobola* is a 'bride price' or dowry, which has to be paid by the prospective bridegroom to the parents of the girl he is to marry.) It was one of the props stabilizing the family in a community where there were no legal or religious sanctions against desertion, and it took a man as much as two or three years to accumulate the full price – which was normally paid by instalments in the form of cattle or goods. In some tribes the young man might move to the girl's village and build his own hut there; towards the end of the betrothal period, the couple might begin to sleep together.

It is not difficult to imagine the anguish which many a young black man of the Rhodesias suffered in the early days of white occupation, when his sweetheart was suddenly taken from him. Sometimes it was the weak will of the girl or of her father, confronted by the white man's money; just as often it was the effective twirling of a loaded pistol by one whose people now held the country by military force. Sir Aubrey reported:

I found that some women had been three parts paid for by Kaffirs . . . and then the white man came along and offered some payment, and the girl's father had let them go. Whenever a Kaffir was treated in that way . . . he hated the white man.

Did the white settlers of Salisbury and Bulawayo make the effort to consider what a legacy of hate they were leaving?

Sir Aubrey ended his speech to the settlers of Salisbury by quoting an old African Chief, who had told him: 'There will never be peace between the black man and the white man . . . until you give our women the protection you demand for your own.'

The settlers gave the old Chief his answer four years later, when they pushed a companion piece of legislation through the

Southern Rhodesian legislature. This made it additionally an offence for a 'male Native' to make 'indecent suggestions' to a white woman. But the act specifically exempted a white man who made such overtures to a black woman.

Before this, the legislature had imposed the death penalty for rape, and for attempted rape as well. The law was not, in print, racial; in practice, it was wholly so. The penalty was not applied if the raper was a white man, whether his victim was black or white. And, curiously, it was not applied to an African if his victim was an African. Clearly one principle shone through all this legal tangle – the purity of white womanhood – the same battle-cry that has inflamed white passions in the southern United States for two centuries.

Rhodesia in those days was under 'Company' control, but the decisions of the British South Africa Company Administrator and his settler legislators were subject to review by the Imperial government. And in those days there was, at least, a watch-dog of the Colonial Office there in Salisbury, in the person of a Resi-dent Commissioner who could, and did, occasionally intervene as the trustee of Native interests. It was a role well understood in India, as in Nigeria and the rest of Britain's African colonies; but it was neither understood nor appreciated by the tough and vocal settler community of Rhodesia.

The Resident Commissioner intervened in 1908, when a black man was due to be executed for rape after conviction by the usual all-white jury, because the evidence seemed remarkably hazy. This was just as well since, after the reprieve, it had all proved to have been a case of mistaken identity; it was another African, equally innocent, whom the white woman in the case had intended to accuse. When the Colonial Office again inter-vened to reprieve a black man in a rape case two years later, there were public protest meetings in Salisbury and Umtali at which – the *Rhodesia Herald* reported – there were speeches pointing out that in the southern United States 'men had found it necessary to lynch and burn blacks who dare to molest women of the white race'.

One of those who drew a special round of applause was a

certain Mr Coghlan, who told the meeting that the settlers would have to resort to lynching if they could not trust the lawful authorities to give their women adequate protection. (There were, in fact, two attempted lynchings in 'Chartered' days, one stopped by the British South Africa police and the other by the eloquence of Dr Jameson.) Mr Coghlan, who was then practising law in the territory, was a South African, like most of the colonists, and had already become one of the handful of elected members in the all-white legislature. But even greater power lay ahead. As the acknowledged leader of the settlers, he was to visit London in 1921 to meet the Tory Colonial Secretary, Winston Churchill, having stopped off on the way, at Churchill's request, to confer with General Smuts in Cape Town. The Smuts–Churchill plan was to incorporate Rhodesia into an enlarged Union of South Africa. Coghlan not only fought this plan successfully; he also proved tough enough to persuade the Tory government in London to bring the period of Chartered Company rule to an end. More than that, his 'kith and kin' argument proved so effective with Churchill, then enmeshed in the Irish troubles and other colonial disturbances, that the loyal white settlers of Southern Rhodesia were rewarded with Crown Colony status, control of the legislature and the franchise, their own armed forces, and a seat at the conference table of the Empire Prime Ministers. Except for control of foreign affairs – and even Canada at this stage was still dealing with other nations through the British Foreign Office – the white Rhodesians were sovereign at last.

Coghlan, the South African, was the man who had done it; he became the first Premier of the new state – the title was later changed formally to Prime Minister – and as Sir Charles Coghlan received his Garter insignia at the hands of the Prince of Wales himself, when the prince made his African tour in the twenties. The body of Sir Charles now rests in the national Valhalla, the Matopo Hills, beside those of Rhodes and other heroes.

If the Charles Coghlan who got up to speak at that public protest meeting about the rape case had, as a thoughtful young attorney, espoused the cause of the black man – or like a subsequent Prime Minister, Garfield Todd – called for liberal reform of that same Immorality Act, then I think it needs no great insight to predict that he would have remained plain Mister Coghlan and speedily disappeared from public life. Two generations later, Garfield Todd's own Cabinet turned against him in the vote to amend the Act, and this defeat was prophetic. Within the year Todd had been turned out of office, and his party machine – what was left of it – annexed by Sir Roy Welensky's United Federal Party. Coghlan, of course, was politically in tune with his electorate on what one may crudely describe as the Sex Issue; indeed, it had bit so deeply into his mind, that he could forget all his legal training and, leaping to his feet at a public meeting, call for a lynching. He might, after all, have remained silent.

The Todd case is important to note, for the almost medical insight it gives into the Rhodesian mind. In forty years of settler politics, only one Prime Minister has been scuttled in office, and this accolade was accorded to the one reformer in power that the system ever produced. Garfield Todd was not, like so many of his countrymen, Rhodesian or South African born. He was a New Zealander, and a missionary to boot. In broad terms his mistake was to break the infallible rule for success in Rhodesian politics – 'Keep Right'. The man who wavers into middle ground soon finds his critics coming up thick and fast on the right. 'Soft on natives,' goes up the war-cry, the hallowed rallying call of every successful opposition party that has emerged so far. Sadly, too, all of Rhodesia's crises have centred on this one, ever-dominant issue of race, rather than on differences over economic policy or other matters normal in other countries.

Todd's final defeat came on the franchise issue: he called for a change in qualifications which would have added between 6,000 and 10,000 Africans to the voters' roll – safely below twenty per cent of the whites on the roll for the foreseeable future, as he pointed out. But that was enough; in defiance of party discipline his colleagues went into private caucus with Sir Roy Welensky and the U.F.P. high command. Mr Todd was cast away, and Sir

Edgar Whitehead invited to take the helm – and give it a good twist to starboard. The Todd Affair, as it is called in Rhodesia's white world, is regarded as a kind of warning buoy to steer the unwary away from the reefs of liberalism. But the franchise issue was only the overt occasion for Todd's defeat. Before it arose, the unlucky Prime Minister, in his outspoken opposition to the Immorality Act, had stabbed the deepest nerve nodule in every Rhodesian. It is a nodule with four components: unadmitted anxiety, a firmly suppressed sense of guilt, repressed lust, and a deep sexual fear of what the African may do if ever his turn for vengeance should come.

The television programmes about Rhodesia scrupulously avoid the sex issue. The normal run of Press comment does not touch on it. Yet the psychiatrists and race-relations experts who have studied the black–white problem in Africa are in no doubt that deep sexual guilt feelings, stemming from the rapine of pioneer days and the fear of future African revenge, are vital to an under-standing of the white man's behaviour where he is still in control of society. It may even be that this unrecognized, unmentioned sexual complex is the central driving force behind all the outward political actions of Rhodesia's white settlers.

No public figure, except the singularly bold Garfield Todd, has even dared to touch on this agonizing psychosis of the well-paid, well-fed – contented? – white Rhodesian. The former Prime Minister of Southern Rhodesia said, before he stepped from office:

We must make it possible for every individual to lead the good life, to win a place in the sun. We are in danger of becoming a race of fear-ridden neurotics, we who live in the finest country on earth.

The Rev. Ndabaningi Sithole, another clergyman-turned-politician, this time in the other racial camp, put his finger on the same raw nerve. Referring delicately to the deep psychological motive of white conduct, he wrote:

The African hates the white man's arrogance, his mania for humiliating him in the land of his birth. One of the reasons the white man fears granting the African full independence is that the African may use against the white man the hateful methods he has seen the white man use against the African.*

Unfortunately for race relations in the Rhodesias, events in the Congo have reinforced the deep-buried sexual apprehensions of the settler minority holding power in Salisbury. Not only were there the sensational Press accounts of the raping of white women in the chaos of the Belgian departure, but a chain of gossip, reaching from the Copperbelt down to the anxious kitchens of Salisbury and Bulawayo, retold with embellishments the eye-witness accounts of the Belgian refugees who came pouring across the border into the Federation during the first few weeks.

I am not at all convinced that the Congo precedent is valid for Rhodesia. Surely the one heartening feature of the hand-over in the English-speaking territories of Africa has been the absence of the very kind of revenge-lust that broke surface in the Congo. In Tanganyika and Nigeria, Ghana, Sierra Leone, and Uganda, there has been a dazzling ordinariness about life after Independence Day. Laconic policemen direct traffic and go about their business, government offices continue to issue dog licences and collect taxes. Of course, there is an important difference between any of these countries and the Rhodesias: in the Rhodesias, the African has so far been denied the apprenticeship in parliament, the courts, the Civil Service, and industry which Africans received in British colonies to the north. I have been taken along the long, cool verandas of the ministerial secretariats in Khartoum, four years after independence, and seen Sudanese principal secretaries, and clerical officers of various grades, working as smoothly as on the day before the hand-over. And this is as true of Lagos and of Freetown. One could do worse than remember that, when the U.N. set about bringing order back to the Congo, the two most efficient and disciplined forces, in the opinion of the world Press, were the Ghanaian regiments under Brigadier J. E. Michell and the unarmed Nigerian police under Commissioner Louis Edet.

* Rev. N. Sithole, *African Nationalism*, Oxford University Press, 1960.

It is up to the neurosis-ridden white masters of Salisbury whether or not they proceed to write themselves out a practical insurance policy on similar lines. The record at the moment is disturbing enough. It took the events of 1959–60 to make the Southern Rhodesian government decide to open its Civil Service to Africans after nearly forty years of all-white administration. Until then the Public Service Act had specifically barred Africans and those of mixed blood. In the Federal Civil Service, which under the terms of the 1953 plan is specifically required to be multi-racial, there are five grades. Only in Grade 1, which is administrative, can anything like policy be determined. In this grade there were, at a recent count, some sixty Africans. They were outnumbered by white Rhodesians in the ratio of 240:1. Even more significant was the composition of the non-policy Grades II, III, and IV, comprising 17,000 'drudgery' jobs. As of the end of 1962, how many white Rhodesians held these meaner posts ? None. Not one in the whole Federal service. It is hard to imagine more blatant racial favouritism.

Almost all the other requirements for a Congo situation are ominously shaping. There is not one African judge, not one African magistrate, less than half a dozen African barristers, not one African holding commissioned rank in the Army, not one African of *any* rank in the Royal Rhodesian Air Force, not one African at decision-making level in the Ministry of Finance. In the two northern protectorates, thanks to the Colonial Office presence, the picture is not all that bleak; but here we are talking about the national government and the Southern Rhodesian heartland, where wealth and power have their centre. 'Join the Regular Army of Rhodesia and Nyasaland,' say the posters. To be accepted as an instructor or non-commissioned officer, 'applicants must be physically fit in all respects and British subjects of pure European descent'.

One wonders what scientific processes are invoked as the potential recruits line up for their ethnic test. British subject, born in Soho of Italian parentage . . . suspiciously dark skin. Hmmm. Applicant claiming Welsh parentage. Crinkly hair. Fingernails not quite right. Birthplace given as Cardiff. Tiger

Bay ? British subject, born Kuala Lumpur, claims father was an engineer in the colonial service. Eyelids funny, suggest recheck. . . .

Ludicrous ? Not really. The white Rhodesians have simply started down the slippery slope that leads to the Population Register, the Race Classification Board appeals, the broken families, and all the other needless human wreckage of the South African system. *Somebody* must be busy doing racial classification in the armed forces. It is no accident that the entire Royal Rhodesian Air Force – fliers, ground crews, and all – is 'European'. There must be *someone* who sees that only whites are made officers in the Rhodesian Federal Army.

The whites parcel out among themselves more than ninety per cent and frequently a hundred per cent of the policy-making posts. To suppose that 312,000 white men, women, and children can provide sufficient numbers of *able* administrators to staff a modern state nearly as populous as Holland, spread over an area as large as Western Europe, surely implies arrogance, or greed, or stupidity, or all three at once. It also implies that there must be a great deal of inefficiency, with many a (white) square peg in a (supposedly multi-racial) round hole. Tests conducted by the officer selection boards in Canada and the United States in the Second World War revealed that about one man in four had the necessary intelligence, and leadership, to qualify for posts of command.

In the local, territorial administration of the two northern protectorates, of course, the manpower resources of Britain's Colonial Office are also brought into play. But perversely, the white Rhodesians in command of the Federal political machine are strenuously attempting to eradicate this 'alien' stream of manpower as speedily as possible. Lord Malvern announced that the 'Rhodesianization' of all public services would be his goal, from the moment that the Federation was established, and this policy has been pressed with notable vigour by Sir Roy Welensky since he succeeded to the premiership. Already, in Northern Rhodesia, the proportion of locally based men in what purports to be a purely Colonial Office operation approaches fifty per cent of the territory's Civil Service. And, of course, the Federal Civil Servants in Northern Rhodesia and Nyasaland have been Salisbury-controlled from the outset. This has been a factor of vital importance for Sir Roy and the settler administration in such crises as that over the Congo and the U.N. request to station observers on the frontier between Northern Rhodesia and Katanga. Even if Lord Home and a U.N.-reluctant Tory government in London had wished to cooperate with U Thant, they could have done so only at the risk of a head-on clash with white Federal Civil Servants and settler-controlled Federal troops. The machinery of British enforcement would have been a local Civil Service and a local police force, both now staffed to an alarming degree by settlers whose first loyalty is to their citadel in Salisbury.

Clearly this defensive staffing of the public services is not logical – at least, not in terms of the nation's most efficient use of its resources of managerial material. It is certainly not logical in terms of the proclaimed objective by Sir Roy and all the other white settler politicians of leading the African towards greater responsibility, and an ultimate hand-over of authority to African control. The best insurance policy against Congo chaos, if this were truly the settler objective, would be an accelerated programme of Africanization. That the settlers do not see this is fundamentally a measure of their fear.

An accident of history has created a minority ruling class in Rhodesia, clearly separated from their fellow citizens by the colour of their skins. The record of history suggests that when Bourbons hold power, they do not voluntarily surrender it. The Mandarins in a declining Imperial China, the Tsar and his nobles in our own century – all bear out the same record of human frailty. The privileged minority holding power does not give it up for a very simple, human reason: fear. They fear the consequences of surrender, and fear induces a paralysis not only of political action but even of the thinking process.

To see how things look to the black Rhodesian, you would have to have a kind of topsy-turvy Britain in which, let us say, the West Indian immigrants and all the other racial groups with dark skins, were somehow to take control of the nation overnight. We would still see some white people in the police forces – in the lower ranks, of course – and white recruits would be needed in large numbers to staff the kitchens and do the dirty manual work in the armed forces. But the 'British' army in charge of this black-occupied Britain would, naturally, be officered wholly by West Indians or Pakistanis. The Royal Air Force would be solidly in coloured hands. The pilots and ground crews alike would be men from India, Pakistan, Jamaica, and the rest. White faces would disappear from the House of Commons, except for those of some puppet white M.P.s – about 15 in every 100. The next national general election would consist of white Britons watching the black ones going to the polls, except for those lucky whites whose incomes were so high as to put them into the bracket of the top four per cent. White Britons, now, of course, compelled to carry 'passes' day and night, would be liable at all times to search and arrest by black police, with or without a warrant, under the British Law and Order Act (passed by a black majority parliament). A white man caught in the act of reaching downwards in the street – to pick up a coin he had dropped? – might be arrested by the black security forces on suspicion of intention to throw a stone and be imprisoned for seven months without option of a fine. At C.I.D. headquarters the interrogation of white suspects would be carried out by tough, black-skinned police inspectors; under the Emergency Regulations, a white man might be sent for three and a half years of imprisonment, or even five, without trial or the right of *habeas corpus*, to a special prison camp established for the purpose at Gokwe, in the peat bogs of the north tip of Scotland. Otherwise, your white suspect would go through the ordinary process of interrogation in Creole, the new national language, and trial (again in Creole) before a black, Creole-speaking judge.

The whole nightmare represents no more than what is going on at this precise moment in Rhodesia today – and going on, as the white Rhodesians never tire of reminding us, under the British flag. (My little fantasy, based wholly on existing parallels, did not by any means cover the available injustices such as

battalions of children in the streets for lack of places in schools.)
And, like a nightmare, it all seems wildly out of control. The
312,000 whites say that they are doing all they can for the blacks;
white taxes, they say, are paying for black education. The African
answer is, simply: Who asked you to ? It is a rude and ungrateful
reply, and it goes to the heart of the matter. It is the cliché of an
Africa that is now mostly free that black people are just not prepared to be grateful for favours; they want to make their own
policy decisions.

Wanting – even deserving – is one thing; achieving it is
another. Standing physically in the way of majority rule in
Central Africa at the present time is the Rhodesian Federal Army
and the Royal Rhodesian Air Force. Strengthening these two
highly effective barriers is the British South Africa police, consisting of 1,500 Europeans and 4,000 Africans. The loyalty of
these particular Africans is not in question; they have already
shown on occasions in 1960 and 1961 that they can charge a mob
or hold it. Every police station of the police has its wall (in the
staff quarters) with photographs of leading African nationalist
politicians. There is a bonus for those (white or black) who pass
the recognition test. This means not just recognizing Mr Nkomo,
Mr Matimba, Mr Silundika, or the Rev. Sithole; it means knowing the local and regional party officials, too. For emergency
situations there is the all-white reserve of 11,000 special constables of the police. These men have their uniforms ready; in
store there is enough ammunition for all of them.

Under what circumstances can we visualize the transfer by
these forces of their present allegiance, from the white government in Salisbury to a government made up mostly or wholly of
Africans ? Because it has to be recognized that such a transfer is
an integral part of the independence process, as it has actually
taken place in a dozen different territories of the Commonwealth.
In India there was the ceremonial departure of Admiral Lord
Louis Mountbatten, the last viceroy of India, but the formalities
were given their realism by the physical departure of the British
troopships and the lament of the regimental pipers of the Scottish units as the ships pulled away from the quayside.

If, as in Ghana or Nigeria, you have a great ceremonial occasion out of doors, with the lowering of the British flag for the last time and the raising of the flag of the new sovereign state, it is a British soldier who lowers the one and an African who raises the other. But behind the flag ceremonial, the real transfer of power takes place when a British commander hands over to his African successor, and in the Ministry of Defence a white official hands over to an African Minister. In all the discussion of the Rhodesian dilemma, there is seldom any mention of this actual process. No one, in his heart of hearts, can visualize it. I am sure Sir Roy Welensky cannot, nor his white Minister of Defence, nor his army and air-force commandants.

That is not to say it cannot happen. There were many years during the Cyprus troubles when no one in Whitehall could visualize such a process there. Indeed, before it could come about there had to be a complete shift of political leaders at the top: the replacement of the unlamented governor, Sir Robert Armitage, by one (Sir Hugh Foot) more in tune with resurgent nationalism; and in Whitehall itself, the departure of Sir Anthony Eden from the premiership, and Lord Salisbury from the Foreign Office and Tory leadership in the House of Lords.

It is as well that we should realize the extent of rethinking, and perhaps the replacement of existing political leaders in Salisbury and Whitehall, which must be achieved before a real transfer of power in Rhodesia can be visualized at all. If Mr Butler shows more imagination and courage in the face of settler pressures than did Lord Home and Mr Lennox-Boyd when they were dealing with Rhodesian affairs, it should still be feasible to resume the orthodox process in the two northern protectorates – the process that leads in due course to a flag-lowering ceremony and the departure of the governor.

It is Southern Rhodesia that must inevitably be the final political battleground. The British government cannot recall its governor, because with the appointment of Sir Humphrey Gibbs, the Southern Rhodesians have now had recognized their right to choose a governor from among their own number. No British troops can ceremonially depart; the only hope must be that, in the normal processes of democratic government, there can come to power an African Prime Minister, whose African Minister of Defence would command the unquestioning loyalty of the (all-white) military commanders. Clearly the existence of a Federal government only acts as a confusing and delaying factor in facing up to this central problem; and this explains the bull-dog tenacity of Sir Roy Welensky and his settler supporters in resisting British and African demands that it is time to dismantle it.

Everything, therefore, depends on settler determination to resist any change in the conditions of power in the settler heart-land of Southern Rhodesia. And that, in turn, hinges on the fear, guilt, and other inner compulsions which motivate the outward political actions of the settlers. The basic question, indeed, is whether these motivations can be wholly eliminated and replaced by mutual trust between black Rhodesian and white.

In 1957 Mr Max Buchan, spokesman for the rich white farmers of the Gatooma district, introduced in Southern Rhodesia's all-white legislature, an amendment to the infamous Immorality Act of 1903. This was, by local standards, a 'liberal' motion; its effect was to make it an offence for a male white Rhodesian to have illicit intercourse with an African woman – to balance the existing measure, in other words, rather than revoke it.

Mr Buchan referred to that nightmare never far from the col-lective race memory of the white Rhodesians, the Matabele and Mashona uprisings of 1896–7. After they had been suppressed, he continued, the white males had taken a rather special kind of revenge:

The conqueror considered, in many cases, that one of the fruits of victory was the women of the conquered race. . . . While strong, lusty and victorious men are not likely to be subject to what one might term biological inhibitions, it remains for those who follow on to endeavour to stabilize the position as soon as possible.

During the same debate, a demand was raised by some southern M.P.s that the territory should adopt the South African system of official race classification, so that every Rhodesian would carry a card proclaiming whether he were black, white, or mixed.

The existence of a small and wretched community of half-caste people is often overlooked in the politics of Central Africa's partnership. Here, surely, is the most intimate kind of bridge between the races; these so-called 'Coloureds' are a visible product of racial partnership. Yet, tragically, they are rejected by white and black communities alike. The Coloured worker commands a little more pay than the African, but not enough usually to get him on to the voters' rolls. He is regarded as 'civilized' enough – just – to be liable for military call-up, as the African is not; but, like the African, he will never be made an officer. He is in a legal limbo; mostly he is lumped in with the Asians – i.e. the Indian shopkeepers – with whom he has no particular affinity (except a general similarity of colour and, by settler logic, therefore, a natural identity). He lives, physically, in a no-man's-land between the races, and his crime-rate is proportionately higher – according to the Plewman Report – than that of either the whites or the blacks.

The white Rhodesians do not make the mistake of the outside observer or visiting British Cabinet Minister; they are hyperconscious of their 'Coloureds', who act upon them as a kind of traumatic ethnic warning. The very existence of such people and their pitiful state in society serves as visible confirmation of all the racist theories held by the dominant white minority. There is not a settler who does not instinctively 'spot' the Coloured by some kind of automatic reflex; I have noticed white men do it while walking with me in the streets of Rhodesian towns. It is nothing much: just the momentary pause in conversation; an instantaneous, involuntary shrinking; and the talk continues as if nothing had happened.

The director of the Institute of Race Relations in London, Mr Philip Mason, who has spent tours of many months' duration in Central Africa while on a Rockefeller grant, has tried to unravel the complex strands of settler reaction to this almost unmentionable subject. He points out how, in pioneer days, the first Coloured children were the accidental result of some union of lust, not love. Afterwards, the white man looked on his momentary gratification with remorse and repulsion:

He determined, when he married, that he and his wife and children should be kept pure from such contamination. There must be no more half-breed children, no more marriages between his people and these people. To make sure, there must be no danger of the common interests, the shared misfortunes, that make love instead of lust. Because of his horror, the gap must be widened and fortified so that he should not cross it again.*

The crucial role of the sexual motivation has been cited also by Miss Margery Perham, the Oxford don who has spent months and indeed, cumulatively, years in Africa. In her Reith lectures on the B.B.C., she touched the raw nerve of settler apprehension.

The Germanic-speaking Europeans – British, Germans, Americans and Dutch – share a deep bias against inter-marriage with the Negro race. We cannot avoid confronting this granite-hard fact. It lies at the very heart of our present problem in Africa. This conscious or unconscious fear of race mixture accounts both for the white man's innermost ring of defence and for his outer ring of political, social and economic ramparts. It explains many of the news items we get from the southern United States . . . the Rhodesias . . . and Notting Hill, with the news of occasional retaliatory orgies of raping of white women in the Congo.

The sexual obsession is so integrally a part of Rhodesian public life that it must rank as a decisive force in the minds of today's white Rhodesians when they go into the voting booth. The nation's leading figures, starting with its first Prime Minister, Sir Charles Coghlan, and including a celebrated mayor of Salisbury, have espoused the call for racial purity. From earliest times the newspapers have used three set phrases for the same dreaded assault by the African on the white citadel – 'The Black Peril', 'The Social Curse', and 'The Great Offence'. Under these descriptions, the subject has been publicly and endlessly discussed at hundreds of public meetings and conferences of women's institutes.

* P. Mason, *The Birth of a Dilemma*, Oxford University Press, 1960.

At one of these latter, a principal speaker was Mrs E. Tawse-Jollie, who demanded that the legislature should act to restrict domestic labour by male Africans. She said: 'I do not think in recent years there has been a single Black Peril case which was not traced to a house-boy.' She went on to refer to the 'incredible carelessness' of new settlers in this matter, and blandly concluded:

The introduction of [African] women servants would solve one of the greatest difficulties about life in this country. . . . No native would attempt to rape a white woman if a woman of his own race was any-where near.

These are not the ravings of the lunatic fringe. Indeed, it is salutary to realize just how closely such extraordinary personal complexes are connected with practical politics. Mrs Tawse-Jollie was at that time a leading figure in the Federation of Women's Institutes, and therefore influential in forming public opinion both in print and on the platform. And she was more than that. When the decisive 1949 conference was held at Victoria Falls under the leadership of Sir Godfrey Huggins, the conference that was to call for 'amalgamation of Northern and Southern Rhodesia [with] complete self-government' and lead to the establishment of Federation in 1953, who should emerge as one of the principal speakers but Mrs Tawse-Jollie again. According to the *Rhodesia Herald*, Mrs Tawse-Jollie declared that: 'The bogey of the Black North would come south if there was no unity of government.'

The White Rhodesia Council, founded in 1949 to 'maintain the principle of white supremacy in Southern Rhodesia', is sometimes dismissed as a small, unrepresentative body. Both adjectives are true; the W.R.C. only represents the extreme right-wing of white politics in Rhodesia, and its membership has never been large. But there is a significant difference between its status and that of groups with similar aims in Britain and America. There, it is usual for such bodies to be written off as 'crankish' by the Press and for responsible political leaders to disown them. This was not the case in Rhodesia in 1949, when the W.R.C. was founded, since the new group's leading spirit was

Mr Charles Olley, a former mayor of Salisbury and still one of the most vocal and influential aldermen on the council of the city. As a small businessman with leanings towards journalism, he was able to make his views forcefully known in a very wide circle.

The W.R.C., therefore, was treated solemnly and respectfully by politicians and the Press – even when it was being criticized – whereas in any normal, balanced community it would have been ignored or laughed out of existence. With fanatic zeal, Olley and his associates played on settler fears from the start, in a campaign of innuendo associated with sex and the lavatory. They sometimes attributed the 'cheek of the natives' to the baleful influences of Communism, spreading up from South Africa, and to the British Labour Party; but an official W.R.C. circular, issued at the height of the settler campaign for Federation, gave another reason, calculated to appeal to the deepest ethnic fears:

Natives [are] collecting certain types of magazines depicting white women virtually in the nude. Unfortunately the natives do not see such photographs with the same artistic mind as the Europeans ... much of the insolence and arrogance on the part of the natives comes through this form of familiarity.

With equal fanaticism the White Rhodesia Council began to demand 'separate lavatory facilities' for white and black Rhodesians, hinting at the unwarranted intimacies and the invasions of privacy which might take place, and attacking African standards of cleanliness. The lavatory campaign again stimulated fears in the subconscious of white Rhodesia, and was a prime factor in maintaining total segregation in hotels (and, absurdly, even in parliament) for another ten years. In turn, it was one of the racial humiliations most resented by Africans, and stimulated the determination of their leaders to adopt a more militant African nationalism. When a former African 'moderate' not long ago abandoned his neutrality and joined up with Mr Nkomo and the nationalists, I asked him what had been the most important factor in his thinking. Without hesitation he said, 'the colour-bar and separate lavatories'.

In a nation where three out of four Europeans are now townsmen, the influence of Olley and his municipal segregationists has been disproportionately significant. The unspoken sex fear was revealed again in the municipal swimming-baths battle of 1961. The multi-racial reformers made this the battleground of one of their most successful campaigns. And, as in the American south, they won on technical grounds, though the white supremacists fought a bitter rearguard action that consumed the best part of a year. Afterwards, some municipalities said that they would simply close their pools; others spoke of 'separate but equal facilities', which promised, however, to consume unjustifiable amounts of capital. In Salisbury the baths were promptly put to good use by large numbers of Africans; most white Rhodesians stayed away from them.

As a delaying mechanism, the White Rhodesia Council has been all too effective politically. It campaigned for separate voters' rolls, and may regard the A and B rolls (segregated by income and education, nor race) in Southern Rhodesia's new Sandys–Whitehead constitution as a triumph, since the system replaces the old common roll. It wants all white municipal councils and all-white legislatures, with 'two or more' white men to represent African interests. With this goes an intensive campaign for independence from Whitehall and full Dominion status, and a call for white immigration on a gigantic scale. In Olley's words:

As the natives are so far behind, it is imperative that there shall be white supremacy for hundreds of years. . . . Actually, it is not their country; in fact, less so than that of Europeans from the point of view of [being] conquered territory.

Alderman Olley had no trouble convening an immigration conference in the Council Chamber of Salisbury itself, attended by municipal and Ministry representatives. It was here that Winston Field, a large-scale farmer of Marandellas, made his first public appearance, endorsing Olley's call for the ousting of Africans 'as far as possible in all spheres of employment' and their replacement by white immigrants for whom large tracts of unused land were – and are – being held in trust. At the 1958 election Mr Field's Dominion Party received more total votes than Sir Edgar Whitehead's U.F.P., and only the chance workings of the transferable vote system in certain constituencies prevented Southern Rhodesia then from getting a racist government as extreme as anything Verwoerd has schemed up south of the Limpopo.

Dr Richard Gray, formerly of London University and now lecturing at the University of Khartoum, has summed up the appeal of the W.R.C.:

Some . . . were inclined to dismiss Olley as an extravagant eccentric. But the fears he voiced were, for many, inescapable. And for most Europeans they still formed the hard bed-rock of reality on which they lived and reared their children.

Another British observer who attaches deep importance to the sex obsession in Rhodesian politics is one who himself became a settler and a politician. He is the Rev. Colin Morris, a rugged Lancastrian whose first parish after finishing his studies at Oxford had been among the coal miners of Yorkshire. He originally answered a call from the Free Church in Chingola, to go out to a ministry among the copper miners of Northern Rhodesia. From an original acceptance of segregation in church and parliament, he moved round to urgent espousal of the need for integration. And he put principles into practice, first within the church and subsequently, after resigning his pastoral charge, as a liberal reformer in politics. Behind all the political attitudes of the white settlers, he discovered, lay 'the great unspoken fear . . . so powerful that a conspiracy of silence shrouds it'. His recent autobiography* described the decisive role which, he maintained, this fear plays in the politics of Central Africa:

Every other justification for the colour bar can be annihilated by logic, but not this, for its emotional potential is such that the nerve of many Europeans who are on the point of abandoning their discriminatory attitudes fails them when the abhorrent prospect is described in concrete terms. It is this fear which the segregationist exploits to

* Colin Morris, *The Hour After Midnight*, Longmans, London, 1961.

provide the last and most effective shot in his locker. When he is really cornered ... he can blast his way out with the most overworked projectile in the racial battle: The Question.

'Would you like your daughter to marry an African?' Immediately all kinds of unspoken fears are exposed. The revulsion ... confounds logic. Those who can be persuaded to talk about it think in terms of white purity being ravaged by black savagery. Possibly the violence of the reaction stems from some atavistic dread deep in the primitive psychology of the race ... a tribal instinct for protecting the female as the bearer of the race's posterity.

Let us turn now to one of the most respectable of the segregationist sources, a typical member of the white settler 'Establishment', for this will give some inkling of the power of the sex argument and, by implication, the practical boundaries of political action that are imposed on any government in Salisbury.

Richard Haw was Vice-Principal of Domboshawa, the best-known trade training school for Africans in the Federation, when he wrote his testament of political theory, *No Other Home,* (published by Stuart Manning Ltd, Bulawayo, 1961), with a foreword by the former Federal Prime Minister, Lord Malvern, as the imprimatur of authority. Mr Haw had many charitable things to say about his African charges, and it was clearly a point of pride with him that he bore no burden of race hatred himself. He simply believed that it would be best for everyone if the white Rhodesian remained in political charge 'for the foreseeable future', which is also the only future Africans care about.

It was when he dealt with the great Sex Argument that he displayed the naked tenacity of the white settler to retain power:

One of the great fears of social integration is that it may lead to miscegenation. This fear drives many White to extremes, and is used as a political stick to beat a shuddering electorate. ... Although the process could ultimately eliminate the racial tensions now plaguing us, there exist strong objections to crossing. These are based on a wealth of statistical, psychological and anthropological evidence. Racial crossing ... is concurrently held in check by the mores of both Bantu and Whites. These inhibitions would ... surely be changed if social integration were facilitated. The consequences are undesirable in the present setting in southern Africa.

Apart from the fact that social mixing would encourage miscegenation, there is the fact that . . . racial tensions are thereby needlessly aroused. Infiltration of select areas by people of a different status or class causes these areas to lose their character, and land values consequently fall. . . . To encourage different culture groups and races to live together is sociologically unsound.

I have searched the 131 pages of Mr Haw's book in vain for so much as a trace of that wealth of scientific evidence which he claimed to be drawing upon in establishing his conclusions. As for the sociological unsoundness of mixed neighbourhoods, I wonder if Mr Haw has had the pleasure of living for a time (as I have) in any of the mixed suburbs of Accra, Lagos, Honolulu, Santa Monica (California), or Kingston, Jamaica. Those cities are in countries where in fact the majority race – whether it is white or brown or black – holds political power. I am not saying that they are suburbs without the ordinary stresses of suburbs anywhere. But I have played some very mixed tennis in all of them, and somehow survived the nightmare horrors of racially mixed swimming too, as well as dances in the evenings. Life in such places – provided that there is not a fear-ridden minority screwing down the political safety-valves – can be rather fun.

Mr Norman Manley, when he was Prime Minister of Jamaica, once discussed this subject with me – taking the West Indies as his practical political example. He maintained that a minority white group holding political power is paralysed by the sheer fear of retribution:

They are aware of a hundred unjust things they have done and they fear the vengeance of the black majority if it should ever get power. But this, in fact, is a misreading of human nature. No such vengeance was taken by us; it need not be taken elsewhere. Even where people of two different racial groups inhabit one country – and I say this from experience – there need be no tension if there is simply a normal democratic system, with a vote for every adult. Because the majority race knows that it is not holding anyone down by force, there is no guilt, no anxiety, and no tension.

There, surely, is the supremely practical example from a nation which has been through the racial mill and knows from experience what white Rhodesians insist that they can guess in advance by superior intuition. One of Mr Manley's countrymen in Jamaica put the thing more pungently. He said: 'Some of these white settlers actually become quite bearable, once they know they're licked politically.'

I am tempted to sum up this phenomenon as Manley's Law, and to suggest that it can be seen operating in many communities. I would submit that it applies to the settlers of Tanganyika who (with one or two exceptions) seem to have accepted African rule with a good grace after political power passed to the majority. It most certainly applies to India and Malaya, to take just two other Commonwealth examples. The British community in both countries is numerically larger now than it was in colonial days; the businessmen are doing more business.

It seems to me quite intolerable that the Rhodesian settlers should affront the civilized nations of the world with their pseudo-scientific clap-trap. It is their job to look at political realities as much as it is ours. But then one realizes that Bourbons at bay do not reason logically or argue logically; they rationalize. Here is Mr Haw again:

Social integration leads to miscegenation. There will at first be fraternization on the fringes. . . . Biological factors will inevitably lead to coloured births. There will follow mixed marriages . . . and so the social sanctions will be broken down until only the hard core of opposition remains. . . . With a little encouragement the process could engulf the whole population in a relatively short time.

And finally, having suggested that race classification on birth certificates in Rhodesia would be a safeguard against 'tragedy', Mr Haw steeled himself for the ultimate horror, the 'Coloureds'.

They are a lost people – they cannot identify themselves with either of the pure groups. They have no territory they can call their own, and their aspirations are correspondingly blighted with the hopelessness of their situation.

Mr Haw's book is too recent for it yet to have received the full, detailed dissection that it clearly merits from the academic

267

historians and, indeed, the psychologists of Britain and America. But for our purposes, in immediate political terms, it is an invaluable casebook specimen. I have not dragged out an obscure pamphleteer for inspection. This book, which has already gone through two editions, bears the highest endorsement – from the father of Federation himself, Lord Malvern. In settler circles it has been hailed with the reverence accorded the tablets of Moses, and copies are pressed into the hands of visitors by senior Civil Servants. Its author, a South African by birth, holds a key position in Rhodesia's public service, at an institute which is held to be the prototype for the trade training of Africans. Multiply him by twelve or fifteen thousand, and you have some measure of the solid phalanx of *administrative* resistance (let alone political or military) in the Federation today, facing any real demand for reform.

But Rhodesia's race attitudes have not all been formed by men who, like Mr Haw, have B.A. Honours degrees. In the original impact between white and black, the pioneers of the nineties were concerned with digging gold, claiming land (occupied or not), laying railway lines, taking black mistresses where they could find them – for a night or a few weeks – and hacking out the rough shape of a modern, cash-economy state. The civilizing influences that provided an element of trusteeship in a normal British colony were lacking: the colonial judges and magistrates, the impartial Civil Servants, the patrician governor. Even the mellowing influence of the ordinary professional man was missing; in the absence of the normal colonial framework, they were unready or unwilling to come. A decade was to pass before the Coghlans would arrive; two, before Huggins, and three, before there would be any public authority employing teachers in government schools.

What the African community faced after their military defeat in the 'nineties was, crudely, rape – of their women, their land, their lives. 'The native women in this country are nearly all prostitutes,' said a Bulawayo merchant, giving evidence to the Morris Carter Commission in the 1920s. 'You will never make them anything else.' This was the Commission whose report laid the basis of the now notorious Land Apportionment Act. A total of 1,986 people gave evidence, many of them the actual Pioneers whose initial impact had set the tone of race relations in Zambesia.

The weird world of white Rhodesia's guilt and sexual fears was revealed in the evidence given to the Carter Commission by another man, who was later to play a decisive part in public life. Charles Bullock declared:

Hybridization, however gradual, cannot be contemplated with equanimity. Apart from that danger, it is best each race . . . be given full opportunities of developing according to its biological inheritance.

Bullock argued strongly for a land-segregation policy to prevent what he called 'the evils consequent on a fusion of black and white races'. A few years later he was appointed to the post of Chief Native Commissioner – the key public servant in administering black–white relations.

After retirement, Charles Bullock set to work on the novel he had long intended to write. Entitled *Rina*, it has heavy overtones of Rider Haggard and is set in Zambesia, with a white hero whose life is saved by a beautiful, white-skinned girl he encounters there. She is living with an African tribe; they are attracted to each other and fall in love. Tragedy strikes when he discovers that she has a small proportion of African blood. Marriage is now clearly out of the question, but he is a decent chap and still feels a sense of obligation to get her away from her squalid situation. And so the novel ends happily, with his arranging a post for her as nanny to a white family in South Africa.

I have sought to bring out the sexual factor in Rhodesian thinking for two reasons: first, that it is seldom acknowledged to exist; secondly, that it may well be the hard, final issue in the political battle to persuade the white minority in Rhodesia to relinquish power. In the struggle within every white conscience says Philip Mason, successive generations of Rhodesian settlers have found their thinking strongly influenced by 'an assortment of lusts and fears that were normally kept out of sight and about which it is not polite to talk even today'.

The curiously-weighted laws about rape and immorality, as Mr Mason remarks, have had their effect on Africans.

Why, they wonder, should anyone take so much trouble to keep a woman inviolate unless there is some peculiar virtue or magic influence to be acquired by sleeping with her? If we could eat the forbidden fruit, we should become as gods. ... This can be translated into educated terms; there have been Africans brought up under this code to whom to achieve a white woman has seemed the crown of success – with a touch of revenge about it. This is uncertain ground, but surely all will concede that on the European side, awareness of a sexual danger was one factor – and some perhaps will feel the most important – in the attempt to segregate and separate the native from the immigrant.

This whole obsession with sex by Rhodesia's privileged minority provides a remarkable contrast with race relations in Nyasaland. Ten thousand white settlers there might reasonably be expected to develop even deeper obsessions, surrounded as they are by three million black people, with a mostly black police force which is much thinner on the ground than in Rhodesia. Yet the authorities there told the Bledisloe Commission, in the constitutional process that led up to Federation, that there had not been so much as *one recorded case* of the 'Black Peril' in the territory. Further, Lord Bledisloe was assured, 'any white woman can go unaccompanied anywhere with perfect safety in Nyasaland'.

It is a telling indictment of settler policy in Southern Rhodesia. Certainly it would be ridiculous to suggest that slight differences in geographical situation or climate account in some mysterious way for a totally different behaviour pattern by black people in a white-run country. The Africans themselves are tribally similar and roughly equal in total numbers in the two territories. Indeed, the Nyasa peoples might be regarded as potentially more unmanageable, since they were not brought to heel by military firepower like the Matabele and Mashona. The only reasonable conclusion one can draw is that the white settlers of Southern Rhodesia are enmeshed in a sex-based neurosis of vengeance, guilt, and fear which is wholly of their own manufacture. Even sadder, their hostility has proved to be contagious, and the

Africans whom they rule have become an embittered people, their natural warmth and trust and generosity eroded.

Logically one must ask if there is any sense in passively, neutrally watching the spectacle of 312,000 neurotics attempting a course of self-medication. It is too much to expect any politician in any country to confess that his policies have failed or that he is groping in the dark – though I strongly suspect that a dose of truth-drug might just pry this confession from the deep subconscious of Welensky, Whitehead, and their lieutenants.

Still the neurotics command the citadel. Can it be any wonder that black men on both sides of the Rhodesian frontier have, in desperation, begun considering the necessity of turning to military force?

3 Civilized Standards

> 'It has got to be recognized, once and for all, that when we talk of
> maintaining high standards in the Federation . . . we mean White
> standards. People who have in their minds that we might abdicate
> in ten or fifteen years . . . ought to prepare themselves for a rude
> shock.' SIR ROY WELENSKY

A broad tarmac highway cuts a black, polished swathe through the
limitless forest of stunted trees, bisecting giant red-clay ant hills. On
and on it goes, paralleling the spidery steel pylons which convey the
power by which the Copperbelt lives.

Speeding along this main road in the middle of nowhere, one is so
hypnotized by the bars of light and shade, caused by sun and trees,
which flick across one's sight, that it is a physical shock to breast a rise
and there see stretched out ahead the red and green roofed villas of a
copper town – each house standing amid a generous allowance of
cultivated green lawn, whose rich colour and texture are a tribute to the
all-year-round watering which the dull, dust-coated bush grass does
not receive. Dominating the town is the head-gear of one of the great
mines, etched sharply against the intense blue sky. This could be
Barnsley or South Wales, except that few British colliers have afternoon tea in the garden, waited on by servants in crisp white uniforms.
And you are unlikely to see two motor-cars garaged alongside the
average Yorkshire council house.*

To convey the luxury, incongruity, and privilege of Rhodesia's
white settlers, I cannot do better than quote those words of the
Rev. Colin Morris. He was writing of the rich mining towns of
the north, where the uneasy juxtaposition with Africa is most
sharply apparent to the visitor's eye. But in greater or lesser
degrees, this contrast exists in every part of the Federation where
the white man has established himself.

Self-analysis is not the most general of human characteristics,
and most settlers are genuinely surprised and offended at the
suggestion that they constitute in themselves some kind of upper
class. For this, after all, is a frontier country in the solid North

* Colin Morris, op. cit.

American tradition. It is the Wild West all over again, complete even to such details as hitching posts and broad verandas in the smaller settlements, where the new era of neon signs and Espresso bars has not yet arrived. The visitor feels that he has somehow wandered on to the set of *High Noon* or some other Hollywood Western – the brilliant sunlight, the Victorian false-front shops, the broad dusty streets wide enough to turn a wagon and horses around in, the effervescent air proclaiming the high plateau country.

With the Wild West look go the frontier traditions of free-wheeling hospitality and egalitarianism – 'Howdy stranger, welcome to our town where the colour of a newcomer's money is as good as any other man's' – the open handshake, the quick genuine acceptance. This is why the white Rhodesian is so hurt when he detects that you entertain some reservations about accepting his society on its own terms, just as a Texas rancher would be hurt. For, as in North America, it is an article of faith to be 'just an ordinary guy'. When a glossy magazine in England recently produced a thirty-eight-page colour supplement on the Federation, it carried on its cover an informal picture of the Federal Prime Minister, chosen by himself. It showed Sir Roy in shirtsleeves and braces, wearing no tie.

Closer inspection revealed that he held an inconspicuous object in one hand – the microphone of a very good quality tape-recorder machine. This is the authentic Rhodesian–Texan touch. The supplement, which appeared in *Courier*, was valuable for its display of white Rhodesian viewpoints; several settlers had contributed articles.

'White society,' said one, in introduction, is 'much less hide-bound than [in] other territories associated with Britain . . . less clannish and less stuffy . . . less respectful of protocol.'

Southern Rhodesia, the article explained, is the permanent home of many who have known no other home.

They and their fathers made of it a fruitful land from wilderness and danger, building homes, farms, hospitals and missions on land which Lobengula had soaked in blood whilst exercising savage power politics.

T – P.P. – K

A truculent note concluded this introduction.

Nobody but a white Rhodesian can properly understand the problems of this part of the African continent. . . . The Southern Rhodesian feels he has a stake in the land and feels as much a Rhodesian as a West Riding man feels a Yorkshireman. [In Northern Rhodesia] the District Commissioner is essentially a Rhodesian, permanently resident; and no time-serving Whitehall servant, eager to be through with his term and flown back to the softer, duller delights of Britain.

The settler view of the African was revealed by a Southern Rhodesian, Christina Wakeley. She explained why the houseboy there lives on £5 a month and his keep.

Like so many of his fellow Africans, he is incapable of doing any other job but the most menial. This is not his fault; he simply isn't capable of anything more. . . . Maybe this generation of children will all have a chance of going to school, but today the large bulk of the African population is incapable of doing anything which requires skill or learning.

Miss Wakeley concluded with what might be called the Settler's Creed, for it is heard so often from so many white Rhodesians by a visitor to the Federation today:

This is a country which was built by pioneers; men and women who trekked behind the indomitable CECIL RHODES; who sought a new life . . . who suffered the heat, disease, ignorance and poverty which was Central Africa, and built a country from nothing. Half of all the white people who live here now are of British stock, many of whom know no other home. . . . One continues to marvel at the African agitators [and a few Europeans] who can create unrest and discord in the minds of a people who knew nothing of life but mud and strife before the coming of the European.

This is the argument that leads inexorably to the policy slogan whose prime champion today is Sir Roy Welensky. In repeated public speeches he has called for 'the maintenance of civilized standards', and it can be assumed that when he puts this argument in private, to British Cabinet Ministers, he drives it home with plainer speaking. But even in public he makes no secret of his view that such standards are European standards; that it is up to the African, if he wants the vote, to achieve these standards. And it is also implicit, though never spelt out in so many words, that the one who sets the rules and judges if the African has qualified is, of course, the white settler.

To the African, these standards seem excessively concerned with money, physical possessions, and lavish recreation. The *Rhodesia Herald* not long ago quoted with some satisfaction the words of a visiting New York editor:

The Rhodesian way of life outclasses that of America . . . something so pleasant and comfortable that Americans cannot conceive of it. Anyone who says that the American way of life is better or more luxurious is talking absolute nonsense.

An adopted New Yorker, Dr Thomas Franck, conducted careful interviews with officials of the copper-mining companies during his last tour of Northern Rhodesia, when the copper boom was at its height. He discovered that £2,390 was the average take-home pay of European employees that year. And, on top of that, were subsidies for housing, water, and electricity, having a total cash value of £177. A curious discrimination qualified the payment to Africans. The white miner's income of £2,390 included a copper bonus amounting to fifty-seven per cent of the basic wage. By any logic, this sort of product bonus should have been distributed at the same rate to all men in all categories. But for black miners the rate was set at twenty-three per cent. And average African wages in that boom year, bonus included, came to less than £150, or less than *one-fifteenth* the handsome total taken home by white miners. It is hard to imagine black men in this position voting for partnership. But then, of course, on that rate of pay, the African is a good £500 below the annual income necessary for entry to the general voters' roll, so the problem does not arise.

The above figures leave out the special compensation pay for a miner who contracts silicosis. It is £600 if he is white, £80 if he is black.

It might be thought that the affluence of the white miners is recent, or transitory, or both. But in fact this state of colour privilege has been a feature of the Copperbelt for some time. Ten years ago the visiting correspondent of the London *Times* wrote:

Apprentices are earning £1,000 a year, ordinary artisans £1,400 and occasional rock crushers £3,000. They are provided with magnificent clubs and recreational facilities. On a gala night nearly everyone is in evening clothes, smoking Havana cigars.

When the Rhodesian talks about preserving civilized standards, he is thinking in realistic, tangible terms. Cyril Dunn of the London *Observer* put it this way:

Luxury guest houses with Old Masters on the walls, the latest novels on the bookshelves, and housekeepers lately in the service of the nobility supervising the kitchens. White miners from the afternoon shift driving home in Jaguars; huge country clubs, sports stadiums and a yacht club operated on water pumped up from the mines; and African townships fitted up regardless of cost. All this set in a circumference of primeval bush hundreds of miles deep. It is an African fantasy beside which Timbuktu and the Mountains of the Moon are trifling.*

Only by providing lavish amenities, and the prospect of lavish bonuses and overtime pay, can the mining companies – they say – hope to attract the sort of white miners who are necessary for efficient operations. (A black government in Northern Rhodesia would hardly accept the necessity; just across the border in Katanga there are twenty-eight categories of mine jobs filled by Africans which are not open to the Africans of the Copperbelt because of the stubborn resistance of the white mine unions.)

Inducements, then, bring the white man to this frontier country, and it would be naïve to suppose that he feels any sense of partnership with the black men of this baking landscape. As for considering guardianship, or earnest projects to foster inter-racial mixing, these tough extroverts have neither the time, the energy after work, nor the inclination. Take a straw vote in any white man's pub in Chingola, and you'll discover the same ambition almost every time: early retirement when the bankroll is big enough; then departure from this God-forsaken bush for

* Cyril Dunn, *Central African Witness*, Gollancz, London, 1959.

South Africa or England, to buy that little farm, or seaside hotel, or family business that has been a long objective.

It is the complaint of Kenneth Kaunda and the other African leaders that such 'settlers' have no stake in the country, that they are hardly settlers at all. Yet in its wisdom, the white man's administration in Lusaka, in Salisbury, and in far-away London, decrees as a matter of course that each of these transients, including the high percentage who actually hold South African passports, shall have the vote. For it is virtually impossible for a white miner *not* to qualify, by his income or possession of property, regardless of his education. And so, by definition, he is civilized. For it has been hammered home often enough by the white men who devised Federation that the franchise is reserved to those who have achieved 'civilized standards' and are prepared to maintain them.

The Africans, of course, are not fools; if you talk to them about this delicate subject (which the white miner will not), you will be told time and again of the absurdities which result. One of their favourite examples, cited to me by Mr Kaunda's U.N.I.P. men in the north and by Mr Nkomo's Z.A.P.U. officials in the south, resulted from the hasty repeal of a 'pinprick' law, after the 1959 emergency, which enabled Africans to buy tickets in the state lottery. A couple of months later two penniless Africans, who had never voted in their lives, won the £30,000 top prize money. By this magic they were transformed overnight; they qualified for the voters' roll and so became, in the twinkling of an eye, civilized men and fellow-defenders of civilized standards.

It has since become something akin to treason for a white Rhodesian of critical mind to cite this lottery incident. For white Rhodesians are collectively defending their citadel of privilege, and the carefully controlled franchise is equivalent to the castle walls. The maintenance of 'civilized standards' provides the whole intellectual foundation for that system of rigid franchise control, and an assault upon the foundation may bring the walls themselves crashing down, never to be rebuilt.

Living with a race problem, day in day out, seeing themselves collectively as an island of white civilization in a sea of black barbarism, must be a very substantial psychological burden for the white Rhodesians to bear. And so the settlers have shown persistent ingenuity in persuading themselves that they are living in a white community after all, not very different from Queensland or Ontario or some other part of one of the older dominions. The Union Jacks, flapping comfortably and ubiquitously from so many flagpoles, before the Federal Assembly and in the gardens of hundreds of ordinary (white) citizens, flourish a reassurance. The terrible thunder of Mosi-Oa-Tunya becomes somehow less frightening when the place is renamed Victoria Falls. People in Salisbury go for a picnic to the Mermaid's Pool; near Melsetter, they can to go the Bridal Veil Falls.

The Edwardian pioneers of Central Africa built themselves men's clubs in the style of Pall Mall and St James's. Today the standards of white civilization are preserved in buildings just as derivative. Salisbury thumbs its nose at the jungle with American-style skyscrapers. When the Pearl Assurance Company had reared its triumphant oblong of glass and steel, it spent a further £15,000 to cap the building with a triple-armed structure sustaining a mighty pearl. At night, illuminated, this beams out its message as far as the airport and beyond: this, it says, is Civilized country.

Indeed, one cannot help feeling, as one searches deeper into the Federal way of life, that in their heart of hearts the white Rhodesians bear a wordless wish – that the Africans would disappear. If only they would diminish to a manageable quantity, like America's Red Indians, how much simpler it would all be politically! Indeed, it was on the American premise – a false premise as it proved – that the first wave of Rhodesian pioneers set up the framework of their state.

There is a curious link between the Americans and Rhodesians of those pioneer days, in the person of Frederick Courteney Selous, the resourceful and seasoned hunter who was hired by Rhodes and the British South Africa Company as chief guide for the all-important march of the Pioneer Column. A few years later, having helped to crush the Matabele Rebellion, Selous departed for Washington at the behest of President Roosevelt, to join him on a big-game hunting expedition into the mountains of Wyoming. After that came further hunting trips, in Western Canada, made possible by the newly completed Canadian Pacific Railway, and later yet another link-up with Roosevelt, when Selous agreed to accompany him on his African hunting trip. 'Three cheers!' wrote the President, 'I am simply overjoyed you are going out. It is just the last touch to make everything perfect.'

Selous epitomized in his own life the dilemma which has faced the white Rhodesian from that time until the present day – whether to regard the African as a ward who, with care and encouragement, will grow up to control his own affairs, or whether (as in South Africa) to see him as an ever-present enemy. If he is a ward, then clearly you must educate him; and humanity as well as self-interest dictate that you should educate him in your own ways at your own sort of schools. But if he is inherently your enemy then you must, like the Afrikaner, be clear-cut in your thinking and even ruthless. Educate him apart from you, make him live apart and work apart.

And that is where the Rhodesian has, up to now, differed from the Afrikaner. Unlike him, he has not yet resolved his dilemma by assuming, overtly and deliberately, the role of jailer. Nor, however, has he assumed the role of guardian. He has dithered in between.

'When the improvement of the Natives reaches such a pitch that it is impossible for a foreign nation to retain the government,' said Elphinstone, then Britain's duty would be plain. It would be to pull up stakes and go – 'and take the glory of the achievements as our sole reward'. That was the Governor of Bombay a century and a half ago, enunciating the trustee principle which Britain's colonial service has pursued – with delays and interruptions, sometimes costly – from that day to this.

But what should the principle be if those who enjoy the powers of trustees are white settlers, who intend *never* to pull up stakes and go? The systematic and almost complete destruction of the Australian Aborigines does not make pleasant reading; on the island of Tasmania the invading colonists succeeded in wiping out the entire indigenous populace – a Stone Age community – in seventy-three years. The whole sorry tale, with descriptions of the escaped convicts turned bushrangers who hunted the Aborigines for sport and for dogs' meat, can be found in Brewton Berry's detailed account.* Modern New Zealanders are trying, and perhaps succeeding, by liberal legislation to expiate the bloody deeds committed by earlier generations against the Maori. As Toynbee points out, the Portuguese devised the simple but devastating strategy of taking the clothes from recent victims of smallpox and planting them in native villages, thus clearing large tracts of Brazil with swift efficiency. And in Matabeleland to this day the black Rhodesians have a communal tradition, transmitted verbally from the previous generation, that the resourceful Dr Jameson made use of the same device. This is a legend that can never be satisfactorily confirmed or denied; it is known that Jameson had his men vaccinated before the attack on the Matabele began, and that Lobengula, like many of his followers, was stricken with smallpox during those last weeks and may have died of it. The central question is whether Jameson's vaccinations were a precaution or a preliminary, and on this point, lacking data, black and white observers are apt to reach opposite conclusions. Perhaps the point that matters is that the suspicion lingers, that politically the harm has been done.

That there can be decisive differences in 'native policy', depending on the political direction at the top, is shown by the contrasting experiences of Canada and the United States. The films have taught us that the American push westwards was a costly conquest, achieved only after numerous encounters between Indian arrows and the white settler's gun. There were even times when the Indians seemed to be winning; Selous out west with Roosevelt must have passed not far from the site of General Custer's last stand.

What is not often realized is that at this same time, on the same western plains of North America, but just on the other side of the 49th Parallel, a wholly different native policy was being

* B. Berry, *Race Relations*, Houghton Mifflin, Boston, 1951.

pursued – and with astonishing success. The instrument of policy was different; instead of the U.S. Cavalry it was the North-West Mounted Police. But otherwise the situation was, in every respect, remarkably the same. There were even native tribes split in two by the white man's imposed and invisible border, as in Africa. The Sioux, Cree, and Blackfoot tribes of the Rocky Mountain foothill country west of Calgary are but three examples. And, like the Yao of Moçambique who trekked north to the trusteeship of Sir Harry Johnston's Nyasaland, so these Indians of the American West 'voted with their feet'. The branches of the tribes south of the border chose to trek north and settled down with their cousins in Canada.

This is not to say that Canadian policy was without stain; there was much to criticize in it. But there is one single, telling fact that reveals how enormously it differed from the policy pursued south of the border. In American territory there were, as every schoolboy knows, pitched battles – sometimes between Indians and forces of the U.S. Cavalry, sometimes between Indians and the settlers themselves, desperately pulling their covered wagons into a circle, nose to tail, going into laager like the trekkers of South Africa. In Canada, too, the wagons were rolling west, though on a much smaller scale than in the United States, where the white population was twelve times as great. Still, it was a westward-flowing tide of white settlers, spreading out across the wheatlands of half a continent. But not in all the decades of expansion was there a single pitched battle between white Canadians and the indigenous peoples. It is a remarkable difference, and one which has increasingly teased the minds of transatlantic historians. A difference in degree would be less difficult to explain. Factors of geography, population, resources might be adduced. But it is not the case that the Canadians simply had fewer armed encounters than their settler cousins to the south; they had none at all.

I should make it clear that in making this comparison I am not referring to the earlier era of white settlement on the eastern seaboard of North America, when armed encounters were plentiful, but the Victorian era of 'wagons west', exactly comparable to the northward march of the Pioneer Column. To give Rhodes credit, it should be noted that he was aware of the Canadian example and made notable efforts to copy it. He decreed that the British South Africa police should be formed very much on the lines of the Mounties, and he and Frederick Selous were agreed that the pioneers of the Column should strive by every means to avoid armed encounter with the Matabele – which they did. Yet within three years there was inter-racial warfare from which the white emerged triumphant.

It is worth noting, perhaps, that in Canada the push west was not a shoestring operation like Rhodes's, nor one carried out under the flag of a private company. Mid-way in the process, the politicians in Ottawa, fed up with the obstructionism of the Hudson's Bay Company, bought it out. Up till then the Hudson's Bay Company had dominated and administered the Canadian West exactly like the British South Africa Company in Central Africa; indeed, there are indications that Rhodes consciously took it as his model. Certainly, the troopers of the North-West Mounted, later to become the Royal Canadian Mounted Police, were under the clearest instructions, issued to every recruit passing through the gates of the training post at Regina, to regard their relationship towards the Indians as one of trusteeship. Indeed, their jackets of scarlet and gold were so designed as to proclaim a careful connexion, for the Indians, with the British 'Redcoats' they learned to trust in the colonial days before 1867.

This is not to say that all was perfect in Canada's race relations then – or now. The system of Indian 'reservations' was as reprehensible in its way as the Land Apportionment Act. But the basic fact remains that in Canada – as indeed, Selous himself was able to see – there had been a clear and deliberate policy decision in favour of trusteeship. And since warfare was successfully avoided, there *was* a basis of trust.

What the Rhodesian pioneers did not know, of course, was that their race-relations problem had entirely different proportions from that of the North American settlers. Sheer numbers do count. In India the British gradually came to realize that they were outnumbered in the ratio of something like 1,500:1 and devised a trusteeship policy accordingly. In Canada, because the white settlers were few at first, they walked softly. Those south of the border, twelve times as numerous, carried 'a big stick', in the immortal phrase of Teddy Roosevelt, and encountered the consequences. The Canadian pioneers carried a small stick, and pointedly did not use it.

The North American Indians, as Selous himself remarked with horror, were swiftly being exterminated by the white man's brandy and the white man's diseases, like syphilis and tuberculosis, as were those Australian Aborigines who had survived the gun. (Not until the arrival of anti-biotics many years afterwards would the downward line on the population graph halt and turn upward at last, after whole tribes had disappeared.)

It seemed reasonable for the white Rhodesian of that time to suppose that he could create a new 'White Dominion' on the Canadian or Australian pattern, in which a declining, disease-ridden African population would become no more than a manageable minority or vanish in time altogether. Only with the opening up of the country, and the counting of heads in one census after another, did the white settlers realize at last that they were vastly outnumbered by a black population and likely to remain so. Even then they were not prepared to accept defeat. Lord Malvern, as Southern Rhodesian Prime Minister, embarked at the end of the Second World War on a massive programme of white immigration which achieved spectacular results – though it nearly bankrupted the nation. Starting with a white population of 82,386 in the year 1946, the territorial government brought in the almost incredible total of 85,000 more during the next seven years, until the establishment of Federation. It has been estimated that the total cost of this operation, in terms of public and private money, was £2,210 million. Much of this was offset by the system of advances and repayments; but still an enormous burden fell upon the state. It brought protests in the legislature, and Malvern was forced in 1951 to scale down the programme by thirty per cent in order to avoid disruption of the social services. Even so, Southern Rhodesia entered Federation with a debt of £88·4 million, which it shifted on to the shoulders of the Federal government.

But, as even the most obdurate white settler must know, it was a case of too little and too late. This explains the note of hysteria or desperation that sounds through the legislative debates from the earliest times; while conducting themselves as though Rhodesia was a white man's country, the members of the all-white legislature were uneasily aware that what lay outside was not Ottawa, or Canberra, let alone Westminster.

Thus the settler in Central Africa found himself launched on the debate which continues unresolved to this day: what are 'civilized standards' to be, and who shall impose them? For if you accept the role of guardian, it follows inevitably that you will end up with a society that only makes sketchy contact with the one to which you are used. External pressure from Whitehall is now, in the 1960s, bringing this new society about in Nyasaland and Northern Rhodesia; it is in Salisbury that the battle to save 'white civilized standards' will be fought in the end.

Every Rhodesian white child grows up with an acute consciousness of the horror that so nearly overwhelmed white civilization in his father's or grandfather's day. School and story books carry brave etchings: the Last Stand of the Shangani Patrol, Captain Spreckley organizing the Laager in the Market Square of Bulawayo. The visitor to the Federation is constantly having these historic landmarks pointed out: 'There is the jail where the women and children were taken for protection when the Mashona rose.' It is an ever-present event, a communal memory of all white Rhodesians.

And it is well to remember that this bloody clash between black and white in Rhodesia has been given fresh, contemporary political impact by events in Kenya. To people in Britain and other far-off countries, Mau Mau was something horrid and yet almost unreal; it lasted seven years and brought death by butchery to 2,481 people (the victims) and to 10,548 members of Mau Mau shot by the security forces.* It tied up twelve

* Final official totals obtained from the Kenya Government.

battalions of the British Army, and it cost the taxpayers of Britain and Kenya £71 million. In the Rhodesias, it was anything but remote. The two white communities are linked in many ways: settlers visit each other and often have relatives in the other territory. In a continent where the whites are now acutely aware of being a five million minority among 250 million black people, a neighbourliness born of fear and the instinct for self-protection has – in the post-war period – drawn the settlers together. And, in the jet age, travellers to Salisbury can and do break their journey at Nairobi, which is the next stop on the overnight air-route to Europe. White Rhodesians are prosperous people who, proportionately for their numbers, travel a great deal. In particular, Rhodesia's politicians, journalists, those who make policy and form public opinion, are closely in touch with Kenya just as they are with events in the Republic to the south.

With the turn of the political tide in Kenya, the trek southwards speedily began. In parts of the territory like the Eldoret district, which were heavily settled by Afrikaners at the turn of the century, as many as a third of the white farmers and their families had left for the Rhodesias and South Africa by the middle of 1962. An informal poll conducted by the Kenya Convention, comprising the colony's 2,600 master farmers, showed that seventy-nine per cent were planning to leave – when they could find purchasers for their properties. Tom Stacey reported, in the London *Sunday Times* during June 1962:

Virtually all property in Kenya, whether land or houses, is unsaleable. In Nairobi, scores of European houses stand blind and vacant, rank weed and high grasses re-establishing themselves – homes the absent owners would jump at selling at half their pre-1960 values.

In settler eyes, down in the Rhodesias, these bleak events in Kenya seem a foretaste of what awaits them if a 'Butler Constitution' were to lay down a formula for black rule in their country on the lines laid down for Kenya in 1960 and 1962 by the Macleod and Maudling plans. In the *Sunday Times* report there appeared a very good example of the outrage felt by the settlers at the betrayal of their kith and kin by the far-off politicians in Whitehall. The speaker was Jim Hughes, whose 503-acre farm was worth £35,000 – before the last Lancaster House conference – and was now unsaleable. He had built it up from scratch, starting with raw bush and a bamboo shack for his wife and himself:

I'm not a philanthropist, not a missionary; I hate the sight of the bastards. But I came here to farm and to look after these fellows, the Africans. They look up to you as their mother and father; they come to you in all their trials and tribulations.

We built this house. We got the stone from the forest. I taught them how to cut it, how to use a square. We carried our own cement. We carried every single thing; we cut every single mortal thing from the forest – there was nothing here. Why should I let it go – go to rack and ruin? Do you think the British government will pay for it? There are a few people over here who might create a bit of trouble . . . somebody might get hurt . . . somebody might get killed.

And, the report continued, he brought out his treasured pair of Colt ·45 revolvers with the ivory handles he had carved himself, and declared that he was ready to use them.

I have referred to Kenya because of its prime political importance for Central Africa. A third of a million white Rhodesians are watching closely every move made by Britain in Nairobi, as a clue to what may lie ahead for them as well. A minority of liberal Rhodesians believe that the Macleod–Maudling plans have proved their worth in establishing a basis of accommodation – even trust – between black and white, and thus heading off the fresh bloodshed of another Mau Mau. Most, however, reject the plans, feeling that the pace in Kenya was too hot and that it could be forced by Mr Macleod and his successor only because they had the Coldstream Guards in Kahawa Barracks as their ultimate sanction. No such British sanction exists in Rhodesia.

Trust, as Iain Macleod said when giving up his task at the Colonial Office, has always been the crux of the problem in seeking an accommodation between the races in Kenya and the Rhodesias. Talk to the settlers of the Zambesi country and you'll be told time and again how they came there half a century ago and found the Africans, or – in their favourite phrase – the 'raw natives', uncivilized, 'just down from the trees'. Here is Mrs Nora Kane, herself of pioneer stock and a trusted friend of Lord Malvern, in her book brought out to mark the establishment of Rhodes's goal, the Federation.

The Bantu alone, of all races, has contributed nothing as yet towards the many civilizations the world has known. Perhaps his contribution is yet to come. Continued contact with inferior people brings those of a high level of civilization down to the level of the lower. The government of Southern Rhodesia, realizing that the European can only retain his own status by raising the black races from their savagery . . . is doing everything within its power to help the African to attain a higher standard of living. The work has been slow and tedious, but . . . the African is beginning to take pride in lifting himself to the level of his white neighbours.

Life in Southern Rhodesia is based on social and residential segregation. This is understandable in a society where a civilized race lives cheek by jowl with one still in a state of semi-savagery. Both white and black sections prefer to live their own lives . . . and the idea of integration and miscegenation is as repugnant to the majority of Africans as it is to the European.

No casual visitor or distant critic can understand and appreciate the relationship of the black man to the white in Central Africa. . . . The two races would be best left alone, to work out their own future free of outside interference. . . . Political maturity as evolved by the British people over seven centuries cannot be acquired overnight by a race who have had no political background. The African . . . has yet to develop reason and an unemotional, unbiased outlook in his political life; he should learn not only to accept benefits but to take responsibility as well; above all he should cultivate tolerance, for this is the hallmark of a civilized man.*

In the suspicious atmosphere of present-day Rhodesian politics, the African nationalist leader is apt to look at Mrs Kane's use of the word 'tolerance' in that statement and conclude that it merely means 'submission'. One of the factors that continually bedevilled colonial Africa during the 1950s and 1960s was the lack of a firm deadline by which black as well as white would have to get their house in order. Only in Tanganyika and Somalia, where the accident of U.N. trusteeship had imposed an external

* Nora S. Kane, *The World's View*, Cassell, London, 1954.

control, was a timetable of advance resolved – with remarkable results. In neither country was there the barren, vindictive inter-racial struggle which has scarred the face of Africa elsewhere. Confronted with the imminence of responsibility, the African threw all his energies into the task of preparing for it.

When Sir Roy Welensky maintains that political equality for the Africans must wait until they are civilized, he is in effect hurling a double challenge at every African. First, the African wants to know what body or committee is to lay down the rules, and judge the degree of 'civilization' achieved (suspecting that it will continue, as at present, to be the white Rhodesian electorate, whose authority derives ultimately from control of the armed forces). Secondly, he wants to know if there is to be any time-table or deadline (suspecting that, as at present, the date of his emancipation will always be placed beyond the 'foreseeable future').

Inevitably, the African has come to the conclusion that the white Rhodesians, of their own volition, will never surrender their political control; and he seeks, in consequence, to bring an out-side force to bear – if not the British government, then the U.N. This may infuriate the white settlers; but if they were to give the matter even a moment's imaginative consideration, they would see that only black puppets and bootlickers would submit to the foreseeable permanence of white government. They fail to see that the spirit of Dunkirk, and Bunker's Hill, and indeed Thermopylae, can animate men with black skins every bit as much as men with white ones. And it is unfortunate, perhaps, but also significant that those landmarks in our own Western struggle for individual liberty are all military. The Africans themselves are beginning to draw the appropriate conclusions, and in 1962 the first ominous references – to Cyprus and Algeria in particular – began to appear in the speeches of African national-ist leaders in the two Rhodesias. Certainly, their conclusions have historical justification. The English-speaking races, for all their lip-service to the values of civilization, have shown by their actions in Africa and Asia that they measure people of dark skins with a different scale of values altogether. It is the warrior they respect, and our literature is littered with the evidence, from Kipling's *Gunga Din* to Lawrence's fighting Arabs.

Any Anglo-Saxon respect for the noble savage evaporates when he surrenders. The Matabele were brought to heel in 1893, and, when they rose again three years later, their act was automatically termed a 'rebellion'. It is difficult enough for the master with absolute power to maintain any degree of respect for his human chattel, and the difficulty is enormously increased by a difference in skin colour between the two. It is not surprising, therefore, that the white man arriving in the Central Africa of Victorian times, armed with his superior technology, conditioned in any case to think of people with dark skins as inferior, and finding himself able with relatively small numbers of British South Africa Police and mounted volunteers to subdue half a million people, should have felt little or no respect for the black man he had conquered. It is an attitude one finds reflected in the earliest legislative ordinances, and it is still the central, most powerful attitude motivating Sir Roy Welensky and all the other white politicians of Rhodesia when they challenge the 'interference' of the British government in defence of what they call civilized standards.

Respect, indeed, is the heart of the Rhodesian dilemma today, and the shrewder African politicians have perceived that, if they can only acquire a set of this magic armour, they will soon enough breach the white man's political citadel. This explains in part the constant travelling by Mr Nkomo, Mr Kaunda, and their colleagues; their lobbying in London, their journeying to the U.N., their mounting in glory of high platforms in Addis Ababa and Accra. It boosts their morale, and the morale of their supporters at home. It was, after all, the device employed by General de Gaulle in the war years, when his Free French forces lacked money and prestige, and it was – then – far from obvious that France would be one of the 'Big Four' at the end of the war. Well-publicized journeys to Africa and the Mediterranean, combined with a rigid intransigence, rebuilt his prestige and won him political dividends. 'Then, General, you will make no concessions in this matter, not even one?' Churchill demanded during one of their frequent, angry interviews. De Gaulle's unyielding expression gave the answer even before he spoke it: 'No, Mr Prime Minister, I cannot; you see – I am too weak.'

As de Gaulle regained *la gloire* for his people, so did Kwame Nkrumah.

I saw that the whole solution lay in political freedom for our people, for it is only when a people are politically free that other races can give them the respect that is due to them. It is impossible to talk of equality of races in any other terms. No people without a government of their own can expect to be treated on the same level as peoples of independent sovereign states. . . . No race can be respected at home and abroad without political freedom.*

Among the white Rhodesians, this basic lack of respect for the African is so widespread as to be almost universal. It lies at the root of all the punitive laws, the subtleties of discrimination and the hundreds of invisible barriers that mark race rule in the Rhodesias. In the view of most white Rhodesian voters 'the Munt is not civilized yet'. It is a fundamental conviction, passionately held, and upon it the whole structure of the present Rhodesian state has been erected.

From the start the settler found himself in the position of judge in his own cause; competitor against the African for political power and yet referee in the race as well. And this gave rise to an ambiguity in Rhodesian life that has survived till today. Am I tutor or jailer, rival or guardian ? This is the unresolved question that the white man asks himself constantly in Salisbury and Lusaka, Umtali and Bulawayo. And behind the question is the premise that the black man is, still, a lesser creature than himself in the scale of civilization. The ambiguity showed most strikingly at the time of the rebellions in 1896, when ten per cent of the white settlers were killed by assegais and battle-axes. Selous himself, who considered that guardianship was the right policy to be followed towards the African, revealed in his own words the contemptuous feelings of settlers at the time. Leading a column of armed volunteers, he came upon the remote farm-

* Kwame Nkrumah, *Ghana*, Thomas Nelson, Edinburgh, 1957.

house where eleven people, English and Afrikaner, had been butchered:

> The remains had been much pulled about . . . but the long fair hair of the young Dutch girls was still intact and . . . these bloodstained tresses awoke the most bitter wrath in the hearts of all who looked upon them, Englishmen and Dutchmen alike vowing a pitiless vengeance against the whole Matabele race. . . . You probably know not your own nature nor are you capable of analysing passions which can only be understood by those Europeans who have lived through a native rising, in which women and children of their race have been barbarously murdered by savages – by beings whom in their hearts they despise – as rightly or wrongly they consider that they belong to a lower type of the human family than themselves.

Frederick Selous did not write of the atrocities committed by white against black; and, like him, the settlers remarked the actions of others, not their own. They recoiled from the brutality of black violence with horror, and thought of the 'rebels' as barbarians. Any profession of partnership with such people would have been unthinkable. And what was the evidence of their civilization in times of peace?

> It took a long time for a savage, unused to tableware, brushes and crockery . . . to grasp the different uses of the multitude of strange utensils, to realize that a sock should not be employed as a coffee-strainer and that it is an offence to clean out the inside of a saucepan with his master's hairbrush.

Marshall Hole, who wrote those words, was an administrator for the Chartered Company who arrived from England a year after the occupation. He remarked how the European employer, like settlers in other parts of the world, would garble a houseboy's unpronounceable tribal name into something more manageable for an Anglo-Saxon tongue: Sixpence and Pumpkin were two of the most frequent nicknames; others were Lobster, Monkey, and Jackass. In ways like this, the basic doctrine of race relations was being constructed. From the start there were white Rhodesians who believed that their proper function was that of guardian rather than jailer. But for most settlers, the cry was 'preserve the gap'.

In 1903 the Salisbury Chamber of Mines demanded in a memorandum to the Colonial Secretary 'that restrictions be placed on the present system of Christianizing natives . . . and the utility of labour and general economic principles be substituted'. Soon afterwards, the *Rhodesia Herald* declared that, 'The black peril will become a reality when the results of our misguided system of education have taken root and when a veneer of European civilization struggles with the innate savage nature.'

In the legislature a year later, one of the settler spokesmen, Colonel Napier, urged the need for municipal by-laws 'to restrain Natives from making use of public footpaths' and suggested, in a later debate, that the education grant to mission schools be cut by one-third since 'the uneducated native is the most honest, trustworthy and useful'.

In 1910 a formidable figure entered the debate: Leopold Moore, an irascible chemist-turned-journalist who founded and edited the *Livingstone Mail*:

> We shall consistently oppose the employment of natives where they compete with . . . white men. It is better to pay a white man three times as much as a native than to run the risk of evolving a native – as contrasted with a white man's – state.

Incredibly, he was talking of Northern Rhodesia where even today, after two post-war waves of immigration, and a copper boom, the white man is still outnumbered 40:1. Fifteen years after making that statement, Moore had this contribution to make to the art of race relations:

> It seems to me a well-established fact that Europeans are the only people in the world who are capable of exercising the right of election. Non-European peoples can only be represented satisfactorily by some method of nominating Europeans.

Leopold Moore was speaking those words not only as the editor of the territory's most influential newspaper, but as the leader of the Unofficial Members – i.e. the settlers – in the Northern Rhodesian legislature. A few years later he was an active participant in the campaign that successfully 'sold' Federation to a gullible or conniving British government, and emerged covered in glory, as Sir Leopold. Is it any wonder that the Africans of the Rhodesias tend to be as bitter about knighthoods as they are about the Union Jack?

Throughout the pioneer years, we can see the mould of white supremacy being formed, and setting hard. Let us look at it through the eyes of a distinguished Belgian lawyer, Henri Rolin, who toured the Rhodesias just before the First World War. The translation is by Philip Mason.

The white man will not take his meals at the same table as the black; he will not meet him on the footpath of the streets; he travels by rail in separate wagons . . . he relegates him at night to 'locations' outside the urban centres.

Society is composed, so to speak, of two societies . . . an aristocracy of white landowners, a proletariat of blacks. The whites conquered the country in 1893. They are established there as masters, with the overwhelming superiority given them by their intellectual and moral heritage from Greece and Rome, from the achievement of Europe.

That the Chartered Company's administrators were not entirely happy with the trend of events we know from frequent settler criticisms that the Company was 'too much on the side of the Native'. To get to grips with the basic dilemma, the Company appointed a research worker, Wilson Fox, whose monumental reports in the period 1910–12 are still standard reading for students of Rhodesian politics today. More than any one man, perhaps, he shamed white Rhodesians into recognizing that a policy of white supremacy was neither moral nor intelligent.

How best to elevate and utilize its indigenous inhabitants is the most pressing problem with which Rhodesia is confronted today. . . . Can a system possibly be right or successful that bases itself upon the principle of complete segregation? On the contrary, every European and every native should be jointly engaged in making the most of [the country's] resources.

The Company's administrators hedged, and played for time. But their policy of appeasing the settlers in the legislature was no more successful than appeasement policies have ever been anywhere; the settlers continually demanded more. Having gained control of the legislature, the settler M.P.s, led by Sir Charles Coghlan, set out to capture the inner citadels, the executive council and the Civil Service. As early as 1912 Coghlan demanded in the legislature that the Civil Service should be recruited locally; and he promoted this policy himself when he gained the levers of power at last in 1923, with the ending of Company rule and the hand-over to Crown Colony (or settler) government.

In Nyasaland Sir Harry Johnston, once the unquestioning disciple of Rhodes, had come to the conclusion that white settlers were not always the best judges of how to deal with the black men in their care. In a memo to Lord Salisbury, he wrote:

Where, throughout all tropical and Mohammedan Africa, we merely impose our rule to secure a fair field and no favour for all races, and inferentially for our own trade, there the local government must depend directly on London.

The crucial question to decide was whether the territory was White Man's Country – or Black Man's. Clearly, when he made his break with Rhodes, Johnston had determined that Nyasaland was to be the Black Man's. And one may suspect that in the long-drawn-out meetings of Prime Minister Macmillan with his 'Rhodesia Committee' in January and February 1962, leading up to the publication of the Maudling Plan at the beginning of March, the British Cabinet finally faced up to the truth about Northern Rhodesia – half a century late.

It was the great debate on land that disclosed settler intentions in Southern Rhodesia. Should the territory be split up and parcelled out on racial lines? The Morris Carter Commission in the 1920s laid the basis for the Land Apportionment Act, which has been described by one Rhodesian M.P. as 'the Magna Carta of the European'. Here is what a senior official of the Native Affairs Department at that time – N.H. Wilson – had to say to the Commission:

We are in this country because we represent a higher civilization, because we are better men. It is our only excuse for having taken the land. For us to turn round now and ask the Natives to help us in directing the government of ourselves is ridiculous.

Wilson also wagged the finger of warning about black competition, candidly admitting that since – from his own observations in native administration – there were a good many potentially able Africans, some of the settlers were bound to slither downwards and end up as 'poor whites':

To allow this to come to pass would be a calamity to the state, a cruel injustice to our own race and children, and a gross betrayal to the civilization in which we may be supposed to believe.

Only one Rhodesian M.P., a Gwelo lawyer named Max Danziger, opposed the Land Apportionment Act. Instead of turning the territory into a sort of racial patchwork quilt, he recommended outright partition, with the eastern part of the country made an avowedly White Dominion, and the western part a vast native reserve which might – if the Colonial Office were agreeable – be incorporated with the adjoining territory of the Khamas in Bechuanaland to make one solid African state. It would have cost money and uprooted great numbers of people, but it might have worked. If it were not done, Danziger predicted, the African would inevitably compete with the white man – first in jobs and then in politics – and 'in 50 to 100 years Rhodesia will no longer be a white man's country'.

It is on the land issue that racial battle was joined in white man's Rhodesia, a battle that continues to this day. Joshua Nkomo calls it 'the paramount issue in our struggle; the source of all our bitterness'. One of his colleagues in the early Congress days, Chad Chipunza, described it as 'one of the greatest points of division, if not the greatest, between African and European'. And in moving the second reading of the Land Apportionment Bill, the then Prime Minister, Howard Unwin Moffat, declared land division between the races to be 'the greatest of all problems for this young colony'.

The six-year battle to determine the wording of the Act and its objectives forced white Rhodesians to examine the basic principles of the civilization they were trying to establish in southern Africa. A tiny minority, whose spokesman was Danziger, held that the two cultures could not and would not mix:

that partition and – if it ultimately had to come – a fortified frontier, were essential. Three M.P.s who led the rejection of this viewpoint in the great debate were Huggins, Thomson, and Mitchell. They maintained that partition was impractical simply because the white man needed the black man economically – for his labour and for the revenue he supplied in head tax and indirect (consumer) taxes.

But rejection of partition did not mean integration, then or indeed ever. Most settlers demanded what was, in effect, an internal frontier, a social, economic, and political barrier that would protect white civilization until the African – never in the foreseeable future – learned its ways. 'A curb should be put on the activities of the native' – Dr Huggins told the Carter Commission – though he might have the right to progress 'as long as it is harmless'. The General Manager of the British South Africa Company – by his position the greatest landholder and most potent commercial influence in the Colony – demanded 'some measure of protection' for the settler and recommended that ten per cent of the land was quite enough to grant the native 'for many years to come'. (The final allocation was forty-eight per cent African, fifty-two per cent European, slightly revised in the African's favour during 1961.)

For the M.P.s of Southern Rhodesia there was one uncomfortable day when their own Speaker, Lionel Cripps, who had farmed for thirty-four years near Umtali, gave evidence to the Carter Commission on how the land should be apportioned:

I suppose if you were to act fairly you would have to give them more than the white people really . . . because after all, it amounts to this, that we took the country from them by force, and when they endeavoured to regain it, we said they were rebels.

Happily for the settlers, Mr Cripps and his awkward conscience were soon to disappear from the scene, and with the passage of the Act by the Moffat government – ironically, the Prime Minister was the son of Lobengula's missionary friend, the Rev. John Moffat – the markers of the internal racial frontier could be placed.

Any policy genuinely aimed at helping the Africans achieve 'civilized standards' would have involved a crash programme of education, and deliberate, judicious mixing of the races – first in farm and factory, perhaps, and then socially in the higher income group. Nothing of the kind occurred. Under Moffat and his successor, Huggins, no visible effort was made to propagate 'civilized standards' of education among the Africans; indeed, by the outbreak of the Second World War, there was still no secondary schooling available for any African child in any of the three territories of Central Africa. From 1930 to 1936 the number of African schools in Southern Rhodesia itself actually declined by 133 (the world depression was blamed), though in fact annual government revenue from Africans showed an increase of £60,000 during the same period. By 1938 Southern Rhodesia was spending £360,000 a year to educate its white children, and almost exactly one quarter of that sum (£89,500) on the Africans, though the population ratio was 30:1 the other way round. It worked out at £6 a head for settler children, and 1s. 5d. a head for black ones.

Here is Sir Hugh Williams, M.P., speaking in Huggins's legislature:

The native will continue to be honest if you leave him with his beads and blankets. ... If we could clear out every mission station in this country and stop all this fostering of higher native education, we would much sooner become an asset to the Empire. ... We are simply committing suicide.

It is politically instructive to consider where Central Africa's present African leaders were at the very moment that Sir Hugh was speaking. Kenneth Kaunda was at mission school – thanks to Scots mission money, and no thanks to white Rhodesians. Joshua Nkomo was studying in South Africa – thanks to American Methodist money. Hastings Kamuzu Banda was in the United States, studying medicine – no thanks to the settlers. The wonder is that these three distinguished Africans were able to stomach the idea of a Chequers week-end during the 1960 London negotiations, to sit in church and later to take tea with the Federal Prime Minister whose platform word for them is 'extremists'. Perhaps it was because they are all three very civilized men.

Such advance as was permitted the Africans in Southern Rhodesia, took place in the context of segregation, or as Huggins enunciated it in the landmark speech at the start of his régime, the 'Two Pyramid Policy'. This was to be a system of deliberate 'gradual, differential development', by which a firm white paternalism would determine the scale of civilized values. In purely African areas, Huggins said 'every step of the pyramid must be opened to him except only – and always – the top; the senior administrative officer must be white'. In the European areas, the African should 'merely assist and not compete with' the white man.

Separate development worked magnificently. The village locations near the white towns were showpieces for visitors to the practice of white civilization and the gradual extension of its standards. The wards – some might say inmates – lived, apparently cheerfully, in their cement matchbox houses, row upon soulless row along the curiously nameless dirt tracks that counted for streets. By day they might work in the white man's town – but not eat in its restaurants, drink in its pubs, or visit its hotels or cinemas. At dusk they might drink beer in the barrack-like halls provided by the white man. And by night they were securely segregated in 'black town'. No visitors were allowed without permission from the Superintendent (who was the appointee of the adjoining white municipal council), no visitors at all from 6 p.m. until the next morning; and no resident was permitted to absent himself from the township after 9 p.m. The inmate of the African location might lose his home if he was convicted for sedition, subversion, liquor offences, or failure to produce a pass. Members of the British South Africa Police, medical officers, Native Commissioners, or any official sent by the Ministry of Native Affairs, might enter his home, without the need to produce a warrant, at any time of the day or night. Political gatherings were illegal without the written permission of the Superintendent.

Furthermore, the manipulation of the franchise carefully ensured that the black man could not change the pattern of civilized living to which it had pleased his white master to call him. At the start of the Company's rule, the franchise had been so hedged by minimum income or property qualifications that virtually every white man and virtually no Africans had gained entry to the voters' roll. Just for safety, the qualifications were raised in 1912, to a property minimum of £150. Then, in 1928, Moffat's Cabinet decided that the time for revision had once again arrived. As one of the Ministers explained with perfect candour in the all-white legislature, the new plan for Native Purchase Areas might add considerable numbers of Africans to the voters' roll, and he was sure that neither the M.P.s nor the white electorate would wish to run the risk of a black majority.

The Leader of the Opposition, however, had worked out that some settlers might fail to qualify, if franchise requirements were further raised. Votes were for 'civilized men', as Rhodes had proclaimed, and all white men were, by definition, civilized. 'On no account', said the Opposition spokesman, 'must we keep out a single white voter in this country.' This solemn thought decided the issue. The Prime Minister withdrew the bill, adding that, since there were in any event 22,000 white voters and only sixty-two black ones, it was not urgent.

The way to deal with the question is when the time comes ... we should then definitely face it and decide whether the native is to continue to have a vote on the same terms as the European, or ... grasp the nettle and decide upon some other form of franchise for the native.

There could have been no M.P. present who did not understand perfectly well the meaning of the operative phrase in Moffat's promise: 'when the time comes'. The Prime Minister added that it would be practical to watch South Africa's way of handling the problem, as 'a guide for future action in this Colony'.

In 1936 the South African government under Hertzog and Smuts swept the Africans from the common voters' roll in the Representation of Natives Act; and, by 1938, Huggins had begun publicly to consider following suit. A check showed, however, that there were now 24,587 white Rhodesians on the register, while the black Rhodesian voters had actually diminished to thirty-nine. Action seemed unnecessary. The economic upswing of the war years then prompted Huggins to contemplate franchise adjustments again, and two events in 1948 brought matters to a head. An African strike in April stirred the fears always in the minds of white Rhodesians, and in May Dr Malan and his Nationalist Party swept into power in South Africa to proclaim the ruthless discrimination of apartheid. In the Salisbury parliament, some of Huggins's right-wing critics accused him – incredible as it may seem to us at this distance – of being 'dangerously progressive'. Huggins checked the voters' roll. On 31 March 1948, there were 47,000 white and 258 black voters in the territory.

Huggins went to the country in September 1948 on a pledge to close the common voters' roll to the black man 'for the foreseeable future', starting with a trial period of twenty years. He won a decisive victory and declared that the next step would be the formation of a 'great Middle Dominion of Africa', composing Southern Rhodesia, Northern Rhodesia, and Nyasaland, and so making the vision of Rhodes a reality. Two weeks later he left, in buoyant mood, for the Commonwealth Prime Ministers' Conference in London.

And then, suddenly and unexpectedly, the long-dormant 'Imperial factor' awoke in the form of pressure by the Labour administration of Clement Attlee to keep the franchise system of Southern Rhodesia non-racial in appearance. The Washington factor – today of much greater importance – for the first time entered Rhodesian politics as well. Harry Truman's administration exerted discreet behind-the-scenes pressure through Whitehall. Huggins fell diplomatically silent on his franchise plan, and on his return home announced only that there would be alternative action to protect civilized standards.

The 1951 Electoral Act roughly tripled the money barrier and raised the alternative educational qualification as well. The minimum income figure jumped to £240 (which, a dozen years later, is still *three times the average* for all African wage earners), and the property figure to £500. The requirement of an 'adequate knowledge of English' was enough on its own to eliminate hundreds of thousands of Africans. Through lack of school places, they had either never been to school at all, or had attended only one or two years of primary classes. Even in Salisbury itself, as recently as 1957, only forty per cent of eligible children found places in the first grade of African primary schools.

Huggins was not opening the flood-gates to Africans, or even civilized Africans. But all the same he came under pressure from his party congress in the following year to explain why he had not swept the black man off the voters' roll altogether, in terms of his 1948 election pledge. He replied – and his words have vital significance for the future –

Our action would be misunderstood in the United Kingdom and the United States of America. Although it might be possible for larger countries with more economic strength to flout world opinion, we certainly cannot afford to do so.

The double change of régimes – to the Tories in London at the end of 1951, and to Dulles at the State Department with the Eisenhower victory in 1952 – meant the temporary collapse of Anglo-American pressures on white Rhodesia. Huggins, and his colleagues, could breathe freely again. Defending his Electoral Act in the all-white parliament of the colony, the Prime Minister declared that it did 'almost as much as closing the roll', and that it did succeed in preserving 'what we call civilized government, which is the only important thing'.

This puts us at last in sight of what the white Rhodesian politician really means when he talks about civilized standards. Huggins had one further statement to make on the franchise problem. He was sure the Act was 'a far better way of dealing with it than the frustration it would create if the native was to be told that he was to have no say at any time in any part of the government of this Colony'.

4 The Heart of the Matter

> 'Racial hatred is a peculiar thing. You always find it at its most violent among the least civilized men.' GOETHE

The crux of the Rhodesian problem is this – Do the settlers genuinely intend that majority rule should come, that power should be yielded to an African Prime Minister and a predominantly African Cabinet? Or do they in fact intend, by every legalistic and lobbying device in the book, rather like the white southerners in the United States, to retain rule for as long as possible – perhaps, by some miracle, for good?

As Britain moved into the 1960s, after the débâcle of the 'murder plot' (which wasn't) in Nyasaland and of the tragic shootings in the two Rhodesias when black men died (but not white), it became increasingly urgent for the men in Whitehall with their fingers on the levers of power to judge the true intentions of the settlers.

Natural conservatives like Lord Home and Duncan Sandys – both enormously influential in the shaping of British policy towards Rhodesia as successive Commonwealth Secretaries – have plumped unhesitatingly for the first possibility. It is consistent with the 'civilizing mission' which, they like to feel, the Empire first and now the Commonwealth is pursuing. It is consistent, too, with temperaments that distrust speed, that prefer to let freedom slowly broaden down without giving it a helpful push.

By contrast, another Old Etonian in the Cabinet has apparently had less faith in the good intentions of his kith and kin, once they conditioned themselves to a life of privilege under a comfortable sun. This was the Prime Minister, Mr Macmillan. He appeared to be wavering between the two possibilities.

Among those believing delay to be the true settler intention have been not only members of the Liberal and Labour

Parties at Westminster, but also a good many M.P.s in the liberal wing of the Conservative Party, including a Cabinet Minister or two.

Blinding settler ignorance of the black world all around is one of the most profound impressions awaiting the visitor to Central Africa; the phenomenon is noted again and again by the members of the Devlin Commission in their report on the Nyasaland crisis. It has been remarked on to me by non-Rhodesian members of the Monckton Commission; and in the 175 pages of their report there are recurrent references to the remoteness of the settler – and his political leaders – from African opinion.

And this ignorance is a vital factor, of course, for those in Britain bearing the responsibility of deciding where and when and how to intervene in the present Rhodesian crisis. It was significant that Mr R. A. Butler, the British Deputy Prime Minister, who took charge of the Central African Office in the spring of 1962, found this to be the most immediate of his problems. At his Press conference in Salisbury after making his first survey tour of the Federation, he said that the first priority for all Rhodesians, white and black, was to 'get the facts'. In London, on his return, he said this again. Publicly that was as far as he could go, but in private he found himself forced into the role of political broker, urgently trying to persuade the Federation's white leaders to close the gaps in their ignorance, to meet the African leaders whose true viewpoint was unknown to them.

Mr Macmillan had instinctively recognized this settler ignorance too, during the 1960 Federal Review talks, and had promptly arranged a typical English house-party at Chequers where the white Rhodesian leaders could meet those mythical figures from outer space, Kenneth Kaunda, Joshua Nkomo, and Hastings Kamuzu Banda.

In a normal society these men and their respective supporters would not be separated by the racial void which yawns like some political Kariba gorge across Rhodesian life. The British politician takes the measure of his rivals, and of the electorate, through a hundred delicate antennae. He reads the newspapers that support him, but he reads others, too. He may have known some of his opponents because they were at school or served in the army with him. He gets the feel of the public pulse through social contacts, political meetings, and finally the ballot box. But for the white Rhodesian politician, every one of those fact-gathering, pulse-taking devices is denied him by the system he has imposed on himself. 'This country is run on the pretence that the native is not here,' said a Rhodesian Native Commissioner to Philip Mason of the Institute of Race Relations in 1956. And Mason himself commented that the Commissioners had become wardens over a kind of huge game reserve – 'a national park where those curious creatures, the natives, could live their lives undisturbed'.

The *African Daily News* of Salisbury is a professional, well-edited paper which accurately transmits the various currents of African opinion. Indeed, a former editor, Nathan Shamuyarira, came under pressure more than once from the nationalist parties for not espousing their cause uncritically. The ownership rests with Roy Thomson, the Canadian press millionaire, which puts the operation happily outside the normal arena of white–black relations. Yet white Rhodesians simply will not buy the paper. Mr Shamuyarira's circulation manager told me of the frustrating efforts he had made to set up vendors at street corners in central (i.e. white man's) Salisbury. There were no legal barriers to doing so. White people just wouldn't buy the newspaper, and after a long trial run the costly experiment had to be abandoned. When I am in Salisbury I have to make special arrangements for messengers to get me a copy daily from one of the stalls across the tracks in black man's town, and this is standard practice for every visiting correspondent, because, of course, we *have* to know what the Africans are saying and thinking. The settler, up to now, has decided that *he* does not.

Cut off from African opinion, reading comforting articles in their own white papers, relaxing in the evening with white friends in white suburbs, and forming their views of all Africans on the sketchy basis of houseboys handicapped by a strange language and a grossly inadequate education – is it any wonder that white Rhodesians are living in a cloud-cuckoo-land of their own?

I know that when Sir Edgar Whitehead says that 'most Africans are just not interested in politics' he really believes it. But how does he explain his refusal on one occasion to receive a two-man delegation from the African National Congress (as it then was called, before the 1959 Emergency)? Here were the two key men, George Nyandoro and Robert Chikerema, ready to state their grievances and to outline the views of their followers, and to do so in a civilized way around the table. But the Southern Rhodesian Prime Minister refused to see them. He said that he was sure he knew already what they would tell him. Besides, he believed that they were extremists and not really representative of African opinion; that they were seeking, by the device of an interview, to gain prestige in the African community. (This was the argument offered by settlers time and again for their rejection of the Malawi leaders in Nyasaland. Then Malawi achieved a ninety-five per cent victory in the 1961 election, and the argument has never been heard since.) Nyandoro and Chikerema perhaps commanded more prestige in Sir Edgar's own eyes than he cared to admit. They were among the 495 people whisked away to detention overnight in the Emergency. And nearly four years later they were still rotting in Gokwe camp, among the half-dozen 'hard-core' detainees being held without any charge or trial, until released by the new Field government in 1963.

One of the great shocks for the visitor to the Rhodesias is to discover that the apparently sensible, logical white people he meets are – when it comes to the greatest single problem confronting their nation – operating on the basis of sheer fantasy. On a journey through the Federation, a few months after the declaration of the 1959 Emergency, I was solemnly assured by supporters of Sir Roy's and Sir Edgar's United Federal Party that the basis of the African massacre plot in Nyasaland was 'forty tons of poison delivered to Dr Banda's surgery'. The mind boggled. Was it delivered in huge vans at dead of night? But it is no use scoffing. The white voters actually believed such poppycock.

A senior member of the U.F.P. was at that time solemnly declaring that not only was there a murder plot, but that the police had a complete record of the celebrated Nyasa 'forest conference' of 23 January 1959, taken by a cine camera on colour film with synchronous sound, and that Dr Banda would be convicted by his own words. Considering the clutter of apparatus involved, and the complications of siting microphones, the story sounded unlikely at the time. It took a commission under a British judge to sort out truth from fantasy, to show that there had been no murder plot at all, and that Dr Banda (who had not been present) had probably been unaware of the forest gathering in question. No dramatic showing of any sound film ever took place. But by that time a British Colonial Secretary (Alan Lennox-Boyd, as he then was) had solemnly espoused the 'murder plot' before an incredulous House of Commons at Westminster. In order not to lose face, he then rejected the Devlin Report. A few weeks after that, the Federal jails bursting with 1,322 Nyasas and a costly, protracted campaign of repression being the sole alternative to retreat, Prime Minister Macmillan dropped his Colonial Secretary and appointed a new one. Behind the scenes at Westminster, the Tories were coldly furious.

Clyde Sanger, in his book *Central African Emergency**, recalls that in the two-year period leading up to the rioting and shootings in Nyasaland, the Federal Prime Minister visited the territory twice. On the first occasion, he received an all-white welcome at the airport; Nyasas were excluded. A special, separate meeting was held for Africans; a dozen of them arrived.

At the big meeting he addressed on the Limbe tobacco floors there were a few Africans among the audience of a thousand, and none asked a question. Welensky's comment on this was: 'I don't think they are really interested in politics. Those who are, are represented here.'

In view of the blow-up that was to follow in 1959, and Dr Banda's Malawi triumph of two years later, with an almost complete turn-out of the 100,000 black voters, this pronouncement of the Federal Prime Minister's must go down as one of the truly prodigious political misjudgements of history, along with Marie Antoinette's miscalculation about the price of cake.

* Heinemann, London, 1960.

Welensky's interpretation of the African uprising in Nyasaland was revealing, too. He told a settler audience in Ndola:

The most cogent lesson to be learned from the recent disturbances in Nyasaland is the need for adequate policing of the right sort, properly trained, and with an effective intelligence service.

One more illustration may point up this alarming situation in which white Rhodesians, not only the ordinary voters but their responsible leaders as well, are out of touch with the Africa of the 1960s. On a visit to London in 1962, Southern Rhodesia's Prime Minister, Sir Edgar Whitehead, had very little to say publicly about the possible ways of resolving the Rhodesian dilemma, but a great deal to say in small luncheon and dinner parties, where he was consulted by Members of Parliament – mostly influential Tory back-benchers – and by British industrialists with interests in the Federation. He told a number of anecdotes about the 'Build a Nation' campaign – very much his personal project – and of the various Africans, many of them prosperous farmers, who had joined with the white Rhodesians in the mixed team of several dozen people which was touring the country. He also related stories of community self-help projects in his own area near Umtali, where he himself farms on a substantial scale, and these too were concerned with inter-racial cooperation. His theme was that the African is not interested in 'extremist politics' (whatever that might be) preached by the African nationalists, and that the campaign was achieving solid success. Sir Edgar added that he was optimistic about lower roll registrations for the first election to be held under the new Sandys–Whitehead constitution. (This allocated fifteen seats in a sixty-five-seat house to lower roll candidates, who would inevitably be Africans). He would be very disappointed if less than 50,000 to 60,000 Africans turned out to register; that was a reasonable target to expect. In the event, Mr Nkomo and the Z.A.P.U. nationalist movement declared a boycott of registrations; the total slowly rose to the 11,000 mark, and stuck there. The white-owned *Central African Examiner* described the Whitehead 'Build a Nation – Claim Your Vote' campaign as a sorry failure.

On his way to the U.N. Mr Nkomo told me a story to illustrate his own relations with the Whitehead administration. Like his colleagues in the leadership of Z.A.P.U., he was constantly trailed by members of the British South Africa police. On one particular occasion, he and some of his executive were combining a rally in the country with a visit of his own to Mrs Nkomo and his children at the mission station where they were living. It involved 300 miles of dusty driving, and the police van, with its radio whip antenna and its load of young white constables armed with loaded guns, was never absent from their driving mirror. When the Z.A.P.U. leaders decided to make a 'lavatory stop' in the remote bush country, the police van pulled up smartly, too.

Joshua Nkomo told me:

I was foolish enough to get into the position of being about twenty yards off the road and entirely alone. I heard a click which could only mean one thing; someone with a rifle had slipped off the safety catch. I turned in time to see a young man taking a bead on me; as I turned he faltered, lowered the rifle, and looked embarrassed. I shouted at him 'Have they given you orders to shoot me while trying to escape?' All he would say was that I had better ask them that back at Head-quarters. I walked slowly up to him. He put his safety catch back on. Then we walked back to the road together in silence and got into our separate cars.

Behind these assorted pictures of race relations in the Federation stands the main question, the one Mr Butler has been putting to black and white Rhodesians alike: Do you know the facts of the 1960s – all the facts? The ignorance of many black men cannot be denied – though their leaders are well-educated men, well-travelled and equipped with a negotiating skill in English from their visits to London and the U.N. that Lobengula might have envied. But in a country where the expenditure of public funds on education is £103 a year for each white child and £7 for each black one, where white children may have free schooling to the age of eighteen and black ones pay fees (painfully large in relation to the income of their parents), where 4 out of 5 white children go on to secondary school because there are plenty of places for them, but only 1 out of every 148 Africans – in such a country, is it any wonder that many black people may be poorly informed?

The obligation is clearly on the privileged white citizens to see that the Africans are helped. A federal voting roll that is ninety-eight per cent white quite evidently puts on them the responsibility of acting as guardians or trustees for a voteless multitude of eight million people. Again, the task of negotiating in the name and on the behalf of these eight million Africans in London clearly places on the Federal administration the responsibility of having a close knowledge of their needs and wishes. Or, to put it another way, Mr Macmillan and Mr Butler must be able to feel that when they are dealing with Sir Roy and his Ministers they are dealing with men who are 'in touch'. If not, any negotiations become unrealistic and a farce.

It is in this context that we must examine the ultimate intentions of the white settlers. Until he has an accurate idea of them, it will be a waste of time for Mr Butler or any other British Minister to invite Sir Roy and the Rhodesians to the conference table. Which is it to be: trusteeship leading to African majority rule and the transfer of power to an African Prime Minister? Or permanent white authority in Salisbury and permanent secondary status for the African?

We may call them Choice A and Choice B. If it is A, then it makes sense to persist in the present course: the endless junketings of British Ministers to Salisbury and Federal Ministers to London; the commissions, the conferences, the patient behind-the-scenes manoeuvring. But if it is Choice B, then there can be only one conclusion: the white Rhodesian governments – Federal and Territorial alike – are on a collision course, and it is up to Britain to put the helm over and the engines full astern if millions of people (some of them white) are to be spared calamity.

Rhodesia is an exercise in trusteeship and responsibility. Britain is ultimately responsible for the welfare of eight million black Rhodesians. That is her case before the U.N. If Britain were not the trustee, it would be up to Sir Roy Welensky to name *his* spokesman, who would make his own direct submission to the U.N. on behalf of 312,000 settler-voters as corporate trustees.

But Britain is the trustee. And, as such, she has not only the right but also the duty to ascertain that the settlers, too, accept their trusteeship role. This is the sequence of logical argument, based on the principle of accepting obligations, that has led a good many British Conservative M.P.s – the so-called 'Macleod wing' – to declare that the time has come for the British government to stiffen its back and face squarely up to Sir Roy Welensky at last.

Guardian or white supremacist? Choice A or Choice B?

The answer, according to the father of Federation, Lord Malvern, is that the African must attain 'civilized standards' in order to qualify for social and political rights on equal terms with the white man. This answer was reinforced by Sir Roy Welensky in 1953, a few months after he had received his knighthood in the Queen's Birthday Honours List, as he and Malvern (then still Sir Godfrey Huggins) prepared to lead the Federal Party into the first Federal general election.

We of the Federal Party are determined to see that there is no lowering of European standards, which means that Africans must exert themselves if they wish to rise to a higher level. In the political field the African can enjoy only such a share of political control as he is capable of earning by demonstrating that he has attained civilized standards of behaviour and culture.

The formula – let us call it the Welensky Contract – is crystal clear. Qualify as 'civilized', and you get the vote. If enough of you are black, then it will be your right, if you wish to exercise it, to elect an all-black government. But by this formula, as the black man approaches parity on the voting rolls, the contending political parties will all be 'zebras', their leadership and membership alike a black-white mixture, qualified by policy instead of race. You would move from today's almost altogether white Federal Cabinet (there is one African junior Minister) to one progressively more African. In due course, you would see an African Prime Minister take office, but with white men in his Cabinet, too.

It seems an attractive and credible formula. And it was, so far as correspondents in London could determine, accepted with complete trust by Lord Home, Lord Kilmuir, and Mr Sandys, to name three of the six Ministers in the British Cabinet who were concerned, with Mr Macmillan himself, in shaping the Northern Rhodesian constitution during the winter of 1961–2. (Lord Kilmuir is out of office now, but as Lord Chancellor he was a powerful figure, and – whenever Mr Sandys was away – the policy-maker to whom all papers were referred by Commonwealth Relations Office staff.)

It is tactless perhaps to try lining up the remaining Cabinet Ministers on the issue, since it would suggest that they did not wholly accept the Welensky Contract at face value. Let us put it charitably and say that they tended to suspend judgement. In the 1961–2 negotiations they were the Colonial Secretary, Reginald Maudling; his predecessor, who had become Conservative Party Chairman and Leader of the House, Iain Macleod; and Harold Macmillan himself. All three had visited the Federation; all three had wide knowledge of Africa (Mr Macmillan's contact dating from 1942).

Mr R. A. Butler was then just another member of the special 'Rhodesia Committee' of the Cabinet; Mr Macmillan, as Prime Minister, was Chairman. But after the creation of the new Central African Office in March 1962 (to reduce the load on Mr Macmillan and to stop Salisbury from playing off Colonial Secretary and Commonwealth Secretary against each other) the situation suddenly changed. As 'overlord' for Central Africa, Mr Butler became the key man. Does he now accept the Welensky Contract? Mr Butler is and always had been an enigma, even to his closest friends. He is a man with a clear, cold mind. He has enormous respect for any adversary who demonstrably possesses skill, ability, and the political will to get things done. On this score I should say he respects Dr Hastings Banda at one end of the Central African spectrum, and at the other, 'Taffy' Evans, the ebullient *eminence rose* of the Federal Civil Service, who has been the real brains behind the Welensky team in all the complex bargaining with Whitehall over the years. If I were an African politician I should be far more apprehensive seeing Taffy Evans reach for his slide-rule to do one of his deadly calculations –

where X is the income minimum, Y the optimum constituency boundary, and Z the potential maximum voters' registration – than I would be at the approach of an armed trooper from the British South Africa Police. I know which one can be the more effective warder.

The realistic test of the Welensky Contract is its record in the ten years since it was enunciated. How swiftly have the voteless Africans moved forward to votes and civilized citizenship? What obstacles, if any, were put in their way? Finally – and this, the acid test of the Rhodesian settler régime, must be the central question posed by any book on Rhodesia today – what positive programme has been pursued to help the maximum number of black Rhodesians reach 'civilized standards' as rapidly as possible?

The terrible – and the terrifying – truth about the settler régime in the Federation is that, under its management, on several fundamental matters the African citizen, rather than going forward, actually moved back. In the Federal Assembly, the black man's share of the seats – here I refer to those controlled by Africans – has slipped from 11·5 per cent in 1953 to 6·8 per cent today. The white settler seats have increased from 82·75 per cent to 86·4 per cent of the whole. The common roll of 1953, which was – at least in principle – non-racial, has been split into two separate rolls. To qualify for the 'general' roll, which means the upper one controlling eighty-six per cent of the seats, the income hurdle is now £720 a year, or three times what it was when Federation began.

As for safeguards, the much-advertised African Affairs Board, which helped persuade a reluctant British House of Commons to accept Federation ten years ago, has now been turned inside out and reduced to the status of a sub-committee of the settler-run United Federal Party. Before it was effectively gagged, the Board had protested against the very changes in franchise and seating that I have listed above. Now it has been smoothly dealt with (as Lord Malvern had coolly predicted that it would be), and the Africans would be fools not to draw the appropriate conclusions.

In Southern Rhodesia itself, the Africans have again seen a common-roll system of voting split to provide the familiar 'double standard'. First, as a result of the Todd affair in 1957, came the 'devaluation' system, which created two voters' rolls – one 'General' or, for all practical purposes, white, and the 'Special' or black one – both voting for the same M.P.s but with voters on the 'Special' roll limited in number to no more than twenty per cent of the voters on the 'General' roll. Then, in the 1961 Sandys–Whitehead Constitution, this system was abandoned for an outright split into 'A' and 'B' rolls, each electing its own M.P.s. True, this now provided there would be about fifteen black faces in a legislature of sixty-five, instead of the all-white parliament of thirty which had ruled the southern heartland since the start of settler home rule in 1923. But the 1961 plan ensured by its entrenched clauses that upward revision of the seating in favour of the African could be blocked indefinitely by the settlers, while at the same time the British government could no longer be invoked as guardian of African rights. Mr Sandys had specifically agreed that this power should be terminated, as the price of settler agreement to any revision at all.

In the two northern protectorates, however, matters have gone differently. Both territories have been under Colonial Office control, and the neutral observer would be forced to conclude that the continuance of British trusteeship has served as a buttress against settler attack. It has not always been such a brave, impregnable buttress as it should be – the Welensky forces crashed through it when the Northern Rhodesian Constitution was unheroically dismantled in June 1961. It took the next Colonial Secretary, Mr Maudling, months of work, but by March 1962 he had repaired the breach. In Nyasaland, thanks to the introduction of the Macleod Plan, there was a clean swing over to African majority rule in the local parliament. In the two territories, a new system of franchise put some 180,000 Africans on to the voters' rolls.

It would be a shining argument for the worth of Federation, and for the genuine concern of the white settler to advance his African partner to 'civilized standards', if these changes in the

North had come about through the initiative of Sir Roy Welensky and the dominant U.F.P. But, of course, as the Africans saw themselves, and as the British national Press – even including *The Times* and the *Daily Telegraph* – did not fail to point out, these advances came about despite blatant and determined efforts by Welensky and the settler régime to resist them. The lesson was not lost on the Africans of the Federation.

By their own choice – as enshrined in the list of qualifications for the vote – the settlers have set the attainment of civilized standards in terms of income and schooling. How effectively have the Africans been enabled to reach the white man's standards under these two vital headings?

I. INCOME: Even a distinctly optimistic calculation suggests that it will take two full generations for the Africans to reach the levels enjoyed by the white man today. The most favourable statistics reveal that the average income of African wage-earners rose from £70 in 1956 to £87 in 1961–2. European breadwinners have seen their take-home pay rise in the same period from £1,100 to £1,209. Now if one supposes that the white man's income froze at this figure, how long would it take the African to catch up? Allowing even for the upward curve of logarithmic progression – you might call it 'compound interest' – the most hopeful prediction comes out on the graph paper at forty-nine years.

The other target figure to examine is the minimum income of £720, which enables a man (regardless of colour) to vote on the upper roll in Federal elections, or on the 'A' roll, controlling fifty of the sixty-five seats, in elections for the Southern Rhodesian legislature under the new Sandys–Whitehead Constitution. Even by a calculation based on 'compound interest', it would take forty-one years for the *average* African's income to reach £723 8s. 0d. (A large number of black citizens would still, of course, be receiving pay below that figure and thus not qualify for the higher vote.)

Reduced to other terms, this means that the average African citizen of the Rhodesias will reach the income level to qualify for full adult franchise in 2004, and might achieve an income equal to the *present* figure for white Rhodesians by A.D. 2012.

But, as every African asserts and every settler inwardly knows, the situation will undoubtedly have changed again long before that – if the settlers continue to retain their absolute authority. How else can one reasonably interpret this list of the ways in which the minimum income figure has been continuously revised upward, so as to withhold the adult franchise from the African?

1898	Proclamation 17	£ 50 a year
1914	Legislative Ordinance	£100 a year
1951	Huggins Amendment	£240 a year
1957	Home–Welensky Revision (Federal)	£720 a year
1961	Sandys–Whitehead Revision (Southern Rhodesian)	£720 a year

The normal adult franchise is for the black citizen of the Rhodesias a kind of Sahara mirage; stumbling towards it like a thirsty man towards water, he sees it lifting and moving onwards long before he has even come within grasping distance. Even more tantalizingly, the black Rhodesian can see – as the mirage lifts to go bobbing onward again – that there are contented white Rhodesians lolling comfortably at the oasis labelled 'Civilized Standards', and that there is a full cup of water for every (white) man who dips into the well of adult franchise.

2. EDUCATION: There are complex alternative qualifications, combining income and years of schooling, even for entry to the lower voters' rolls, but the one that is pertinent is the same for both of the white settler parliaments, since the Home–Welensky Federal formula of 1957 was simply transplanted into the Sandys–Whitehead territorial plan of 1961. The voter must have an annual income of £120 plus two years of secondary education. Setting aside the fact that this income figure is a handsome forty-five per cent higher than the statistical average, the educational barrier alone must appear hopelessly high to the African. What

are his chances of reaching and passing the Form II examination at the end of Junior Secondary School? Here are the official figures for 1959–60, showing the number of Rhodesians taking secondary education:

African Enrolment		
Southern Rhodesia		3,300
Northern Rhodesia		2,108
Nyasaland		1,300
	Total	6,708

European Enrolment (including small numbers of Asian and Coloured children)

All three territories	21,671

Further examination of the figures shows that, in Northern Rhodesia, for example, the annual total of African children completing two years of secondary school was 617. For all three territories, a generous estimate would put the annual total at 2,000, out of an African school population of 1,036,617. This represented the 1960 crop of qualifiers for the 'B' vote, and they would still have to clear other barriers, including complex citizenship qualifications which can prevent Nyasas from voting in Northern Rhodesia, and so on. But by the time they reach the age of twenty-one, later in the 1960s, those junior secondary school Africans must also have attained an income level of £120 – well above national average. It will be surprising if the qualifiers, among that batch of 2,000, number as many as 500. And even then, their numbers will only swell the 'B' roll and represent no menace to the settler-dominated 'A' roll, where the real power lies.

The African must be excused if he does not see much hope of achieving eventual political parity, let alone majority rule, through education. He notes that the tiny community of white settlers (plus Asians and Coloureds) was able to get secondary education for *three times* as many children – 21,000 of them – as could the African community of eight million people, outnumbering the settlers in the ratio of 26:1. The African would have to be gullible indeed to see partnership in a system that

spends £6·2 million on the education of 1,036,000 black children
and £6·1 million on 79,000 non-African ones.

In considering whether or not the settler governments can be
trusted to carry out the role of guardian, the African is bound to
look first at income and education, since those are the two keys he
needs to open the gates of the political citadel. But how about
'civilized standards' in general? What encouragement are the
settlers giving to economic, administrative, and social advance?

1. JOBS: The salary of the white still runs as high as ten and
twelve times that of the African, for the identical job. The African farmer still gets approximately thirty per cent less for his
maize, delivered to the marketing board, in a land where this is
the staple crop.

When the economic slump hit Rhodesia in 1960, largely because of the racial clashes, black unemployment soared, while
the white settlers did not noticeably suffer. By the end of 1962
there were 80,000 Africans, who had formerly been in employment, looking for work. Official figures published in May 1962
showed an actual net decline in total African employment for the
period 1956–61 of 1·2 per cent, though the African population
had increased by more than twelve per cent. In the same period
the more fortunate white settlers had a net *increase* in employment of 11·1 per cent.

2. THE CIVIL SERVICE: I have already described how whites, by
virtue of their skin colour alone, are automatically appointed to
Grade I of the Federal public service. The 1960 political riots
provoked the settler governments in Salisbury – Territorial as
well as Federal – into some painful rethinking. Sir Roy himself,
in a phrase that infuriated most Africans by its inadequacy,
talked about removing 'the pinpricks' of racial discrimination.
(In his view these were marginal and vestigial, while to most black
men they were basic, humiliating, and integral to political
reform.)

The Federal government announced a plan to reorganize its
public service on a non-racial basis by November 1961. In June

317

1962 it was discreetly revealed that implementation had again been 'postponed for several months'. It began in March 1963.

The Southern Rhodesian government had operated an all-white Civil Service since the start of settler rule in 1923, continuing the practice initiated by the Chartered Company. The 1959 State of Emergency, however, pitchforked the legislature into action at last, and it is now legally possible for Africans to be admitted to the service. But by mid 1962 there had been only the tiniest nibbling at the outer edges of this dangerous pie and, as the Paterson Report observed, there was 'very great concern at junior levels' among white Civil Servants.

The Native Affairs Department was a case in point. Nine years after Federation had begun, and with it the official policy of partnership, the Department was still a potent instrument of control. By its very name, as well as its functions, it was obsolete in what was supposed to be a society of partners, equal before the law. In London during the 1960 Federal review, Sir Edgar Whitehead assured the British government that reform (including the removal of the offensive title) was imminent. His government had appointed two commissions of inquiry and their recommendations appeared early in 1961, in the Mangwende and Robinson Reports. Later that year the Scottish expert on administration, Professor T. T. Paterson of Glasgow University, produced his massive and definitive report on the public services. It re-emphasized the earlier recommendations that the Department's arbitrary judicial powers be scrapped and its other functions transferred to Local Government and other ministries.

For almost a year Whitehead put off the evil day of having to act. First, publication of the report (which had been rushed through for an October deadline, as Paterson specifically noted) was mysteriously held up for half a year. Then when M.P.s and the Press began to urge implementation, the Whitehead government still held off from what might be a vote-losing decision in an election year. Ironically, it was the riots that followed the banning of Z.A.P.U. that finally brought action. Sir Edgar made a broadcast appeal to Africans to abandon their false gods, and, as an enticement to win their cooperation, at last took the plunge and reorganized the Native Affairs Department overnight. The Africans might be excused for drawing their own cynical conclusions as to what produced results after nine years of far too patient waiting.

3. THE FEDERAL ARMY: In 1956 the Federal government assured the African Affairs Board that provision would be made for the promotion of Africans to commissioned rank in the Federal Army. In the ensuing years there has been no action; no black man has yet been made an officer, nor is there any provision in training methods or accommodation which would make it possible.

4. SOCIAL LIFE: It would have to be conceded by any fair-minded African, and any outside observer, that the roll-back against social discrimination – the removal of the pinpricks – did indeed get under way after the 1960 disturbances had at last penetrated settler consciousness. The Whitehead régime in the south took steps at last to turn permissive into compulsive legislation. The public swimming-pool controversy in 1961–2 ended with victory for the African cause, and the Whitehead government refused to back the obstructionist tactics of the Salisbury City Council and other local (settler-run) authorities.

In *local government*, all municipalities (except Salisbury) in Southern Rhodesia agreed in principle by mid 1962 to having direct African representation on their boards and councils – though Africans have yet to achieve the equality of citizenship implied by becoming ratepayers and being allowed to build houses of their own design on any land in the municipality.

The *Liquor Laws* have been amended to permit Africans to consume beer, wines, and spirits. And though some hotels and restaurants attempted to hold out against African entry by means of technicalities, or high prices, that particular battle had been largely won by the end of the 1961–2 summer. The Association of Citizens Against the Colour Bar, largely made up of liberal-minded whites, had conducted a spearhead campaign which prodded the settler government into action on these matters at last. But it seemed reasonable to wonder if these social advances had not all come too late. 'It isn't enough now for us to swim in the baths with you,' said Joshua Nkomo with bitter bluntness. 'We say it is time to swim with you equally in parliament, too.'

5. POLITICAL LIFE: Mr Nkomo's words flowed from direct, personal experience. Throughout that summer of 1961–2, at the same time as it was lowering the colour bar, the settler régime was cracking down with savage force on those nationalists whom Whitehead considered to be, in his own phrase, 'unrepresentative extremists'. The old African National Congress, after being banned by Sir Edgar in 1959, had been succeeded by the N.D.P. – the National Democratic Party – again with Mr Nkomo as its national leader.

The London Review Conference in December 1960 had been nearly wrecked by Whitehead's refusal – reluctantly withdrawn under considerable British government pressure – to recognize Nkomo and sit down with his N.D.P. representatives at the same conference table.

A year later, while Joshua Nkomo was actually away in Dar-es-Salaam for the Tanganyika Independence celebrations as an honoured guest of the Nyerere government, Whitehead had banned the N.D.P. Yet in Tanganyika Nkomo was present on equal terms with such guests as Duncan Sandys, and the representatives of other Commonwealth states.

In the first three months of 1962 Nkomo found himself, along with eleven out of thirteen members in the national executive of their successor organization Z.A.P.U., effectively gagged. These leaders of the new Zimbabwe African People's Union, as it was called, were under constant police surveillance, day and night, to ensure that they did not break the order banning them from addressing public meetings. It was largely for this reason, Nkomo told me, that he chose to take his country's case to the Committee of Seventeen at the U.N. in New York.

As part of this deliberate harassment, Nkomo's two chief deputies were subjected to special attentions. A month before his untimely death in 1962, the late Dr T. S. Parirenyatwa was summonsed on a trumped-up traffic charge and had his car impounded. Leopold Takawira, a former headmaster and distinguished educationist, was charged under the Law and Order (Maintenance) Act and sentenced to nine months' hard labour.

Here is how the *Central African Examiner* reported the first incident:

A posse of white police walked without so much as a 'by your leave' into a home in Highfield (the African township outside Salisbury). A guest in the house had carelessly let his back wheel slip into the ditch and been helped out by passers-by. The police informed the guest that since he had failed to report an accident his car would be impounded – which it was, until he took the matter up with the Minister of Justice. That the person concerned was Dr Parirenyatwa, Deputy President of Z.A.P.U., ought to have made no difference to the police. Did it? One wonders.

The same issue of the *Central African Examiner*, in June 1962, reported the extraordinary case of a white police officer who was taken into custody at one in the morning by African constables of his own force. They did not know who they were arresting because the officer had been dressed and made up to look like an African. The incident occurred in Highfield township, across the tracks from white man's Salisbury, and the paper claimed strong circumstantial evidence that the disguised officer was running away from a house whose window had just that moment been broken by a stone. The house was the home of a 'moderate' African, well-known as a supporter of the present system and an opponent of Mr Nkomo and the nationalists.

This matched, of course, the unsavoury incident of 'intimidation' in Nyasaland at the time of the 1961 election, when the home of an African supporter of Sir Roy Welensky and the U.F.P. was burnt to ashes. In court it was proved to have been the work of a group of minor U.F.P. officials, who were sentenced to terms of imprisonment. Yet, before the case had come to court, parties of British M.P.s on tour as guests of Voice & Vision Ltd, the Federal government's publicity agents in London, had been shown the remains of the hut as a typical example of 'Malawi intimidation'. So that the outcome of the episode should not be forgotten, a back-bench Tory M.P. of the Macleod wing, Nigel Fisher, rose in the House of Commons and read out the details, which were recorded in Hansard. (See Appendix to this book.)

It is a measure of the remoteness of Rhodesia's settler politicians from the feelings of eight million Africans that the United Federal Party should have chosen the time they did for their 'Build A Nation Campaign'. Such a campaign might just conceivably have had some chance of success if its launching had been made to coincide with dramatic political concessions to the Africans, but hardly in early 1962.

The answer, pathetically, seems to be that the U.F.P. high command, starting with Sir Roy and Sir Edgar, genuinely believed they were doing this. The very modest assault on the social colour bar – letting Africans enter cafés instead of having to buy a sandwich and eat standing on the public pavements outside – was the kind of concession that apparently seemed prodigious to U.F.P. eyes. True, considering the fanatic opposition of white supremacists, the roll-back in social discrimination represents a triumph for the patient (too patient ?) manoeuvres of Sir Edgar who by his own lights, is a liberal in politics. But it was again the tragic case of too little and too late.

The Africans of the Federation can now go to the white man's cinema in the centre of town and see a first-run feature, instead of having to wait (as has been the case for half a century) to see it six months late or not at all, in a squalid flea-pit of a back-street building where the diet is an endless series of cowboy second features. But this seems trivial now, when the eight million Africans of Tanganyika right next door are running their own nation.

The white Rhodesians may overlook Tanganyika's independence – and its nightly broadcasts across an invisible white man's border – but the Africans do not. One of the minor tragedies of 1962 was the departure from Salisbury of Herbert Chitepo to become Tanganyika's Director of Public Prosecutions. After eight years he was still the only practising African barrister among Southern Rhodesia's three million black people. For him, a special clause had had to be drafted in the Land

Apportionment Act (the Chitepo amendment) so that he could have chambers in town adjacent to other lawyers – and the courts. He had moved, in those years, from a cautious middle position in politics to outright association with the nationalists. By mid 1962, with long prison terms threatening them, the Z.A.P.U. leaders thought it better to have their best legal brain out of the country, assisting their struggle from the security of an independent African state, and gaining experience of use to a future black-administered Rhodesia, than rotting in jail with them. He returned in 1963 to defend Joshua Nkomo.

It is an old rule of Southern Rhodesian settler politics that the government in power should, and indeed must, demonstrate that it is pursuing a 'firm Native policy' before it goes to the country. Sir Edgar Whitehead was shrewd enough to see in mid 1962, with his 'Claim Your Vote' campaign a disastrous failure – hardly a sixth of the Africans he wanted had registered for the 'B' roll – that there had been an impressive display of Z.A.P.U. nationalist strength. Either that or and this was the explanation that Sir Edgar himself clearly favoured – there had been a skilful campaign of fierce intimidation conducted by those much-maligned but seldom-visible creatures, the 'Z.A.P.U. thugs'.

In either event, the profitable political strategy – by precedent – was obviously the same. The time had come for an impressive, wide-scale show of force. If this seems a cynical reading of events, the reader is referred to the near-disaster of the 1958 election, when only a mathematical miracle had saved the U.F.P. By sheer chance the tough men of the party caucus, who had thrown out Todd and his franchise formula for Africans, had neglected to throw out another Todd innovation – the transferable vote. (It had been part of his plan for moving towards non-racial politics.) In the first ballot the right-wing Dominion Party had actually topped the poll, with more than 18,000 votes to less than 17,000 for the U.F.P. Fortunately for the Whitehead forces, however, this had left for redistribution the 4,705 votes (1,700 of them African) which had gone to the small new party hastily formed by Todd, and these voters had named the U.F.P. as their second preference. The final outcome had therefore been a narrow victory for Sir Edgar, though on a straight vote the Dominion Party would have emerged with a seventeen to thirteen majority in the legislature and power to pursue its vigorous programme of full-blooded apartheid on the South African model. During the election campaign, indeed, the D.P. had promised, if successful, to end the fuzzy policies of 'partnership', to get the African right off the white man's voting roll, to adopt a 'tough' policy on land, and to erect a strong frontier-line of segregation through the whole uneasy terrain of Rhodesian political and social life.

Whitehead recognized in the election results that he faced a real rival for power from the traditionally most dangerous direction – the right. His skilful presentation of the constitution in 1961, and its acceptance in the (practically) all-white referendum which followed, were no guarantee that the Dominion Party would not sweep to power at the polls. Humiliated by the successful Z.A.P.U. boycott of his 'Build A Nation – Claim Your Vote' campaigns, Sir Edgar decided to play for time. He postponed the general election to late 1962, and proceeded to inflict the ritual crack-down that settler tradition demanded.

The details of this punitive campaign appear in a later chapter; it is enough to note here that the measures devised by the U.F.P. high command and proclaimed in August 1962 gratifyingly, perhaps brilliantly, succeeded. The vicious amendments to the Unlawful Organizations Act, and the Law and Order (Maintenance) Act produced a tidal wave of protest from what might be called the liberal wing of the white electorate.

One can only speculate on the silent chagrin in the camp of the Dominion Party extremists and their other right-wing allies, now reformed under the banner of the Rhodesian Front. Sir Edgar's actions effectively stole their thunder. If proof were needed, the white voter had only to refer to some well-tried barometers. Cries of protest came from such liberal critics of the U.F.P. as Sir Robert Tredgold and Ralph Palmer.

Mr Palmer, leader of the liberal Central Africa Party, was the man who, in two nights of hot work from hotel rooms, had bridged the gap between Whitehead and the N.D.P. nationalists, and brought Nkomo and his colleagues to their seats at Lancaster

House. When the August 1962 crack-down came, he joined fourteen members of the Southern Rhodesian bar in claiming that the new amendments would empower the Minister of Justice to 'stifle all political opposition'. Sir Robert, the former Chief Justice of the Federation, said that the measures effectively removed 'the last vestiges of doubt about whether Southern Rhodesia is a police State'.

The unprecedented petitions and delegations from the Churches, and the dramatic resignation of Sir Roy's junior Minister, Jasper Savanhu, all added up to making one thing clear to 70,000 white settler voters: Whitehead and his territorial U.F.P. organization had moved sharply to the right. Neither he nor his opponents could be sure just how effectively he had split the right-wing vote. But the Whitehead crack-down had achieved its essential tactical objective; it had established the U.F.P. in settler eyes as being just as 'safe', just as dependable and solid, as its strident white opposition.

Was Whitehead wrestling with his soul as he put through his Draconian measures in 1962? I do not believe he was. As a paternalist, wildly out of touch with the real thoughts and aspirations of the mass of Africans, he seemed, in conversations with political correspondents at that time, to be genuinely convinced that Z.A.P.U. was no more than the fraudulent structure of a minority group of ambitious men. In the Whitehead–U.F.P. view, Nkomo and Silundika and all their nationalist colleagues were simply a small group of educated but aggressive opportunists. I myself and other correspondents were solemnly assured that they were greedy, unrepresentative Africans, out to get the easy jobs, the long black cars, and the lush living that would go with the capture of government. A devilish combination of Liberia and Haiti in their least attractive aspects, was how Lord Malvern himself had expressed it.

Whitehead's own farm near Umtali is, by most accounts, a reasonably happy place where paternalism is the pattern of living. Africans who are not impatient, who do not insist on a timetable of progress or the guarantee of political equality within 'the foreseeable future', find that they can be perfectly contented there. And so, seen through Sir Edgar's paternalism-tinted spectacles, the calm clear contented world of Rhodesia is rendered unstable only by the frenetic, grasping activities of a small band of unrepresentative African fanatics. If Nkomo and his aides could only be removed from the scene and politically neutralized, then the 'gentlemen settlers' of the old school, who really care for the welfare of the ordinary African, could get on with their plans, and could afford to ignore the raucous competition from the Rhodesian Front and the right wing.

By this line of reasoning Sir Edgar conceives it his duty to see that he and his fellow-liberals are returned to office, in order to pursue a humane Native policy, rather than let in the crude men of the right wing who might well precipitate a racial explosion. Thus does the slippery slope of pragmatism lead the paternalists to the detention of their African opponents without trial or even charge of any sort, and to the Draconian legislation of August 1962. To be returned to power the U.F.P. must present the 'brand image' of firmness to the white voters who constitute 98·5 per cent of the only electoral roll that matters. The two Prime Ministers who failed to observe this rule were the ex-missionary, R. S. Garfield Todd, and the missionary's son, Howard Unwin Moffat. The demise in each case was swift, and the attack came from the right. Moffat was politically butchered by Huggins; Todd, by his own U.F.P. colleagues in a palace assassination conducted under the benign imperial gaze of Sir Roy Welensky. The Matjaha warriors of the Mbesu Regiment, dispatching old Lotje on the bloody slopes of Thabas Induna, could not have been more ruthlessly efficient.

Confronted with this spectacle of pragmatism rampant, it would be a naïve African politician indeed who concluded that all was for the best in the best of all African worlds; that he and his compatriots could rest assured they were being led forward by their white partners to civilized standards and the vote. Indeed, it may be pertinent to ask – as the Africans are asking – whether the white men who hold supreme military, economic, and political power in Rhodesia today are any longer capable of judging what civilized standards are. The ordinary British voters, and even the Ministers in Whitehall, have no convenient tape measure by which to gauge events in the Rhodesias. But they are, in fact, confronted with a shrill example of Lord Acton's famous dictum – absolute power corrupting absolutely. Like Anthony Eden over Suez, the white rulers of Central Africa are irascible, out of touch, and in full possession of the means to wreak enormous damage before they can be removed.

This is the frightening aspect of the political dilemma in Rhodesia today. There is the strong possibility that the ship of state is in the command of a band of Captain Queegs who have lost their bearings, and their self-control. It is not long since Lord Malvern solemnly told an astonished British House of Lords that 'all Africans are liars', thus making it pretty clear that they would not attain civilized standards – and the vote – as long as he had an influence over the policies of the U.F.P. Here is the key-sentence about ultimate objectives, as he put it to his own legislature in 1952, when requiring a mandate for Federation:

We are trying to enlarge and fortify a unit of the Empire which is at present small, thinly populated, industrially of small importance ... into a country well populated, highly developed and its immense natural resources employed to the benefit of mankind.

I have quoted this for its *implicit* racialism, since the actual phrases are unexceptionable. It is surely preposterous to talk of the Rhodesias as 'thinly populated', when there are seven (now eight) million black citizens living there. Indeed, an African Prime Minister of Rhodesia, speaking at that same moment, might have justifiably said 'one of the largest, most populous states of Africa'. For in land area, resources, *and* in the number of its inhabitants, the Federation exceeds Ghana, Kenya, Uganda, Morocco, Tunisia, Liberia, Sierra Leone, and a dozen of the French-speaking states that stretch across the map from Senegal to the Brazzaville Congo.

This is the perhaps fatal blind spot of the privileged white people who inhabit the Rhodesias. They see themselves, and only themselves, as 'the nation', and the fact that they hold this

view sincerely does not make the view itself any the less dangerous. Here is Sir Roy Welensky in 1957, as he spoke to the white
electors of Salisbury, before leaving for London to negotiate with
Lord Home the shrewd concessions which were to increase white
control of the Federal parliament:

It is time we took a stand – the stand which I am now taking – on
the issue of whether civilization is to remain here. That is, whether you
and I, as Europeans, are to remain and whether all we set store by is to
remain, and whether on that basis this Federation is to go forward.

The excerpt is from the *Rhodesia Herald* of 9 February that
year, and I have felt the strongest compulsion sometimes just
to run off a translation in French for Sir Roy to send to his
friend, M. Moise Tshombe, the defender of civilized standards
across the border in Katanga. But then, consistency has never
been a marked characteristic of the settler declarations. The
overt statements vary to suit the day and the hour; what matters
– and what the African politicians have cynically learned to
detect – is the very consistent basic doctrine which runs deep
down beneath all the oratory. Many a white politician in Salisbury will say that African majority rule must come 'during my
lifetime', or 'by the time my children have children of their
own'. And he may even think he means it. But the unconscious
principle on which he conducts public policy is that such a
change will NOT come *during his term of office*. It is like the pot of
jam in *Alice in Wonderland* which is always just around the
corner. In Rhodesia the Africans are coming to realize that it is
never jam *today*.

It is as well to remind ourselves that when these rich Rhodesians talk about their standards, they are talking not only about
standards of parliamentary government, but about a standard of
living that is well beyond the reach of the average British taxpayer. The British wage-earner might do well to keep in mind
the picture of his contented Rhodesian cousins – the miners in
their Jaguars, the thousands of households where cheap black
labour makes living so easy, the take-home pay thirty to fifty per
cent higher than Britain – before expending too much sympathy

on statements like another of Sir Roy Welensky's, made on his departure for negotiations in London.

We, the Europeans of the Federation, are striving to preserve the very standards which Britain sets herself. I shall not be slow to argue the case the Europeans of the Federation have to offer.

And if by 'standards' Welensky does not refer to Jaguars and house-servants and luxury holidays, but to democratic government, then one is bound to ask if it is civilized to suspend habeas corpus (when the prisoner is black), to keep people in concentration camps (for that is what Gokwe is), and to restrict the vote to 1·5 or 2 per cent of the Africans. In the words of Colin Leys:

A rough comparison would be a franchise in Britain open only to surtax payers. The official view is that only this tiny minority of Africans is civilized and responsible, whereas all Europeans are.

The words of Welensky in the speech I have just quoted provoked a thoughtful comment from the Interracial Association of Southern Rhodesia, a group led by members of that lonely minority, the genuine white liberals. The I.A.S.R. said that the Federal Prime Minister clearly regarded himself 'as a representative of the white section of the population rather than the people as a whole'. And it continued: 'He refers to the Europeans as "we" and the Africans as "they" and generalizes about both.'

A classic example of this outlook is the official history of the country, to be found in the Federal Government Handbook. On page 78, referring to the First World War, the Handbook claims:

Southern Rhodesia made a particularly large contribution to the British cause. Nearly 7,000 of its population of 24,000 went on active service, an extraordinary percentage, possible only amongst a very youthful population containing a large proportion of men with military training.

The same unconscious white 'We' appears when the Handbook refers to the intervention of a Labour Colonial Secretary, Lord Passfield, whose policy statement of 1930 reiterated the paramountcy of native interests.

This policy led to bitter hostility against the Imperial Government. The only way of preventing the Northern Rhodesians from being reduced to a state of political impotence now seemed to lie in amalgamation with Southern Rhodesia.

The 'bitter hostility', of course, applied solely to the white minority, outnumbered then at least 50:1. For the black majority, confidence was being restored in an Imperial government which, in the preceding era under L. S. Amery's Tory administration, had seemed to have swung over hard to the settler side and away from the traditional Colonial Office role of trusteeship. And whatever the Handbook may say about 'Northern Rhodesians' and amalgamation, must be read exactly in reverse – if one means the great, forgotten majority.

There are many more examples in the Handbook of the unconscious white viewpoint, but the one on page 113 seems peculiarly significant. Describing the moves leading up to Federation, the Handbook says, 'In 1949 a Conference was held at the Victoria Falls, at which both the Rhodesias and Nyasaland were represented.'

Any detached observer, with some knowledge of geography, must picture a multi-racial gathering; some large room in the hotel by the Falls, with long rows of faces – black and white – as the delegates take their seats. I know I formed that mental image of the conference myself, in response to the sentence in the Handbook. It was only when I turned to other sources that I discovered the delegations of all three territories on that occasion at Victoria Falls had been wholly white. I felt cheated, as many an African politician must feel cheated on altogether too many occasions in Rhodesian politics.

The Africans today – it cannot be stressed too often – are not fools. The submissions by Mr Nkomo and Mr Kaunda to the Committee of Seventeen at the U.N. show a sophisticated grasp of political essentials. And if Sir Roy Welensky and the U.F.P. genuinely expect the Africans to line up for a run at the hurdle marked 'civilized standards', then the contest must be rendered credible.

It must be seen that the conditions are fair, that those who leap the hurdle win the prize, and that those operating the contest are doing so in good faith. Unfortunately for the settlers, the law of Hosea is as immutable in Zambesia as it was in Judea: they have sown the wind and they are reaping the whirlwind now. And the principal sower, throughout the whole course of the Rhodesian tragedy now approaching its climax, has been the Father of Federation himself, Lord Malvern. During his active political career, as Sir Godfrey Huggins, he seemed to revel in the kind of short, cynical remark which delighted most settlers, disturbed the white liberals, and shocked the African. Here are some of his verbal sowings:

We do not want our grandchildren to have as a neighbour a state such as Liberia which has no European guidance. [Report in Johannesburg *Star*, 20 December 1948.]

That was a speech in which, as Prime Minister of Southern Rhodesia, he called for federation with the two northern protectorates. If it was not sufficiently clear what the African's future would be, he made it so two months later:

The natives must be ruled by a benevolent aristocracy in the real sense of the word. . . . Our democratic system does not embrace mob law. [*Bulawayo Chronicle*, 17 February 1949.]

And in that same speech, he maintained that any plan to put African M.P.s into a federal parliament would be 'a farce'. The Imperial watchdogs in London dozed on.

Once the Imperial government have granted this constitution they have lost all control – don't forget that.

That was Huggins two years later, as the constitutional plan was being drafted, speaking to a section of his party executive. Even the staunchest Tory of the 'kith and kin' school should have found his conscience, not to mention his pride, troubled at another remark made by Huggins at that same party conference in July 1951:

In practice the reservations are not worth the paper they are written on.

331

Huggins was talking about the safeguards which were to be written into the constitution of the Federation to protect the political rights of Africans and foster their future progress. The Prime Minister asserted to his party executive that Britain's political leaders of both parties, were perfectly well aware of his views. And he went on to quote from a conversation with the Colonial Secretary in the then Labour government in London:

He [meaning Mr Creech Jones] said to me: 'What happens if you insist on carrying out something which is reserved and we don't agree to it?' I said: 'We just have a general election and go on and do it. You can't do anything.' And he agreed.

Knowing a little of the character of Arthur Creech Jones, a tough and stubbornly principled man, I doubt the accuracy of Huggins's account. But it is the cynicism of the white settler outlook, revealed here, which is relevant. Once Labour had been put out of power in the October election of 1951, Huggins spoke his real thoughts even more blatantly. The last round of talks at Victoria Falls, he told the Southern Rhodesian Assembly, had 'degenerated into a Native Benefit Society meeting, led by the (Labour) Secretary of State for the Colonies'. The quotation can be found in Hansard of 19 November 1951, and the operative word is 'degenerated'. There is the man who was Territorial Prime Minister for a quarter of a century, and first Federal Prime Minister, revealing his real estimate of the African. The wonder is that the new Tory Colonial Secretary, Oliver Lyttleton, now Lord Chandos, could reasonably believe that such a man would pursue a policy of trusteeship towards the African. And Huggins did not reserve his cynical sneers for Labour governments only. Three months after the Tory triumph in the British election, he was in London for negotiations with Lyttleton, and had this to say at a news conference before returning home:

It is terrible that the people elected to look after the drains in Shoreditch should really have control of huge territories in the middle of Africa.

It is very seldom that the rich, remote, and urbane Lord Chandos has been made to look foolish and naïve, but Huggins did it. What is more, he succeeded a few months later in achieving the establishment of Federation. Lyttleton and the Tories had placid faith in the good intentions of the settlers to guard and advance African interests – 'We have put our trust in Sir Godfrey Huggins and Sir Roy Welensky,' said Julian Amery in a notable emotional outburst during the final debate at Westminster – but Huggins himself made no effort to hide his own more cynical view. Could the Africans flood the Federal roll and swamp the white voter, asked an anxious U.F.P. supporter at a public meeting in Rhodesia? Such fears, replied Huggins, were absurd, since 'the Europeans can always alter the law to prevent this'.*

Huggins's good friend, Richard Haw, the educationist whose book *No Other Home* has already been quoted, gives the settler view of the 'chaos' that would result if normal adult franchise were ever introduced in some burst of misguided liberalism:

Parliament would automatically become almost entirely composed of Bantu members. It is scarcely conceivable that the Bantu would vote for White candidates, except in rare cases. Once entrenched in Parliament, the extremists would proceed to reverse all policies and legislation. They may be expected to fill the Civil Service with as many Bantu as possible, lowering qualifications where these stand in their way.

The Whites are maintaining their position and interests by ensuring that only civilized persons are enfranchised. . . . Partnership . . . can lead only to dominance by the majority race, and the majority of Whites in Southern Africa not unnaturally wish to avoid this conclusion.

And Mr Haw goes on to advocate the ultimate policy of despair – the partitioning of Central Africa into settler zones and black Bantustans.

This policy is now being frankly advocated for the Rhodesias by those members of the Dominion Party, and other racist right-wing groups who came together in 1962 to form the Rhodesian Front. They are calling for apartheid – they publicly use the word – on the South African model. Yet this is nothing

* Report in the Johannesburg *Star*, 29 July 1952.

fundamentally new. As long ago as 1957, during the great Todd affair, the Dominion Party itself had served notice on the African leaders of what the alternative settler policy would be, if the U.F.P. were ever turned out of office. Its Franchise Memorandum of the same year claimed that the U.F.P. method of measuring 'civilized standards' in terms of education and income was much too open to abuse. The draft regulations of the D.P. would require each would-be African voter to secure testimonials from ten people (presumably white) already on the voters' roll, certifying that 'the applicant has lived after a civilized manner of life for a period of 10 years, is educated to the understanding of a liberal democracy, and is of good general repute'. After that the applicant would be required to appear before a five-man Board of Franchise Examiners. None of these stipulations would apply, however, to a white person applying for the vote since the European was, by inheritance, 'tolerant, fair, reasonable and liberal-minded'.

In the election that followed, the Dominion Party, together with its Franchise Memorandum, was narrowly defeated, thanks to the transferable vote. But it is worth remarking the implications of the 'raw' percentages:

Dominion Party	46 per cent
U.F.P.–Whitehead	42 per cent
Todd liberals	12 per cent

To any thinking African, there could be only one deduction: nearly half the white settlers in Southern Rhodesia actually agreed with the crack-brained view of what constituted a civilized African in the Dominion Party programme. Every second Civil Servant, more or less; every other white officer of the British South Africa Police; and, most important of all, half of all the white men making up the Rhodesian army and air force, were then, in 1958 – and probably still are – going about their daily business with their heads stuffed full of crude race supremacist philosophies.

And this is putting it at the minimum, for the supporters of the U.F.P. also talk – and act – as though the black Rhodesians will never be civilized enough to get the adult franchise in their lifetime. Time and again the correspondent visiting Rhodesia is told by settlers that 'it took us two thousand years to get where we are'. Whitehead and Welensky never tire of the theme, and it is repeated in a hundred private conversations.

This is sometimes known as the 'Race Memory' theory, and it has been laboriously examined and disproved a dozen times in such genuinely civilized places as Vienna, Zürich, London, and New York. Progoff has dealt with it exhaustively in his *Jung's Psychology*, as has Kammerer in *The Inheritance of Acquired Characteristics*. On a simpler plane, the point has been proved in reverse by the 'Wolf Boy' cases, where a child has retrogressed in one generation (his own) to cave-man status, simply because he grew up in a jungle environment instead of a civilized home.

It is convenient for the Rhodesian settler, desperately rationalizing as the frontiers of independent black Africa move inexorably south, to resuscitate the discredited theories of race memory. This was the shabby battle cry of the O.A.S. and the settlers of Oran in their unlamented last stand. The truly civilized attitude to the problem of having culturally backward peoples in your midst is to provide the practical means by which they might advance.

If this means anything, it means a real obligation on every last one of the fortunate white adult citizens of Rhodesia today. His black neighbour, pathetically poor, with one-fifteenth of his own income and no accumulated backlog of books and other treasure, desperately needs help. And the hard fact is that a cheque-book alone cannot provide that help. It means communally mixed living, however distasteful that may seem; for how else is the black man ever to absorb the standards that he is being urged to acquire? It means an end to the present legal separation of white children from black in schools. This is one of the important inner citadels that the white man is most reluctant to yield. Yet it must be done if the settler's professed policy is to be achieved.

Here we are at the heart of the matter. Do the settlers, and their political leaders in particular, really want to raise African standards at all?

Certainly, in terms of their published statements, their frequent protestations to Lord Home, Duncan Sandys, and other sympathetically inclined Cabinet Ministers in successive British governments, there can be no doubt of the answer. The whole concept of partnership is a public commitment to do just this. And yet the true answer is, on the record, clearly different. It may come to something like this: we want to advance our African neighbours socially; but to ensure that the white community *en bloc* is always economically ahead. We want them to become westernized and conform wholly to a European way of life; but until that day actually arrives, we are determined not to mix with them socially, since that might dilute or alter our present standards. And, to secure these standards, we will never let real political power slip from our grasp, though we are prepared to take verbal steps to placate public opinion in Britain. But if the British government tries to intervene, effectively so as to delete or reverse any part of that policy, then it will be time to stage our own Boston Tea Party; time, with our military power as the ultimate sanction, to declare independence and go it alone in Central Africa.

5 The Politics of Privilege

> 'It is a sin against all reason, a criminal madness, to train a semi-ape to become a lawyer.' ADOLF HITLER

Disraeli, in his novel *Sybil*, was moved to write: 'I was told that the Privileged and the People formed Two Nations.' He could hardly have known that some eighty years later, in a British colony, a policeman would give this report, in evidence to a parliamentary commission:

I found little boys of about seven to eight years in the tobacco factory. They are trying to work because their fathers have no support for their children. They live in dark and dirty places and most of them were coughing. They will not grow into good men. They will die before they come to be men.

That was an African constable at the Makabusi police cantonment in Rhodesia. And one of his colleagues testified – in evidence to the Howman Committee – that on pay of less than £5 a month, the fathers of families could not possibly make ends meet. At about the same time, the Batson Survey in Salisbury found that nearly half of all African families were not *just* below the 'poverty datum line' of £7 7s. 4d. income a month; they were *more than fifty per cent* below it.

All that was twenty years ago, and most white Rhodesians would like to think that such days are now far behind them. But the truth is very different; present-day surveys arrive at the same cruel results. The settlers, of course, do not encourage scrutiny: the prying of visitors is not welcomed, and most of the white people who make their homes in the territory never go near the African 'locations', where the plain, unpleasant facts are distressingly on view.

Sir Edgar Whitehead, to give him credit, recently criticized his fellow countrymen on this score, and estimated that apart from those government officials whose work took them there, probably not more than fifty white Rhodesians had been down to their local African township in the previous year.

If they had been, they would have found conditions not much changed from those described by the Plewman Commission on Urban African Affairs, which reported in 1958. Indeed, with the economic slump which began after the riots of 1960, and the rise in African unemployment over the last two years, it is possible that the Africans may actually be worse off now. The Commission itself had been appointed by Mr Garfield Todd before he fell from power, in response to the Salisbury bus boycott and a big railway strike by Africans in both the Rhodesias. Poverty, not race, had proved to be the basis of both campaigns; and there had been rioting at Harare and widespread hooliganism as a bitter aftermath. The break-down of the bus company's finances had shown that the income from the heavily used African routes was being used to underwrite the thinly patronized services to the white suburbs; in other words, a subsidy from the poor to help the rich. African bus fares were abruptly reduced.

An Appendix to the Plewman Report contained the latest survey on the 'poverty datum line'. The compiler, Dr Bettison of the Rhodes–Livingstone Institute, calculated the bare minimum required to provide a man and his family with food, clothes, and shelter in some kind of decency. By this standard, not some, but *all* African families in the Salisbury locations were spending less on foods containing protein, fats, and vitamins, and more on foods with a high carbohydrate content, than they should have been doing. And an analysis of their total expenditure showed that they were spending less overall on food than was necessary to preserve proper standards of health.

Below the 'poverty datum line', Dr Bettison drew another line, thirty-five per cent lower down the graph. This he called the 'extremely impoverished' line, and he found that 57·1 per cent of the African families were living *below this*.

In Northern Rhodesia he conducted a parallel survey, in the capital, Lusaka. He calculated that for a couple with three children the 'poverty datum line' would be £14 11s. a month; in fact, the actual average monthly income for an African family of five members was £8 8s. 10d.

An observer for the Institute of Race Relations in London surveyed the Federation in the light of this report.

There is really no room to doubt that from one-fifth to two-fifths of urban Africans in the Rhodesias are not earning enough to keep their families; and of those with two children or more, the majority are undernourished and underclothed.

How do these people manage? The question thumps harder and harder in the mind of the visitor, the more he travels through the Federation. There is a curiously disarming factor at work, too – the habitual cheeriness of the African people themselves. The downtrodden peasants and slum dwellers in European films may have long faces and a general air of despair; in Rhodesia's sunlit slums they are apt to be smiling bravely, and beating out the time to the tune of a penny whistle while the youngsters dance in the dust.

Obviously the health of these people suffers. Doctors and nutrition experts have frequently linked his poor diet to the slowness and 'laziness' of the urban African worker. And, to be fair to the white governments of Rhodesia, the problem is not unique to their territory. There are undernourished Africans in every country of the whole continent. But what remains politically inexcusable is the presence of this 'extreme impoverishment' directly alongside the wealth of the white community. For it is well to remember that the white Rhodesian is not just a transplanted Englishman, in slightly happier circumstances. The 1962 figure for the *average* annual income of British wage-earners came to £780. The black Rhodesian wage-earner, as we have seen, gets one-tenth of this amount. The white Rhodesian gets a comfortable fifty per cent *more* than his British counterpart – £1,209. One may question the political wisdom of this, in the Africa of the 1960s, and one may share the suspicion of the Africans in the Federation that this luxury standard of living is being sustained at their expense.

What seems a perpetual miracle is that the Africans should

keep themselves going, economically. The answer, perhaps, is that they live by their wits – like the Cockney townsmen of Dickens's day. In this, as in their demand for redress through the franchise, they are not so very different from many of our Victorian forebears.

They steal, they gravitate (in daylight hours) across the tracks to the white man's town to look for a fast shilling or two, they supplement their incomes by brewing illegal beer. Many an older brother treks home to the Reserves – if the family still has links with one of the tribal areas – to get supplies of food or simply to eat a little better for a week. The girls, sadly, turn all too often to the desperate business of selling their bodies; most visitors from overseas have had the distressing experience of being solicited by teenagers who ought to be in school.

In the suburban comfort of Greendale and Mount Pleasant, the settlers write all this off as 'loose morals', though the desperate rioting in the townships during recent months has begun to stir deeper, more searching thoughts, at last. And meanwhile, to buttress their safety, there is the Vagrancy Act, which Joshua Nkomo described as a measure to turn 100,000 unemployed Africans into 100,000 criminals. Even the London *Times* was moved to express suspicion over this curious law:

If it was intended as a social welfare measure, as the Minister introducing it to Parliament claimed, why was it rushed through the House and enforced in the land in a matter of days, before the Re-establishment Centres were even ready to receive the 'vagrants' – roped in in their hundreds in police sweeps, as the ink was drying on the Act?

The period of mounting racial clash in 1959–60 also saw the introduction of the Preventive Detention Act, and the notorious Law and Order (Maintenance) Act. This last, which produced drastic new curbs on the freedom of speech, movement, and assembly, provoked the Chief Justice of the Federation, Sir Robert Tredgold, to resign his post, sacrificing a handsome salary and pension to re-enter politics and campaign for a programme to halt and reverse the decline in race relations. His was a voice in the white wilderness. The last months of 1962 saw the Whitehead government bring in amending legislation to tighten up the Unlawful Organizations Act and increase the severity of the Law and Order (Maintenance) Act. The Africans claimed that these Draconian measures, supposedly non-racial, were directed almost entirely at their community. The sole Independent in the legislature, Dr Ahrn Palley, produced statistics to bear this out. In terms of the Law and Order (Maintenance) Act, he said, during the first eighteen months of its operation, 1,220 Africans had been convicted – and TWO Europeans.

As for the Plewman Report, with its authoritative analysis of African poverty, Sir Edgar Whitehead's administration 'took note' of the recommendations, but did not accept them.

It might reasonably be asked: if conditions are so appalling for Africans in the urban areas, why do they not return to their tribal reserves? Indeed, Sir Edgar Whitehead often talks of inducing the natives to go back to their 'ancestral homelands'. It is a favourite settler myth. And it is cruelly fantastic.

There are ninety-seven million acres of land in Southern Rhodesia, and until the revision of the Land Apportionment Act in June 1961, the ratio had been weighted heavily in favour of the settlers. For just over 200,000 white people, there had been a total of forty-eight million acres; for nearly three million black people, forty-two million acres of land; with the remainder allocated to forests and national parks. The 1961 revision shifted the balance slightly, removing some land from European possession and allocating two million acres of it to the Africans either for distribution or sale. The rest was devoted to forestry or put into a holding 'pool' as Unreserved Land. The changes produced this result:

(in millions of acres)

European Land:

General	37
National Parks	4
Total	41

African Land:

Native Reserves	21
Native Purchase Areas	7
Special Native Areas	14
Additional Native Land	2
Total	44

There are, obviously, basic absurdities in the whole arrangement. The white man had been putting land aside for his own use at a rate which favoured him over the black man in the *per capita* ratio of 15:1. The 1961 revision made this ratio 11:1. The African share 'advanced', but not very far. And vast acreages of European land still lie idle, awaiting the thousands of white immigrants who, it is hoped, will one day arrive to reinforce the ranks of the tiny settler community already in occupation.

There is a wilful blindness to African sensitivities which extends even to recreation. Where but in a community obsessed with racial differences could anyone seriously create a land category entitled 'European National Parks'? Yet this is the official term used, and it is only the visitor who remarks on this curious contradiction in terms; for the privileged citizens of this lunatic society, there is nothing odd about it. But, for the African, the joke is really too big to be funny; there are four million acres of European National Parks.

The 1961 reform was not without benefit to the Africans. For the first time it became possible for those living in African urban areas to buy land or property there. And in all African areas there would for the first time be access to outside capital on a mortgage basis. But the amended Land Apportionment Act still fell far short of African aspirations. Africans would still not be permitted to acquire commercial premises in the centres of towns, nor move into any of the white suburbs. (This prohibition has ended in Northern Rhodesia and Nyasaland, under British colonial rule.)

As for safeguards, there were two shocks in store for the Africans. The Board of Trustees administering their lands, it turned out, would consist of six men, four of whom would be government appointees subject to the direct pressure of the Prime Minister. And the Board itself was given discretionary powers to grant use of tribal land to 'persons other than tribesmen' when it was 'in the public interest'. In that phrase the apprehensive African could hear the clanking of the settler steamroller. He could hear it again in the further provision that all arrangements covering the apportionment of land were specifically excluded from the Declaration of Rights under the new Sandys–Whitehead constitution of 1961. Existing discrimination remained frozen on the statute books and could not be challenged before the new Constitutional Court.

Not all white Rhodesians, however, are deaf to African complaints. Sir Edgar Whitehead himself was moved, early in 1962, to declare that he accepted the recommendation – made by a select committee of the legislature in 1960 – that the Land Apportionment Act be gradually repealed:

The arbitrary division of land between Africans and Europeans through the Act is having the effect of leaving land unused when there is a land hunger in the country. For this reason, if no other, it must go.

That set the territorial cat among the federal pigeons. The London *Times* reported that 'the right wing of the U.F.P. is critical of the speed at which Sir Edgar is moving' and added that the Federal Prime Minister, Sir Roy Welensky, had clashed with the liberal wing of Sir Edgar's administration. The Salisbury *Sunday Mail*, which espouses Sir Roy's views on most matters, commented, in a double-column editorial:

We do not believe white Rhodesians are prepared to see responsible government pass out of their hands at the speed Sir Edgar Whitehead's behaviour makes inevitable.

But nothing, apparently, could arrest the Prime Minister of Southern Rhodesia in his headlong plunge. The liquor laws for Africans were amended, to enable them to drink ordinary beer (as well as the weaker 'kaffir' beer), light wines, and spirits. The swimming-pool controversy had ended in victory for the integrationists; and though just a single courtroom victory, Sir Edgar had not intervened to erect new barriers afterwards. In February 1962 he announced a plan to move 50,000 African families on to the land before the year was out, giving them six acres each, while his Minister of Native Affairs, then Mr Quinton, said the aim was to deal with between 400 and 600 African farmers a month.

It all looked like the change of heart that the Conservative right wing at Westminster had predicted would come about in Rhodesia, if only the 'left-wing critics' would stop sniping at the settler governments. Yet six months later the whole policy of concession had collapsed in the August–September crisis, with Sir Edgar ramming through another round of punitive legislation and banning Z.A.P.U., the effective voice of the politically conscious Africans. What had happened?

It did not escape the notice of observers that the full spate of Whitehead liberalism had come in the month before the Prime Minister's mission to London, seeking financial aid, a mission that was rewarded a few months later with a British loan of £3·5 million. The contrast between the two settler leaders, in terms of tactics, was revealing. Sir Roy flew to London at the end of 1962 in a last desperate bid to stop the British government from announcing the Maudling Plan for Northern Rhodesia, a move which threatened to open the way to African majority government. His technique was all bluster and threat; resisting any shift of power into 'irresponsible hands', and letting slip his fatal phrase about 'going the whole hog, if necessary' in order to secure the Rhodesian way of life.

By comparison Sir Edgar was all sweetness and light. To Mr Macmillan and the other British Ministers he portrayed a Southern Rhodesia firmly moving into a new era of enlightened partnership. He told them of his 3,000-mile whistle-stop tour of the territory, to launch his 'Build a Nation' Campaign. He spoke with quiet pride of the other campaign, to persuade fifteen times as many Africans as had ever voted in the past to register for the new 'B' roll, which would elect fifteen out of sixty-five seats in the new parliament. Sir Edgar was not, like Sir Roy, rigid about the present structure of the state; he was open to new constitutional ideas, he was proceeding rapidly to relax racial discrimination, and – he stressed this hard in private conversations – would initiate substantial land reform. It made a big impression. It was the music that the Tory front bench at Westminster wanted to hear; how much better for everyone – including the Conservative Party – if there would be no political explosion over Rhodesia when the Prime Minister was fully occupied in the Common Market negotiations.

Unfortunately it proved to be just one more demonstration of an old settler stratagem: always be liberal in London and conservative at home. The Whitehead crack-down, when it came in August, was more savage than anything the Africans of the territory had experienced this century. The government deployed 20,000 men – troops and armed police with tear gas, loaded rifles, and machine-guns – around the African townships: a force which is very nearly equal to half the strength of Britain's N.A.T.O. commitment in Germany, the British Army of the Rhine.

Yet it would be wrong to suggest that Sir Edgar was cynically determined to have his great crack-down in 1962, regardless of other events. When he was in London in March, he seemed to believe his own propaganda about the campaign to register African voters. It was many months before he realized that it was a sorry failure, having taken half a year to reach only twenty per cent of its target. And in the meantime he and many another settler had been infuriated because Joshua Nkomo, leader of the Z.A.P.U. party which was boycotting the campaign, had by-passed Salisbury and Westminster to take the African grievances to the U.N. As late as June of 1962 the 'liberal' Whitehead programme was still in operation. In that month the government announced the purchase of 500,000 acres of land from a property and mineral syndicate, to be allocated to Africans for farming and tobacco-growing. But Z.A.P.U. was not impressed. The deputy leader, Dr T.S. Parirenyatwa, who was to die a few weeks later in a mysterious car accident, said that far greater land reform was needed. There were sixteen million acres, he said, which were either not being used at all or else held by absentee landlords in

Britain and under-used. Africans might be squatting on some of it, but had no legal rights there and could be moved off at any time, at a few hours' notice and with the loss of any crops. Faced with this 'ingratitude', and the knowledge that opposition by Z.A.P.U. leaders to his paternalism would only increase, Whitehead took his decision to outlaw the African organization.

Like Sir Roy Welensky, Sir Edgar still believes that the basic problem in Rhodesia is economic. If the government can just rid itself of the impatient extremists and greedy self-seekers among the African politicians, and enjoy a few years of peace and quiet, it can develop the country, eliminate poverty, and lay the groundwork for real partnership in a prosperous and happy nation. But this, of course, is flying right in the face of human nature. As Kenneth Kaunda said in Northern Rhodesia: 'Why should we wait like dumb cattle? If British people were caught in the same humiliating position that we are in, they would never wait. They have too much of the Dunkirk spirit.'

Professor Franck, whom I have quoted earlier, comments:

The Federal government has proceeded in the honest belief that the African masses have no cognizable intellectual basis for political choice and that, therefore, they do not really hold political convictions. They merely follow like cattle the leaders who have thrust themselves forward. Change the bulls and you change the direction of the herd. The history of African and Asian colonialism has revealed time and again the folly of these assumptions. The only effective way yet discovered by which Europeans can replace irresponsible native leadership is to give the irresponsible leaders political responsibilities. The Federation appears determined to wage a lonely, losing battle against history.

This lonely, losing battle of the settlers has taken the form of carefully stripping the African nationalist parties of their leadership, usually by bans and arrests, sometimes by money and the promise of prestige. The attractions of a Ministerial or Ambassadorial post have proved overwhelmingly tempting to some men. Godwin Lewanika who founded the African National Congress of Northern Rhodesia in 1948 ended up as a U.F.P. stalwart in the sixties, holding a safe seat with an almost all-white electorate, a junior Ministry in the Federal government, and a firm resolve never to make public speeches in the African townships again after the fearful heckling which followed his last appearance there some years ago. Mike Hove, one of Nkomo's colleagues in the old days, slipped into another safe U.F.P. seat in 1953, again with a ninety per cent white electorate, and got his ultimate reward in 1962 with his appointment as Rhodesian High Commissioner in Nigeria.

Occasionally there are angels who fall from grace, like the astonishing Jasper Savanhu, who had also been weaned away from the African nationalists to a safe seat with a white electorate. Raised to the post of junior Minister, with special responsibility for race relations, this forty-five years old ex-teacher was in many ways the linchpin in the Federal government's whole programme of partnership. Yet even his very appointment showed, alarmingly, the true attitude of the settler voters. When the London *Economist* got wind of Savanhu's prospective promotion, just before the Federal election in 1958, it promptly became a bitter election issue. Welensky had sent word of his plan to his good friend Lord Home, since it was just the kind of multi-racial music that the Tory Cabinet in London wanted to hear. It confirmed them in their view that putting trust in one's 'kith and kin' and in gradualism was the right path to follow. The fact that, under the new electoral arrangements, African voters were almost all restricted to an inferior roll, with effective control over barely half a dozen seats in a Federal Assembly of fifty-nine, was less remarked in Whitehall.

The Dominion Party, then the chief opposition to Sir Roy's U.F.P. and now reorganized as the Rhodesian Front, seized on the Savanhu affair as a real election winner. 'African Cabinet Minister – Secret Leaks Out', screamed the scare posters which the D.P. plastered all over Bulawayo. The ordinary Africans, who had already written off Savanhu as a collaborator, watched sullenly on the sidelines. (Only two per cent of them, in any case, had the vote.) After the election, Welensky held off from the promised appointment, and did not announce it until disturbances had broken out in Nyasaland and States of Emergency declared there, in Southern Rhodesia, and parts of Northern Rhodesia. The Africans cynically concluded that stirring up trouble was the only way to spur the settlers into racial advancement.

Even then Savanhu's difficulties were not at an end. As a Minister, he was entitled to an official house, and the Federal government sought to build him one in a white suburb of Salisbury, near to the university. But the Land Apportionment Act stood in the way, and the Salisbury City Council refused to cooperate. The government then built him a showpiece home for £8,000 on the outskirts of Highfield, the new African township. But this soon became a kind of landmark to the Africans, a monument to the advantages of 'cooperation' but also to the will of the dominant white settlers to hold intact their racial citadel. I have never yet been taken past Highfield by an African without his pointing out the house and asking if I know the story.

The final chapter of the Savanhu affair has a certain bitter justice about it. Four days after Sir Edgar Whitehead tabled his punitive amendments to the Unlawful Organizations Act and the Law and Order (Maintenance) Act in August 1962, Jasper Savanhu resigned in a blaze of angry publicity. His letter of resignation to Sir Roy Welensky said, in part:

Your government, in spite of strong representations from the African party members and other quarters, has failed or has no intention of implementing a policy of partnership.

And in a subsequent Press conference, he maintained:

Europeans are quite incapable of treating other races fairly. No African who thinks he can influence events can continue to hobnob with a European party which has no intention of practising what it preaches. Only an African-dominated government would put partnership into practice. Southern Rhodesia is on the verge of exploding. I wish to identify myself with the African people.

He said that he was not resigning his seat in the Federal Assembly; he would remain as a watchdog for African interests. He had never, he insisted, been a 'stooge'; he had simply taken the U.F.P. at their word, assumed that they really meant to implement partnership, and given them whatever help he himself could. But Federation was moving into its tenth year, and still the Africans had failed to catch more than a fleeting glimpse of the pot of gold at the end of the rainbow.

Savanhu ticked off the list of failures: land, schooling, jobs, and so on. He particularly mentioned the Federal Civil Service, which he said had been lamentably and inexcusably negligent in failing to give Africans a fair share of the opportunities. Hardly any had been accepted into the top grade, and he himself had been used by the settler government as 'window dressing' to impress the Tory government in Britain.

Sir Roy's reply the next day rejected this criticism, claiming that partnership was being implemented in the Civil Service as swiftly as could be done 'without a sacrifice of those standards which are essential to good government'. No fewer than 315 Africans, he said, had already been appointed to the Grade I category.

This statement puzzled people at the time, since the figure 315 did not square with any known statistic. The Federal Information Service insisted that Savanhu was wrong in suggesting that 'only nine Africans' had qualified for top Civil Service jobs in nine years of Federation, and produced a report a week later which was intended to show the remarkable state of African advancement. The report was remarkable for what it omitted.

At no point did it make clear that Europeans – all 13,000 of them – were all automatically taken into Grade I. The report did say that there were also '305 non-Europeans' in Grade I. (Was this the source of Sir Roy's 315?) But it became clear, in the next line of the Federal government's own report, that two-thirds of these were not Africans. The 305 non-Europeans, it said, were made up of '199 Asians or Coloureds and 106 Africans – who have complete parity with European officers'.

Now it must be obvious that 13,000 white Civil Servants and their 305 non-white companions cannot all be heads of departments. They staff the whole clerical and administrative machine of the Federal service, and their salaries range as low as £387 a year, the level where most of the Africans are to be found. So to say that 106 Africans have leapt the barrier into Grade I is not, as Sir Roy's statement implied, to say they have all reached supervisory positions. And this, of course, was what Mr Savanhu meant when he said that only nine Africans had reached top Civil Service jobs.

If Grade I is very nearly all-white – ninety-eight per cent, in fact – the racial injustice throughout the rest of the Civil Service is no less blatant. By deduction, reading between the lines of the government's report, it is possible to calculate that the remaining 24,000 employees in Federal service are all non-white. Half of them are African messengers and orderlies, who make up Grade IV. Grade III contains the great majority of African employees – obviously much lower-paid than their European colleagues two grades further up the salary scale. And the report is less than frank about the 324 student nurses in Grade II. These are African women who have taken the same training and examinations – carefully segregated into separate hospitals or, at least, separate wards, of course – as their white sisters. When they come to join the Federal service, equally qualified, it is Grade I and high pay for the whites, Grade II and a more modest stipend for the blacks. This, after ten years of federation, is partnership! And it is only one of dozens of discriminatory examples which are well within the purview of any really determined government, Federal or Territorial, to change. One doesn't have to ask how long such discrimination would last under an African government. Not a moment longer than the transfer of power, I should say.

Indeed, the guilty knowledge of this itself acts as a barrier against political change. It would be reasonable to suppose that out of the 312,000 privileged white citizens of the Federation, many must be sheltered, benefited in varying ways above their capabilities – not necessarily slack or unqualified for their jobs, just protected and overpaid in relation to the eight million black citizens. It gives the whites of the Federation a vested interest in resisting change, if it means the kind of African advance that Lord Home and other trusting Tories optimistically expect.

The Civil Service is certainly no showpiece for partnership.

By the Federal government's own figures, only 0·5 per cent of Grade I posts are now held by Africans, after ten years. And in the territorial service of Southern Rhodesia, reluctantly opened to Africans after the 1959 riots had prodded the settlers to action, progress has been even slighter. The Paterson Report of 1961 made it clear that white Civil Servants in the lower echelons were fiercely resisting change – a familiar enough phenomenon in southern Africa, where the unskilled white worker, conscious that he has no intrinsic superiority over Africans, only the advantages of colour, is the bitterest opponent of African advance. In the police great numbers of white recruits are still taken straight into ranks like those of Sub-Inspector without examination, while qualified Africans are but rarely selected.

The settler governments have been far less concerned with African advance in the Civil Service than with putting pressure on colonial Civil Servants, sent out originally by the British government, to accept Rhodesian status and acknowledge Salisbury as their national capital. The objective is clear enough: if Salisbury is to set the pace of racial integration, there must be no risk of challenge from either of the northern protectorates. And the risk is real, because African advance has been proceeding with relative swiftness in Northern Rhodesia and Nyasaland. In the former, the decision was taken in 1959 to merge the African and European services, and many black Civil Servants have moved up to policy-making and supervisory posts. In Nyasaland, since Dr Banda and his Ministers assumed power in 1961, all barriers have been dismantled.

The Federal government has repeatedly charged that white Civil Servants in the two northern territories 'owe no abiding loyalty to Central Africa' (Sir Roy's phrase) and are inclined to sentimental and 'Fabian' attitudes towards Africans. It is frequently alleged that they do nothing to 'sell' Federation to their people, as do the settler Civil Servants in the south. Sir Roy came triumphantly back from his 1957 negotiations in London with Lord Home, not only with the revised plan for Federal Assembly and franchise which entrenched settler control, but also with the concession that 'in principle all civil services in the Federation would eventually be locally based and look for their future to the Federal Area'. Swiftly on the heels of this decision, came the campaign to make Civil Servants 'go Federal', and already some 8,000 have been persuaded to do so. Others have resigned, rather than surrender their Colonial Office status and link with Britain.

The settlers, it is plain, want absolute authority over the security apparatus of the state – the Civil Service, the army, and the police – to support the highly effective control that they already wield over the Federal and Southern Rhodesian parliaments. Welensky's objective, which Whitehead also pursued, was one single national Civil Service. This was to guarantee the vital 'allegiance' to Salisbury and remove such embarrassments as speedier African advance in a particular territory. Whitehall's 'sentimentalists' would be safely removed from the scene.

Starting in 1959, after the Nyasaland disturbances, Welensky directed pressure towards gaining control of the information services in the two northern territories; it had been embarrassing for him to have Colonial officials in Lusaka and Zomba following a line different from Salisbury in relation to African political advance. And in one respect at least, the Federal government succeeded.

In radio and television, the dominance of the Federal authorities was for a long time nearly unchallengeable. Day after day, night after night, two of the most powerful media at the service of any government – in a continent where illiteracy is high – pump out the settler viewpoint. The commentators of the F.B.C. are staff men whose opinions rarely stray from the clear, Federal line. When one of the white news editors on duty at headquarters in September 1962 prominently reported the views of Joshua Nkomo, after the banning of Z.A.P.U., he was quickly disciplined by Sir Edgar Whitehead.

The editor in question, John Appleby, was roused from bed at midnight and paraded before the angry Prime Minister at his official residence. Sir Edgar pointed out that Mr Nkomo now had no status other than that of a private citizen, and that by giving prominence to views he had expressed in the neighbouring territory of Tanganyika, the F.B.C. was 'aiding and abetting' the underground activities of the outlawed Z.A.P.U. organization. The Prime Minister further warned all editors, including those of news agencies and newspapers, that reports on these lines would be 'actionable' under the security legislation which had been rushed through parliament earlier in the month. Foreign correspondents were warned that they, too, came under the law while in the Federation.

It is entirely improper for the Executive thus to usurp the functions of the Judiciary. If the editors were culpable, then it was for Sir Edgar to use the machinery of his public law officers to lay a charge and attempt to obtain a conviction. As a politician he had no authority to summon Mr Appleby, or any other editor, in the way he did.

Nor, as Territorial Prime Minister, did he have authority to summon Federal employees at all. He began his crack-down on the F.B.C. by telephoning the *Federal* Information Officer, Colin Black, at his home, and ordering him to bring the offending *Federal* employee to his residence. Such are the realities of Rhodesian life today. Who can doubt that, in a crisis, the white Rhodesians will scrap all the elaborate structure of 'Federation' and retire to their southern fastness, where – thanks to sheer military might – they believe themselves unchallengeable ?

There are already signs of strategic retirement in the broadcasting field. The F.B.C. suddenly announced in August 1962 that it was ceasing to have any liaison with the Tanganyika Broadcasting Corporation, and that facilities for T.B.C. reporters in the Federation would, from that day, be withdrawn. For an election campaign had begun in Northern Rhodesia. Harry Nkumbula and his African National Congress had managed – with the blessing of the U.F.P. and the Federal government – to forge a profitable link with the Tshombe régime across the border in Katanga. Sir Roy's good friend, President Tshombe, had agreed to let the A.N.C. use Radio Katanga to appeal to the African voters of the northern territory in their own tongues. This had neatly avoided the problem of granting air time on the Rhodesian F.B.C., for it was the larger and more potent African party of Kenneth Kaunda, U.N.I.P., which represented the real threat to settler rule. And it had suited Welensky very well to have Kaunda and his men denied the powerful assistance of broadcasting, while Nkumbula could use Radio Katanga to build up the A.N.C. and split the African vote. This, however, had reckoned without the forces of pan-Africanism. Radio Tanganyika had come to Kaunda's rescue, just as it had done for Dr Banda in the Nyasaland election campaign a year before. It had taken up the challenge of the Nkumbula–Tshombe–Welensky combination and carried the voices of the U.N.I.P. leaders to the three million people of Northern Rhodesia.

In Nyasaland, the U.F.P. forces have now accepted defeat. Yet as recently as 1959, when the emergency was on and Dr Banda was a new and untried force in Nyasa politics, the settler politicians in Salisbury confidently asserted their control over the Colonial Civil Service in the territory. Under pressure from Welensky, the then governor, Sir Robert Armitage, sanctioned the sending out of a letter (kept deadly secret at the time) to the headmasters of all the schools. It said, in part:

The government is concerned to learn that on occasion government officers have failed to do their utmost to stimulate confidence in Federation. I must ask you to ensure that you and all *European* officers serving under you are fully aware that it is the duty of every officer to promote great confidence in Federation . . . Should any officer wish to criticize any action of the Federal government . . . complaints should be conveyed to me in secret, and I will take such action as is necessary.

The subversion of the colonial service to settler ends had still one stage further to go. On 6 May 1959, after Dr Banda and more than a thousand fellow nationalists had been arrested and dispatched to prisons which, significantly, were in Southern Rhodesia, the government information office in Zomba sent out this notice about the African National (now Malawi) Congress:

Do you know of any member of Congress living near you who has not been arrested? Do you know of any group of Congress members near you who are plotting to cause trouble? If you do you must tell the Boma [local government officer] so that these wicked people can be arrested. . . . You can either report personally to a government officer or, if you prefer to remain anonymous, send an unsigned letter to your District Commissioner or Police Officer, giving the name and address of any Congress member still at large. There is no need to put a stamp on the letter.

The inference for any African was clear. Their government in Zomba was now the agent of the settler government in Salisbury. For had not Dr Banda and his party leaders in 1958 warned their people that the settlers aimed to achieve full and final authority over them in 1960? And had there not been alarming confirmation of their warnings when the Federal government, with unique stupidity, had chosen 12 September – Southern Rhodesia's 'Occupation Day' – of that year for a 'show of force' in Nyasaland? At dawn, the all-white troops of the Royal Rhodesian Rifles, 500 strong, had swept down by plane on Nyasaland in what must have looked to any ordinary African like a genuine military invasion. In full kit, with rifles, machine-guns, and plenty of ammunition, these 500 white men had presented a picture of rampant military power.

Belatedly it had been explained that this had just been an exercise. But, to the Africans, it had seemed too much of a coincidence that this piece of elephantine military diplomacy had come at the time when Welensky and his U.F.P. were campaigning among a ninety-eight per cent white electorate for a mandate to seek full independence by 1960. Welensky had made his meaning clear in the white man's parliament at Salisbury:

We go forward to the conference table in 1960 firmly believing that the achievements of Federation fully justify the granting of independence. Should we fail . . . then will be the time to take stock and decide what other action is necessary. I personally would never be prepared to accept that the Rhodesians have less guts than the American colonists had.

Lord Malvern, before his retirement from the Federal leadership, had already made the same point in a speech to the Assembly in August 1956:

We have complete control of our own Defence Force. I only hope

355

we will not have to use it, as the North American colonies had to use theirs, because we are dealing with a stupid government in the United Kingdom.

What African politician could have got away with two speeches like that? Guy Clutton-Brock, himself detained in the 1959 Emergency, asked this question in his book, *Dawn in Nyasaland*. The Public Prosecutor in Salisbury had never turned a hair or raised a finger in protest. It had been enough to convince the Africans that drastic measures were needed if settler control was ever to be escaped.

Lacking any channel of redress in the courts, with only half a dozen representative Africans in the Federal Assembly, none in the Southern Rhodesian legislature, and less than half a dozen in the parliaments of the two northern protectorates, there had seemed only one logical course: to kick up such a row that the politicians and the public in the United Kingdom would be forced to pay attention. Kenneth Kaunda and his party in Northern Rhodesia had decided to boycott the local election. There had been widespread outbreaks of fighting and rioting, Kaunda's Zambia Congress had been outlawed, and he with other nationalist leaders taken into detention. The blow-up in Nyasaland had been much more dramatic. Thanks to rugged terrain, with tree-lined ravines, mountains, and good cover, the Africans had been able to immobilize traffic over much of the country, felling trees to block roads, sabotaging bridges, burning public buildings.

The uprisings served their purpose. The Devlin Commission on the Nyasaland disorders was followed by the much wider-ranging Monckton Commission in early 1960, with the task of surveying the whole Federal scene and all its problems. At Westminster there were angry scenes at Question Time, and full-scale debates so fiery that observers in the press gallery could recall nothing as emotion-charged since Suez. In the Commons and the Lords alike, the speeches flowed, hour after hour, filling volumes of Hansard. The name of Dr Banda became a household word. Lacking under the British system the constitutional safeguards, the rights of appeal through the courts, that are provided in written constitutions such as that of the United States, the

Africans had realized that their only channel of appeal had to be political. They had had to exert pressure on London – and they had done it. Who can reasonably say that if they had failed to mount their campaign in 1959, Welensky and the settlers would not smoothly and quietly have achieved their objective? That there would not have been yet another transition, as deceptively optimistic as the transfer of power to the white South Africans in 1909, by the Act of Union?

After the immediate hubbub of the Emergencies, the British public began to learn at last of the discrimination practised in their name throughout Central Africa. Hostility was stirred as anomaly after anomaly was dragged into the light of public examination, and voters in this country – including great numbers of Tories – saw that Africans were being asked to put up with indignities that no Britisher would willingly endure. And here the new logistics of the jet age came into play, for not only were British correspondents able to visit Central Africa themselves and cable back reports to their newspapers, but the African leaders were able to descend on London and use the full machinery of the Press conference, the television interview and the quiet chat with M.P.s at Westminster in order to ram home a case that could not be ignored. How very different the tortured history of the Federation might have been, had these forces operated in the buccaneering days of Cecil John Rhodes!

Homes, schools, jobs, social inequalities – these were the grievances which the Africans of the Federation were now able to present to the British public. It was a public already largely sympathetic because of the traumatic shock administered by Sharpeville. The killing of sixty-seven African men, women, and children there had sounded a terrible warning-note of the tragic direction which settler politics might take. At the other end of Africa, the terrible war of attrition and waste in Algeria was moving into its closing stages. There were many in Britain who sensed that there might still be time – just time – to avoid a third calamity in Central Africa.

There are those who regret the African decision to boycott the Monckton Commission; who say that it showed African

357

immaturity. But to politicians at Westminster and to the Commissioners themselves, this angry decision was indicative of something much more profound. It revealed a yawning gulf in race relations, a deep and bitter distrust between black and white. I believe that in retrospect historians will see the boycott decision as the right one; it was the final spur to conscience that made the Commissioners determined to remove the political land-mines in the Federation before they all exploded.

I have dealt with some of the main African grievances already: the denial of basic rights to Africans in parliament and the public service. Some of the others may be itemized here:

I. THE RHODESIAN ARMY: In theory Africans may aspire to any rank, but none has yet been commissioned in the nine years of Federation. Commissioning an African officer would, in fact, raise costly and embarrassing problems of housing, mess arrangements, discipline. Would his wife 'fit in'? Would white subordinates be cheeky? These problems have been solved in Ghana, Nigeria, Kenya, Sierra Leone, and all the French territories of Africa. The settlers in Rhodesia reject such solutions.

There is no cadet training for Africans in schools – undoubtedly deliberate. Army barracks at Llewellin Camp (Southern Rhodesia) and Lusaka (Northern Rhodesia) have inadequate African quarters; relatively luxurious white ones. Whites get housing, fuel, and servants' and marriage allowances. The rate of pay for a white private is *twelve* times that for the African. Africans get twenty-eight days leave a year; Europeans, fifty-two to fifty-nine days.

Schooling is fully laid on for children of white soldiers, but is haphazard for others. At most camps, it is no higher than Standard I (third year primary).

The Defence Regulations of 1956 made no provision for Africans to get commissioned rank. The African Affairs Board, then under the chairmanship of Sir John Moffat, objected, and the Federal government gave assurances that opportunities would be equal. There are still no African officers.

When the British Army operated in the two northern protectorates, before the establishment of Federation in 1953, Africans could go to trade schools and study communications, metalwork, auto engineering, etc. But this system was scrapped within months of coming under Federal Army command, in consequence of bitter opposition from white officers of the Southern Rhodesian forces.

2. FEDERAL RAILWAYS: Job advancement for Africans on the railways is scandalously slow. Staff consists of approximately 10,000 whites and 25,000 Africans. Expenditure on housing is, *per capita*, for whites *12·5 times as much* as for blacks.

White crewmen held tenaciously their exclusive right to drive and fire trains during the first seven years of Federation; the ban was then officially lifted, but the number of Africans actually operating locomotives is still pitifully small. When the supply of white drivers and firemen ran short in 1956, the Federal government spent public funds to introduce totally untrained Greeks and Italians, whose sole credential was their colour.

The absurdity was vividly shown when trains from Katanga or Portuguese territories would arrive at the Rhodesian border, and African drivers and firemen would climb down from cabs to be replaced by members of the European Railwaymen's Union (Sir Roy's old trade union).

The ban against African customers in railway dining-cars was lifted in 1957, after the intervention of the Federal Transport Minister. Diners are now open to Africans, providing that they are 1st- or 2nd-class passengers. Two-thirds of all African passengers, however, travel 3rd or 4th; no dining-cars are provided for them.

3. LAND: The schedule of the original Land Apportionment Act of Southern Rhodesia (1930), running to twenty-five pages of close print, sets out a coherent and detailed system of agricultural apartheid.

Dr Huggins (later Lord Malvern) said, when the Act was passed: 'I welcome this as the first step in the social segregation of the native, getting him into separate areas.'

When re-enacted in 1941, the Minister of Native Affairs said:

'The ultimate aim is to raise the African from his lethargy and make him in mind and vigour a counterpart of the Europeans.'

Roughly half the territory is available for the use of 225,000 Europeans; the other half, for the use of three million Africans. But this is not the whole story. Ken Brown, an English agriculturist who served in Rhodesia for six years as a land development officer and left 'for political reasons' at his own request, has since written:

Most of the Native Area is poor soil, usually granite-sand known as Class III. In many parts of the country it is quite embarrassing to drive through a European Area into a Native Area. The change in soil-type coincides almost exactly with the boundary line and is startlingly obvious; an example is the Salisbury–Shamva road.

In various reallocations down the years, Africans who have occupied, with their forebears, a particular area for as long as three centuries, have found themselves classified (without appeal) as 'squatters' and ordered to move. Ken Brown, Professor Franck, and others have concluded that the Rhodesian authorities are more efficient than the Nationalist government of South Africa in organizing these mass evacuations. In the ten-year period to 1960, some 110,000 Africans were shifted from what had become European land. Bulldozers were used, where necessary, to demolish huts, as in South Africa, but operations received much less publicity than in the Republic.

Land allocation has been a settler obsession since pioneer days. A Land Commission met immediately after the crushing of the Matabele rebellion, demarcating (without visiting) two African Reserves. Marshall Hole of the British South Africa Company wrote of one, the Gwai Reserve: 'It proved quite unsuitable, the bulk of it being waterless, and the natives never settled in it except on a small portion.' The other, the Shangani Reserve, proved to be infested with tse-tse fly.

The visitor to Rhodesia is constantly astonished to find large tracts of European-designated land unused. The official explanation is that they await the arrival of the immigrants who will help make the country a white dominion. A select committee of the legislature, appointed by Todd, reported: 'It is clear that the present percentage of European-held land under crops, approximately three to four per cent, is deplorably low.' An earlier commission (1949) reported: 'Large tracts of useful land in European areas lie idle because of the large size of the farms, or are held for speculative purposes. The present owners of a very considerable number are not even known or cannot be traced.' Bishop Lamont of Umtali said in 1959 that it was easy to see why the African was 'swayed by subversive propaganda, when close beside him there lie hundreds of thousands of acres of fertile soil which he may not cultivate, nor occupy, nor graze'.

Three-quarters of European land is within easy access of the railway or main roads; for African land, the position is almost exactly reversed. White farmers can accordingly send produce to market cheaply and swiftly, while the Africans face delays and substantial transport costs.

The Land Apportionment Act is continually being amended because of gross absurdities. The 'Chitepo' amendment enabled the first African barrister to have chambers in the centre of town like his white colleagues. Further amendment was needed for the multi-racial College of Citizenship and for the University College of Rhodesia and Nyasaland in Salisbury. All cities and towns are in areas designated as European. In fact, of course, the (white) land commissioners deliberately drew boundaries to provide for this.

The Land Husbandry Act (1951) has brought sorrow to countless African families. At least in part, the intention was admirable – to reduce the overload of cattle on native lands which tended to strip the surface, and so cause gullying and erosion. In theory, there was to be no more than one family to every six acres of (sandveld) soil, with intensive cropping and a limited number of cattle (5) providing manure. In practice it was found that the plan would entail the forcible removal of 128,000 African families from the lands they occupied. The Africans were hostile to the plan, in any event, because they had never been consulted, and their hostility made the Act even less workable than it would otherwise have been. Now many farms are down to two or three acres, are insufficient to carry their load of cattle, and erosion rages unchecked. Everywhere, in the rural areas, the visitor encounters the spectacle of 'broken homes': the father forced to work for the white man in the nearest town and live in 'bachelor' quarters, the children growing up without proper guidance, the wives bitter and in need. The three- or six-acre plots constitute a bitter contrast to the *minimum unit* of 750 acres automatically allotted to each white immigrant.

Native Purchase Areas: In 1957, when there were 10,000 Africans on the waiting lists, the lists were closed. The *Rhodesia Herald*, one year later, defending the policy of keeping land unoccupied in European areas, commented: 'Today Rhodesia needs people more than anything else. You have got to have inducements to get people out to small-holdings which are necessary for agricultural prosperity.' Presumably the word *people*, as used by so influential a newspaper five years after the start of racial partnership, did not mean *black* people. Africans have reasonably concluded that white settler governments are incapable of change. Chad Chipunza, writing in the *Central African Examiner*, maintained: 'The ownership of land has been one of the greatest points of division, if not the greatest, between African and European.' In 1962 it was estimated that 50,000 Africans a year were being forced into the towns by land hunger and overcrowding.

Northern Rhodesia land policy: 94·5 per cent of Northern Rhodesia is allocated to Africans, either as Reserves or as trust land. Half of the territory is infested with tse-tse fly, however, and useless for cattle or mixed farming, while a further twenty-five per cent possesses poor soil. The best farming land lies along the 'line of rail' stretching northwards across the territory to the Copperbelt; not surprisingly, this rich strip, extending approximately twenty miles either side, is more than ninety per cent European-occupied. In other parts of the protectorate, rural Africans are packed in densities of up to 240 per square mile on soil too poor to support them.

The effect of this, and of the coercive 'head tax', is to drive the African men to work in the towns and on the copper mines.

Yet the picture is not altogether bleak. Because of British Colonial Office control, the Northern Rhodesia administration was relatively generous when Africans had to be moved from the banks of the Zambesi River to make way for the Kariba Dam. Compensation paid to Batonga tribesmen totalled £330,000. This was in sharp contrast with the policy pursued on the southern bank of the Zambesi, in Southern Rhodesian territory. The settler government paid not one penny in compensation; it simply removed 20,000 'natives' from the area and gave them two years' basic food supply. The episode showed the striking difference in outlook between the two governments: one sees itself as a trustee exercising persuasion; the other, as a conqueror issuing orders.

Lack of any major racial clash over farm land in Northern Rhodesia, however, has not been due to firmness of Imperial purpose in discharging a 'trust', but to the basic fact that most of the territory is unfit for farming and did not attract white settlers. The colour-bar was not long in appearing after the big copper strikes of the 1920s and the subsequent boom in white immigration.

Nyasaland: The happiest land distribution exists in Nyasaland, thanks to the 'Certificates of Claim' introduced by Governor Sir Harry Johnston after he broke with Rhodes, the Company, and the whole concept of a settler-run 'white dominion'. Johnston stopped further land sales (1891) to white men except, by special certificate, 'to protect the rights of the Natives'. As in Northern Rhodesia (1947), a Native Trust Lands Law was passed in Nyasaland (1936), reserving more than eighty-five per cent of the land surface of the territory for African occupation. Subsequently, the colonial government actually *bought* back from white owners land to be allocated to Africans; this amounted to 430,000 acres in all, and reduced European acreage to 3·2 per cent of Nyasaland. This is, however, by far the best land, producing no less than fifty-seven per cent of the territory's total export sales.

Thangata is a system of tied tenancies, with a punitive rate of rent amounting to a quarter of a man's earnings. Sir Sidney

Abrahams in his report (1946) recommended a 'clear-cut remedy, not compromise', to release 49,000 families from this form of Victorian bondage. There were still 17,000 living under Thangata when Dr Banda and his Malawi Congress came to power in 1961. Legislation was drafted at once, and the Private Estates Bill put before parliament in 1962. Dr Banda declared that its purpose was 'to free the Africans of this country from the vicious, pernicious and degrading system which has reduced them to the status of menial serfs on the lands of their fathers'. His words might have been deliberately chosen as a battle-cry for the frustrated Africans of Southern Rhodesia. News of Nyasa reform quickly travelled throughout the African rural areas of the Federation.

4. AGRICULTURE: *Crop Allocation* is practised only by the Southern Rhodesian government. The Tobacco Marketing Board uses its powers to prevent African farmers from growing the higher-grade, flue-cured Virginia types, on the argument that they do not know how to produce better-quality product, even though Nyasa and Tanganyika African farmers *are* growing Virginia and curing it successfully. The effect, of course, is to reserve the high-revenue crop for white farmers alone.

Cattle Buying: The Southern Rhodesian Cold Storage Commission buys its full requirements from white ranchers alone; African cattle, regardless of quality, are just bought for 'boys' meat' – food for African house servants.

Land Purchase: The Southern Rhodesian government operates a scheme for the limited freehold purchase of land in designated areas by Africans, who must not only have the money but be certified as master farmers. Europeans, however, may buy unlimited acreages (3,000 is normal), are not asked for proof of ability, and may proceed to farm it well, inefficiently, wastefully, or not at all. Some recent immigrants have been townsmen from Britain or Europe with no farming experience, who have soon failed and moved from the land.

Maize Marketing Boards: Legislation of great complexity in both Northern and Southern Rhodesia favours the European maize producer, especially in the south. As maize is the staple crop of the Federation, and the chief constituent in the average African diet, this is obviously political dynamite. It is seldom reported in the Press, rarely mentioned to visitors unless they go to the farming areas, and is a burning issue to the impoverished rural African farmer.

Between the wars all African maize was automatically regarded as Class D, the lowest of six grades, because it was considered dirty and of poor quality. Since 1945 it has not been graded like that, but the old suspicion lingers. A white farmer selling to the Grain Marketing Board gets the guaranteed price, which has recently been running at the rate of 38s. a bag. The African, providing he can argue that his maize is of equal quality, receives 38s. subject to three levies: 3s. 9d. for the Native Development Fund; 3s. 9d. for the trader's handling margin (a hangover from the old Class D grade system); and 5s. for 'transport equalization fund charge'. Deductions accordingly total 12s. 6d. The African goes home with 25s. 6d., compared with the full 38s. received by his white competitor. It is true that he will draw some indirect benefit from the Development Fund, but this is paternalist control over the spending of his own money, and most Africans suspect that a great deal is frittered away on the salaries of white Civil Servant administrators.

5. PUBLIC SERVICES AND BENEFITS: Many public services are available to whites alone: white farmers may borrow from the Land & Agricultural Bank; white industrialists may apply to various loan boards for assistance; the small miners (whites only) can get government subsidies to buy equipment and, ironically, receive government help in hiring African labour; Civil Servants (white) may borrow public funds for house mortgages; whites who are unemployed or without sufficient funds after retirement age are eligible for public assistance – Africans are not.

6. INDUSTRY: With the establishment of Federation in 1953, there was a complete reversal in tariff policy. The white Federal government deliberately applied charges to cheap consumer

goods, notably kitchenware and cotton textiles from India, so as to foster manufacturing in the Southern Rhodesia heartland. For the African consumer, the cost of this policy was considerable. The cheap black cloth he bought for making work clothes rose from 1½d. a yard to 9d. Hong Kong shirts went from 10s. to 15s.

Dr Banda warned that he intended to wipe out these penal charges when taking Nyasaland out of the Federation and renaming it 'Malawi'. He denied the Welensky argument that secession would cost Nyasaland £3½ to £4 million a year – the estimated gap between revenue and expenditure covered by Federal grants. The Nyasas argue instead that, by running their own economy, they will regain their missing customs revenues (lost since 1953) and attract the foreign capital which the Federation, since race troubles broke out in 1959, has notably failed to get.

From an insignificant place in the Southern Rhodesian economy, manufacturing (all under white settler control, of course) has leapt to rival chrome and tobacco as a money spinner, doubling its size up to the time when race riots brought on the 1960 recession. With Northern Rhodesia and Nyasaland as captive consumer markets, the settler-industrialists of the south have had things all their own way. Racially it may make sense (it has sprouted visually in the shape of Salisbury's spectacular skyline), but economists have their doubts. Professor W. J. Barber of Nuffield College, Oxford, has commented:

It has been an axiom of policy to promote expansion in the money economy and thereby to attract European immigrants. The major institutions of racial policy have served this economic end. ... The European employer could operate profitably while paying artificially high wages to European workers, as long as African labour cost him little. Increasing the African's skills would call for sweeping amendments in the fabric of Rhodesian society. This threat may be minimized. With more expensive technology the African can produce more without an improvement in his industrial status. And what is equally important, new jobs can continue to be created for Europeans to fill.

And Professor Barber concludes that 'a more modest promotion of industry, combined with agricultural reform and urbanization, would far better serve the long-term interests of the African'.

7. TAXATION: The austerity programme introduced by the Welensky régime in August 1962, to cover a current deficit running at the annual rate of £2 million, produced taxes on African mass consumer goods like soap and matches. It was not the first time the black Rhodesian had been made to pay for the economic whims of settler governments. Indirect taxes, like a couple of shillings on a cheap shirt, may not hit the higher-paid white consumer at all. And if it does, the 2s. means a great deal less to him than to the African who earns £7 a month.

Past tax increases have followed this general pattern. In the 1956 Federal budget, it was the cheap cigarettes smoked by Africans that bore the brunt. The next year it was African clothing. The Minister of Finance stressed that the increased duties were 'aimed at the very cheapest garments'. The legislature did not have to have that phrase translated; it meant, in settler double-talk, that the Africans would be paying.

With the flat rate levy of the head tax on Africans, grossly unjust because it is based solely on skin colour and not related to income, it is possible for a black Rhodesian to find himself having to hand over the equivalent of two or three weeks income to the state. Professor Barber has written:

Direct taxation pinches more sharply on the African than the European. The aggregate sums paid into Central African treasuries by Africans do not yet equal those paid by Europeans. But judged by the standard of the ability to pay – a principle to which Western governments in the main subscribe – it is the European, not the African, whom the Central African structure lets off lightly.

8. INVESTMENT: It is the firm conviction of virtually all the economists who have examined the workings of Federal finance that Southern Rhodesia has received the lion's share of public investment, Northern Rhodesia has come a poor second, and Nyasaland a very poor third.

In the Federal government's 1957–61 Development Plan, the Kariba dam and hydro-electric scheme took £55 million and Rhodesia Railways £29 million. This was a total of £84 million out of the £122 million allocated for the plan as a whole. Neither could affect Nyasaland; neither the power lines nor the railways go there. And, within the allocations listed, the major share of benefit went to Southern Rhodesia.

In the six-year period to 1959, out of £261 million in loan money spent in the Federation, Nyasaland received only £10 million. This works out at $\frac{1}{26}$, and it has been noted by various economists that the fraction bears a remarkable similarity to the ratio between white people in Nyasaland (10,000) and those in Southern Rhodesia (225,000). The share of public investment allocated to Northern Rhodesia has tended to follow the same formula, based on her white population of around 80,000. Deliberate or instinctive? It is hard to say. I rather believe that it is the latter.

But there can be no doubt that Kariba was deliberately planned for the benefit of the settlers. The power station is situated on the south bank, and Sir Edgar Whitehead has himself pointed out on various occasions (with a slight smile), in conversations with newspaper correspondents, that this places the vital part of Kariba on Southern Rhodesian territory. The implication is clear enough; if the North goes black, the South can still hold the electric power supply and dictate the terms of use.

The Federal (settler) government in Salisbury favoured Kariba because it was safely within the settler heartland. In taking this decision they overrode the advice of engineers who had doubts about the location (and indeed something like £1 million is now having to be spent on a cementing operation because the rock is porous). Economists favoured either the Shiré scheme in Nyasaland, or the Kafue project in Northern Rhodesia, which would have provided immediate farming opportunities on a vast scale for Africans, as well as yielding power. It was the Kariba scheme that was adopted.

It tied up virtually the whole of the Federation's public borrowing power from 1959 to 1965. Now in operation, it is running below capacity and its output is therefore more costly per unit to use.

The objective, of course, is easy to discern. It is to build up the manufacturing potential of the Federation; in other words, to buttress that part of the economy which is white-directed and encourages white immigration. Only the 1959 Emergencies, and the riots which have disfigured the Rhodesian winters of 1960–2, resulting in an outflow of capital and a near standstill in private investment, have frustrated this plan.

The Rhodesian Central Bank performs its functions with a pronounced settler-manufacturing bias. Professor Franck writes:

They are interested in maintaining a relatively tight-money economy, uninflated by credit or deficit-financing, and have created a Central Bank which can promote this by manipulating the percentage of demand liabilities which commercial banks must deposit with it. In each case, these policies do not coincide with the best economic interests of the African population.

And he concludes that the present policy, of making any African prosperity the mere by-product of European economic growth, must be totally reversed 'to avert political catastrophe'.

Professor Barber reaches a similar conclusion:

The government's commitment to support a large-scale industrial establishment is likely to absorb the bulk of the funds which it can mobilize. Little may remain to finance other urgent requirements, particularly those which have the most immediate bearing on the African's economic prospects. This presupposes that governments would be willing to finance major improvements in indigenous agriculture and urban housing for the African.

9. SCHOOLS: In 1958 Sir Edgar Whitehead announced that Southern Rhodesia was doing more for the education of its Africans than any other government on the continent. He based his claim on the percentage of the budget (twelve and a half to fourteen per cent) devoted to education, and the percentage of African children for whom school places could be provided (eighty-five per cent in 1962). It is an effective propaganda ploy; British spokesmen on the defensive at the U.N. have used it, and

R. A. Butler referred to it in a speech in London in July 1962 after his tour of the Federation: '. . . African education is farther ahead than in any of the critic countries where no such educational scheme exists'.

The real situation is rather less impressive. In aiming for a programme of mass primary education, the Southern Rhodesian authorities have diverted funds from the necessary development of secondary schooling. This is not to disparage the actual increase in educational expenditure which has taken place. The Southern Rhodesian budget was £1·6 million as recently as 1956 and reached £4·5 million in the 1962–3 vote. Enrolments have risen in twenty years from 100,000 to 552,000. It is frequently pointed out by white Rhodesians that the sum allocated for African schools alone is more than all the revenue received by the government from Africans in taxes. But this is not a just comparison, of course, since Africans pay less than Europeans in *direct* taxes, but much more in the indirect charges – like the levies on matches, soap, and clothing – which a white legislature imposes on cheap (i.e. African) consumer goods.

Whitehead's self-congratulating reference to percentages conveniently ignores the fact that the Southern Rhodesian government is regional, so that its budget does not include items like national defence. The educational item therefore bulks relatively larger for the Southern Rhodesian than for national governments elsewhere in Africa. Even so, the Southern Rhodesian percentage of twelve to fourteen per cent is not the highest. Uganda spends eighteen per cent – a figure I ran across purely by accident while investigating something else – which makes one wonder just how carefully the Southern Rhodesian statisticians have based their claim. Did they really run through the budgets of thirty national governments, including the half that are French-speaking?

The most damning indictment of settler-controlled education was contained in a recent article (1962) in the *Central African Examiner* by James Lauderdale, which maintains that there is built into the whole Rhodesian system 'a very marked bias towards European economic interests . . . in education particularly noticeable'. Expressed as expenditure per head, the figures for 1960 were:

White children in all territories	— £103
African children in Southern Rhodesia	— £8
African children in Northern Rhodesia	— £9
African children in Nyasaland	— £3

This works out to a national average of £7 per head spent on African children out of public funds, and *fifteen times that sum*, also from public funds, for the children of settlers. Incredibly, this is not the whole story: African parents must also pay fees, ranging from £3 to £60 a year. All white children are guaranteed places at government schools (in contrast to the fifteen per cent of all African children who are simply turned away), and there are no fees. One Salisbury school for white children was closed recently for lack of sufficient pupils. In September 1962 the Principal of Nyatsime College for Africans, A. M. Wakatama, said – in evidence to the belatedly appointed Education Commission – that he had received 1,100 applications for sixty-two available places.

When the British government granted its £3·5 million loan to Southern Rhodesia in August 1962, a sum of £200,000 was immediately allocated for African schools, and a similar sum for building houses and offices to accommodate an additional 500 police.

The 'low triangle policy' – broad based but coming to a point almost at once – means that the eighty-five per cent intake of African children swiftly peters to about one per cent in the tenth year of schooling. The average black child gets two to three years of instruction, barely learning to read and to count. White children provide a sharp contrast: all of them start school and virtually all complete their primary education, while seventy-three per cent reach School Certificate level, Form IV (compared to 0·5 per cent for Africans). A table compiled by Lauderdale from official figures shows the rapid decline of African children in the two Rhodesias from the year of initial attendance (1947) to the completion of secondary schooling (1960):

		Southern Rhodesia	Northern Rhodesia
Intake year	1947	81,821	27,845
Standard II	1950	23,366	11,920
Standard VI	1954	4,429	1,889
Form II	1956	1,888	339
Form IV	1958	379	117
Form VI	1960	15	28

As a result of this low triangle policy, all three territories are woefully deficient in Africans with the secondary education needed for the Civil Service and senior posts in industry. The total output of Nyasaland's secondary schools at School Certificate (G.C.E. 'O') level was eighty in 1960. Told that output was scheduled to reach 260 in 1964, Dr Banda said on assuming power that the rate would have dramatically to be increased by a crash programme. The Education Minister, Kanyama Chiume, stepped up secondary-school intake fifty per cent during his first year of office, and declared that the 1965 School Certificate output would touch the 1,000 mark. Also, because of deep dissatisfaction with the policies of Southern Rhodesia, where the University College of Rhodesia and Nyasaland is located, and as a protest against Federation, the Banda government declared that Nyasaland would build its own university. Mr Chiume announced that sixty Nyasas had been sent overseas for courses, forty-five of them at degree level. He had discovered, on taking office, he said, that the Federal government had blocked by administrative controls, offers of scholarships to Nyasas from India, the United States, Canada, Australia, and New Zealand which would have come to two dozen a year. Salisbury had also refused an offer of four experts from U.N.E.S.C.O. to go to Nyasaland.

Africans in the other two territories also complained bitterly when they learned of the blocked awards. A total of sixty-six American scholarships had been earmarked for East and Central Africa, said Mr Nkomo, and of these sixteen had been offered to Africans from Southern Rhodesia, on condition that the home government paid the passages. Kenneth Kaunda declared that ten of the American awards had been offered to Northern Rhodesian Africans but that the Welensky government had categorically refused to pay any passages. U.N.I.P. had given £1,500 to establish its own scholarship committee, and the first six scholars had left for degree courses abroad.

Mr Nkomo charged the Southern Rhodesian government with deliberately blocking African educational advancement:

Angola has more Africans studying abroad. In our territory we have only 2 African barristers, 1 solicitor, 10 doctors, about 100 graduate teachers, no engineers and no other trained people. One has to see the numbers of African students from independent states [studying] in Europe, Russia, the United States, Canada, etc., to see what African governments are capable of doing for their own people.

Self-help: When schools opened in January 1962, the Southern Rhodesian government found itself overwhelmed with the cumulative effects of the unemployment crisis and the drift to the towns brought about by the Land Husbandry Act. At the Highfield African township, outside Salisbury, the eight primary schools were inundated by hundreds of extra, unexpected applicants. They proved to be 'illegal'; their parents were 'lodgers' in the township and as such were not entitled to send their children to local schools. Police used tear gas to disperse a crowd of 1,000 outside one particular school; police cars were stoned and the school windows broken. At two schools, Nyandoro and Mutsas, teachers let 500 'illegal' children into already packed classrooms. The Management Board Secretary, K. Gutu, estimated that approximately 1,000 Africans between the ages of five and fifteen were without school places. In further clashes with police, four children were arrested. Inspectors arranged a two-shift system.

Then the Africans acted. By March they had formed the Highfield Community Association and with help from individual white Rhodesians, had collected £2,000 in pennies and shillings, got thirty-eight volunteer teachers and the loan of fifteen Protestant church buildings. When classes began, a total of 1,600 African children registered. The whole project contravened the Southern Rhodesia Education Act, but the Whitehead government pointedly turned a blind eye, especially as the campaign had been widely publicized abroad.

At the start of the same school term, two Coloured children were accepted at a white secondary school. The Federal Education Department ordered them to leave by the next day; in terms of the law, schools were to remain racially separate.

University: The settlers originally planned an all-white University of Southern Rhodesia, with a separate though associated institution for Africans, and in 1948 the Salisbury municipality offered a splendid site measuring 250 acres, later increased to 474, in the white suburb of Mount Pleasant.

Three events coincided in 1953, just as the university board was about to ask the Southern Rhodesian Assembly to pass the necessary legislation: Federation was established; a Commission of Inquiry (of the Central African Council) recommended that a Federal university should be set up on non-racial lines, in Lusaka if the Southern Rhodesian settlers would not accept integration; and Britain offered financial help, on condition that the new university had no colour-bar.

The bargain was struck. The non-racial University College of Rhodesia and Nyasaland was incorporated by Royal Charter, and the British government gave to it a handsome grant of £1·4 million – since increased. Classes began in 1957 with seventy-one students, only eight of whom were African, and these were accomodated in a separate hostel. Soon, however, the students were eating together, and the initial objections of white students to mixed accommodation were overcome. By 1959 the university was integrated, and the students themselves have opposed any colour-bar in their university jazz orchestra, rugby teams, and other extra-curricular activities.

Then came the Chidzero affair. Dr Bernard Chidzero is one of the most distinguished academic figures ever to have emerged from British Central Africa; he had taken his Ph.D. in Political Science at McGill University in Canada, and an American foundation was prepared to provide a special research fellowship for him at the university in Salisbury. He would be the first African member of staff, if the university authorities would have him.

The answer was a delighted yes, and Dr Chidzero prepared for his return to Southern Rhodesia. But the authorities then discovered that he had just got married – to a Canadian girl whose colour was unquestionably white. They announced that the post was no longer open, and admitted that his mixed marriage was 'a major factor' in their decision.

The move drew warm praise from such right-wing settler papers as the Salisbury *Sunday Mail* and the *Citizen*, but the criticism of Press and academic circles throughout the English-speaking world. Perhaps in an effort to recoup its prestige, the university has since shown considerable resistance to white supremacist pressures. It continued to employ a lecturer, Michael Faber, despite the open hostility of the Federal Cabinet to his views. Mr Faber was still on the staff – and on leave in England – when the Welensky administration refused him permission to re-enter the Federation for the start of the next academic term. Two other lecturers, also openly critical of U.F.P. 'partnership' and sympathetic to African political advance, have been John Reed and Terence Ranger. By 1962 they had gone so far as to join Mr Nkomo's Z.A.P.U. movement and had been elected to committee chairmanships. They had jointly edited a newsletter, *Dissent*, and Dr Ranger had sprung into the news as founder and leader of C.A.C.B.A. – the Citizens Against the Colour Bar Association. (He was pushed, fully-clothed, into a Salisbury swimming-pool during one of the C.A.C.B.A. demonstrations.) Throughout all this, over more than three years, the university has not sought to interfere with these controversial 'outside' activities. In the crisis of September 1962, when Z.A.P.U. was banned and hundreds of its members detained, Messrs Reed and Ranger were served with restriction orders confining them to a three-mile area. In 1963 Dr Ranger was deported – without reason – from Rhodesia, and accepted a post in Tanganyika.

Unfortunately – and this is not the fault of the university authorities – the student body reflects, in terms of numbers, the disparate opportunities open to Southern Rhodesian citizens in terms of colour. From about twelve per cent at the start, the African fraction of the student body has slowly grown, to thirty-two per cent by mid 1962, or 61 in a total of 235. There were also some students of Asian extraction and a few from beyond the Federation, leaving 162 white Rhodesians. A breakdown of the figures is revealing. It shows that among the white community of the Federation, some 52 out of every 100,000 are able to study at a university (the number is actually much higher, as many white Rhodesians study at British and South African universities). For Africans, the figure is a mere 0·7 in 100,000. Or, putting it another way, since the white settlers are outnumbered by their African fellow-citizens of the Federation in the ratio of 26:1, one might expect a similar ratio at the university. But instead of one student in every 26 being white, the actual number is 18 out of 26.

10. LOCAL GOVERNMENT: Constituting one of the last bastions against integration are the municipal councils and town management boards. These were all white, even in Nyasaland with its tiny white population of 10,000, until the Banda administration began 'Africanization' in mid 1962. The Southern Rhodesian government also acted in the same year to make it possible for Africans at least to take part in the management of their own townships; hitherto the direction and finance had been wholly in the hands of the (white) councils of the adjacent European municipalities. The Bulawayo City Council, which has given the lead in race relations more than once in the past, and which is proud of its model African townships (one of them a real showpiece), went even further and proposed that there should be seats for Africans on the City Council itself. The Mayor, Mr Pair, offered four seats for Bulawayo Africans as a beginning. And though seven municipalities and twenty-five town management boards turned down such reform, Fort Victoria voted to follow Bulawayo's lead, while the Selukwe Town Management Board invited Africans to attend its meetings as observers.

Police: at the time of the 1959 Emergency, only nine African policemen in Nyasaland had achieved the rank of Inspector Grade II, the rank at which every white recruit enters the force. On taking office in 1961, Dr Banda and his colleagues served notice that a full programme of Africanization would at once be pursued.

In Southern Rhodesia the British South Africa Police has had separate training and different uniforms for its African constables, who could not be promoted above the rank of 'African Sergeant'. By 1962, however, there were signs that this clear dividing-line might be fading; on the social side, the police abandoned separate sports days and from 1960 have been holding their annual athletic meeting jointly.

Salisbury itself continued recalcitrant. After the Federal Supreme Court ruling on municipal swimming-pools, ordering that they be opened to all citizens regardless of race, the Mayor and Council, while reluctantly complying, passed a resolution 'against the principle of multi-racial swimming'. The same Council voted in 1962 to refuse a lease on thirty acres of land for a proposed multi-racial sports club, since the land was in 'a European area'.

11. SOCIAL COLOUR BAR: The Salisbury *Sunday Mail* sympathized with the Salisbury City Council over multi-racial swimming. It said:

What Europeans here feel is that the economic barrier would not apply to swimming baths, and that instead of entry being limited to the better type of non-European, their pools would be swamped by hordes of bathers whose notions of hygiene often fall far short of Western standards.

They also dislike – and this is probably the strongest feeling of all – the idea of their wives and daughters being exposed to the gaze of African men. These are facts; regrettable possibly, but facts nevertheless.

But the *Sunday Mail* was behind the times. The great swimming-pool controversy of 1961–2 can be seen in retrospect as the high point in a successful campaign by Dr Ranger of the C.A.C.B.A., his colleague S. N. Mehta of the Asian Association, and many individual citizens to breach the walls of an ancient citadel. Social privilege was not ended, but had its end begun?

Those two staunch supporters of the U.F.P., the Argus news-papers in Salisbury, recognized that a social revolution had occurred.

The *Standard* spoke of 'certain realities which people will have to face, whether they like them or not: colour-bar is dead ... discrimination on grounds of race alone is finished'. And its companion, the *Herald*, maintained, 'We cannot, with an honest face, purport to be building a nation without trying out non-racial swimming-pools for a reasonable period.'

An African returning home to Southern Rhodesia in the middle of 1962 after an absence of, say, five years, would accordingly have found so many substantial changes in the social sphere that he might well have assumed that Lord Home and Duncan Sandys were right: that the settlers were moving in the right direction, and that if outside critics would only be tactful enough to keep quiet, all was bound to go well.

In sport, for instance, the dark year of 1956 – when the Rhodesian all-white team had been ruled inadmissible for participation in the Olympic Games – was now far behind. In 1960 the Federation was able to send a mixed team to the Olympics in Rome; there were only one or two Africans, to be sure, but still, it was a beginning. There were still some rugby and cricket leagues maintaining a colour-bar, but most had dropped their restrictions; almost all boxing was inter-racial, and so were athletic meetings. The U.F.P. at its annual conference in 1961 had voted to repeal the Land Apportionment Act (after the next election) and make all racial discrimination illegal; it was a brave decision, which in fact led to its defeat in 1962 by the Rhodesian Front. But a returning African would have been astonished to see that at least some cinemas and hotels in every Southern Rhodesian town had been opened to black men. In Northern Rhodesia, by legislative action, all such bars had been dropped. In the changing mood of the times, the Colonial authorities were now more anxious to placate Mr Kaunda and U.N.I.P. than the former bogey of the Afrikaner miners.

Africans – a few at least – were being trained at last as firemen and engineers on the Federal Railways. The first African Clerk of the House – at a salary of £1,300 a year – had been appointed to the Federal Assembly. The first African school inspector had been appointed in Southern Rhodesia. Even the pass system had been simplified in Southern Rhodesia under the Pass Laws (Repeal) Act so that since March 1961 no African had had to carry more than one document – either the standard 'Situpa', or the Identity Card for 'emergent' (more sophisticated) Africans.

Hard liquor was on sale to Africans, and enough bars and pubs, restaurants and hotels were open to black Rhodesians to make civilized encounters with white friends feasible (at last) in the centre of towns like Salisbury and Bulawayo. In Northern and Southern Rhodesia alike legislation was opening apprenticeship and extending workmen's compensation to all races. A cautious step forward had been taken in opening some categories of work (hitherto all-white) to black miners, a step approved by a majority vote of the European Mineworkers' Union on the Copperbelt. The (hitherto all-white) Rhodesian T.U.C. had even formally abandoned its colour bar. The Southern Rhodesian Civil Service had been opened to Africans (1961). African home ownership schemes had (years too late) been initiated in Northern Rhodesia (1959) and even Southern Rhodesia (1961), though the high prices (minimum £750 in Northern Rhodesia, £2,500 in Southern) would limit benefits to the few rich Africans.

Africans might now buy lottery tickets and bet on horses, both 'privileges' having been hastily rushed through parliament in 1959 after the Emergency, when the settlers had first been shaken into realizing that their half-century of insulation from the realities of Africa was ending. 'There must be an immediate and massive lifting of colour-bar,' Garfield Todd, the liberal former Prime Minister had declared.

Welensky, however, provided the settler perspective. 'We must remove the pinpricks,' he said. It was a fatal belittlement of African impatience and the temper of the times. Indeed, many observers of the Rhodesian scene are, in retrospect, coming to the conclusion that this was the moment when the settlers threw away their last chance of an agreed solution and a peaceful transfer of power. It was Welensky's Rubicon; instead of taking the leap, he paddled timorously at the water's edge and then drew cautiously back to pause, and consider, and do nothing at all.

If I have heard enraged African politicians snort out that foolish word 'pinpricks' once, I have heard them do so a dozen times. Like Welensky, the average white Rhodesian cannot get inside the skin of his black neighbours to feel just how deeply all the indignities penetrate, from second-class taxis and second-class prices for their maize, to second-class votes in the polling booth (if they have any vote at all). Herbert Chitepo, Rhodesia's first African barrister, has written that partnership failed not only in parliament and in industry, 'but in the shops, on the staircases, and at office counters where someone denied to the African his essential dignity as a person, and violated his sense of justice and self-respect'. Mr Chitepo was talking from his own experience. He had been asked, in office buildings in Salisbury, not to use the lift or the stairs, but the fire escape – the proper place for 'boys'.

His wife, Victoria, had once tried on a pair of shoes in a Salisbury shop, and seen the manager come up to the salesgirl who had allowed this and fire her on the spot. In 1960 a group of Salisbury housewives, mostly U.F.P. supporters, decided to remove these 'pinpricks' with what they called a Courtesy Campaign. It helped, but about as much as one bucket of water when the forest is ablaze.

Whatever good the Courtesy Campaign may have done was virtually wiped out by contrary conduct, when a group of settlers dug in their heels to hold the line. An African doctor, one of the two who had qualified in Southern Rhodesia, was ordered to cease performing post-mortems on the bodies of white people. One should not 'ride roughshod', explained the Federal Minister of Health. And in 1963 the new Winston Field government began a "roll back" against integration, starting with segregated swimming.

12. THE NATION'S HEALTH: The Federal budget for health services has declined (as a percentage of the whole), while defence costs have doubled in the past five years. And the same inevitable bias favours the settler in health services, as in other departments where public funds are spent. The provision of hospital beds

(1960 figures) revealed a rate of 8·5 a thousand for white Rhodesians and 2·9 a thousand for Africans. The occupancy ratio is
equally significant: in Southern Rhodesia it was sixty-four per
cent of capacity for beds in European hospitals, and 138 per cent
for beds in African ones. In other words, more than a third of
the beds in white wards are usually empty, while African wards
are crowded thirty-eight per cent beyond capacity. The supply of
doctors reflects the same bias: 755 in Southern Rhodesia, 336 in
Northern Rhodesia, and only 97 in Nyasaland. Yet the number of
Africans is about the same in each territory – roughly three
million. It is with the number of white settlers in each that the
supply of doctors almost exactly correlates. Similarly, the preventive control of diseases like malaria and bilharzia has been
concentrated in 'urban' (i.e. white) areas. African student nurses
(whose pay is a fraction of European ones) are unable, because of
segregated training facilities, to take courses in radiography,
physio- or occupational therapy. European and Asian children must, by law, be given regular medical inspection at their
schools; there is no such provision for Africans.

Health Finance: The average cost a day for an African in
hospital varies between 10s. and 18s.; the government foots the
bill. For Europeans, the cost is calculated to be £4 a day; the
patient contributes £1, and the government pays the rest. This
subsidy for settlers consumes £1 million a year, about fourteen
per cent of the national budget for health, which seems a trifle
generous for a group that constitutes only four per cent of the
total population. The Monckton Commission, noting this persistent settler bias in health services, recommended that they be
'de-Federalized' and handed back to the control of the individual
territories.

These are perhaps the main areas of public life – there are
others – in which the black Rhodesian, to use the phrase so often
on the lips of his leaders, finds the dice loaded against him. It is
the overwhelming sense of injustice that has brought race relations in the Federation to such a pass of bitterness. The African
has learned from countless disillusionments always to doubt, to

suspect. When the settler government announces another surprise package to benefit the nation, the African searches for the bomb beneath the fancy wrapping-paper.

The Kyle Dam project was officially opened in 1961 by Sir Edgar Whitehead, who told the crowds at the ceremony how the desert would be made to blossom. Over an area of 18,000 acres, the yield of cotton, sugar, citrus, and wheat would produce crops worth £200 an acre, as a result of irrigation. The Southern Rhodesian government had supplied a third of the £3·25 million needed, so presumably the dam was to benefit the territory's citizens, regardless of race. And, indeed, Sir Edgar said precisely that. To start with, there would be enough sugar to make the Federation self-sufficient and so cut the current import bill of £2 million a year. And there would be employment opportunities. A government announcement at the time put it in these words:

> Five years ago the local tribes lived in the kraals, poor in health from nutritional deficiencies, without ambition, and without hope or desire for a change. Next year ... some 30,000 Africans will be living on the estate on a balanced diet, with health, educational and welfare facilities ... their own brick-built living quarters complete with cookhouses and ablution blocks. This is an example of partnership. ... Empire building as a term may have fallen into disrepute, but this is the fulfilment of all that is best in pioneer vision. The construction of something, where nothing was before, is the most satisfying achievement of mankind.

There is an evident sincerity in the announcement. But two points must be made.

First, as with almost every other project in Central Africa starting with Federation itself, the Kyle irrigation scheme was a white man's project from start to finish – concept, planning, construction, right down to those 'ablution blocks'. No one had asked 30,000 voteless Africans whether or not they would care to live on the estate. They had no M.P. who could, if the terms were not right, storm into the office of the Minister of Lands and object. They were expected to be grateful; and if they were not, well that was just too bad.

The second point is specific to Kyle. The project is being enlarged by the building of a dam at Bangala, at the cost of a further £1·8 million, and with the combined reservoirs there will be water enough to irrigate 28,000 acres. It is provided that one of the two companies already involved in sugar production at Kyle, the Hippo Valley Estates, will at that point – the government has announced – inaugurate a large-scale land-settlement scheme. Who will these lucky people be, in a territory where African land hunger is now desperate ?

Harsh economic facts suggest that white Rhodesians will have first choice; after all, they have capital and the black man has not. But the Hippo Valley Agreement does not just leave this to chance. It says:

The Government shall . . . assist the Company with the selection of suitable Settlers, all of whom shall be of European origin.

Does Sir Edgar Whitehead seriously suppose that he can go out to Kyle now and persuade those 30,000 Africans to accept his 'Build a Nation' and 'Claim Your Vote' campaigns at face value ? The answer, incredibly, is yes. Sir Edgar *does* suppose he can persuade them. And if they are sullen, and support the Z.A.P.U.-called boycott, then to him this is proof of the evil influence exerted on the 'ordinary African' by the ambitious, self-seeking 'extremists' who have captured the Z.A.P.U. leadership.

The Kyle affair illustrates the political booby-trap that awaits the 'moderate' African. Suppose you are a Z.A.P.U. leader who feels that – with the roll-back of racial discrimination begun in 1961, the modification of the pass laws, the throwing open of hotels, cafés, and cinemas to Africans, the hints of land reform – you should take the advice of Lord Home and Duncan Sandys and give the Whitehead government another chance. Suppose, indeed, you are persuaded that the Kyle irrigation scheme is a further advance and you go out there in the middle of 1961 for the opening ceremony, to see 'the fulfilment of all that is best in pioneer vision'. There are handshakes all round, cups of multiracial tea, flourishes of partnership. And then everything blows up

383

in your face. With the revelation of the race bar in the land-settlement scheme, you, an African political leader, supposedly guarding the interests of your people, are shown to be gullible and stupid.

Is it any wonder that the word 'moderate' is so discredited, has now become a term of bitter reproach at African gatherings? There have been too many Kyles in Rhodesia; too many spectacular let-downs for the trusting African moderate. The settlers have thrown away their most precious asset, the best guarantee they had for their physical security in the unpredictable years that stretch ahead. They have thrown away any trust in their word.

Even the simplest African 'voter' - if he had a vote - can work out for himself that if an African government came to power in Salisbury tomorrow, there would be no more 'white settler' clauses in land schemes like Kyle. Can anyone seriously imagine them today in Tanganyika? Nigeria? Senegal? Tunisia? Such a change of government would immediately lead to a change of policy on education, land, health services, wages, taxation, the social colour-bar. And, since white Rhodesians are also well aware this would be so, they stiffen their resolution to hold on to what they have; to resist at all costs the forces - in Africa and at Westminster - which threaten to bring about change.

The savage blood-letting, arrests, and detentions which marred the last months of 1962 in Southern Rhodesia ought to serve as a warning-light to the settlers - ignorant or not. So should the transformation wrought in Northern Rhodesia by the October general election, and the promise of secession taken home by Dr Hastings Banda from his November conference in London. One wonders when that strange little white community in the south, hitherto insulated by ignorance, will at last hear the winds of change blowing up around it to gale force. It might like to consider the words of a pioneer student of colonialism, Edmund Burke, who looked on two revolutions - the American and the French - and said this:

Freedom, not servitude, is the cure of anarchy. People crushed by law have no hopes but from power. If laws are their enemies, they will be enemies to laws. And those who have much to hope, and nothing to lose, will be dangerous.

Part 5: The Time of Decision

'I do not hate the white man; you see, his position of
domination has placed him in a position of
moral weakness.'
CHIEF ALBERT LUTULI

1 The Westminster Factor

> 'Europeans here are sensible enough not to care two hoots what is
> said in the British House of Commons. The formula for those in
> control of the Federation must be; for overseas critics as much
> contempt as you can; and for our own people, keep the public
> sweet.' LORD MALVERN

The view from Westminster Bridge is deceptive. Those of us
who are not professional politicians look out across the river and
see the Mother of Parliaments, where freedom broadens down
from precedent to precedent. A fortress of democracy. In our
own lifetime it has withstood the assaults of the Nazis, both physical and spiritual; when we are gone it will still be there, as
timeless as the river.

That is the simple view of Westminster, the view of the voter
who can play some part in determining the affairs of his country.
It may also be the view of the visitor from Canada, India, Jamaica,
or any of the other sixteen sovereign nations which have taken the
Westminster system home with them and made it their own.

But this is not the view that presents itself to the black
Rhodesian, or to the man from Basutoland, Bechuanaland,
Swaziland, or any of the other territories where colonial rule still
persists. As he sees it, there will be time enough for sentimental
abstractions about parliament and justice later on – after independence has been won. What he sees before him, here and now,
is the Westminster of the lobbies, the pressure groups, the whole
machinery of political bargaining.

In the spring of 1961, when the controversy over the release of
Jomo Kenyatta was at its height – coinciding with the struggle
between Macleod and Welensky over a new constitution for
Northern Rhodesia – it was solemnly announced in Nairobi that
the Governor would consider a number of factors in determining
whether or not to release Mr Kenyatta from detention. Tom
Mboya, asked to comment, said simply: 'The decision will not be
made here; it will be made by the 1922 Committee in London.'

His reference to the influential – if generally unseen – group of Tory back-benchers showed that at least one Kenyan politician had a shrewd grasp of where power actually lay.

It is doubtless all wrong that the fate of Colonial peoples should depend upon the fluctuations in party politics at Westminster – especially the fissions or threatened fissions within the Conservative Party over colonial policy. One might like to think that the great decisions had been taken, down the years, by dispassionate and well-informed administrators at the Colonial Office. But this just would not be true. The most that such men can do is to marshal the facts and press for action when delay seems dangerous. And then the morning comes – usually a Tuesday or a Thursday – when the Colonial Secretary descends from his first-floor office to the black official car parked at the kerbside in Great Smith Street, that waits to whisk him off to Downing Street. There, at the meeting of the Cabinet, you may be sure, the realities of domestic party pressures and of Britain's own national interests will loom rather larger then the immediate needs of any particular colony. Kenyatta's release was postponed from February to July because it threatened to produce a Tory back-bench revolt which might conceivably have brought down the Macmillan government. From Kenneth Kaunda's point of view, as it happened, this was probably a good thing. Iain Macleod, as the Colonial Secretary of the day, rated the danger in Northern Rhodesia a shade more critical than the one in Kenya. And so any decision over Kenya was delayed in order to keep the Tory parliamentary party together at Westminster for the immediate task of resisting Welensky and pushing through the 'February Plan'. But by June of that same year, 1961, the priorities had changed. Harold Macmillan wanted to have a united Conservative Party behind him when the moment came in July to announce Britain's application for Common Market membership. And meanwhile it seemed necessary to release Kenyatta, in order to avoid widespread disturbances in Kenya; either that, or fly out troops (which the Army Reserve could not spare). If there were to be any emergency airlifts of troops, Berlin and Kuwait clearly had first claim. And for the Persian

Gulf crisis – the clash between Kuwait and Iraq – the British bases in Kenya were essential: the R.A.F. at Nairobi, the Guards at Kahawa, the Navy at Mombasa. In the circumstances, the Tories had no room for manoeuvre; Welensky's delegates in London (Greenfield and Evans) gained the settler concessions in the Northern Rhodesian constitution that they had come for, and Kenneth Kaunda left London disappointed and angry. It was to be eight months before the Westminster factor would once again be propitious, and a final revision of the Northern Rhodesian constitution – which half-satisfied the Africans and infuriated Welensky – could be made.

Anglo-Rhodesian relations, or – to put it more crudely – the process of political bargaining between British and Rhodesian politicians, can be said to have covered a period of some seventy years. I can write from personal experience about only a small fraction of this period. But from all that I have seen, which has at least covered the period of Federal experiment in Central Africa, I have grown more and more convinced that, in the shaping of all Colonial politics, the Westminster factor is paramount. And I have no doubt that this is the view of most, if not all political correspondents in London.

Three men whose judgement was wrong over Cyprus were all deeply involved in the Nyasaland crisis of 1959–60. Henry Hopkinson, as the Tory Minister of State at the Colonial Office, had toured Central Africa a few months before the establishment of Federation and said that 'ninety per cent of the Africans know nothing about it at all'. He strongly backed Federation as something whose benefits the Africans would come to appreciate in time, and he assured the House of Commons in the final debates that it could safely entrust the care of the African – and his political advancement – to the settlers. But the Tories began to doubt this Minister's political judgement some months later, when he acquired questionable fame as the man who said 'Never' to Cyprus. The Cypriot agitation for independence or union with Greece had, up till then, taken only non-violent forms. After Hopkinson's speech in the House of Commons, when he said that Cyprus – for military reasons – could 'never' achieve independence but must always retain colonial status, it was only a matter of a few weeks before General Grivas and the first boat-loads of smuggled arms arrived, and guerrilla warfare began on 1 April. The Cypriots I have talked to have all declared that the Hopkinson speech and the April explosion were cause and effect.

The unfortunate governor, Sir Robert Armitage, who had mis-calculated the force of Cypriot nationalism, was transferred – to the place which Hopkinson predicted would long be quiet and contented – Nyasaland. There then entered upon the Central African scene another Cyprus veteran, in the person of the Colonial Secretary, Alan Lennox-Boyd – a kind and thought-ful man in private life, but in politics somewhat addicted to the techniques of the dungeon. His banishment of Archbishop Makarios to the Seychelle Islands in the Indian Ocean had been a notable failure. It had ensured a dramatic stiffening of Cypriot resistance, and a hero's homecoming to the Archbishop when the British government was at last forced to release him.

The year 1959 was to be a fateful one for Lennox-Boyd. He flew to Somaliland and made nonsense of everything that Britain was preaching in its other colonies about the need for staged pro-gress in the advance to democratic government, by granting the Somalis immediate adult suffrage and the freedom to choose independence. The reason? The embryo Somali Republic next door was prepared to take on Somaliland (relieving Britain of budget and defence problems) by an agreed amalgamation when U.N. trusteeship ended in 1960.

This domino tripped off others. Kenya is Somalia's southern neighbour, and Tom Mboya together with his colleagues saw no sense in accepting a minority of seats in a settler-ruled legislature if Lennox-Boyd could grant democratic government to Somali-land when the right pressures were brought to bear on him. The Africans of Nyasaland, meanwhile, saw signs that Lennox-Boyd would give in to the pressure of Welensky and the settlers, per-haps granting them full independence in the 1960 constitutional conference drawing near. When they rebelled, the police told the lurid tale of the 'murder plot' to Armitage, who believed it and told it to Lennox-Boyd. He not only believed it but recounted it to an incredulous House of Commons. That was in July 1959. The Tories stonewalled on Africa, won an autumn general election, and appointed a new Colonial Secretary in the person of Iain Macleod.

He inherited log-jams in Cyprus, Kenya, and Nyasaland, all of which Lennox-Boyd could not have dealt with for reasons of 'face'. Macleod proceeded to take action. In Kenya and Cyprus he offered swift concessions that his predecessor would not have considered. Next Nyasaland: he ordered the release of Dr Banda from detention in Southern Rhodesia, called a constitutional conference in London which granted handsome (and realistic) concessions to African demands, and recalled the unfortunate governor whose usefulness was at an end. (Dr Banda, at the farewell party, made a gallant and generous speech to the man who had jailed him.)

It may be asked by the ordinary newspaper reader, when he has ploughed through yet another sea of print about Rhodesia: 'Well, if the settlers are being so difficult, why not do what Macleod did in Kenya and just push through better terms for the Africans, whether the settlers like it or not?'

This seems logical enough, but it assumes that Britain's network of control is the same in Central Africa as in the rest of her colonial possessions. But of course it is not. The Rhodesian Federation is the one British dependency where Britain has no troops. Indeed, it constitutes the sole instance where this has been allowed to occur in a colonial history that embraces three centuries and five continents. Britain cannot summon Sir Roy Welensky or any other white settler leader to the conference table in London, because the troops who hold Central Africa are Rhodesian troops, paid by the settlers and under their command.

All this makes utter nonsense of Britain's solemn submissions at the U.N. in 1962, when Sir Patrick Dean, Lord Home, and Sir Hugh Foot (until he resigned in despair) argued that Southern Rhodesia remained a British dependency, but insisted at the same time that, because it was a 'self-governing colony', Britain could not intervene in its internal affairs. One felt embarrassment

391

for distinguished public servants like Sir Hugh and Sir Patrick, who had to support such a ramshackle structure of sophistry in the solemn deliberations of a world forum. But one needed to waste no sympathy on Lord Home in his predicament, since, as one of the architects of Federation, the dilemma was of his own making. No wonder the Chairman of the Committee of Seventeen, Mr Jha, said at one point in utter exasperation: 'Well, is this place a colony or isn't it?'

If the word 'colony' is to retain any meaning at all, the plain answer seems to be that it is not. Southern Rhodesia is an independent state with its own Legislative Assembly, Cabinet, Treasury, tax system, judiciary, Civil Service – and troops. It has been so since 1923, and no amount of fancy window-dressing can alter the fact. But pride – Imperial pride – has prevented successive British governments from facing up to it. The establishment of Federation in 1953 did nothing to obscure the fact. By 1963, with the Federation disintegrating, the same fact was apparent, more obtrusively than before. In the post-war world of 1953, Britain could not properly grant formal independence to a settler government in Salisbury which would obviously attempt to hold its black citizens in permanent political subjection.

On the other hand, Britain had no means of enforcing a policy of African advance on to the stubborn members of a thirty-man (all-white) legislature, backed by their own Civil Service, police, army, and air force. Federation seemed to be the ideal answer; it postponed the evil day of settlement. By linking the white supremacist colony with the two northern territories where African advancement was accepted, the British government naïvely hoped that liberal ideas would somehow prove infectious. The settlers, for their part, quietly counted on spreading their own ideas northwards. They saw Federation as a method of halting African advance north of the Zambesi, of making the two northern protectorates into buffer states against the southward flowing tide of African nationalism. In 1951 Sir Charles Arden-Clarke had released Dr Kwame Nkrumah from prison, and, in the jubilant reconciliation which had followed, the British government had agreed to a timetable of self-government (it was to last for six years) leading to independence. For the settlers of Rhodesia, this had been the ringing of the alarm bell.

The campaign mounted by the white Rhodesians under their leader, Sir Godfrey Huggins, was skilful and determined. But it was not without its tactical mistakes. The failure to invite Africans of any kind to the second Victoria Falls Conference was a major error of judgement, and there were other omissions which made the settler leaders vulnerable to outside criticism. What saved them was the last-minute change of government in Britain, just as the series of scheduled conferences had reached its climax. Attlee and Labour went out; Churchill and the Tories came in. And that put an end to all the shuffling in Whitehall, the deep soul-searching at Transport House and Westminster. The new Prime Minister knew Africa; he knew the Colonial Office well, from tours of duty at decisive moments in history when race relations in southern Africa had been the problems at issue; and he knew the settlers. But even greater than his knowledge had been his resolve – to stop the outflow of Imperial power set in motion by Attlee, to wrench the controls hard over and shut the sluice-gates tight.

Churchill and his Colonial Secretary, Oliver Lyttleton, were the two best allies Huggins and Welensky ever had; within a few weeks Federation on settler terms was assured. For Churchill the dismemberment of Empire, which had led to the loss of the Indian sub-continent, had to stop. And it is noteworthy that, from his return to power until his retirement four years later, Churchill put British colonial policy firmly into reverse and held it there. As long as he was at No. 10 Downing Street, not one square foot of Imperial soil was handed back to its original owners; as much of the map as was still painted British red remained so.

It is with genuine reluctance that I find myself having to criticize the man who was a nation's hero in war and who has borne the illnesses of retirement with such fortitude, good humour, and nobility. My embarrassment is increased by the great courtesy and kindness that Sir Winston has shown me whenever we have met. On one occasion, he was quick to take up something I had written for my paper (which numbers him among its regular readers). It revealed a gap in the law, he said, which could only be closed by legislative action. And unlike many politicians he saw to it that the necessary legislation was passed.

Having said this, I may as well go straight to my central thesis on the disaster in British Central Africa and say that, in my view, the key to it has been the Westminster factor, rather than the machinations of the white settlers themselves. And the man who turned the key – wrongly and disastrously on the two vital occasions in this century when it had to be turned – was Sir Winston Churchill.

For his decision that established Federation in 1953 was only the second, and lesser, of the two decisions that had to be made. The first one, which started Rhodesia down the hazardous path to white supremacy, was the decision of 1921 that resulted in the creation of a 'self-governing colony' in 1923. And, by one of those unlikely coincidences of history, the Cabinet Minister whose job it was to receive the settler deputation in 1921 and agree to the terms under which the Rhodes era and British South Africa Company rule should be ended, was the then Colonial Secretary, Winston Spencer Churchill. On his shoulders must rest the heavy responsibility of deciding then to let the settlers gain supreme military control of Southern Rhodesia, with their own little army and air force, to run their own affairs without budgetary control from Whitehall. There was to be not one member of the Colonial Office in the territory, save the Governor whose limited powers made him a figurehead. (And today even he is a Rhodesian, not responsible in any way to Whitehall.) The only limitation was that Rhodesia's foreign relations should be conducted by His Majesty's government at Westminster. But even this was, in practice, largely obliterated by the Balfour Declaration and the Statute of Westminster in 1931. For, by another anomalous decision, it was agreed that the Rhodesians should have a seat at the Commonwealth Prime Ministers' Conferences. It is an important point, overlooked by non-Rhodesians when they criticize Sir Roy Welensky for conducting an independent foreign policy over Katanga and the Congo, that in fact he does not only hold the portfolio of Prime Minister. He is, as well, Minister of External Affairs. And as such he presides over a small but expanding Ministry, which has diplomatic missions in London, Washington, and Pretoria as well as consuls in Katanga and other key-points in Africa.

This is the heritage of Churchill's 1921 decision. Those of us who are pessimists about Central Africa feel that then was the fatal moment when the dragon's teeth were sown. The crop will soon be ripe.

By the 1950s, therefore, Britain had effectively lost control of her unique (and indefinable) self-governing colony. As long ago as the 1930s it had become a military power in its own right; small by comparison with its neighbour, South Africa, perhaps, but still a power on the continent. Inevitably, in groping for a solution to the Rhodesian puzzle, we find ourselves thrown backwards in successive leaps through history. The Churchill–Lyttleton decision of 1953 followed from the decision of thirty years before. And the 1923 decision had its roots in conflict before the First World War, just as the Company Charter was due to end. What remarkably emerges is not only that the Westminster factor was crucial on each occasion, but that Churchill himself was throughout personally involved: with Smuts, in the campaign to unite Rhodesia and the Union; with Dr Jameson at the Imperial Conference of 1907; with the Rhodesian volunteers in the Boer War. Churchill's early life might have been a deliberate preparation for the settler-sympathizing politician later on; the making of a kind of political Janissary.

The whole framework of his early life – as student, soldier, war correspondent, and rising politician – was Africa. As a schoolboy, he had heard his famous father, Lord Randolph, describing his adventures in Matabeleland just after the March of the Pioneers – tales of Lobengula, and his savage warriors with their assegais; personal recollections of encounters with Rhodes and Dr Jameson; a view of the great new Dominion which might arise if only, as Rhodes hoped, the two Boer republics could somehow be added, with Zambesia, to British South Africa.

After Harrow and Sandhurst had come, in 1895, the Spanish–American war in Cuba. Churchill was twenty-one, and he volunterred to fight – on the *Spanish* side. It was consistent with his vision of Empire and the virtues of enlightened Victorian colonialism. For we must try to see that far-off world as Churchill saw it, a world in which 'wog' and 'Fuzzy-Wuzzy' were not quaint, antique words, but part of the everyday language. Churchill saw many of such people when he took part in the Egyptian campaign; at Omdurman in 1898 he rode against them as an officer of the 21st Lancers in what is said to have been the last great cavalry charge of the British Army. It would have been unthinkable to give such people votes or a share in responsible government, in an era when one still spoke of 'the Lesser Breeds without the law'.

There was the mystic bond of Empire, and loyalty to one's kin and the all-uniting Crown:

> A Nation spoke to a Nation,
> A Throne sent word to a Throne:
> 'Daughter am I in my mother's house,
> But mistress in my own.'

That was Kipling's effort to define the role of Canada and her sister dominions – white dominions, of course – which were emerging into nationhood while staying within the Empire. No one fretted in Ottawa or Canberra when the summons came from London to attend the gathering of Prime Ministers known as the Colonial Conference. And, when Asquith announced a change of name at the 1907 meeting, no one took umbrage at the new title: the Imperial Conference. Churchill met Jameson there, for Dr Jameson was by that time Prime Minister of the Cape, and young Winston was junior Minister at the Colonial Office. As such he had made his mark the year before in the Commons by eloquently advocating a policy of conciliation towards the Boer states, to unite them with the two English colonies into a new Dominion. And, of course, as a correspondent, Churchill had seen the people of whom he was talking. He had spent his twenty-fifth birthday in a Boer prison before his daring escape;

a year later he had become a Tory M.P. and was launched on his political career.

His personal views were shaped by the great imperial questions of the day: Egypt, Suez, India, Ireland, and South Africa. He had heard Lord Randolph saying, 'Ulster will fight and Ulster will be right!' He thought of Gandhi almost with disgust; he was aware that the little Indian barrister had been busy with his first Congress activities in Johannesburg in 1906, and stirred Indian demonstrations against the 'Asiatic Ordinances' of the Boer régime. Since his aim was reconciliation with the Boers (for the larger goal of a new Dominion) he was bound to feel impatient with Gandhi – a busybody, and a pacifist to boot.

For four years from the end of the First World War, up to the fall of the Coalition in 1922, Churchill was directly involved in all the Imperial crises; first as Minister for War and Air, then as Colonial Secretary. From Washington, men like Woodrow Wilson, with no practical knowledge of colonies or empire, were actually preaching self-determination. When Gandhi, now back in India, proclaimed 'Hartal' in 1919, General Dyer gave his controversial order to fire and 379 civilians died in the Amritsar massacre.

As a Minister, Churchill was closely involved in Indian affairs, though by this time he also had the Irish 'troubles' on his hands – another unwelcome erosion of Empire. He and his Cabinet colleagues were even more appalled by Gandhi's next campaign: the strikes and anti-tax riots in 1921 which were deliberately timed to coincide with the royal visit of a future Emperor of India, Edward, Prince of Wales. There is a consistency to Churchill's views on imperialism; he could not abide MacDonald's slogan of 'Indian autonomy', and his opposition to the Indian Reform Bill of 1931 led to his exclusion from the National government. This is worth noting as a key to the ardour of his views on Imperial dominion and the inherent rightness of British rule over millions of brown (largely voteless) people.

But 1921 was the year of decision for Rhodesia, and the British government was then, as now, under conflicting pressures from other quarters. Egypt had been set ablaze by a nationalist now long forgotten, Zaghlul Pasha, who was the De Valera of his day. His independence campaign was reaching a peak in 1921, just as Churchill had his hands already full with Ireland, Gandhi, and the prospective arrival of Sir Charles Coghlan and his Rhodesian delegation. For Egypt, Churchill's formula was a commission of inquiry, headed by his old friend, Lord Milner. And for Ireland, Churchill was able to call on another recruit from South African days, General Smuts, who had been a gallant and loyal ally in the war just ended. Smuts it was who drafted the 1921 Belfast speech, in which King George V appealed 'from a full heart' for reconciliation. And that led to the visit of an Irish delegation, and the talks which lasted in London through the second half of that year. The upshot was peace, with Ireland accepting Dominion status and – a curious condition of the bargain – an oath of loyalty to be taken by every Irish M.P. That was the Churchill touch; the emissary who had conveyed it to De Valera had been Smuts. In that summer of 1921, therefore, when the Rhodesian delegation led by Coghlan arrived at the Colonial Office, Churchill viewed a world in which disloyal men were trying to dismember the Empire, to strip it of territories vital for its security: Ireland (naval bases), Egypt (Suez), and India (manpower). What a relief it must have been to see arriving in Great Smith Street a group of men whose loyalty was undoubted – Sir Charles (who had been knighted for his part in the conferences leading up to South African Union in 1910), and other loyal white Rhodesian settlers, who had sent a corps of volunteers to fight in the South African war, and had provided more than 5,000 volunteers – the greatest *per capita* contribution of any colony – for British forces in the world war just ended. Coghlan himself was being described as an 'Empire statesman' – the same term already applied to Smuts.

Could any British Colonial Secretary in those circumstances have quibbled about native policy, and subjected these loyal Rhodesians to a cross-examination on their intentions? The answer is: other men, perhaps, but not Churchill. His only real concern was to try and persuade the settlers to reconsider the possibility of union with South Africa. For that would bring about the Federal Union of Rhodes's and Milner's dreams. When Coghlan and his colleagues politely refused, and asked for immediate responsible government instead, Churchill bargained for time and persuaded them to put it to a referendum. And early in 1922, before the voting took place, Smuts journeyed up to Salisbury in the role of Churchill's intermediary and put his final proposition before Coghlan: a seat in the South African Cabinet, money for irrigation and railways, and perhaps one day the Union Premiership.

Empire building was Winston Churchill's real interest in the Rhodesian question; 'native policy' was marginal and unimportant. As for the idea that British forces should be stationed on the soil of this most loyal of colonies, it was unthinkable. And so, on this highly emotional basis of kinship and loyalty, Britain's normal instrument of ultimate policy control in every colonial dependency was discarded. The trump card had been thrown away.

Coghlan politely turned down the Smuts–Churchill offer of amalgamation and went on to gain a decisive victory in the (all-white) referendum of 1922, when the settlers showed that they preferred to go it alone. Nearly 9,000 votes were polled for independence (tactfully described as 'responsible government' on Coghlan's posters), and just under 6,000 for joining the South African Union. The referendum also marked the final disillusion of most settlers with the policies of the Chartered Company, which, with the great mining houses and their subsidiaries, the Rhodesian newspapers, had come out in favour of union.

'Rhodesia for the Rhodesians' had been Coghlan's winning campaign slogan. It was significant on two counts. First, it revealed the aggressive self-confidence which characterized the settlers then, as it characterizes them today. Though they were surrounded, in the colony, by a million Africans, outnumbered in the ratio of more than 30:1, they were convinced that they could maintain full administrative and military control. Secondly, Coghlan's slogan demonstrated very clearly the settler blind spot in race relations. 'Rhodesians' meant white Rhodesians; no one doubted that. The Africans just didn't count politically, and no one gave them a moment's thought.

If there was any lesson to be drawn from Churchill's attempt at Empire-building in 1921–3, it was that the most profitable course for any settler government to pursue was the elimination of the Westminster factor. Such, indeed, has been the constant object of white Rhodesian agitation, as it has become, since 1953, the major object of Federal government policy. The link with London is, of course, to be retained, but only as an economic one. Long experience has taught the settlers that any wisp of imperial political control means interference sooner or later in racial policies. The do-gooders at Westminster, particularly those in the Labour and Liberal Parties, are always ready to interfere.

The suspicion is generally reciprocal. The men of Westminster learned long ago that white settler communities overseas tend to cause difficulties under two headings: race relations and foreign policy. Rhodes's northward thrust to extend Cape Colony influence into Zambesia is the classic case, combining both elements. But it is far from being unique. Rhodesians are addicted to saying that they are up against a very special, unprecedented problem which can only be solved by 'the man on the spot'. This is a piece of ingenious (and perhaps unconscious) rationalization. The major military engagements with the Maoris, undertaken by the early New Zealand settlers, were a source of constant friction with Whitehall – and of protest by the same humanitarian societies in Britain which interested themselves in Rhodesia. The settler campaign to wipe out the Stone Age aborigines in Tasmania fell into this same embarrassing category. Successive British governors of Lower and Upper Canada in colonial days found themselves forced to assume a guardian role over the Hurons and other tribes; the Royal Canadian Mounted Police in their red coats were a later extension of this guardianship policy. As for engaging in a little local imperialism, the settlers of New Caledonia (as the Canadian west coast was known in colonial days) lost no time in fitting out with cannon the first steamer to arrive from Greenwich – s.s. *Beaver* – and taking on the Americans. The Battle of Goat Island led to a boundary dispute at the highest level, with London and Washington having to bring in the Kaiser to arbitrate. More Canadian tempers exploded when

London was beaten by Washington on the purchase of Alaska. And easily the coolest display of local imperialism was the Australian takeover in New Guinea. Acting solely on the instructions of the Queensland government, a local magistrate named Chester formally took possession of that half of the island not occupied by the Dutch, one day in 1883. His action was repudiated by a Liberal government at Westminster, but quickly endorsed by Lord Salisbury's Tory administration that followed. Formal annexation by Britain followed physical occupation by Australians, and in 1905 under the Papua Act half of New Guinea became Australian sovereign soil, as it has remained to this day. Lord Rosebery, who got caught on that one, complained of the New Zealanders as well; they were enmeshing him into taking over Samoa against Britain's own real interests, he said.

Farther back, of course, there was the local initiative of the American colonists led by George Washington in what they called 'the opening up of the Ohio Lands'. In fact, this was a straight real estate deal (at the expense of the local Indians) and differed hardly at all from the March of the Pioneers into Zambesia a century later.

It is important to list these parallel examples for two reasons. First, they show that settler behaviour in Central Africa has run to a pattern, even including the northward grab of the two protectorates in 1953 – which may be seen as Southern Rhodesia's Papua or Ohio Lands. Secondly, we must ask if these parallel examples offer any guide to what Westminster policy in Africa should be.

I would submit that one clear lesson emerges – intervene massively, or get out. That was the alternative which Clement Attlee faced over India in 1947; he decided to get out. Massive intervention was tried in Canada after the 1837 rebellion, when British troops went into battle against white settlers. It was the second and last time that Whitehall tried such a policy in North America; but then, it is worth noting, the ratio of settlers to 'natives' was about 25:1 in favour of the settlers, or almost precisely the reverse of the Rhodesia ratio. The white Canadians got Lord Durham and his report; the brown ones got the Queen's protection, which has continued (with a number of practical and tangible benefits) to this day.

To what degree did Westminster try massive intervention in British Central Africa? By supplementary charter Rhodes had been able to extend the Chartered Company's control to Northern Rhodesia before Salisbury and the Tories were pushed out of office in the British election of 1892. Rhodes promptly told the new Chancellor, Sir William Harcourt, that if he and Mr Gladstone would like to turn over Bechuanaland and Uganda to the Company, it would run them so cheaply that the British subsidy for each territory could be cut by fifty per cent. The offer was curtly rejected, and Harcourt noted dryly, in a memo to the new Colonial Secretary, Lord Ripon: 'In dealing with these Cape eels it is necessary to have sand on one's hands.'

Ripon was in for another shock. He, like most M.P.s, had always supposed that the Rudd Concession was one of the key possessions of the Company, for it was on this basis that the Royal Charter had been granted. But correspondence left by the outgoing Tory régime, when examined, showed that a curious transaction had taken place. Rhodes and Rudd had continued to hold the famous concession through a subsidiary of theirs, leasing the rights to the Company for fifty per cent of its profits. Then, the Chartered Company had been made to go through the motions of formally acquiring the Rudd Concession in return for one million £1 shares, whose total market value had by that time passed the £3 million mark on the London Exchange. The capital gain on the transaction had been split by Rhodes, Beit, Gifford, and Cawston, and senior Civil Servants at the Colonial Office submitted that this constituted a case for outright cancellation of the Royal Charter.

Furious, Ripon wrote to Gladstone when all this was discovered in 1893: 'These companies are really speculative, got up mainly for Stock Exchange purposes . . . they are not pleasant instruments of administration.' But the charter was not revoked, for by that time the Matabele War had broken out, and Britain's own prestige was directly involved in seeing that a settlement was achieved. But Loch, at the Cape, shared Ripon's disgust, and added his own suspicion that war had been provoked to boost the British South Africa Company's stock prices by a crushing conquest. His secret dispatch,* written after Jameson had mounted the offensive against Lobengula, urged that the British government take over 'the administration of Mashonaland and Matabeleland' as soon as hostilities ended. And he went on:

> I do not much care for the Company as a political device. I consider it advisable on principle that the executive of a country should not be personally interested in the acquisition of the lands and properties they are called upon to govern.

Rhodes was to succeed in thwarting all rumoured attempts at Westminster intervention. He pursued two courses, in both of which he was followed by later settler politicians when dealing with London. He cabled his powerful friends on the Board in London to exercise their influence. And he stressed, with implicit menaces, his local support.

> I certainly intend to settle the question on South African lines. I had the idea and found the money, and our people have had the courage to fight without help from home. I feel I can reckon on the people of the Cape Colony supporting me in this view.

When Sir Roy Welensky lands at London Airport and talks about 'going the whole hog' – as he did during the final round of bargaining over the Northern Rhodesian constitution in March 1962 – his truculence and bluster, with his influential lobbying in London, are in a long tradition. It pays off – most of the time.

Unfortunately for later British governments, both the Liberals, in 1893, and the Tories, when they returned under Salisbury in 1895, could not bring themselves to discipline Rhodes and the settlers. A lone voice in the wilderness was that of Loch who, before he retired, grimly predicted that Mr Rhodes's next adventure would not be just an expedition against local Africans but actual full-scale war against a foreign power. He was not far wrong; Loch knew that something was being planned against the Transvaal Boers. The Jameson Raid followed soon afterwards.

* Col Off., 18 Oct. 1893, file 459.

The essential timidity of British governments, especially Tory ones, when dealing with the white settlers of southern Africa, has become a factor that the settler politicians can count on in their clashes with Westminster. After all of Rhodes's ambitions had been fulfilled in Rhodesia, the Tory Chancellor, Sir Michael Hicks Beach, wrote in a memorandum to Chamberlain at the Colonial Office:

> We can never govern from Downing Street any part of South Africa in which the whites are strong enough to defend themselves against the natives.

Chamberlain, in reply, agreed with Hicks Beach on the need to keep the goodwill of the settlers, since the naval base at the Cape 'forms the cornerstone of the whole British colonial system'.

Rhodesia was just a pawn in this Imperial chess game, with India the vital piece to be held at all costs. But in 1947 India was lost, and in 1961 Harold Macmillan fought a losing battle to keep South Africa in the Commonwealth. It was for this that British native policy had been perverted, and (in 1923) eliminated in Southern Rhodesia, creating an endemic condition of white supremacist thinking among Rhodesian settlers. Here, indeed, was a prime example of the law of ends and means.

The Westminster factor or, as Sir Roy has sometimes expressed it, 'the unwarranted interference of Whitehall', remained a constant thorn in settler flesh. After the Raid, when Milner had installed H.M. Resident Commissioner in Salisbury to keep watch over 'native policy' and other matters of Imperial concern, there came the inevitable clash. The settlers wanted African labour provided where and when it suited them best; in the absence of the normal Colonial Office administration, it was the settlers who made the laws and settler Civil Servants who implemented them. In April 1900 the British Commissioner sent to Milner at the Cape a report typical of that era:

> Neither the Matabele nor the other Rhodesian tribes take kindly to labour in the mines. The Native Commissioners induce the Natives to work and afterwards collect taxes from wages unwillingly earned.

There is undoubtedly discontent among the natives, due primarily to the constant pressure.

And there is a revelation of settler thinking in the petition of the Salisbury Chamber of Mines in 1903, asking the settler legislature to double the African Hut Tax to £2 (which would have taken two months to earn):

Owing to the necessity of a large mounted police force in the country for the protection of the whites from a recurrence of the '96 rebellion, the natives [should] be directly taxed for the maintenance of this force.

Westminster intervened some months later at the climax of the settler campaign and vetoed any increase in the Hut Tax. The decision was transmitted by the Colonial Secretary himself.

It takes little imagination to see that the urge for self-government began to take on the aspect of a settler crusade. Coghlan, who had emerged as the settler leader in the legislature, had formulated his slogans of 'Responsible Government Now' and 'Rhodesia for the Rhodesians', even before the First World War. In 1912 he pushed through a legislature which now had a settler majority, the policy of a home-based Civil Service. Rhodesians had to have first preference, he declared. As for Englishmen, 'the gentlemen in the universities have the whole Empire at their disposal'.

From there, with the interval of the war years, it was but a short leap to the 1921 deal with Churchill. The storm signals had not, of course, gone unnoticed by the Africans, who had learned to turn to various agencies in Britain, especially the missionary societies, to lobby for them at Westminster. The first African students, with missionary help, began looking towards England as the place to gird themselves, educationally as well as politically, for battles ahead. The settlers were appalled that any black Rhodesians should attempt to bring the Westminster factor into play, and the Committee on Native Affairs, set up at Coghlan's initiative, had this to say about the dangers of letting Africans go for higher education anywhere except South Africa:

When he returns he is filled with a spirit of unrest and dissatisfaction with his surroundings, and is imbued with ideas which, if communicated to the people among whom he settles, may become a source of danger to their peace and quiet.

It was far wiser to see that any young African went for his education to the Union, where natives were taught to know their place.

Matabele Thompson, the old hunter who had trekked north years before to the court of Lobengula, recalls how around this time he encountered one of the senior chiefs he had known in the days before settler rule. Their last meeting had taken place in the Royal Kraal; this one was at a drab railway station, and the chief was now a ragged old scarecrow without position or power.

'O Tomoson, O Tomoson,' he said, 'how have you treated us after all your promises which we believed.' Thompson records this in his autobiography, and adds: 'I had no answer.'

There is an ironic twist to the story of the successful settler campaign that led to the setting up of Federation in 1953. Essentially this was a device to create a buffer zone, to insulate the whites against the African nationalism which – one day in the future – might sweep southward to the Rhodesias. But the practical effect was to hasten the very process which the settlers so dreaded. Instead of the infection's being brought south by 'foreign natives' at some far future date, the epidemic broke out on home ground, as a direct result of the imposition of white supremacist policies. In the south the Africans had developed a sort of sullen submission to settler rule, but once they saw the alarmed and hostile reaction of their comrades in the two northern territories, they were seized by the same frenzy too.

Margery Perham, the Oxford historian, has written of the slow discovery made by the peoples of Africa in the 1920s and 1930s that, by virtue of their dark skins, 'they could never escape from the livery of scorn'. But only in one or two of the largest African cities, at least until just before the war, 'did the scanty vanguard of the young politically-minded define their discontents'. In this inter-war period, the racial outlook of the dominant Europeans shaped the structure of government, as she points out:

The European rulers of Africa believed that Africans were not only almost immeasurably inferior to themseves in development, but were inherently, permanently inferior as a race. Here lay the fundamental, damaging mistake. Science and experience, certainly my own personal experience of African pupils and friends, have taught most of us to abandon this view. We suspect it was cherished by our predecessors largely because it seemed to justify the subjection, the indefinite subjection, of Africans.

The Westminster factor, as it operated in Rhodesia after the surrender of power to the settlers in 1923, took the form of intrusions by the Colonial Secretary aimed at persuading the settlers to take a liberal view more in harmony with the concept of trusteeship. The first move came almost immediately after Churchill's departure from office. The Colonial Secretary, the Duke of Devonshire, was a Tory of the guardianship (Livingstone) school rather than the nakedly Imperialist Churchill one. And most significantly he promulgated a 'doctrine of paramountcy', designed to act as a brake on white settler aspirations throughout British Africa. It has become famous as the 'Devonshire Declaration', and says in part:

His Majesty's Government think it necessary definitely to record their considered opinion that the interests of the African natives must be paramount; and if and when those interests and the interests of the immigrant races should conflict, the former should prevail. ... His Majesty's Government regard themselves as exercising a trust on behalf of the African population, and they are unable to delegate or share this trust.

The Duke was too well-bred to comment on Churchill's hasty 'delegation of trust' in Rhodesia, but he must have hoped that he was locking the barn door in time. On paper, at least, there remained a safeguard. Any Southern Rhodesian legislation (passed by the colony's all-white parliament) which endangered the status or rights of Africans, had to be submitted to London for 'His Majesty's pleasure'. In practical terms this meant that the British Cabinet of the day did the vetting and took the decision, while M.P.s had the right of question and comment. With the wisdom of hindsight, we may feel that something less loose, more the preserve of the judiciary than the executive, would have served the Africans far better. For in the thirty-nine years during which this safeguard was supposed to operate, British Cabinets did not once, in fact, intervene. A legal safeguard, as provided by a Canadian or American type Bill of Rights, on the other hand, would have enabled the Africans themselves to take steps for their own protection. This is a case where British insularity, the compulsive urge to pragmatism, and the pride in lack of a written constitution has worked to the dire disadvantage of black people living in a very different sort of society overseas.

L. S. Amery, another Tory Colonial Secretary in the Imperialist tradition, was the one who established the unfortunate precedent of non-interference in Southern Rhodesian affairs. In 1926–7, two Acts passed by the Southern Rhodesian Assembly were remitted to London for examination and approval before the royal assent could be granted. The Native Juveniles Employment Act and the Native Affairs Act have since proved cruel and discriminatory in practice; the Monckton Commission singled out the latter especially for urgent revision. They were, like so many Southern Rhodesian statutes, modelled closely on prevailing South African law. And in the House of Commons they attracted sharp criticism, especially from the opposition Labour benches. Was it this that provoked Amery perversely to defend them ? The two Acts were approved, and by the end of Amery's five-year term in office, the precedent had been firmly laid down that Westminster did not interfere in Southern Rhodesian affairs, even when 'African interests' were involved.

The erratic nature of the Westminster factor – for that is how it has always appeared to the settlers – was shown by the next abrupt swing of the pendulum. Amery had not been content just to nod approval of settler antics, for in his White Paper of 1927 he had gone as far as he could – short of directly affronting his Tory predecessor – to repudiate the Devonshire Declaration. Now a distinguished Labour humanitarian took office as Colonial Secretary – Lord Passfield. In his 1930 Memorandum on Native Policy, he decisively reversed the Amery white paper and reaffirmed the African paramountcy doctrine of the Devonshire Declaration. And, as a practical man, he did not leave it at that. He directed the Governor of Northern Rhodesia to take 'immediate steps to ensure conformity': equal opportunity for Africans to take up Crown land, an end to the coercion of labour by head tax devices, and a shift in Northern Rhodesian budgetary policy to make African development the 'first charge' on public funds.

Lord Passfield's dispatch fell like a bomb among the Northern Rhodesian settlers, and was taken by white Rhodesians south of the Zambesi as terrible warning of the interference that could be expected from any Labour government at Westminster. And the immediate result, on both sides of the border, was to trigger off the demands for 'amalgamation' that led to Federation in 1953.

Sir Leopold Moore, whose dinosaur views I have referred to earlier, now led the settler M.P.s in the drafting of an angry memorandum of protest:

The natural trustees of barbarous and less developed races are their more civilized neighbours. The assumption of trusteeship by the Imperial Government is uncalled for and inadvisable. . . . Interference, directed by uniformed or misinformed authorities, resident many thousands of miles away . . . can lead only to resentment and antagonism. . . . Faced with the declared determination of the Imperial Government to prefer the interests of alien and barbarous races to those of their own, they may seek and find sympathy and aid (interested though it may be) from neighbouring colonies enjoying freer institutions.

This last was a clear reference to Southern Rhodesia, and when Lord Passfield turned down their demand for an immediate round-table conference, the settlers proceeded to carry out their threat. The first emissaries visited Salisbury soon afterwards, to sound out the possibility of making common cause against interference from Westminster. They hoped by amalgamation to slip safely behind the barricade which the Southern Rhodesian settlers had successfully erected: their own legislature, with no 'outside' influences such as the British Governor or senior Colonial Office officials who still held the majority in the north.

For the southern settlers, the idea of union with the north had begun to have attractions as well.

Rhodes had laid the original plan, and Dr Jameson in his capacity as President of the Company had travelled from Cape Town in 1913 and again in 1915 to push hard for 'amalgamation'. He had introduced the word into Rhodesia's political vocabulary, and his aim had been to implement Rhodes's imperial vision and reduce the Company's operating costs at the same time by a joint operation north and south of the Zambesi. But by then the settlers had launched their litigation in London and were well on their way to ridding themselves of Company rule. In any case, there had been little inducement to take over 'a desert of anthills and scrubland, and a million black problems', as one of the settlers had tactfully put it.

But the big copper finds of the 1920s had changed all that. It was becoming clear that Northern Rhodesia contained one of the largest copper deposits in the world, and men were trekking north to share in the sudden economic promise. One of these (in 1924) had been a young drygoods salesman and amateur boxer, Roy Welensky, who had started on the footplate as an apprentice fireman at the big railway headquarters near the Broken Hill mine. By the time that the Passfield affair blew up, he was already a leading figure in the trade-union movement, and he must have followed the controversy closely. For when he entered the legislature he made a point of reviving the issue of African paramountcy and pursuing it until the matter was resolved on terms acceptable to himself and his supporters in the European Railwaymen's Union.

In the south, the recurrent crises over the need to submit Southern Rhodesian legislation to the British parliament for approval acted as a prod to settler action. Amalgamation, or, as it later came to be described, Federation, seemed to promise a possible escape from the constant threat of intervention. True, no British Cabinet had ever asserted its right of veto, but the right itself was seen as a humiliation by the settlers. The Westminster encounters continued. The 1936 Native Registrations Act set up a comprehensive pass-law system – modelled closely on South African legislation as Lord Hailey somewhat anxiously pointed out. But the Tory Cabinet gave its approval; though this law, too, would be singled out more than twenty years later by the Monckton Commissioners as a major cause of failure in race relations. African chickens may not always be recognized for what they are from the Cabinet Room in Downing Street, but they still come home to roost.

In 1947, there was an uproar at Westminster over another Huggins initiative – this time, again copying South African practice, to remove the Africans from the common voters' roll. Two Labour M.P.s challenged their own government in a motion calling upon the Attlee Cabinet to implement the long-dormant British right of veto. *The Economist* swung its support behind the move: 'Cannot Southern Rhodesians learn from the deteriorating race relations in the Union ? To limit the franchise would solve nothing.' This was as near defeat as the settlers ever faced. Huggins withdrew his proposal, and decided to suspend action until a more propitious occasion.

Westminster, however, was not always as quick as its opponents in Salisbury. The Subversive Activities Act of 1950, modelled closely on the Riotous Assemblies Act of South Africa, was the evil precursor of all those Draconian laws which have since savaged the Southern Rhodesian statute book. It empowered the Minister of Justice to control the movements of individuals 'spreading subversive propaganda or promoting feelings of hostility', and even some white trade unionists grew alarmed. But the Prime Minister emphasized its colour basis, and, sure enough, it was only implemented against African politicians. Benjamin Burombo and his African Voice Association were its first victims. Joshua Nkomo and George Nyandoro, looking on, were jolted into active politics.

The rough passage that such items of settler legislation experienced at Westminster – even though the British Cabinets always acquiesced in the end – served each time to intensify settler demands for some new formula that would permanently exclude the possibility of Westminster intervention. Irritatingly, too, in Northern and Southern Rhodesia alike, there were signs that the Africans were awakening from their long political sleep.

In the north the first African strike occurred – the first real demonstration of African resistance since the arrival of the white man – in belated response to the Churchill surrender of power in the south twelve years before. The Africans of Northern Rhodesia had lost their trust in Colonial guardianship, particularly when – under settler pressure – a new governor, Sir Hubert Young, began openly to retreat from the Passfield Memorandum. He 'reinterpreted' the declaration to make it cut both ways; white interests, he maintained, would therefore never be subordinated to native ones. A few months later, in May 1935, African fears erupted in strike action. The tribesmen swarming to the newly opened mines had been complaining of their inferior amenities, the ubiquitous colour-bar, and, especially, of the lack of schools for their children (4,000 of them on the Copperbelt had no school to attend, according to the government's own survey). The strike broke out suddenly when the African mine workers learned that a revision of the poll tax had been decided, mistakenly assuming that even harsher rates would be announced. (In fact, a graduated scale was to replace flat rate.) Since it was already taking them two to three months each year to save enough money for the tax, the Africans decided that the dreaded era of white paramountcy must have arrived. The governor called out reserve (white) police, and then troops. In the shooting that followed six Africans died. It was the first blood spilt in a racial clash in the north.

This crisis in turn shattered any illusion the Europeans of the Copperbelt might have possessed that they still had decades in which to resolve the 'native problem'. The immediate result was urgent consultation between them and the settler government in Salisbury, leading up to the first Victoria Falls conference in 1936. This was an all-white affair, even including the delegation from Nyasaland where the settlers were outnumbered by more than 300:1, but no public surprise was voiced at that. There was only one jarring note in an otherwise successful conference; Huggins's right-wing critics in the Southern Rhodesian Assembly protested that the racial barriers had not been clearly enough marked in the north under Colonial Office rule. They would only agree to amalgamation if the resulting government were assured of a free hand on 'native policy'. The conference agreed, but the British government found the demand unacceptable.

Britain did, however, agree to a Commission of Inquiry, which visited Central Africa in 1938. The Bledisloe Report (1939) was indecisive, but it satisfied Huggins by recognizing some kind of political association as an objective. It considered the three territories fundamentally similar in administration, economic needs, and other essentials, and held that 'identity of interests would lead them sooner or later to political unity'. Almost in passing, it noted that Southern Rhodesia's race policies were 'in some respects restrictive' and that Africans in the two northern territories seemed tenaciously attached to their protectorate status under the Crown. Fundamentally, however, the report was a settler triumph. The federal campaign had won formal recognition.

The war intervened, but, as soon as it was over, one recommendation in the Bledisloe Report was implemented — the establishment of a Central African Council for joint economic and social cooperation. It began work in 1945, and not only took over the coordination of many existing links in farming, public health, currency control, and secondary education, but swiftly expanded into finance, air services, and cooperatives as well. Indeed, the Council seemed rather too successful, since it knocked the bottom out of the settler argument that amalgamation was vital in order to obtain economic benefits. A few more years of the C.A.C., and it would have been impossible to campaign for Federation without disclosing to Westminster that the real settler motive was political control.

Meanwhile, nascent African nationalism was making speed imperative. During the war years some 14,000 Nyasa men, including many of the best educated, had served abroad with the British forces. (Southern Rhodesia had been careful to draw on the services of no more than 1,505 Africans – most of whom were not involved in the use of firearms.) The Nyasas had come home with new ideas of African progress, and the territory now had a thriving African National Congress movement. Some of the 18,000 Nyasas working in Northern Rhodesia had founded A.N.C. branches there, and from these had sprung a vigorous local Congress movement. Its first leader was Godwin Lewanika, a Barotse aristocrat, who was later to tumble from office and find sanctuary in Sir Roy's U.F.P. The new team that took command consisted of Harry Nkumbula and Kenneth Kaunda; partners then, rivals later, and partners again in the 1963 coalition.

Also during the war years had come another fierce African strike on the Copperbelt; in the riot that followed, seventeen Africans had died and sixty-five had been wounded, from bullets fired by white police and white army officers. In both northern territories the governors had been compelled to recognize the upsurge of African nationalism; in 1948 the first two African members (nominated by the governor) took their seats in the Northern Rhodesian legislature, and in the following year two Africans entered the legislature in Nyasaland.

Mr Welensky, as he then was, had won his seat in the Northern Rhodesian legislature on a pledge to fight for amalgamation, and he was now demanding union 'under a constitution similar to that enjoyed by Southern Rhodesia'. This was not racially explicit, but the settlers understood the significance well enough. And so did the Africans. An honest broker appeared on the political scene in the person of Sir Stewart Gore-Brown, an old Harrovian and ex-Guards officer who had hacked himself a vast isolated farming estate out of the bush in Bembaland and built himself a Scots baronial fortress on it for a home. In one of the post-war debates, when Welensky was again submitting a motion for amalgamation, the spry figure of the old colonel rose ramrod straight in the legislature:

I am now convinced that there are two quite different ways of dealing with the African. One consists of treating him well but keeping him a servant. The other ... regarding him as a potential partner. I am convinced the African is right when he opposes amalgamation, because he fears he would be handed over to the first of the two alternatives, what we may call the South African ideology.

That may well have been the first time that Welensky heard the word partnership used politically; at any rate, he was not slow to steal his opponent's slogan and give it his own special interpretation. Meanwhile he was busy with his campaign to extract for Northern Rhodesia a share of the British South Africa Company's lush royalties from mineral rights, royalties which today produce anything from £8 to £10 million a year and are not the product of any special skill or investment. The argument was eventually settled, after deputations to London, when the Chartered Company agreed to pay a twenty per cent tax to the Northern Rhodesian government until the expiry of its rights in 1986. It was during one of these trips that the Labour Colonial Secretary, Mr Creech Jones, remarked that he was hoping to see the first two African members appointed to the Northern Rhodesian legislature. Welensky reported to his fellow M.P.s when he got home – the sentence can be found in the territory's Hansard of 3 December 1946 – 'I expressed the opinion that it was premature to give direct representation to Africans.' That was also the year when the Labour government at Westminster decided to give the Africans of the Copperbelt a helping hand, by arranging with the T.U.C. to send a skilled organizer, W. N. Comrie, into the area. The unions that he founded are flourishing today, but such outside interference earned the unyielding hostility of the territory's white mine workers.

The settler efforts to attain amalgamation were intensified, and on one of his London visits Roy Welensky called on a former Conservative Colonial Secretary, Colonel Oliver Stanley. He received the profitable advice – as he revealed later in his own legislature – to try federation instead of amalgamation as a compromise which might be considered more acceptable by Westminster. Welensky persuaded Huggins, and the two settler leaders launched their new campaign.

The second Victoria Falls Conference opened in February 1949, with Huggins and Welensky as the two key figures. No Africans were invited, but Sir Stewart Gore-Brown who had an automatic right of attendance as an M.P., offered to appoint himself their watchdog instead. The opening words of Huggins's keynote address were notable: 'For some time to come, Africans must be ruled by a benevolent aristocracy.' African fears and antagonism grew throughout the northern territories as the conference pursued its insidious course in secret session. When it was over, the chairman spoke mysteriously in metaphor. The delegates had not only laid the foundations for the Federation, he said, but built the house itself. 'All that remains is to move in the furniture and the fittings.'

The Africans were by now thoroughly alarmed, for the settlers had begun to make preparations for a full-scale assault on Westminster. And at the same time they had managed to score a diplomatic triumph by getting the British government to concur in the final, definitive denial of the Devonshire Declaration.

Bourbons forget nothing, and this doctrine of African paramountcy still rankled in settler memories. Welensky had singled it out as his target long before getting into the legislature. Once he had become an M.P., he set about his bulldog attack with ardour. Having got his teeth into the Chief Secretary's leg – 'to ask whether the British government has modified its views on the paramountcy of African interests' – he kept returning again and again to the subject with questions and formal motions. When the Labour government's Colonial Secretary, Arthur Creech Jones, announced that he would be visiting the Rhodesias in 1949, the Northern Rhodesian officials with profound relief prepared to hand the paramountcy problem over to him.

Mr Welensky had been proving impossible to placate. The announcement in 1948 that one ministerial seat would be granted to a settler M.P. had failed to stop his truculent attacks. He demanded a larger role in policy-making, and threatened to cross the floor and go into full-scale opposition, with the other settler representatives, if he was denied. In defiance of all protocol he even announced his intention to table a motion on finance, declaring, 'If that permission is refused, there will be trouble in this country.'

His strategy succeeded. Within weeks Welensky and his colleagues had been granted not one ministerial seat, but four.

Creech Jones arrived for his tour, and was forced by events to give his blessing to the change. (The British government had a straight choice: to approve, or else fly in extra British troops. And this was the period of both the Berlin Airlift and the outbreak of the Korean War.) Westminster had surrendered to the settlers once again.

But Creech Jones made a point of seeking out African organizations in the Rhodesias – some dozen all told – and listening to their grievances. And before catching the plane home, he told a Press conference that in terms of the Devonshire and Passfield Declarations, the British government had an obligation to the Africans. 'Permanent white settlement in Northern Rhodesia,' he was reported as saying, 'needs to be controlled.'

Settler reaction was strong and immediate. The *Bulawayo Chronicle* proclaimed the need to 'look further south . . . for support in a battle of survival'. And Welensky exploded into the first of the 'Boston tea-party' threats that he has been making for a dozen years since:

The Colonial Secretary's statement is completely unacceptable. If the British government wants to implement it, they will have to bring their troops to this country to carry it out. The European community will not under any circumstances recognize the paramountcy of African interests. I shall not hesitate to appeal to the people of South Africa for support in counter-action. I shall also contact the elected members of Kenya to make sure we take concerted action.

These words have to be read and reread, if one is to savour the true, pungent fanaticism of the white Rhodesian politician. I have considered typing them out on a little card, to have ready in my pocket when some Tory M.P. of the 'Rhodesia Lobby' corners me at Westminster and hectors me for suggesting that Sir Roy Welensky is committed to a policy of permanent white supremacy.

And how incredible it is that, five years after Welensky spoke those words, a Tory M.P., Julian Amery, (the son of L. S.) should solemnly have rebutted Labour critics during the debate on the Federation Bill by saying: 'We on this side of the House, and the honourable members opposite, have put our trust in Sir Godfrey Huggins and Sir Roy Welensky.'

It may be gentlemanly and admirable to do so, but it is certainly not realistic. President Eisenhower did not put his trust in his fellow white man at Little Rock, Governor Faubus; nor did President Kennedy express faith in the kindly intentions of Governor Barnett at Oxford, Mississippi. The Americans have experienced the cruel consequences of a rabid white supremacy; furthermore, they have a good Intelligence service. I doubt if, when Julian Amery delivered his naïve reproof, he had ever read those words of Welensky's. The remoteness of Rhodesia is the finest political smokescreen that the settler politicians can have. It means that they can say one thing on one side of it, and another, quite different, in London.

In the struggle over paramountcy, peace was dictated on Welensky's terms – and in such a way that a devastating slap in the face was delivered to the African people. Their main source of news, the *African Weekly* in Lusaka, appeared with the statement that Creech Jones had, during his visit, reaffirmed the principle of African paramountcy. At the next opportunity Welensky raised the issue in the legislature, and it was clear that he was bristling for a fight.

The Chief Secretary read from some notes. He stated that the African newspaper had made a mistake. 'Previously', he declared, there had been a theory of paramountcy about what would happen if interests conflicted. But that was now regarded as 'a purely hypothetical situation', and 'no longer had any force at all'.

This might have satisfied lesser men, but not Welensky. He bounded up with his supplementary question:

Could I ask if my Hon. Friend would state categorically in simple language that paramountcy is dead, and that the policy followed in this country is a policy of partnership . . . in the interests of all its peoples ?

By inference, his question provides a most valuable clue to the meaning that the settlers attached to the doctrine of partnership. The official reply sealed the matter:

If by paramountcy the Hon. Member means a policy of subordinating the interests of one section of the community to those of the other, then I can say that paramountcy is dead.

The wretched white miners of the Copperbelt could breathe easily again. Scraping by on £1,500 a year, they now had the assurance that they would no longer be subordinated to the ruthless, powerful men of the African unions, who earned £80 a year (and possessed no vote).

For the bewildered readers of the *African Weekly*, there was – under the British colonial system – no judicial channel of redress. American Negroes can, and do, file an action under the Bill of Rights, which is entrenched as an amendment to the American Constitution. In Lusaka, on the day of Welensky's great victory, the Africans had no such recourse.

The settlers were now confident that they held the initiative and that the time had come to push Federation through Westminster. One of Sir Roy's present colleagues in the U.F.P. was then, like himself, an M.P. in the Northern Rhodesian legislature. Mr van Eeden did not disguise the object of the campaign:

The main reason we need a Federal State in Central Africa is because this will enable us to loosen the grip of the Colonial Office on the territory.

Huggins, as we have seen, had been equally candid when speaking to the white voters in Southern Rhodesia. In one of his outbursts, he declared:

I gather the United Kingdom government would require representation of Africans by Africans from the start. I am quite sure the time has not arrived for that; there are not yet enough civilized natives to justify one constituency.

He added that African Federal M.P.s would be 'a farce', and that democracy in Rhodesia did not include 'mob law'. In London such remarks were not reported.

Still – despite the enchantment lent by distance – things were not going all that well there for the settlers. Creech Jones had made a close study of colonial affairs; his whole parliamentary career had been in effect a preparation for resolving Britain's problems in Africa. He resolved not to be pushed.

Around him, among his officials, there were a good many who were already convinced of the virtues of Federation. They based their case on economic grounds, on the need for 'larger units' in a Great Power world. They pointed out that Nyasaland was chronically dependent on Colonial Office grants for all its capital development, and frequently for balancing current budget as well. French policy in Africa at that time favoured large units; a dozen little states had been grouped into the administrative blocks of French West and French Equatorial Africa, with one regional capital and governor-general in each. It would not do for British Africa to be Balkanized, to stagnate economically, and find itself unable to compete.

But Creech Jones knew that these arguments neglected the views of the Africans themselves. To this objection, officials like Gilbert Rennie and G. H. Baxter had a ready answer: the Africans had no grasp of economics and no concept of continental problems. If Federation were established, the resultant prosperity would soon enough preach its own moral.

While Creech Jones paused to consider, the settlers marshalled their forces. Welensky asked and got from the Northern Rhodesian governor the 'loan' of two key Ministers, the Financial Secretary and the Attorney-General, to travel with him to Salisbury for the meetings of the new joint committee that he and Huggins had established. For in Africa as well as in London, there was solid support among Civil Servants for the Federal plan. In retrospect one reason seems obvious enough: the new Federal service would have to be staffed, and those Civil Servants already in the territories would move to bigger jobs. Besides, many of them had been infected with settler views, and the economic argument was persuasive too.

Commander Thomas Fox-Pitt, a Provincial Commissioner in Northern Rhodesia who happened to reach his retirement at that time (1951), later told a conference in Oxford about the change in Civil Servant attitudes:

The honest wish to do the best by the Africans changed to a willingness to give up the struggle and let the settlers have their way for better or worse. I don't believe the change came suddenly; it grew from a relaxation of effort to a final surrender over a few years. . . . The Civil Servants began to accept [settler] disparagement of things African. They travelled less in the African way and more by motor-car. They saw less of the Africans in the setting where they were superb, as watermen and hunters; more of them as misfits in urban and industrial life.

In the Northern Rhodesian legislature, Sir Roy Welensky was shrewd enough to conjure up a bogey – the new Nationalist government of Dr Malan and his racial dogmatists who had swept to power in 1948 on the new (to Britain) slogan of apartheid. In a future war, said Welensky with one eye on London, South Africa might be a republic outside the Commonwealth, pursuing a neutralist policy. Britain might be glad of the chance to establish bases in a friendly Federation. And he introduced a motion requesting the British government to act by calling a formal constitutional conference.

In the greatest alarm the Africans turned to Sir Stewart Gore-Brown and the other settler M.P. representing African interests. The two announced that, with the two African M.P.s, they would oppose the motion. Sir Stewart declared:

We feel that in view of the universal African opposition to Federation, we cannot honestly say the time is opportune for Britain to take the lead in creating a Federal State.

The ten white settler M.P.s voted solidly together, while – to the dismay of Africans – the Colonial Office M.P.s abstained.

When London still failed to move, Huggins took a turn at exerting pressure. In January 1950 he announced that Southern Rhodesia would formally withdraw from the Central African Council at the end of the year. He also had it informally conveyed to the British government that, if there were no action on the Federal issue, Southern Rhodesia would have to open negotiations with South Africa. (This was confirmed by Creech Jones in a pamphlet written after Labour fell from power.) Officials in London took the threat at its face value.

Fate now took a hand, for, in the British general election of February 1950, Arthur Creech Jones lost his parliamentary seat. Mr Attlee, back with a perilously small majority, had a limited number of senior colleagues from whom to choose his new Colonial Secretary. James Griffiths, the veteran Socialist who now took the post in the 'lame duck' administration of 1950–1, was a man with little experience of African affairs. He readily agreed to the concerted request of the settlers for a Conference on Closer Association, limited to Civil Servants only, which would explore the possibilities on a 'practical, factual basis'.

It was a brilliant, calculated risk by Huggins and Welensky, and it worked. Both men had been to London to see the new Colonial Secretary, and had turned on their considerable charm. They had felt out the ground. Now they were sure they could win. One stunningly simple factor was in their favour: since only top Civil Servants would be taking part in the conference, all the delegates would be white. And the largest single block, from Southern Rhodesia, would be under Huggins's direct control – personal friends (for Salisbury is a small town) and Federationists to a man.

In the chair was the Assistant Under-Secretary for Commonwealth Relations, the late G. H. Baxter, who had resolved to use his key-role in the furtherance of Federation. Several years later he reminisced to a B.B.C. interviewer: 'It suddenly came to me, almost with the force of a conversion, that this change had to be brought about.'

There were no outsiders, no newspaper correspondents at the conference to ask awkward questions, and, of course, there were no Africans. The result was, frequently, a grotesque twisting of the truth; for there was no check on the 'data' which the Southern Rhodesian delegates – supremacists all – might choose to submit. The conference documents, published later, contain some statements of lurid fantasy, or naked political fraud.

One of these (H.M.S.O. 8233) stated that under the Southern Rhodesian system of Land Apportionment, there were 'special European and Native areas'. But *it did not mention the ratio* (which was then 15:1 in favour of the settlers). The same document declared that 'Europeans and Africans share a common roll', but again *did not mention the ratio* (ninety-eight per cent white, thanks to the income hurdle). In one of the working documents (H.M.S.O. 8334), it was flatly stated that the Southern Rhodesian government was based on 'universal adult suffrage'.

These were not impartial White Papers, but propaganda pamphlets, intended to make Federation palatable to those who had the power of final decision – 634 M.P.s on the other side of Parliament Square. They glossed over the fact that Southern Rhodesia did not permit the registration of African trade unions, that there was then an all-white Civil Service in the colony, and that Southern Rhodesia did not intend to permit African participation in municipal government – issues on which the practice in the two Northern Protectorates was precisely the reverse. Document No. 8233 suavely noted that some differences existed in political development, land, employment, and trade unions. But these were swept aside in the enthusiastic summing-up:

The most striking conclusion which we draw is the degree of similarity between the policy and practice of the three governments rather than the degree of difference. The ultimate objective of all three is broadly the same: namely, the economic, social and political advancement of the Africans in partnership with the Europeans.

The conference of officials then proceeded to recommend a detailed Federal scheme; and one may be sure that the firm hand of Huggins busied itself behind the submissions of the eight-man Southern Rhodesian team. Finally, the South African bogey was produced – though most Southern Rhodesian laws on African administration had been modelled on South African ones, even to identical turns of phrase – to scare British M.P.s into accepting Federation as a bulwark against apartheid.

A curious argument was put forward by the officials, based on hopes and hypotheses, but not on observable examples of settler behaviour in the past. It was seriously suggested that the act of Federation would, by some unspecified chemistry, reverse the political outlook of the Southern Rhodesian settlers. They would abandon their own local apartheid, and any lingering thoughts of links with South Africa, in favour of a new policy of African advance and ultimate majority political control of the whole Federation. But surely this had never been the view of the Southern Rhodesian settlers? Federation was a device to preserve their privileges, not surrender them.

How did Huggins and Welensky get away with it? To that one must reply that the Westminster of 1951 saw African affairs very differently from the way it sees them today. There had not been much trouble in Africa; the headlines were concerned with India, Berlin, Korea, Europe, and Asia. Everyone connected with the African colonies felt that there was still lots of time to play with; it would be decades before the final decisions would need to be made. I can remember myself how, as late as the summer of 1958, the name of Dr Hastings Banda meant nothing to any British newspaper reader, or to many correspondents. His farewell Press conference, when he was leaving London for home (and the five-month crisis that would culminate in the State of Emergency) took place in a shabby room in a side-street below Charing Cross Station. It was hot and stuffy, the floor-boards squeaked, and the handful of 'pressmen' present were mostly well-wishers from Fabian and Church groups. The one representative of a national paper present apart from myself was a young man who had never spoken to an African politician before in his life and who belonged to the 'Diary' staff of his newspaper, responsible for a daily column of bright jottings. He called the Nyasa leader 'Dr Hastings' throughout the Press conference, and so the name appeared (as a bright little jotting) the next day. Two years later, the same newspaper was ready and eager to lay out £300 in air fares to send one of its top correspondents to Nyasaland to interview 'Dr Hastings' when he came out of jail.

Perhaps the greatest asset which the settlers possessed at Westminster in 1951 – and which they possess no longer today – was the uncritical trust of most British people in the settler parliaments. The names of Welensky and Huggins were not much known; to talk to, they appeared (and still do) courteous and friendly men. The race-supremacy policies of South Africa were already making headlines, of course; but these were regarded as peculiar products of Afrikanerdom. The 1953 debates on Federation at Westminster were full of confident tributes to the 'men of British stock' who seemed certain to behave decently towards their African partners in the great new experiment of Federation. And not all these tributes came from the Tories, either.

In the draft plan for the Federal Assembly, therefore, there were no rock-ribbed safeguards. The African Affairs Board, originally to be headed by a Cabinet Minister, emerged from the final bargaining a far less significant and much weaker creation. And – incredible as it may seem to us now – there were no detailed franchise provisions. Nor was any machinery provided for the gradual extension of African participation in government. All was left to the wisdom of the first Federal Assembly, though it was known even then that at least seventy-five per cent of its M.P.s would be white men. Britain trusted her white settlers in those days.

Did anyone at Westminster worry about the franchise in those critical months of debate? Since Britain burnt her fingers in Central Africa, she has grown more cautious. At later conferences on Kenya, Uganda, and half a dozen other territories, with Colonial Secretaries like Lennox-Boyd, Macleod, and Maudling in the chair, it has become standard practice to set up a sub-committee on the first day to deal with franchise, a bill of rights, and other safeguards. After much wrangling, the final formula is settled in the most precise legal terms before the delegates leave for home.

The revelation of the African's political inferiority in Central Africa came in 1953, when the 'electors of Southern Rhodesia' went to cast their votes on Federation. There were 45,975 white voters and 380 Africans. (The balloting went 2 to 1 in favour of the Huggins–Welensky plan.) In Northern Rhodesia the imbalance was even greater. On the day Federation began, the voters' roll there consisted of 15,505 names. Of these, *eleven* were Africans.

In two debates before Federation, when the question of the franchise was raised, Tory Ministers reassured the House that justice would be seen to be done. John Foster, Q.C. and Cuthbert

Alport (now Lord Alport, the High Commissioner in Salisbury) said that a common roll 'based on fair qualifications' would be introduced. If it proved, in fact, to exclude most Africans, then that would be an issue for intervention by the African Affairs Board, they said. It was taken by the House as a pledge.

But in fact Huggins triumphantly declared after the conference of officials that 'once the Imperial government have granted this constitution, they have lost all control – don't forget that'. He was compelled to be a shade indiscreet; his object, after all, was to sell the new plan to the Southern Rhodesian voter. But his indiscretions were noted by Africans, and signs of opposition began to manifest themselves. In the north, the Northern Rhodesia Congress changed its name (in that same month, July 1951) to the African National Congress. In London, Creech Jones – no longer an M.P. – counselled his friend Jim Griffiths to let the Africans have a good look at the draft constitution, and ensure that Africans took part in the next conference, wherever it took place.

The new Labour Colonial Secretary decided to tour the three territories in August and September, in company with his colleague Patrick Gordon Walker, the Commonwealth Relations Secretary. The tour ended in yet another conference – the third and last – at Victoria Falls. The governors of Northern Rhodesia and Nyasaland had brought with them this time not only the white settler M.P.s but strong delegations from the African advisory councils in their territories. This was the one eventuality that Huggins had sought to prevent; indeed, he has since said that he tried to get the conference postponed in the hope that the Labour government would soon be swept from office. His worst fears were realized. The Africans made all the running, with their specific objections to discriminatory features in the draft plan, and the conference never got to that part of the agenda where the settler delegation from Southern Rhodesia had planned to request further watering-down of African safeguards. The African representatives demanded a precise definition of partnership (the Tories came to power a month later, and the definition was never made) and insisted on written undertakings by Britain that the special Protectorate status of the Africans would never be withdrawn unless a majority of the inhabitants (not voters) so desired. This pledge at least finally appeared in the famous Preamble to the 1953 Constitution.

By its third day, the conference had not only reached deadlock, but admitted it in the final communiqué. Huggins then blandly suggested that the Africans from the two protectorates should withdraw – his own Southern Rhodesian delegation was, naturally, all-white – so that there might be straight bargaining between the elected M.P.s from the two Rhodesias. Gordon Walker promptly described this as an ultimatum, and rejected it outright.

Attlee had named an October election date while the Victoria Falls conference was still in session. Churchill swept back into power and promptly named as Colonial Secretary a man whom he had originally induced to enter politics, Oliver Lyttleton. An Establishment figure *par excellence* – he is now Lord Chandos – he 'knew everyone' and was himself the son of a former Tory Colonial Secretary. Within a month of taking office he announced that the British government was convinced of the 'urgent need for Federation' and would reassemble the adjourned Victoria Falls conference in London in July. Soon afterwards Huggins visited him at the Colonial Office, and it was officially announced that the conference date had been advanced to April. Clearly, the settler tactics were to head off further African obstructionism by rushing Federation through Westminster. Meanwhile Lyttleton announced abandonment of the Labour policy of 'Federation only by consent'. If the Africans could not see the benefits of Federation, they would get them anyhow.

Churchill had not become the Queen's First Minister to preside over any further dissolution of her Empire; he gave Lyttleton the green light to hustle through whatever scheme he liked for setting up a new Dominion in Central Africa. He also gave him as running mate, and co-chairman of the April conference, another man with 'Empire' views on Africa, the redoubtable Lord Salisbury, whom he had put in charge of Commonwealth Relations.

James Griffiths, now in the political wilderness as an Opposition M.P., warned the Tories that the forthcoming conference must not consist of white settlers and officials alone: 'This matter has been bedevilled by conferences of white people, with black people shut outside.'

In fact, the two Northern governors had the greatest difficulty in persuading significant African representatives to come to London. The African leaders seemed to feel that their presence at Victoria Falls was now being used to claim that they had rubber-stamped Federation even before the terms were final. The Northern Rhodesian African National Congress announced plans for a Mass Action Campaign, 'realizing that the Tory government is about to attempt to force through Federation against the unanimous wishes of the African people'. And in London the Rev. Michael Scott assembled a committee and founded the Africa Bureau. Labour and Liberal support was plentiful, and he managed to recruit an outstanding Tory stalwart in Lord Hemingford.

The two Africans from Southern Rhodesia, invited to attend the conference by Huggins and Whitehead, were Joshua Nkomo and Jasper Savanhu. They reacted differently to their experiences. Nkomo went home and stood in the first Federal election against one of Huggins's nominees, Mike Hové, later to be the Federation's first African High Commissioner in Nigeria. He was defeated and plunged into African nationalist politics, a course much less profitable or safe than that followed by Hové. Savanhu tried 'cooperation', accepting a safe seat offered him by Huggins, but broke with Welensky and the U.F.P. in the August crisis of 1962.

The other five Africans – two Nyasas and three from Northern Rhodesia – came to London in 1952, called on Lyttleton at his own suggestion, and were formally invited to attend the conference. But when they asked to see an agenda, he refused. They had first to agree to attend. All of this fantastic interchange was set out in the letter which these Africans later sent to *The Times* after they had announced their decision to boycott the conference. They declared they had a right to see an agenda in order to

428

consider and offer their submissions and modifications; after all, the settlers had been doing nothing else for two years.

The letter also outlined their fears that Federation would extend Southern Rhodesia's racial policies to the north, and that the real settler objective was to achieve Dominion status 'before the African inhabitants are politically conscious and active'. The five announced that they had no faith in the 'professed safeguards for African interests', and they appealed to British voters 'to protect us from the machinations of the European minority among us and not to be deceived by their plots'.

Above all, they rejected the idea of attending a conference that was to be held behind closed doors. Their hunch was right; in secret session the conference chopped away the main provisions that might have made the African Affairs Board an effective safeguard. It was also agreed that the three 'African' M.P.s from Southern Rhodesia would be elected by the (ninety-eight per cent white) voters, and not nominated by the governor. Various Federal powers were increased. Colin Leys, the Oxford don, wrote subsequently that the whole scheme was 'a bargain made in secret so that the extent of concessions on both sides could be minimized in public'.

The publication of the Draft Scheme set the alarm bells ringing. Press opinion began to swing from approval of Federation in principle (especially on account of its economic benefits) towards a position of suspended judgement until it became clearer how effectively African interests were to be protected. *The Economist* declared that 'the economic case for Federation is not convincing; a transport union, a customs union and some common administrative arrangements would meet the case as well'. The *Manchester Guardian* maintained that while the British government might be retaining the power to preserve existing African rights (though this was by no means certain), it was clearly giving up the power to insist on the gradual increase of those rights. *The Times* agreed, and so did constitutional experts like Professor Vincent Harlow, Sir Keith Hancock, and Miss Margery Perham.

At Westminster, the Labour and Liberal Parties were wholly committed to opposing the Federal scheme as it had now taken shape. Griffiths, as chief spokesman for the Opposition, demanded rejection because the safeguards proposed were ineffective and all African political advance would depend upon whether settler M.P.s felt inclined to grant it.

Protests issued from the London Missionary Society, the Fabian Society, a number of prominent Quakers with knowledge of Africa, and the International Confederation of Free Trade Unions. The Archbishop of Canterbury joined his counterparts in the Church of Scotland and the Free Churches in sounding a warning of the need to try, even at this late hour, for African consent.

A final revision conference was called by Salisbury and Lyttleton for January 1953. Not even the two Southern Rhodesian Africans were willing to attend. It was hardly a good omen for the 'great experiment in multi-racial partnership' that the fifty final delegates should all be white. Nor did it seem right that once again the meetings were to be held in secret. *The Times* criticized this, declaring that the conference ought to be a public attempt to fulfil pledges publicly given. In particular, it expressed suspicion that the safeguard of the African Affairs Board would once again be diminished. Its suspicion proved well-founded. In its final form, the Board was no longer an independent body of six outside critics, but had become a standing committee of six Federal M.P.s. The white settlers had simply to capture enough seats to gain political control of the Board. Welensky achieved this four years after Federation began, and the Board has never been heard of since. It is the watchdog that was quietly killed.

Everything was now set for the big debate on 24 March 1953. Lyttleton was complacently sure that the settlers would never discard their humanity: 'I have faith that the spirit which has animated our race in the past will continue to animate it in the Federation.'

'Everything,' said *The Times*, 'depends on the honest goodwill of the men in Salisbury.'

The Tories ordered a three-line whip and pushed approval for Federation through the House of Commons with a margin of forty-four votes, after some of the most passionate and bitter debating heard there since before the war. We now know that some sixty of the Tories who voted for Federation were men with business interests in Central Africa; presumably they felt that sound economic progress (for the benefit of African and European alike) required solid settler control for a few years more.

Two last desperate efforts were made to stop Federation, both with the help of Rev. Michael Scott and the Africa Bureau. Paramount Chief Mwase of Nyasaland, with the support of 120 fellow chiefs, prepared a Petition to the Queen. Thousands of Nyasas contributed pennies and sixpences to raise the air fares of a small delegation, which duly arrived in London, hopefully requesting an audience at Buckingham Palace. The Tory government advised the Queen not to receive their petition in person, and the visit did not take place. The other attempt came at the U.N., where Scott tried to have Federation discussed in the 4th Committee. It was blocked by the British delegate, Lord Hudson. In Nyasaland, Congress declared a civil disobedience campaign. Before the riots ended, seventy-two people had been injured and eleven killed. All of them were Africans.

2 Contending Pressures

'Will you tell me,' said Alice, 'why you are painting those roses?'
LEWIS CARROLL

Suez has a special place in Tory mythology. Disraeli first, and the great Lord Salisbury after him, contrived to turn it into a kind of Holy Grail for the Party. Possession of it would solve all problems for Britain, slaking Imperial thirsts forever. Yet, each time the chalice was seized and sipped, it proved to contain bitter gall.

Anthony Eden in 1956 was only the last in a long line of Tory romantics who sought the Grail. But his adventures were such as to stir the whole Afro-Asian world. The independent states of Asia and Africa suddenly found a common bond and purpose in resistance to this latter-day Imperial guest, while, within Africa itself, Eden succeeded in unstoppering the great bottle from which the genie of Pan-Africanism had been struggling to escape. And I doubt, *pace* Lord Grey, if we shall see that genie put back again in our time.

In the Federation the effects were immediate and profound. Three years of the crucial experiment in partnership had brought few benefits; indeed, on such fundamental issues as the Federal franchise, constitutional safeguards, and political progress in the constituent territories, the Africans had experienced only severe setbacks. After Suez they saw little reason to place any great hopes in the prospect of beneficent Imperial intervention on their behalf in Central Africa. Suez showed them, to put it crudely, that white people stuck together in a crisis, and would not hesitate to unleash armies and aircraft against non-white people in the interests of their own security or power. Africans today do not habitually go around discussing Suez, any more than Europeans do. But if you talk politics to Africans, many Africans of different callings, you are bound to be struck by the great numbers of politically conscious ones among them who return again and again to the theme.

Suez jolted Egypt into modern Africa. Our maps still show the country as a kind of European appendage, down in the right-hand corner, and a good many Egyptians thought of it in just that way themselves, before 1956. After Suez, however, President Nasser declared:

We cannot under any circumstances remain aloof from the terrible and sanguinary struggle going on in Africa today between five million whites and 200 million Africans. We shall not stand idly by in the belief that it will not concern us.

A cynic might say that Nasser had had his eye on the Pan-African movement for some time, and that Suez merely gave him the chance to grasp at the leadership. If so, this provides a poor comment on sophisticated Western diplomacy.

No correspondent – and no African politician – can visit Cairo today without sensing the atmosphere of dynamic new policy and the energy with which it is being pursued. The affluent West may consider contemporary Egypt unimpressive, but that is not how it looks to Africans. They have observed how, when the Anglo-French pilots were withdrawn, the predicted break-down in canal traffic did not occur. They see today that more ships than ever are being piloted through the canal, and they regard the men who are doing the job not only as Egyptians, but as Africans too. The Aswan Dam project has had the same sort of effect: Africans can 'do it themselves', and the element of Soviet aid makes little difference to the general impression.

An embassy in Cairo is one of the first essentials for each new African state that achieves independence. Most of the political parties in British Africa have their 'man in Cairo'. It is a manda-tory stop-over point for most of the African leaders in the Federa-tion: Kaunda, Nkomo, the Wina brothers, Dumbutshena, Mainza Chona, and many more in a long list. This is not to say that they accept Nasserism in uncritical bulk. They may have their own reservations on points of policy, which they keep to themselves. But the essential point is that the link is there; the network is established; the money flows. And for this the nationalist leaders in the Rhodesias, as in other parts of Africa, have reason to be grateful to their original benefactor, Anthony Eden.

They have had another source of support, besides Nasser, from the moment that Ghana entered on the Pan-African scene as an independent state in 1957. We will return to this, and the whole network of interlocking influences which has become so potent a political force in the Federation today. Meanwhile, it is necessary to examine internal political developments in the Rhodesias and Nyasaland from the moment of settler triumph in 1953.

(i) First African reactions

In Nyasaland the first reactions to the establishment of Federation were the riots and deaths of the civil disobedience campaign. In Northern Rhodesia the African National Congress and the trade unions joined forces to launch the mass campaign of resistance which their leaders had threatened earlier, before Lyttleton took the final decision. Soon after the fateful vote in the House of Commons, Dixon Konkola, the President of the African Railway Workers Union and an important figure in the A.N.C., led the first group of Africans into the 'European section' of the post office at Broken Hill. Disturbances mounted till, in 1956, the whole Copperbelt was disrupted by 'rolling strikes'. And the boycott of colour-bar shops – where Africans were served through side-hatches and could buy only second-grade goods like 'boys' meat' – had grown so effective that white shopkeepers faced ruin, and were appealing to Salisbury for Federal help. Rioting broke out, and the inevitable African arrests followed at once. The governor declared a state of emergency in the whole of the Western Province, and the subsequent commission of inquiry conceded a strong case for the African sense of grievance. They had scored a notable victory. One magistrate discharged those brought before him – they were members of their Urban Advisory Council – when they were able to establish by means of correspondence that they had been trying *for two and a half years* to arrange a meeting with the settler-run

Chamber of Commerce in Mufulira, so as to discuss the very grievances which by 1956 had exploded into violence.

In this Northern Rhodesian struggle, the new Federal government played no part, though its local U.F.P. supporters were visible to the Africans on the other side of the political barricades, bitterly resisting any change. If 'partnership' was ever to be implemented, as these Congress leaders interpreted the slogan, the change would come through their own initiative, they realized, not Welensky's.

(ii) Federal intervention in Nyasaland

African morale was high in Nyasaland as Federation began. The Nyasa Congress movement, with its branches for migrant Nyasa workers in the other two territories, had acted as the yeast of African nationalism. From it had grown the A.N.C., first in Northern Rhodesia, then in the settler stronghold of the south. Dunduza Chisiza, while he was working in Salisbury, developed close links with George Nyandoro, who in turn organized the A.N.C. in Southern Rhodesia and invited Nkomo to assume the leadership. Chisiza himself went home (he was deported as a dangerous radical by the Southern Rhodesian government) and was to emerge as junior Finance Minister after the Malawi victory in 1961.

The terms of Federation had explicitly stated that constitutional advance in the member territories would not be restrained. Lyttleton, when questioned sharply in the Commons, reaffirmed the point. Yet the Nyasas were to learn, in the revision of 1955 and the frustrated revision plan of 1958, just how potent the intervention of Salisbury could be. For Northern Rhodesia, the same lesson would come in 1961–2.

There can be little doubt that the riots at the time of Federation, and the impressive collective action taken by the Nyasa chiefs, acted as a prod to the Colonial Secretary. But when he called for submissions on constitutional change in Nyasaland, the Federal government was quick to demand its right to be 'consulted'. The word 'consultation' had never been defined (possibly deliberately), and from the start was taken in Salisbury to mean 'permission'. It soon became clear that it meant the best bargain it was possible to strike at Westminster in the light of lobbying strengths.

The Nyasas knew that Huggins – now Lord Malvern – had been to London in 1955 while constitutional advance in the territory was under review, and they assumed that he had been responsible for ensuring a settler majority in the new legislature: six non-Africans to five Africans (with officials holding the overall balance of power). And that had seemed to be only part of his lobbying success. The Provincial Councils, heavily packed with traditional chiefs and headmen, were to act as electoral colleges for the five African seats, instead of a voters' roll based on adult suffrage. But if Malvern thought that the chiefs might provide a challenge to the nationalists, he was speedily proved wrong, because the Councils returned five militant Congressmen, notably Kanyama Chiume and Henry Chipembere. They immediately began demanding the introduction of ordinary ballot-box voting for Africans, while Chipembere declared: 'Moderation will never get us anywhere. The only language which British imperialism can understand is the language of conflict.'

At the Colonial Office, Alan Lennox-Boyd (by now occupied with the Cyprus disturbances) sniffed trouble, and in 1957 transmitted a message to the governor. It was designed to be read and printed publicly, and called for 'an eager, indeed adventurous searching after some better form of constitutional arrangement'. The message arrived only just in time to postpone real trouble for a little while longer.

(iii) Southern Rhodesia

Garfield Todd, the ex-missionary, took over power from Malvern in Southern Rhodesia to inaugurate what many hoped would be a new era of African political advance. But the very establishment of the Southern Rhodesian A.N.C. in 1957 was seen by the settler right wing as the sort of defeat that the white man inevitably suffered if he gave way even a little. Pressure was put on Todd to prove himself capable of being 'tough with the natives'. He doubled the head tax (actually devoting the increased proceeds to African schools) and cracked down hard on African strikers at the Wankie coalfields by calling in Federal troops.

But these sops to right-wing intransigence did not convince the settlers that Todd was 'sound'. And when he introduced a reform that seemed to threaten the inner bastion of settler privilege – a plan to give the vote to more Africans – his downfall was precipitate. Todd's 'heresy' was to suggest that the number of Africans on the common voters' roll might be increased from two per cent to a maximum of twenty per cent, with the ceiling figure fixed by law. Terrified that the right-wing Dominion Party opposition might sweep to power by making an issue of the proposed reform, Todd's own party staged a palace revolt and cast their leader into the political wilderness. Sir Edgar Whitehead, who had been Minister of Finance in the Huggins Cabinet, and had gone off to Washington as the Federation's chief diplomatic representative in the United States, was recalled to assume the Premiership and lead the party to success at the general election on a "safe franchise" policy. In the final franchise revision, the Africans emerged worse off than they had been before.

(iv) Malvern and 'technical independence'

In his last year of office as Federal Prime Minister, Malvern took a secret diplomatic initiative. While in London for the Commonwealth Prime Ministers' Conference, he proposed to the British government a new constitutional advance – to 'technical independence'. When this leaked out in the Federal Assembly, he explained his proposal as a means of raising the status of the Federation in the eyes of the outside world: 'This would enable us to talk to other countries as a separate state, not as someone else's child.'

Wellington Chirwa, the Federal M.P. from Nyasaland, declared in the Assembly that such a change was legally impossible. The British government concurred, pointing out that the Malvern proposal was incompatible with the protectorate status of the two northern territories, still directly under Colonial Office care. The proposal itself was dropped, but the Africans were now alarmed at the way the settler wind was blowing.

(v) The April 1957 deal

As Welensky assumed the Federal leadership, external pressures were threatening the settler *status quo*. The Gold Coast became independent in March 1957, and promptly changed its name to Ghana. Welensky was probably familiar with Nkrumah's stated policy.

> Freedom for the Gold Coast will be a fountain of inspiration from which other African colonial territories can draw when the time comes. Independence for the Gold Coast is meaningless unless it is linked up with the total liberation of the continent.

Ghana's independence, as Welensky later admitted, was the most urgent reason for his mission to London in April. But he was pressed as well by the new pan-Africanist policy of Cairo, begun since the unsuccessful Suez escapade of the year before. He had the necessary excuse for his trip: the Federal general election was due in 1958, and it would be necessary to have the franchise issue settled before then. Besides, since the Todd affair, the British government was surely aware that the 'moderate' United Federal Party, the defenders of partnership, were under severe attack from the settler right wing. The Dominion Party was showing dangerous affinities with the predatory racialism of the Nationalists in South Africa, and its spokesmen had promised that they would clear the Africans right off the voters' rolls if they came to power.

This argument had (and still has) a profound effect upon Tory Ministers in London. They were themselves committed to proving that Federation, rammed through the Commons despite Labour and Liberal opposition, widespread public criticism, and overwhelming African hostility, was sound and workable. They had a vested interest in Welensky's survival. After five days of private talks, Lord Home and Mr Alan Lennox-Boyd agreed that it would help if Welensky could be given 'something to take home'. This, although no one would have been so tasteless as to say it, was a euphemism. The political interests of the Africans were surrendered to those of the settlers. Welensky gained four concessions: (a) Britain yielded the right to initiate legislation having force in the Federal area. (*b*) All civil services, including those of Britain's Colonial Office in the two northern protectorates, would eventually be 'locally based'. (*c*) The constitutional review conference would be held no later than 1960. (The original proviso had been for some date in the period 1960–2.) (*d*) The review conference would 'consider a programme for the attainment of such status as would enable the Federation to become eligible for full membership of the Commonwealth'.

As Welensky was himself to make very clear, the first concession ruled out the possibility that, if the British Labour Party returned to power, it might 'endeavour to inflict some of its half-baked ideas on us by legislative act'. The final concession was simply settler – and Whitehall – double-talk for complete independence. When the Africans read this in their newspapers – and they do read papers, whatever settlers may think – they knew that they were to expect the worst.

It duly came. The Constitution Amendment Act of 1957 and the Federal Electoral Act of 1958 split the common voters' roll into upper and lower rolls, with most Africans relegated to the lower one, and increased the Federal Assembly from thirty-five to fifty-nine seats while diminishing the effective African representation. It was a clever ploy. There would be more Africans in the Assembly, but almost all would be 'stooge' ones, elected in constituencies where anywhere from eighty-seven to ninety-eight per cent of the voters would be white. (Welensky found candidates all right. The salary of a Federal M.P. is eighteen times the average African's income.)

The African Affairs Board, with a Liberal M.P., Sir John Moffat (of the missionary family) as Chairman, went into action at last. It declared both measures to be discriminatory; attacked the slick device of making black M.P.s dependent on white votes (something that the British House of Commons had not anticipated in 1953); and obliquely criticized the British Cabinet by pointing out that constitutional revisions – pursued by private negotiation in London with no chance for the Africans to make their own submissions – was a breach of the contract to refrain from Federal changes until the 1960–2 conference.

After an uproar in the British parliament, Lennox-Boyd and the Tories over-ruled the African Affairs Board and rammed through approval for both measures. The Rev. Andrew Doig of the Church of Scotland in Blantyre, a lifelong friend of the Africans, declared the Board to be a farce and resigned. At the 1958 election Welensky used his power as Prime Minister to pack it with his nominees, and it has never been heard of since. Contrary to what most Africans believe, it is actually still in existence.

(vi) Nyasaland erupts

Welensky's triumph took place in April 1957. Dr Hastings Banda, who had given up his medical practice in London in 1953 and moved to Ghana, received a full account of the four concessions made by the Tories and the shameful treatment meted out to the African Affairs Board.

Leaders of the African National Congress – many of them political disciples who had consulted him in London when they were students – pleaded with him to come home. He prepared to do so; and meanwhile Congress drew up a memorandum demanding major reforms, including direct elections on the basis of 'one man, one vote'. The governor, Sir Robert Armitage, the veteran of Cyprus, seems simply to have lost his nerve or all power of decision as these pressures mounted.

The A.N.C. demand for constitutional reform was formally placed before the governor in September 1957. The A.N.C. leaders heard nothing and called again in November. The governor said he would be going to England on leave in March and would take the matter up with the Colonial Secretary then. In the summer of 1958, Dr Banda went to London and led a deputation to Alan Lennox-Boyd in June. In August he returned home to a tremendous welcome from 5,000 Nyasas gathered at Chileka Airport. The settlers grew alarmed.

On the last day of October the governor at last saw Dr Banda, but he had no news to give him, and no real explanation of the delay. What had happened to Lennox-Boyd's clarion call of 1957 for an 'eager, indeed adventurous searching'? By January 1959 the truth began to sink in. The governor was terrified of Welensky. Confirmation of a kind came in February, when the local white settler leaders submitted their own plan for constitutional revision and at the same time announced that they were all joining Sir Roy's U.F.P. (They had campaigned as Independents up till then.) In February the governor announced that all submissions were now before him and that he would begin to consider possible changes. But he offered no timetable to indicate when a conference would begin, or when any new constitutional plan might come into effect. And meanwhile, in the Federal general election at the end of 1958, Welensky and his U.F.P. colleagues had campaigned on a platform of demanding Dominion status at the London Review Conference in 1960. The embittered Africans of Nyasaland could draw only one logical conclusion; their own governor dared not stand up to the U.F.P., excuses would be found to prevent them having an election in time, and then, in the first convenient week of 1960, a conference would be assembled at which Nyasaland would be represented mostly by its white settlers, who numbered less than 10,000 in a population of three million.

There was one last chance. The Nyasas had learned the importance of the Westminster factor and they approached a friendly M.P. to put a question for them in the Commons. On 25 February 1959, he asked whether Britain still stood by her guarantee to the African peoples of Northern Rhodesia and Nyasaland.

Julian Amery, who by then had become junior Minister in the Colonial Office, rose to make the reply: 'Her Majesty's Government have never departed from their pledges given at the time Federation was introduced.'

In the subsequent questioning, the junior Minister stood by his exact wording. He would not emerge from the past tense into an undertaking for the future.

The inference was clear enough to the Africans of Nyasaland, and in March widespread disturbances rocked the territory. The governor declared a State of Emergency, and white troops were flown in from Salisbury. Fifty-two people were killed. All were Africans. Those detained without trial totalled 1,322. All were

Africans – and they included thirty-four out of the thirty-five Nyasas holding university degrees. And, despite the claim made by the Federal government, the governor of Nyasaland, and the British Colonial Secretary alike that the Africans had plotted widescale murder, no white settler, no white policeman, and no white soldier lost his life.

In the view of today's Malawi leaders, the sacrifice was not in vain. In July of the same year, 1959, the British government was once again asked in the Commons where it stood in regard to its guardianship of the African people in the protectorates. And this time it was not the junior Minister, nor even the Secretary of State, who answered the question, but the Prime Minister himself. Mr Macmillan said:

We want to make it abundantly clear that the purpose of our policy is, as soon as possible and as rapidly as possible, to move towards self-government in Northern Rhodesia and Nyasaland. . . . The British government will certainly not withdraw its protection. When all the units are agreed that British government protection is no longer needed, then – and only then – can the whole Federation go forward to independence.

Professor A. J. Hanna, the Commonwealth historian, drew this conclusion from the disturbances in the two northern protectorates.

It is idle to blame the Africans for reacting so violently. Had they accepted Federation with quiet resignation they would almost certainly have seen the last of Colonial Office control in 1960, and a predominantly white electorate would have been given full legal competence to preserve its oligarchical rule for all future time.

And Professor Hanna concluded, as many historians and newspaper correspondents have done, that the very act of establishing the settler dominated Federation proved to be the building of a hothouse for forcing the growth of African nationalism. It was Huggins and Welensky who had been 'too clever by half'.

But they were not men to regard a single set-back as defeat. The British government appointed the Devlin Commission of

Inquiry as a convenient means of playing for time, on the theory that a period of 'cooling off' would be the best thing for Central Africa. One might reasonably have supposed that Welensky and the settlers would have felt a certain sense of embarrassment; the very desperation of the Africans, no matter how much London might deplore violence, seemed a serious enough indictment of 'partnership'.

But this was to underestimate the ability of the settlers to ignore whatever they found unpleasant. They felt no sense of shame or disgrace, and indeed the two governors in the north soon found themselves being bombarded with letters from the Federal Prime Minister. He was, as one colonial official in Lusaka put it to me at the time, 'clamouring for the review and almost driving Benson dotty with endless messages'. This was a reference to Sir Arthur Benson, now retired, who held the governorship in Northern Rhodesia during that critical period. Welensky wanted an early decision, and still thought that the British government would give in to pressure. But in London, where the review conference was to be held, attitudes were hardening against white settlerdom in general. And after the Sharpeville massacre in South Africa, in March 1960, public opinion in Britain clearly favoured reform.

The U.F.P. strategy was to race to the level-crossing before the gates were shut. As keepers of the gates, Lord Home and Lennox-Boyd seemed anything but firm. Their indecision was a positive encouragement to the settlers to declare that, if the barriers closed, they might have to call out the Federal forces and shoot their way through.

The story of the origin of the Monckton Commission has never been printed. But I understand it to have been this. Benson sensed the kind of London review conference that Welensky and the settlers wanted. As at the Victoria Falls, in London in 1953, and in the negotiations for the April 1957 deal with Lennox-Boyd and Home, it was to be a private gathering behind locked doors, with a minimal statement at the end, and then weeks later, when all the participants had dispersed, a complicated White Paper in which the constitutional land mines were well concealed under a welter of incomprehensible electoral provisions.

Sir Arthur also sensed that Welensky hoped to enlist the cooperation of the British government, rather than risk a head-on collision. The governor said that he was prepared to accept a review in 1960, providing that there was proper preparation – a basis of solid, indisputable facts assembled by an utterly impartial tribunal – and he initially proposed a Commission made up of three High Court Judges from Britain.

At first Welensky would have nothing to do with the idea. Long experience, quite apart from instinct, tells the settlers that whenever they allow an outside disinterested body to examine their affairs, the verdict is generally unfavourable. The Devlin Report, which appeared in July 1959, provided a classic example of this, though its Chairman was a High Court Judge (and a life-long conservative), and the other three members were Establishment figures (two knights and the Warden of Rhodes House, Oxford).

The publication of the Report, indeed, altered the whole political balance between London and Salisbury. Although Macmillan and the Tories made a show of solidarity with Welensky and the Federal government, behind the scenes they were coldly furious. The Report made it clear that Whitehall had been gravely misled by Salisbury; the settlers under Welensky had been so obsessed with their goal of a review conference in 1960, when they would achieve Dominion status and so put an end once and for all to the possibility of intervention from Westminster, that they had deliberately painted a false picture of harmony in Nyasaland. Any disturbances, and the Nyasa efforts of 1957–9 to get the franchise and a new constitution, had been discounted as the work of 'unrepresentative extremists'. The settlers had carefully swept the dirt under the rug, until 1960 and the big review conference would enable them to do their cleaning up in secret and security.

The Devlin Commission found that there had been no 'murder plot' and produced some devastating criticisms of the settler régime in Salisbury. 'Even amongst the chiefs, many of whom are loyal to the government and dislike Congress methods, we have not heard of a single one who is in favour of Federation.'

The Commission described Nyasaland as 'no doubt only temporarily, a police state', and the actual sentence was carefully drafted with specific, limited reference. But the description hit the headlines all over the world, and politically that was what mattered. In one sledgehammer paragraph, the Devlin Report effectively crushed the hopes of the settlers that they could manoeuvre a quiet, private little conference in London where the transfer of power would be arranged:

The [Federal] government's view is that these nationalist aspirations are the thoughts of only a small minority of political Africans, mainly of self-seekers who think their prospects of office will be worse under Federation; and that the great majority of the people are indifferent to the issue. We have not found this to be so. . . . It was generally acknowledged that the opposition to Federation was there, that it was deeply rooted and almost universally held.

In the House of Commons there was uproar when Lennox-Boyd, as Colonial Secretary, formally rejected the Report on behalf of the Tory government. Tempers had not been as hot since Suez, and the cries of 'Resign' from the Opposition benches at times drowned out what the Minister was saying. But the Cabinet was able to rely on traditional party loyalty to see it through the crisis. What the Tory back-benchers did not know then was that Macmillan would call an autumn general election within a few weeks; the government simply could not afford to admit that the Devlin Report was right. And to have dismissed Lennox-Boyd would have been tantamount to admission. Happily for the Tories, voters have short memories, and in any event it is prices and pay packets that determine elections, not colonial affairs.

Macmillan won the 1959 election; kicked Lennox-Boyd upstairs to the House of Lords; and brought in Macleod to begin a new era at the Colonial Office. And here we see another aspect of the Westminster factor at work, for a government can behave quite differently after an election – though its leadership is the same – from the way it behaved before.

The week that the Devlin Report appeared, there was a

445

reception at Oxford, and one of the Devlin Commissioners was receiving the guests in the foyer of Rhodes House. Two Cabinet Ministers who attended could not bring themselves to shake hands, and stalked by, cutting him dead. That was an indication of how strongly the Tory high command felt then.

The last ten months of the administration were marked by a solid freeze-up in Colonial affairs; the Devlin Commission had been appointed – ironically – as a stopgap until the autumn election. But, after the Conservative victory at the polls, caution was cast aside, and the new Colonial Secretary felt ready to attack the outstanding problems with vigour.

Macleod, with Macmillan's backing, made it clear to the settlers that Britain would take a strong stand on the affairs of the Federation. And in particular, since Sir Roy and his U.F.P. colleagues had been so misleading on African opinion in Nyasaland, the government decided to accept the proposal of the Northern Rhodesian governor for a commission which would compile the basic facts, and so provide the review conference with a practical working document.

Welensky gave in, but on two conditions: that the commission would not be empowered by its terms of reference to consider whether Federation itself should continue; and that there should be as many commissioners from inside the Federation as from beyond. Sir Roy drew up a list of thirteen members; Britain matched it (including one constitutional expert from Canada and one from Australia); and that produced the rather unwieldy team of twenty-six, which was captained by Lord Monckton, a former Tory Cabinet Minister and a notable figure at the English bar.

The Commissioners were appointed at the end of 1959 and went out to the Federation in February 1960, and it is from this time that we may date the birth of the 'Rhodesia Lobby'. Its companion body, the 'Katanga Lobby', was to form itself later in the same year, a few days after Congo independence at the beginning of July, when Tshombe established his breakaway régime.

Welensky had learned the importance of organized political

pressure back in 1952, during the conferences that led up to the establishment of Federation. Through friendly industrialists in Rhodesia, he had been put in touch with a public relations firm in London which handled the accounts of many of Britain's largest industrial companies, particularly those with operations overseas.

That had been a short, but successful operation. Now, with the Nyasaland disturbances and the Devlin Report, the United Federal Party and the settlers badly needed a large-scale effort to remove the aroma of disgrace and to project a favourable 'public image'. And Sir Roy had an idea which, at the time, seemed brilliant – to place the Federal government's account with Colman, Prentis and Varley, and their wholly owned subsidiary, Voice & Vision Ltd. It was this firm which had handled the Conservative Party account in the successful 1959 election campaign. Therefore, if news of the Federal initiative came out, the Tories could hardly object, since Welensky and the settlers were only doing what they themselves had done. Further, the choice of V. & V. offered immediate access to 365 Tory M.P.s in whose hands political power would now repose for the next four or five years. One of the Voice & Vision directors, Brigadier Terence Clarke, was himself a Conservative M.P. And through its close contact with the Tory machine during the campaign, Voice & Vision would have the lists of names, the addresses, and, most important of all, the personal contacts, that led upward to the ultimate power centre, the Cabinet itself.

The initial votes and supplementaries covering 'information services' in the Federal Assembly are so phrased as to make it impossible to disentangle a precise figure for the Voice & Vision account. The contract was administratively arranged – no doubt at the highest level. And the problem is further complicated because there is no parliamentary opposition, in the normal sense, for prying out facts like these. The Dominion Party then, and its successor now, the Rhodesian Front, is critical of the U.F.P. only for not being far enough to the right. On an issue like the Voice & Vision campaign, the settlers stand together.

Estimates have, however, been made by members of the small Liberal opposition among the settlers, who have their own means of finding these things out in Salisbury. They calculate that the expenditure on the campaign in Britain ran to a sum between £136,000 and £160,000 in the first year alone, including the cost of enormous full-page advertisements in the British national Press. In 1962 there was a partial switching of this public relations expenditure, to coincide with the appointment of Mike Hové (the former U.F.P. African M.P.) as High Commissioner in Lagos. Some £55,000 was allocated for improving the Federation's 'image' in Nigeria and other African countries. And the first delegation of Nigerian politicians – conservatives from the Moslem North – came to the Federation on a guided tour.

This is one settler activity that particularly enrages African politicians. 'They are spending our tax money on it, which we could be using for schools,' said Mr Chiume in Nyasaland. Kenneth Kaunda regards the lavish use of funds as 'simply immoral, when our people are in need'.

Whole-page advertisements in British papers can cost anything from £1,000 to £8,000. The series that broke upon the British public in the latter half of 1960 was headed: 'Good News From Africa – Let Facts Have a Hearing', so cunningly suggesting that someone was trying to smother the settler case. The multi-racial university – so often the target of settler criticism – was displayed in pictures. There were photographs of white and African nurses working together in hospitals; but no mention was made of the disparity in their rates of pay or of racial segregation among patients. The advertisements tactfully avoided any reference to the tiny percentage of Africans possessing the vote. They spoke instead of how a new nation had been born seven years before, 'conceived in the faith that Africans and Europeans could live and work together as partners'. The text went on to declare that Africans were 'rising quickly to the opportunities which the European has brought' and that they were being taken into 'the partnership and electorate of a modern state'.

The other chief activity of Voice & Vision on behalf of the Federal government – apart from arranging Press conferences and luncheons for Rhodesian politicians when in London – was the organizing of group tours. British M.P.s were first choice, of course, but the tours have also included journalists, and representatives of the Church of Scotland, the National Farmers' Union, and the Federation of British Industries. Ian Waller, chief political correspondent of the *Sunday Telegraph*, a stoutly Tory paper, examined the Voice & Vision campaign in a long article for the magazine *Encounter*, late in 1962. Of the forty M.P.s who had accepted free trips to the Federation, he said, the Labour group of twenty did 'not include a single Labour Party specialist in colonial affairs'. What rewards did the settler politicians reap for their investment? 'Their most conspicuous success was the fact that several Labour M.P.s abstained from voting for an opposition motion criticizing the Federation last year. One can also point to pro-Welensky articles written by the M.P.s on their return – not only in national papers but in local ones and trade-union journals. There are lecture tours and reports back to constituency parties, and the influence the M.P.s may have on their colleagues and other leaders of opinion.' And Mr Waller concluded that one particular victim of the campaign was the Colonial Secretary himself. 'It played no small part in building up hostility to him and culminated in a damaging back-bench revolt.'

Mr Waller noted in passing that M.P.s as a whole have a considerable stake in industry, much of it involving investment and sales abroad. There is nothing secret or scandalous about these directorships; they are publicly listed and well-known. No fewer than 280 Tory M.P.s (seventy-eight per cent of the total) and fifty Labour ones are listed as directors, and in all, the M.P.s, including Liberals, hold 490 directorships, of which 260 are senior ones (managing, chairman of the board).

This is not to suggest corruption in any way; M.P.s usually 'declare their interest' when it bears on the subject of debate. They have a perfect right to be directors. But it should not therefore surprise us if some fifty or sixty members of the Rhodesia Lobby at Westminster have a perfectly mundane, admitted interest in the welfare of industry and commerce in Central Africa. The pertinent point, politically, is whether Federation is any longer the best way to preserve these interests. By the beginning of 1963 an observable shift was taking place in the attitude of British industry. Some of the copper companies were beginning to wonder if it would not be better to get Northern Rhodesia politically stable by abandoning the 'fancy franchise' and the system of devalued votes, encouraging a strong African majority government on full adult suffrage, and, if necessary, cutting the Federal links as well. Stability, rather than the skin colour of the ruling politicians, is what matters most to businessmen in Africa.

Perhaps before going further into the labyrinths of the Rhodesia and Katanga Lobbies I had better declare my own interest. I am well aware that my reports and my articles in the *Guardian* long ago caused the settler M.P.s in Central Africa to regard me as very 'left-wing' – a member of the Labour Party at least, if not something worse. In fact, I am a property-owning democrat and, at the time of writing, a supporter of the Liberal Party. I accept the essential function of the Stock Exchange (and have a few shares myself) but hold with the Roosevelt view of capitalism as a tiger that needs regular taming. I do not feel any personal hostility towards the settlers of Central Africa. For, despite any criticisms I have made, I regard the white Rhodesians as being themselves victims of circumstance, whose political behaviour is running strictly to a predictable pattern. Most of them, indeed, are personally courteous and kind. But I still would not like to be an African, living under their rule in a 'township', and subject – at the point of a loaded gun – to their decisions.

The Rhodesia Lobby and the Katanga Lobby, as they emerged at Westminster in 1960, were both centred on the same 'hard core' of Tory M.P.s. And to find the touchstone of their sympathies one has to go back four years – to Suez. The original 'Suez rebels' of the Tory right wing were the men who deplored the British government's surrender to the dictates of Washington and the U.N. In their view the British forces should have ignored the U.N. resolutions, together with American Treasury pressure on the pound, and completed their military action. Once in full physical possession of the Canal, from Suez to Port Said, Britain could have 'dictated terms' to Nasser; or so they believed.

The fact that such a policy would have flown in the face of

modern African realities – and would have ruined Britain's diplomatic dealings with the whole non-white world – had no effect on the thinking of these 'Empire men'. They looked back with nostalgia to the days of the great Lord Salisbury; they saw Suez and Central Africa in that context; and most of them considered Harold Macmillan a spineless left-winger, who gave way at the vital moment. Their common hatred of U.N. interference automatically put them on the side of Tshombe in the Katanga breakaway, and with Welensky and the settlers when Kaunda, Nkomo, and other Africans took their case to the U.N. in 1962.

The present Lord Salisbury, known to some as 'Bobbity', is the king-pin of both lobbies. He broke with Macmillan over the 'surrender' to Makarios (the Cyprus settlement), and resigned his leadership of the Tories in the House of Lords as a protest. He marked his departure with a long letter to *The Times*, so as to cause maximum embarrassment to Macmillan. Now, driven by an inner flame of moral wrath, he is much more dangerous than any hypocrite.

During the critical 1960–1 assault on the Macleod policies in Central Africa, Lord Salisbury was a director of the British South Africa Company. He has now resigned because of ill health, but continues as a shareholder. And since the Company still owns all the mineral rights in Northern Rhodesia (until 1986) and draws from these a revenue of some £8 to £10 million a year – a concession which could be ended by legislative act in the Northern Rhodesian parliament – it is clear that the Company has a vested interest in maintaining the *status quo*, both in Salisbury and in the northern capital, Lusaka.

One of the most bitter critics of the Macleod policies – and one of the staunchest defenders of Sir Roy Welensky – at Westminster during the same period was the then Chairman of B.S.A., the late Lord Robins. In the 1959 debate on the Nyasaland Emergency (Hansard 215/55), when he was aged seventy-five, he made a speech which included these observations:

Dr Banda and his lieutenants came out into the open and declared their objective was to throw off British control and set up an independent state on the West African model. So, my Lords, we need now be under no illusions as to the aims of these self-appointed leaders.

No one can fail to have sympathy for the aspirations of the African people to progress economically, socially, educationally and politically. I put the importance of their progress in the order I have stated. ... This unrest is confined to a handful out of the 2½ million inhabitants, and violence has been resorted to by only a hard core of agitators and self-appointed leaders, whose aims no one can describe as disinterested.

The Chairman of the Company was making three points, and on all three he was extravagantly wrong. The Devlin Report a few months later was to make it shatteringly clear that the uprising had had the mass support of all Nyasas, even the traditionalist chiefs, and had not in any way been the work of an ambitious 'hard-core'. The paramount importance of economic progress, with political advance listed last in the table of priorities, is an illusion shared by Sir Roy Welensky to this day – the theory that by some miracle Africans (though not white people) can be persuaded to bury any interest in votes for the foreseeable future, while they turn their hands to the struggle for higher wages. The Africans are interested in the 'foreseeable future', no less than whites are. Finally, Lord Robins was wrong about Dr Banda's objective; it was to throw off the control of Salisbury, but certainly not that of Britain. As he had said himself many times, he had no quarrel with the Colonial Office, but simply wanted it to resume its proper role as the protecting power.

Another Company director took part in that Nyasa debate. He was Lord Malvern who, as Dr Huggins, had ruled Africans for a quarter of a century as Southern Rhodesian Prime Minister and then as first Federal Prime Minister, and he said this:

Now this may shock your Lordships. These Africans, until they are very much advanced, are all liars. I can explain that; it is not anything wrong in their world, it is one of the defensive mechanisms provided by their Creator. We were not brought up like that.

And Malvern went on to confirm what had been suspected: that the 1959 State of Emergency in Southern Rhodesia – the territory had been politically calm at the time – had been declared at the behest of the Federal government (and actually been made effective two days before the governor's proclamation in Nyasaland). He said 'It was decided that the Southern Rhodesia African Congress must be put behind wire so they could not create a diversion and prevent the sending of necessary police to Nyasaland.'

In other words, you do not hesitate to imprison people (who happen to be black) without charge or trial of any kind for the military convenience of the Federal government. If anything was needed to confirm African distrust of Federation as an institution, this extraordinary giveaway by Lord Malvern came as stunning proof. It also contained a crucial inaccuracy. No doubt it sounded better to tell the British House of Lords that 'police' had been sent to Nyasaland. But the men who had been airlifted had been Federal soldiers in full kit, with arms and ammunition. The British South Africa Police, if Malvern was referring to them, are a local force controlled by the territorial Prime Minister, operating only within their own territory. If Africans are liars, they are apparently not the only people capable of inaccuracy.

The debate included a reference to another politician-turned-businessman, who might almost be regarded as the founder of the Rhodesia and Katanga Lobbies. He is Captain Charles Waterhouse, one of the original 'Suez rebels' of the 1956 era when he was still a Tory M.P. Soon afterwards, he resigned to take up the Chairmanship of Tanganyika Concessions Ltd (Tanks), with headquarters in Salisbury, and his year is now divided between that office and his other office in the 'City' – London's financial quarter. In one public speech in Salisbury, Captain Waterhouse declared that full democracy was inappropriate for Africans: 'It should be made quite clear that there is never going to be any question of ruling this country by counting heads.'

We should be quite clear what these lobbying groups are out to do. Very simply, it is to bring down the existing leadership of the Conservative Party and replace it with a Cabinet of 'Empire' men, who would order a standstill in Africa, back Tshombe and Welensky to the hilt, and defy the U.N.

The settler politicians want independence, as soon as possible. Hence their references to 'going it alone' and Boston tea-parties. But independence without clash of arms would be preferable. Indeed, a real conflict with the British government might even destroy what settler control already exists. And so the settlers resort to a lobbying job in London. If only they can paint the roses, now faded after nine years of disillusionment, if they can only make the Federal garden still look lovely to Conservative eyes, keeping the paint job fresh for long enough to convince the British Cabinet that it can safely hand over power – that it even has a moral duty to do so – then the white Rhodesians can control the political barriers as South Africans have since 1910. They can lock the garden gates and proceed at their leisure to enforce any native policy they choose.

The existence of a powerful pro-Federal group of M.P.s and industrialists in London encouraged Huggins and Welensky to sign their contract with Voice & Vision. And then help came from an unexpected quarter. I happened to be in the Federation in February 1960 when Sir Roy dropped his first Katanga bombshell. He invited Rene MacColl of the London *Daily Express*, an old friend, to visit Kabwe for a private chat. And there he told him how he had a 'huge file of correspondence' from 'certain interests' in Katanga, proposing some kind of link-up with the Federation. This would mean that Tshombe and his supporters among the Katangese would declare their own little republic and break away from the Congo when it became independent at the beginning of July. The identity of this group has remained an official mystery, but in Salisbury it is believed that some Union Minière officials in Katanga were prepared to defy their parent board in Brussels and give their full cooperation to Tshombe.

In the two years that followed, throughout the crisis over the Northern Rhodesia constitution, when Welensky fought to prevent Britain from granting the Africans a majority in the territorial parliament, the links with Katanga were strengthened. Sir Roy had at least four known private talks with Tshombe, but there may well have been more, because extreme secrecy has always surrounded their meetings. One of these took place at the time of the Hammarskjöld plane crash; when the U.N. plane failed to arrive, Tshombe flew on to Salisbury Airport and had a two-hour chat with Sir Roy while the world's attention was directed elsewhere. Another of their meetings – in the middle of 1962 – was revealed by Kenneth Kaunda, whose U.N.I.P. supporters had run across evidence while checking on Tshombe's link with their electoral rival, the A.N.C. of Harry Nkumbula.

At the height of the Northern Rhodesia constitutional battle, the Rhodesia Lobby at Westminster fired its biggest gun – the Turton motion.

In the summer of 1960 the new Colonial Secretary had chaired the Nyasaland Conference in London which resulted in the granting of a clear African majority in the legislature, and a limited franchise in which 100,000 African voters (only the higher-paid, better educated) would be dominant – though the 10,000 European residents would still enjoy disproportionately high representation and special safeguards. Now, in the winter of 1960–1, Macleod was trying to find a satisfactory constitutional formula for the three million black and 75,000 white citizens of Northern Rhodesia. Each revision up to 1958 had given the settlers greater power, and the loss of only one constituency (by five votes) was all that had prevented the U.F.P. from getting *de facto* control of the territory in the 1959 election. Kenneth Kaunda and his movement – then called the Zambia Congress – had boycotted the election because of the 'racialist unfairness' of the Lennox-Boyd constitution as he and his supporters saw it. When the African boycott had threatened to turn into mass disturbances, the governor had banned Zambia and rusticated Kaunda, together with most of the movement's other leaders, including the Wina brothers and the philosophical Simon Kapwepwe, to detention camp in the north. Mainza Chona, the first African in the territory to qualify as a barrister, had then launched the successor organization. Critics try to insist that U.N.I.P. is racialist, but in fact its name – United National Independence Party – was deliberately chosen to enable Northern Rhodesian citizens of any skin colour to join. And Chona, who became Secretary-General in 1961, will point proudly to the fact that more than 300 white Rhodesians are members, among them Sir Stewart Gore-Brown, who accompanied Kaunda on his mission to the U.N. in 1962.

Welensky was determined to hold the wealth of the Northern Rhodesian Copperbelt within the Federation, and as a northerner himself had an emotional stake in preventing any breakaway. He could see that Kaunda intended, like Banda, to capture a majority in the territorial legislature and then demand secession from the Federation. The Monckton Report, which appeared in October 1960, had recommended majority African rule in the north, and the right of secession from the Federation for all the constituent territories. And the brief, formal session of the 1960 Federal review conference, which assembled in London just before Christmas, had proved indecisive. There had been seventy-four delegates in all, from Britain, the Federal government, and the various territories, and after interminable speeches from almost every one of them, the conference had adjourned. Three years later it has still not reassembled.

Before the Macleod Plan – to grant greater African representation in the Northern Rhodesian legislature – was announced to the Commons in February 1961, the Rhodesia Lobby made a major effort to frighten Macmillan into retreat. This was the same five-month period when Kenyatta's release and the Common Market application were two other issues threatening Conservative unity, and on both, as on Rhodesia, the 'Empire men' campaigned for standing fast on the *status quo*.

The Turton motion – warning Macmillan in phrases of general principle to turn his back on the Macleod Plan – was tabled by Robin Turton, an ex-minister whose lawyer son had emigrated to Rhodesia. It was wholly a Tory back-bench initiative, and among the first to sign were Suez rebels like Paul Williams, Anthony Fell, and Captain Kerby. They were joined by Dr Donald Johnson, John Biggs-Davison, F. M. Bennett, Brigadier Clarke (of Voice & Vision), Patrick Wall, and an increasing host of anxious Tories, who genuinely appeared to think that the course of honour, with loyalty to their kith and kin in Central Africa, demanded that they attach their names to the motion. Doubtless the motives of many were noble, but the objective was the same: to deny the extension of the franchise to black Rhodesians.

Obviously, with 365 Tory M.P.s in the House, the danger-mark would be reached with 180 signatures, if not sooner. The total rose, over a two-week period, to 102, and then began to slip. It settled at eighty-seven and stuck there, and Macmillan and Macleod knew that they had escaped defeat. In part it had been the work of the party whips; in part it was the result of hard counter-lobbying by the 'Macleod men' – M.P.s of the liberal wing, most of them with some knowledge of contemporary colonial politics, who knew that trying to turn the clock back in Africa would only produce an explosion. At the critical moment the leaders of this group – Nigel Fisher, Humphry Berkeley, and Christopher Chataway – tabled a counter-motion and rallied some forty signatures, which brought the battle of the lobbies to an end. It proved to be only one battle in a war which still continues.

Like all wars, it is ruthless. M.P.s had first realized the power of the Rhodesia Lobby at the annual Conservative Party conference in Blackpool during October 1960. While the conference was still in session, the long-awaited Monckton Report was published. All such documents have an official release time, and because of the key nature of this Report, H.M. Stationery Office kept meticulously to the timetable. Motor-cycle messengers left Whitehall on the dot, taking their time from Big Ben, to distribute copies in Fleet Street. But the joke was on the national Press. The Rhodesia Lobby had beaten the British papers by a clear two hours. Officials of Voice & Vision in Blackpool had distributed their own, somewhat selective summary to Tory delegates – M.P.s and private citizens alike – two hours before the official deadline. The source of their information has never been revealed, but the Monckton Report was, of course, being distributed on the same day in Salisbury by the Federal government.

Clearly, no holds were barred, and this was shown once again by the intervention of the Rhodesia High Commission office in London when the Macleod Plan was about to be tabled in the House on 21 February 1961. Until the Colonial Secretary rose at half past three in the afternoon, the vital documents were strictly embargoed. But because of the agreed protocol on consultation with the Federal government, a full copy had been sent to Salisbury. Someone had evidently cabled the contents back, because twelve Tory back-benchers, including F. M. Bennett, M.P., had been invited for a little private briefing – arranged by Voice & Vision – at Rhodesia House in the Strand at 12.30 on the very same day, and there Sir Roy's Federal Law Minister, Julian Greenfield, took them through the Plan point by point. The twelve Tories were well primed to throw awkward questions when Mr Macleod rose in the Commons three hours later.

The power of the Rhodesia Lobby to insinuate itself into Tory high places was shown again in preparations for the 1961 annual conference. The East and Central Africa Committee consists of several M.P.s, with party stalwarts, who may be peers, or industrialists, attached. It was known that still a third revision of the Northern Rhodesian constitution was going to be undertaken during 1961–2 by the new Colonial Secretary, Reginald Maudling, and this was the vital committee in which the policy line for the party conference would be drafted. Some of the younger Tories objected, after the meeting had got under way, that they had 'spied strangers'. Present in the room was Lord Robins, the chairman of the British South Africa Company, a director of 'Tanks', and close friend of Sir Roy Welensky. With him was a senior Rhodesian Civil Servant, Mr Nicholas, who is of course a Rhodesian citizen and, as an official at Rhodesia House, a member of his country's foreign service. Some Tories thought that the visitors should withdraw; others said that they had a right to stay. On this note the meeting broke up, and the committee went to Brighton that year with its agenda in disarray.

The Conservative Commonwealth Council, an autonomous body connected with the party, was dominated during 1960–2 by Tories favourable to Welensky, Whitehead, and the U.F.P. The Vice-Chairman, Patrick Wall, M.P., was a man who had praised the native policies not only of the Rhodesian settlers but also of Salazar in Portuguese Africa, while the Council itself had – and still has – strong links with financial quarters in the City, through men like Patrick McDonagh, a prosperous stockbroker who supports Welensky, and Geoffrey Kitchen, the Chairman of Pearl Assurance, the company whose floodlit skyscraper dominates Salisbury's skyline.

A counter-force to the Rhodesian Lobby developed in London during this period. First in the field was the Bow Group, an organization of young Tories who sought to modernize their party's outlook on social welfare, schools, housing, and many other things besides Africa. Two of its leading members, Christopher Chataway and Charles Longbottom, are Tory M.P.s. Another, James Lemkin, a solicitor, regretfully broke with the Conservatives and joined the Liberals in 1962 at the time when Lord Home appeared to be swinging his support behind Tshombe against the U.N. plan for uniting the Congo. In 1960 the Group declared that Dr Banda should be released from prison and that Kenya should advance to independence. It caused a sensation at the time, though both proposals were to become official Tory policy. With many of their more radical suggestions, the Bow Groupers had the merit of making Macleod's reforms in Rhodesia seem, by comparison, cautious and middle-of-the-road.

In reaction against them, a number of young right-wing Tories in 1961 founded the Monday Club, with Lord Salisbury as patron, at about the same time that Sir Roy Welensky, on one of his frequent visits to Britain, was staying as a week-end house guest with the Marquess at Hatfield. Its major policy statement, a pamphlet called *Bury the Hatchet*, was produced in February 1962 to coincide with the final week of contorted bargaining between London and Salisbury before Mr Maudling announced the third and final plan for the reform of the Northern Rhodesian constitution. This statement perpetuated some of the favourite Welensky myths: that chiefs and 'other moderate Africans' constitute the majority of black Rhodesians; that a 'loyal' government in Salisbury could offer Britain a military base (for what purpose?) after she lost the three in Kenya; that 'multi-racialism' is threatened by detribalized extremists who use intimidation to disguise their lack of popular support.

There are strong patrician family ties, as well as financial ones, linking members of the Rhodesia and Katanga Lobbies. Lord Salisbury and Lord Chandos are both descendants of men who shaped Britain's Africa policy when Rhodesia was young. Lord Lansdowne, who was Lord Home's choice of (uninvited) emissary to fly to the Congo and intervene directly with Mr Hammarskjöld over Katanga, is the descendant of the Lansdowne who was Foreign Secretary to the great Lord Salisbury and who backed the policies of Rhodes against the Liberals. Lord Selborne, one of the directors of 'Tanks', has lobbied Mr Macmillan personally at vital times during the Rhodesia crises. He is a descendant of the British High Commissioner at the Cape who bitterly opposed Liberal policies at the turn of the century.

Lords Clitheroe, Selborne, and Coleraine, whose financial interests link them to the Federation, are among the inveterate writers of letters to *The Times* and *Daily Telegraph*, putting the case for Welensky, the U.F.P., and 'partnership'. With equal energy, they speak out for the settlers during debates in the Lords.

Clitheroe and Selborne, who are directors of British companies linked to Union Minière, are two members of a remarkable club. The 'Rho-Kats', if one may borrow a Stock Exchange word to describe them, are men who themselves straddle the worlds of politics and finance, as their business interests straddle the Katanga border. They had been valiant fighters on behalf of M. Moise Tshombe since he led the Katanga breakaway in 1960, and have been quietly working away behind the scenes at Westminster for a dozen years, helping to push the settler view of the Federation.

M.P.s and political correspondents were made dramatically aware of the Katanga lobby, and Britain's own special breed of 'Rho-Kats', by a bold move to get *de facto* British government recognition for the Tshombe régime within a month of Katanga's defection from the Congo Republic in 1960. I happened to be one of about half a dozen correspondents who had heard via the African grapevine that something unusual involving Katanga might take place in or around the Foreign Office on 7 August. It was an understatement. A seven-man delegation from Katanga arrived in London under the sponsorship of four back-bench Tory M.P.s with powerful connexions in the City, and under the blessing of the Moral Re-Armament movement. In mid after-noon the seven men were conducted into the Foreign Office Courtyard off Downing Street by their new-found British friends. One of the Katangans was in military uniform – and sweltering, as it was a hot day. Another proved to be M. Thomas Tshombe, the 'President's' younger brother. And the leader, a certain M. Kimba, has of course since emerged as one of the triumvirate holding power in Elizabethville and 'Foreign Minister' until the end of Katanga's secession in 1963.

The group did not offer then, or later, any kind of briefing or Press conference. An air of deepest mystery cloaked their whole London visit. And indeed the seven had barely appeared when police from the near-by Cannon Row police station arrived to clear the Courtyard – a procedure no one could recall in living memory, when we questioned the building staff afterwards. The Foreign Office denied calling the police, but a wink and a jerk of the thumb from a young constable had already satisfied us that an order had come to them from 'on high'. No official record has been kept of the visit, and the group was firmly kept from seeing Lord Home as they lacked official status.

Nevertheless, the four M.P.s gave a gala reception that evening at a luxury flat in Eaton Square, to celebrate 'success'. They were doubtless putting a brave face on failure. The M.P. hosts were Colonel Neil McLean, Paul Williams, Anthony Fell, and Philip Goodhart – all Tories, and two of them 'Suez rebels'. Before leaving London the next day, the seven Katangese were also entertained by M.R.A.

This turned out to be just a rehearsal for the more public ex-ploits of the 'Rho-Kats' during the following winter at West-minster. Most of them rallied to support the Turton motion condemning the Macleod Plan for Northern Rhodesia. And, in May 1961, the Katanga Lobby scored its biggest victory when ninety-one Tory back-benchers were persuaded to put their signatures to a motion calling on the Macmillan government to work for the release of Tshombe, then held prisoner by the

Congolese Central government. The principal sponsors of this move were four of the leading 'Rho-Kats': Anthony Fell, John Biggs-Davison, Paul Williams, and Major Neil McLean. Vigorous support came immediately from Captain Kerby, Lord Hinchingbroke (now the Earl of Sandwich), Lord Balniel, and a former Chairman of the Conservative Party, Lord Clitheroe.

The episode seems to have impressed Lord Home, or encouraged his till then prudently silent sympathies. It was that same spring, just after the outbreak of African rebellion in Angola, that he sanctioned a goodwill visit by H.M.S. *Leopard* to the Portuguese territory. The storm from this had scarcely died down before Home and the Foreign Office permitted the sale of two Royal Navy frigates to Portugal, while in June the Portuguese Chief of Staff, General Camera Pina, arrived from Lisbon on what Opposition critics declared was an arms-buying mission. In May Home himself had gone to Lisbon on a goodwill visit for purposes never specified. And though it was not reported at the time, he was met there by Lord Clitheroe, a director of associated companies of Tanganyika Concessions Ltd and linked, thereby, to Union Minière du Haut Katanga.

Selborne scored one of his neatest successes later that year before the big parliamentary debate on Britain's rejection of U Thant's request for aerial bombs to be used by U.N. forces in Katanga. He was received by Mr Macmillan himself, and had half an hour with the Prime Minister at Admiralty House, just before dinner. Presumably, as a director of Union Minière, he put the case for not encouraging military actions against Tshombe's capital that might also harm U.M.H.K. installations.

British financiers gave the original impetus to the founding of this extraordinary concern, which virtually owns Katanga and has substantial interests in Belgium as well. George Grey, a British mining engineer prospecting for Tanganyika Concessions Ltd, was exploring in Northern Rhodesia at the turn of the century and crossed the frontier to seek African copper diggings of which he had heard. He traced them to a rich vein of copper which, as the Prince Leopold Mine, is still being worked today. 'Tanks' then linked up with the Société Generale de Belgique to form Union Minière du Haut Katanga, and the British firm today holds fourteen and a half per cent of the shares and controls twenty per cent of the voting rights in the joint company. Because of political troubles and the blocking of remittances by the Tshombe government, U.M.H.K. passed its interim dividend in 1961 and reported profits in 1962 forty per cent below normal, which forced a cut in the final dividend as well.

This was occasioned (so far as one can tell) by Tshombe extravagances. Tshombe and his colleagues had been retaining for their own use, since the 1960 breakaway, the revenues which legally are payable to the Congo state as a whole. This money used to meet seventy per cent of the whole Congo budget, so it was not surprising that the Adoula government in Leopoldville was short of funds, while Tshombe was able to buy arms and fleets of jet aircraft, and pay his mercenaries £300 a month. In the last normal year, 1959, total U.M.H.K. payments in taxes, royalties, and dividends amounted to £37 million, and 'Tanks' took a healthy slice of this sum. During 1962, when Tshombe allowed only partial transmission of dividend payments abroad, some doubt began to develop in financial circles over whether there would be any dividend at all in future. Captain Waterhouse, as Chairman of 'Tanks', had put his trust in Tshombe, but there were increasing signs that his loyalty might be misplaced.

Meanwhile, the U.M.H.K. production of copper continued at around its all-time peak rate of 300,000 tons a year – or some eight per cent of the world total. The company also produces annually some 330,000 lbs of silver, sixty per cent of the world's cobalt, most of the world's radium, as well as cadmium, germanium, manganese, uranium, diamonds, gold, coal, and tin. U.M.H.K. controls the exploitation of hydro-electric power in Katanga, and operates railways, chemical factories, banks, and insurance companies. In diversifying abroad, it has acquired a considerable stake in Belgian industry, and has joined with Harry Oppenheimer's Anglo-American and Rhodesian Anglo-American Corporations to purchase control of the Wankie coalfields in the Federation.

The London *Financial Times* puts the market value of

U.M.H.K.'s assets at £145 million, but other estimates have run as high as £500 million. Captain Waterhouse has made no bones about his support for Tshombe. In his 1961 annual report, he referred to the secessionist régime as 'the established authority', and declared that Union Minière and 'Tanks' 'have played no small part in enabling the independent African government of the province to establish itself'.

Various tangible links hook Katanga into economic alliance with Rhodesia and South Africa, quite apart from the Tshombe Ministerial delegations which have been warmly received in Salisbury and Pretoria. Harry Oppenheimer, who is Chairman of the great complex of South African gold- and diamond-mining companies first constructed by Cecil Rhodes, holds directorships in both the British South Africa Company and in Tanganyika Concessions. Before the Katanga troubles began, the British South Africa Company had holdings in 'Tanks' of which it managed to dispose. This enabled the late Lord Robins, at the 1962 annual meeting of the Company, to state:

> Attacks have been made on our whole group in parliament and the Press, alleging that financial interest in Katanga has led us to give active support to the Tshombe régime. May I say at once that no company in our group holds a single share in any concern operating in Katanga.

This declaration rang a little hollow for two reasons. First, at the time of speaking, Lord Robins himself was – and had been for many years – a director of 'Tanks', the part-owners of Union Minière. Secondly, it is widely supposed, a substantial block of shares in the British South Africa Company – not a majority but enough to ensure control – had been acquired by Harry Oppenheimer through Anglo-American or one of its investment subsidiaries. Oppenheimer himself sits on the British South Africa Company Board, as does his colleague Mr A. Wilson. And, at the time Lord Robins spoke, both he and the man who succeeded him, Paul Emrys-Evans, had seats on the board of Anglo-American. Robins himself was a director of De Beers as well.

464

Lord Salisbury was a British South Africa Company director until mid 1961, and Lord Malvern has continued to be one. Since both men are devoted friends of Welensky, sharing his views on the black evils of African nationalism and his admiration for the Tshombe régime, an African politician would have to be curiously artless to suppose that the Chartered Company is neutral in the great political battle now raging. The British South Africa Company was one of the big companies which backed Welensky and the U.F.P. from the start of Federation; its annual contribution to party funds is thought to have totalled at least £60,000. The existence of this financial alliance was confirmed when Sir Ronald Prain and the Rhodesian Selection Trust group of mining companies publicly withdrew their support from U.F.P. campaign funds. Since the big mining concerns and the Company itself are all centred in Northern Rhodesia, Sir Roy Welensky is not only battling to save Federation; he is also fighting to hold on to the U.F.P.'s financial lifeline, by keeping physical control of Northern Rhodesia. It would take a book in itself to trace the full extent of the financial network behind the Rhodesia and Katanga Lobbies, but the British South Africa Company with its annual income from mineral royalties of £10 million is, it would seem, deeply enmeshed.

3 L'Envoi

'All peoples have the right to self-determination.' U.N. GENERAL ASSEMBLY, Resolution of 14 December 1960

The dawn breaks suddenly in Africa. Out of the night, man stirs, and in the first pale light takes up his burden and starts again upon his way.

The birds break into song. The darkness turns to gold. The sun is up. Day has come. Mankind is on the move.

Through the grass thatch of countless daub and wattle huts the smoke filters blue, and joins the morning mist. The porridge cooks in the blackened pot, poised on three stones above the glowing logs. A girl pounds the corn with steady crunch. The man inspans the oxen and cracks the thick hide whip; the woman handles the plough, and a child leads the large-horned plodding team. The earth is turned; the seed is sown.

The women go with perfect poise, clay pot on head, to carry water for the day. The children hasten along the sandy track . . . to the school. The old men gather under the big tree, and talk.

When Guy Clutton-Brock wrote those words, he was deliberately returning in time to the days before Federation, describing the earlier Africa of the missionary and the British colonial administrator. Today the word dawn – '*Kwacha*' – has a special meaning for the Africans. Dr Banda made it the slogan for his people, and it has been adopted by the other black citizens of the Federation, as something between a greeting and a challenge.

Mr Clutton-Brock, of course, is one of the white men who in the Central Africa of today have become identified as 'pro-black' and are now politically disgraced. He was arrested and imprisoned; now he is one of the 'unwanted immigrants' – a company of honourable men. One wonders where the Federation's greatest explorer and teacher would fit in, if he were to return now to the country that he helped to create.

And this is the supreme irony. For there is no question in my mind that if David Livingstone were to reappear on Federal territory now, saying and doing the things that he did in his lifetime, he would not last a week. If deemed to be a citizen of the Federation, he would be dispatched in ignominy to the malarial prison farm at Gokwe, along with other thinkers of dangerous thoughts like George Nyandoro. If not a citizen, he would join the distinguished company of prohibited immigrants.

What we are watching in Central Africa now is the final clash between the two traditions which the white man brought to Zambesia – the Exploiter tradition of Rhodes, with the settler-politicians as its guardians, and the Tutor tradition of Livingstone. Where are its guardians? South of the Zambesi the Livingstone ideal received a near-mortal blow in 1923; in the north it was precariously maintained by a diminishing band of Colonial Office servants against the calculated onslaught of the Federal machine.

All the odds favour victory for the Rhodes tradition; we need only look across the River Limpopo to the South African Republic to see its progress when all the checks have been removed. In the Federation, ten years of dither, misplaced trust, and good grey compromise by successive Tory Cabinets in London offer no tangible hope of sudden, massive support for the Livingstone ideal.

But decisive battle has now been joined; that is the essence of the Rhodesian crisis today. And even if the British Cabinet seeks once again to evade unpleasantness through compromise, it cannot do so. Either the Rhodes tradition will triumph in this last engagement, or Livingstone will at last emerge victorious.

There are curious parallels in the lives of the two men. Both of them made the long sea journey from Britain to begin their African careers at the continent's southern tip. Both felt the urge to push north and open up the unknown interior; but for Livingstone it was an escape from a society whose race policies he found repellent, while Rhodes's aim was to extend the frontiers of that society – warts and all.

Each man showed the traits of character that accompany achievement: relentless drive and concentration, no interest in money for its own sake, and, at the end, death for his cause when there was still so much to be done. Each man had the gift of inspiring others to join him, disciples to carry on when he was gone. In the case of Livingstone, of course, many of these men have been black.

Livingstone consciously set out to free Africans from slavery. Rhodes, whatever his professed aims, sold into slavery the black citizens of the nation he founded. There is a sad and illuminating contrast in the thoughts of the two men as they faced their last illness.

Rhodes prepared specific instructions for his burial place at the crest of the Matopo Hills – down to the wording on the gravestone and the sculptured frieze near by to commemorate the Shangani Patrol. Symbolically, whether he knew it or not, he was declaring the supremacy of white over black. He, Rhodes, had taken over the Matabele Valhalla. Beside him would lie the warriors who helped defeat Lobengula. He had fastened his name on a country, and on his deathbed at False Bay he ordered his staff to take the necessary legal steps to ensure that it should be 'Rhodesia' forever.

Victorian piety has nearly turned Livingstone into a stained-glass saint, which he was not. The Rev. Cecil Northcott of the London Missionary Society has, in this decade, tramped over some of the same routes and talked to Africans along the way. He writes that Livingstone 'still raises the vital questions about Africa and her peoples; though he has been dead over eighty years, he dominates the Central African scene'.

His arrangements for death were simple and practical. He told Susi and Chuma that he hoped he might be buried at home, but made no special request. None of them in that little hut by Lake Bangweulu knew that a nation would give him its greatest honour, that his body would lie with poets and kings in Westminster Abbey. At the time of his last illness, Livingstone was only concerned to get an ordinary, rather practical message to London. He had arranged, for his next home leave, to reserve modest lodgings near Euston Station, and he wanted the mission office to cancel the reservation.

In death, the two founders each left a spiritual legacy to the nation. 'Commerce and Christianity' was Livingstone's phrase, and he called the land-route to Zambesia 'God's highway into the Interior'. Rhodes said his formula was 'philanthropy plus five per cent'; the land-route was 'the Suez Canal to the North'.

Today, if you visit the villages or mission stations in the North, the inhabitants will still tell you, with quiet pride, the remarkable story of Livingstone's last trek. And there is a curious detail which the Africans will insist on stressing, though to us it may possibly seem repellently physical. Before the body was wrapped in bark and sailcloth for the long journey to the coast, Susi and Chuma removed the heart and buried it deep in the earth. David Livingstone, in death, represents the real race partnership Rhodesia needs – and he left his heart in Africa.

Somewhere during the tortuous power struggle that has twisted the whole nine-year history of the Federation, Britain has managed to get her priorities wrong. It is not just that she has tipped the balance slightly against the Livingstone tradition and in favour of Rhodes. She has come close to obliterating Livingstone altogether.

This is morally indefensible, and politically stupid in the Africa of today. We may grow tired of being told that the whole continent is slowly uniting, but it is nevertheless true. And it is much truer today than, for example, it was in 1957, when Lord Home and Alan Lennox-Boyd held their (secret) April conference with Welensky in London and granted the four concessions that so enormously strengthened settler control over the lives of the African majority. 'The entrustments now made are considerable,' Sir Roy told *The Times* on 26 April. 'They give the Federation the fullest practical independence.'

If Britain has any political credit left with the Africans, it is because of their charity and not because of her honour. 1962 was significant as the year when Joshua Nkomo and Kenneth Kaunda by-passed London and took their battle straight to the U.N. Mr Kaunda continues to deal with London as well. But

Mr Nkomo and the other nationalist leaders in Southern Rhodesia declared, many months before the 1962 Whitehead crackdown, that they had lost all faith in London and would no longer appeal to the British government. They refused to meet R. A. Butler on his tour of the Federation in May, and refused to meet the four-man advisory team, sent by Mr Butler, which paid visits in July and September.

The blunt fact is that, for shrewd tactical reasons that are no doubt obvious to Lord Home, Britain has decided to pursue diametrically opposite policies in different parts of Africa. Trusteeship, leading through self-government to full independence, is proper for Ghana, Nigeria, Sierra Leone, Uganda, and Tanganyika. It is even permissible (after a struggle that nearly split the Cabinet) for Kenya. And when the Africans of Nyasaland put up enough of a fight (and it is known that Sir Roy never wanted this 'Imperial slum' in the first place) then it becomes solemnly logical to release Malawi from settler control.

But in the Rhodesias Britain has apparently decided that she can abdicate her duties of guardianship, take no action against white supremacy, and still keep her political credit with the Commonwealth and the world. She is backing Welensky and sheltering Tshombe with reckless, obstinate disregard of the results for her enemies and her friends. The Soviet policy planners for Africa must be rubbing their hands (if that is what Soviet planners do) since Britain's Rhodesia policy 'proves' all their propaganda: imperialist leopards are incapable of changing their spots. And at the same time she is driving her friends in Ottawa and Washington to despair. The U.S. State Department, with its excellent African division headed by Governor Williams and Wayne Fredericks, found throughout 1962 that its efforts in the Congo and southern Africa were vitiated by Britain's inexplicable Katanga–Rhodesia policy. At the Commonwealth Conference, Howard Green of Canada felt obliged to criticize it sharply.

What is holding Britain back from fulfilling her proper and historic role in Salisbury? It cannot be fear of Harry Oppenheimer and big business, surely, for she has seen (with the case of the Williamson Diamond Mine) how the great Oppenheimer corporations can take the political somersault, from white to black, in their stride. That mine is in Tanganyika.

The crudest pragmatic opportunism, if nothing else, dictates an immediate reversal of policy in the Rhodesias. And this is not to ask Lord Home or Mr Butler to explore dangerous new political country, but simply to revert to a tried and trusted policy of guardianship that has served Britain well throughout the rest of Africa. And such a policy must be pursued in both Rhodesias, not just the North (where it will be easier). When the great Lord Salisbury sanctioned Rhodes's Charter and the British South Africa Company initiative, he did not for a single moment regard this as releasing Britain from her Imperial trust over the welfare of the native peoples.

Two traditions have been at war with each other in Zambesia since the beginning of white occupation – a war that in other colonial dependencies has been suppressed or eliminated. One we may call the traditional British role of political tutor. The other is the South African tradition imported by Rhodes, which amounts to permanent white supremacy regardless of whatever fancy phrases or euphemisms may be devised for it.

Long, long ago a flash of intuition told Huggins and Welensky how to wield power. They would proclaim the first of those traditions as their avowed principle – and practise the second. That is the way to neutralize the Westminster factor; indeed, to take it right off the chess-board. Conservative governments in London are inherently reluctant to intervene, and will only do so when compelled by constitutional provision.

And this is why, paradoxically, the African nationalists have repeatedly said that they would much prefer to see the 'middle road' U.F.P. swept away and replaced by the Rhodesian Front. That, at least, would remove the smokescreen of hypocrisy, and force Westminster to recognize that the choice has to be made between white supremacy and democratic rule.

The leading African nationalists of Malawi, Zambia, and Zimbabwe – to give the territories their African names – have a very special claim on Britain to resume her tutor role. All three

471

have adopted the Western moral code as their own. Dr Banda is an Elder of the Scottish Church; Mr Kaunda is a son of the same Church, and a deeply religious one; Mr Nkomo is a Methodist preacher who turned to social welfare work and trade unionism as a practical way of implementing his religion. I must confess that the ignoble suspicion has occurred to me that it is precisely because we know these are moral men that we have treated them so shabbily.

But in today's Central African crisis there is no more time for a leisurely examination of motives. Hard, even unpleasant, political decisions must be taken. For the white settlers themselves have reached a stage of moral paralysis.

No one is suggesting – as Lord Home and Mr R. A. Butler seem to think – that Whitehall should cut the collective throats of 312,000 settlers. Rather it is the case that British intervention now is just about the last chance of saving the moral fibre of the settlers themselves. Perhaps Mr Macmillan would appreciate a double reminder from sources he would respect.

'Unlimited power is apt to corrupt the minds of those who possess it.' That was a great predecessor, William Pitt, first Earl of Chatham. And again: 'We know that power does corrupt,' said the Duke of Omnium in Trollope's novel, *The Prime Minister*. Acton said it too, but that was later. Surely, if ever men were given corrupting power, unchecked by any restraint, it is the rich white settlers of southern Africa. They have turned into pigs under the spell of the goddess of Easy Living. That is their Circe; surely it is clear by now that they themselves are powerless to break the spell.

In asking Britain to assume the role of Ulysses one is being practical as well as moral. Here at Westminster and in Whitehall is a vast reservoir of expertize, built up over the years when a great oceanic Empire had to be administered. In little more than a dozen years that empire has been reduced from 700 millions to less than 30 millions. Take the Indian Civil Service alone: consider the store of experience accumulated by the governors, chief secretaries, and all the rest. Look at the I.C.S., the state and national parliaments – all living monuments to their skill.

Outnumbered 26:1, the settlers of Rhodesia are too proud – or too fearful – to let any 'outsider' come in and straighten out the mess. But this, surely, is just the old phenomenon of the child biting the doctor's finger. Action, not pampering, is what a sick child needs. 'You must give us credit for knowing the African a little better than people in London,' says Sir Roy Welensky. This argument is not only sincere; it is also tragically wrong. Granted that the Matabele, the Mashona, and indeed most of the three million Africans in each territory, are poverty-stricken politically as well as economically; it is not a knowledge of their particular tribal ways that matters. What is needed is a special kind of expertize on the tutoring of politically inexperienced people and the subsequent handing over of power. In India this was trustee-ship or the 'guardian' policy. But there has been Britain's experience in Africa, in Malaya, in the West Indies as well. Suppose, for convenience, that we call this sophisticated process 'political tutoring', then it can be concluded that in Britain at this moment there are not just dozens but literally thousands of men who have guided the process in one country or more. How many political tutoring experts can the white settlers of Rhodesia muster? There may, conceivably, be one or two in Federal service. But among the Welenskys, the Winston Fields, and the rest of the politicians the answer is crystal clear: there is not one.

The British political tutors have this further advantage: having barked their shins on the whole process at every stage, they must in retrospect be able to see mistakes that could be avoided a second time round, time and money that could be saved, short-cuts that could usefully be taken. No such expertize is being brought to bear on their own problem by the white settlers of Rhodesia at the present time. It is as if a man were to refuse to call the fire brigade because he knows the firemen have never yet done any firefighting on his particular piece of property. Not only that, but timid offers of help from any quarter are brusquely turned down as well.

'Stand back, everyone!' cries the white Rhodesian as the flames crackle and roar, and begin to leap dangerously towards the vital parts of the main structure itself. Then voices start calling out from somewhere in the cellar. Twenty-six people, it turns out, are trapped down there. They are mostly poorly educated and badly dressed, but their leaders are not. They call out, saying they can help with the firefighting.

'No good, old chap,' comes the reply. 'I can tell by the colour of your skin that you've no experience at firefighting.' The words are spoken in a friendly, paternal way, without rancour and with utter sincerity.

The black men in the cellar are becoming desperate. Some of them call out that in fact they *have* taken extensive firefighting courses themselves. Others suggest calling in neighbours – who happen to have black skins also – because they have dealt with fires like this in the recent past. Both sets of suggestions are ignored.

Two white neighbours arrive on the scene: Mr Nosey from Fleet Street and Mr Parker from Whitehall. Both of them recognize the kind of fire that has broken out, because each has seen this kind in other parts of Asia and Africa before.

'It looks like a Self-Determination fire,' they call out. 'How about getting the London Fire Brigade in to help? They've got lots of experience at this sort of thing.'

'No good, old chap,' replies Mr Settler. 'I'm afraid you don't realize what I'm up against here. This isn't an Asian type of fire. It isn't even an African fire, of the ordinary kind. These are special, peculiar, Rhodesian-type flames I've got to tackle here.' And once again this refusal of help is spoken with utter conviction and deep sincerity.

Now there is a lot of angry shouting and cries for help coming from the cellar. Mr Nosey discovers that the twenty-six Africans seem to be blocked from getting out. He decides to ask, at the risk of a snub, if the white householder knows this and whether it might be a good idea to let them out to help fight the fire.

'You must give me credit for knowing my own Africans a little better than someone from 5,000 miles away,' comes the reply. 'I know these people; they've shared this house with me since 12 September 1890. Why, I can speak to them in their own language.' (He calls out 'Be patient down there' in fluent Sindabele.)

The men in the cellar call out that the householder only chats to the cook and the garden boy, that he has never invited any of them into his living-room and that any attempt at conversation on the level of equal exchange is called 'cheeky'. Mr Settler retorts that the twenty-six men are in the cellar because they prefer it there, and get food, shelter, and clothing practically given to them.

But the flames are now burning fiercely, and when Mr Nosey and Mr Parker start to frame their next suggestion it is apparent that Mr Settler has entirely lost patience. He reaches suddenly inside his jacket and produces a loaded pistol, and orders Mr Nosey and Mr Parker right off his property at once. Then, still brandishing the pistol, he leaps with surprising agility for the entrance to the cellar and padlocks it.

As Mr Nosey and Mr Parker take their departure they are presented with a final vignette of despair. Some of the men in the cellar, reckoning that the flames might set them free, have made improvised bellows and are setting to work with a will. The fire is now roaring out of control. Mr Settler, looking hot and exasperated, comes out on to the stoep, sits down with his back to the flames, puts his pistol carefully by his right hand, and opens a little booklet entitled *Manual of Firefighting*. As the scene fades we hear his exasperated words: 'All I need is time.'

Perhaps the foregoing sounds preposterous, but I would contend with the greatest seriousness that this, in metaphorical terms, is precisely what is going on in the Central African Federation today. The political masters of the Federation are wrong on two vital counts.

First, it is not at all certain that they know their own Africans better than outsiders.

Secondly, whether they do or not is relatively unimportant; what matters at this point is knowing not the patient but the disease. And in this particular case the kind of doctor that needs to be called in is a kind that does not exist in the Federation. He is called a political tutor and experienced men in this field are to be found either in Britain or else – God save the mark – at the U.N.

As I've said enough to raise the hackles of every follower of Whitehead and Welensky, I may as well go the whole hog and quote from a source that never fails to infuriate the present privileged white minority: the Labour party.

It was one of the patron saints of Labour, Bernard Shaw (whose books I was pleased to see occupying a prominent place in Sir Roy's personal library at his home in Salisbury), who commented about people of privilege in his own time:

We have no more right [he said] to consume happiness without producing it, than to consume wealth without producing it.

I have often thought of those words – Shaw's Law for the Privileged – as I watched Rhodesia's new breed of happy Bourbons at work and at play in Central Africa. Piling up the money and mowing their irrigated lawns in the new Klondike of the Copperbelt. Driving safely home from the white-run territorial legislature in the heart of Salisbury to the all-white security and comfort of suburban Greendale. (You can, as I have said, do it without the disturbing experience of driving past the impoverished squalor of Harare township.) Or bowling down to Beira on a broad, black ribbon of tarmac where once the ox-wagons of the pioneers toiled upwards only two generations ago, for a luxury holiday in 'Portuguese East' on the shores of the Indian Ocean. (No problem on £1,733 a year and no income tax.)

I marvel at the rhinoceros-hide skins that ordinary mortals develop – so quickly – in such circumstances, that enables them to enjoy their privileged delights, without the dilution that would come from a momentary backward glance to see how the other ninety-seven per cent are enjoying themselves. Does it ever occur to these new Bourbons, these happy Californians of Africa, that there are fellow citizens who will go through life without ever knowing what it's like to own your own car and say 'Fill 'er up'? Without having a family holiday? Without being able to have – ever – enough shirts or shoes to look anything but tatty and second-rate? Without a hope of secondary education? Without the tiny luxury of picking up a glossy magazine at a news-stand for a couple of shillings?

Does it occur to them that these luxuries are denied, not just to some of their fellow Rhodesians who happen to be black, but to more than ninety per cent of them?

Let us accept that the Rhodesian Bourbons have acquired the knack of convenient deafness to blot out unpleasant sounds, as their predecessors carried nosegays or pomander balls to ward off the unpleasant aromas exuded by the poor in the streets. Let us accept that outside advice, especially from Liberals or the Labour party or from Shaw, falls on deaf ears. Despite all this, perhaps they would heed – not advice but a word of warning – from a Conservative who also had deep understanding of the power of nationalism? When Daniel O'Connell said 'nothing is politically right which is morally wrong', there were Bourbons in his country too. They are there no longer.

Postscript

> 'In Government, a great deal may be achieved by severity; more by love; but most of all by that impartial justice which pays no respect to persons.' JOHANN VON GOETHE

'My people have been patient for too long. They cannot be expected to go on respecting imposed institutions. We call on the British Government to intervene in Southern Rhodesia to avert disaster.'

Thus Joshua Nkomo, the lay-preacher turned nationalist, when he emerged from his three-month sentence of rural detention in 1963, soon after the defeat of Sir Edgar Whitehead and the coming to power of the new government under Winston Field. Mr Nkomo was not advocating violence. But he was desperately trying to shake a dormant administration in London into realizing that the era of violence had begun.

During the election campaign in December it had, in fact, become obvious that Mr Nkomo's Z.A.P.U. movement had lost control of the nationalist campaign. Banned by the Whitehead government, and stripped of its leaders (who had been arrested by heavily armed police in a country-wide round-up in September), it was starting to lose ground to the menacing new underground organization calling itself the Zimbabwe Liberation Army.

There were about fifteen bomb explosions every day for a fortnight before polling day, according to Z.A.P.U. figures, though neither the British South Africa police nor the few Z.A.P.U. officials still at liberty seemed able to pin down the shadowy group directing operations – a kind of African E.O.K.A. For the first time since the far-off Matabele Wars sixty-seven years previously, Africans were making direct attacks on settlers' houses. The desperate men of the 'Liberation Army' were using petrol bombs of the crudest sort. Most of them were ineffective, but there was one spectacular success when the Lancaster clothing factory was burned to the ground. There were about four dozen bomb explosions on election day itself.

The Z.A.P.U. leadership realized that they themselves were facing a challenge on the left from the Z.L.A., just as the political initiative in South Africa seemed to be passing from the law-abiding Congress movement of Chief Luthuli to the terrorist gangs of Poqo. In *The Spear*, their banned journal which now circulates clandestinely, the Z.A.P.U. leaders made a desperate appeal to Britain to act:

The 2,000 Africans arrested for non-existent political offences are determined to build up a State of Zimbabwe which will be democratic and non-racial. They will win. Do we have to wait until European blood is shed ? There are now more than a hundred Africans killed by police in the name of white supremacy. There has not yet been one European killed by Africans in the name of majority rule.

It is the undisputed authority of the [Z.A.P.U.] leaders that controls incidents of violence. But such leaders cannot put an end to violence, arson, and sabotage unless they can show that, by so doing, political freedom would be won. If there were a constitutional conference in the offing, violence would be ended. Without the prospect of one, violence and more violence, ending in the bloody defeat of the settlers, is inevitable. If the British Government are bent on granting Southern Rhodesia independence, then the Africans must be very tough ... against the settler government of Winston Field.

Whatever the future may bring, these words of the Z.A.P.U. leadership must be looked upon as a last warning from civilized but desperate men. Indeed, as those words appeared, Z.A.P.U. had already set up exile headquarters in Dar es Salaam (with the goodwill of Dr Julius Nyerere and the Tanganyika government) and had named the Rev. Ndabaningi Sithole, its national chairman, as Leader-in-Exile. He, in turn, addressed one last appeal to Britain by flying to London and asking to see Mr Butler at the Central African Office. He took with him a long, detailed document which up to the time of writing remains confidential. But he also issued a public statement. This said that if Britain were to grant independence to a minority white government, then the

African people of Southern Rhodesia would resort to ultimate sanctions:

We shall regard such a step as a declaration of war and will not hesitate to form immediately a government in exile, and, as a government, enlist material aid from other governments in and outside Africa. If fair constitutional means are denied to us, we shall be prepared to solve the problem with our blood.

It is this savage change of mood that points to the politico-military climax in Rhodesian affairs which cannot be long postponed unless there is decisive intervention by Whitehall. Perhaps the gravest warning from the Africans came, not in words, but in a tiny incident at Gwanzura Stadium near Salisbury at one of the last Z.A.P.U. rallies permitted by the white authorities before the movement was banned. Mr Nkomo had returned from a tour of African countries to be welcomed by a crowd of 30,000 weeping, cheering, and nearly hysterical black people. Gone were the western clothes he used to wear; now he was in national dress with a Matabele fur hat. With the drumming and the dancing, and the sea of black faces lining the route, it took him two hours to get from airport to stadium. And there the incident took place.

A wizened man of ninety was led forward; he handed Joshua Nkomo a curious object which proved to be a Matabele battle-axe, and told him he 'must fight to the bitter end'. Later that evening in Salisbury's comfortable white suburbs, settlers smiled cynically over their sundowners and said 'they'll never fight – the monkeys have no guts'. But is it true? That man of ninety was a deliberate link with the past; he had been a youth of eighteen when Lieutenant Tyndale-Biscoe hoisted the flag at Salisbury on September the 12th, 1890, after the March of the Pioneers. At twenty-one he had fought as a soldier of his king, Lobengula; at twenty-four he had seen the final Matabele defeat in the Matopo hills. And now, in the 1960s, that same man was calling on three million fellow-Africans to bring the settler chapter in Zambesia's history to a close.

Emotion is the effective fuel of the political machine; Churchill's great broadcast appeal for 'blood, sweat, and tears' after Dunkirk should convince us of that. But leaving emotion and sentiment aside, cold political logic suggests that by the spring of 1963 Britain was confronted with a very real threat to national self-interest if she failed to intervene. Kenneth Kaunda, speaking at the United Nations, had described Sir Roy Welensky as 'a desperate man prepared to use firepower' and went on to warn that if the Federal Prime Minister ordered his troops into action 'then the world will have on its hands a second Algeria'.

The threat to Britain's interest that is developing now is something that half a dozen years ago would have seemed inconceivable: a split in the Commonwealth. Yet the threat is real enough, and the potential tragedy is that if Mr Macmillan (or his successor) fails to act decisively when the crisis comes to a head, then the split could be permanent. The storm clouds on this one have, in fact, been gathering for more than three years – ever since Sharpeville. At the conference of Commonwealth Prime Ministers that followed that tragic event it was not the hot-blooded African radicals who made an impulsive call for action, it was that notably conservative Malayan prince, Tunku Abdul Rahman. He planted the idea then, in an impassioned twenty-minute speech, of reading South Africa out of the 'club'. When the Prime Ministers arrived for the 1961 conference in London, their diplomatic weapons were loaded and ready. Strong backing for the Malayan stand came from Canada (Diefenbaker), India (Nehru), and Africa (Nkrumah and Abubakar). But many, like myself, who covered that conference, are convinced it was the 'invisible veto' of Dr Nyerere that turned the trick. He was not present at the conference since Tanganyika at that time was still eight months away from independence. But he asked the other Commonwealth leaders, in individual letters, to act on the South African issue since, if they did not, then Tanganyika would feel obliged on reaching independence to leave the Commonwealth.

The Commonwealth leaders acted – decisively. And the ultimate factor that forced Mr Macmillan to concur was the certain knowledge that the alternative would have been to split the Commonwealth association, perhaps irrevocably.

Fortunately for the Macmillan government the Rhodesian issue

481

was sidetracked at the 1962 conference of Commonwealth Prime Ministers because normal protocol was suspended in order to concentrate on the Common Market issue. Yet, even so, the Canadian foreign minister, Howard Green, forced the delicate issue of Katanga on to the agenda and it became apparent that Britain's attachment (through Lord Home) to the Tshombe–Welensky axis was something that aroused grave misgivings among her Commonwealth partners.

To the door of Marlborough House, on the opening day of that conference in September 1962, came Mr Sipalo of U.N.I.P. and Mr Chirimbani of Z.A.P.U., with separate copies for each of the sixteen Commonwealth Prime Ministers of a petition from Mr Kaunda and Mr Nkomo. This described Sir Roy Welensky as 'an impostor' holding down nine million Africans by 'brutal force' and representing only a few thousand Rhodesians. By the time the next Commonwealth conference is summoned, Britain may well come under extreme pressure from her partners in the club – and not only those of the African states – to rectify injustice in a British dependency, namely Southern Rhodesia. In January 1963 the Prime Minister of a now sovereign Uganda, Milton Obote, ordered home three of his M.P.s who had gone to Salisbury for a meeting of the Commonwealth Parliamentary Association. Similarly, Dr Nyerere refuses to have official contact with Salisbury now. Anticipating the crisis that seemed likely by 1964 at the latest, a member of Mr Field's victorious Rhodesian Front, J. R. Ryan, said that his party's object was independence as soon as possible, and since it was likely that the Afro-Asian nations of the Commonwealth would object, 'it may not be possible for us to do anything but get out'.

A Conservative back-bencher, Humphry Berkeley, has warned the Tory government in a recent Central Africa debate that whereas Canada and other Commonwealth countries abstained at the United Nations in the 1962 vote on Southern Rhodesia, they were unlikely to do so again. It was up to the present British government to rectify 'this most extraordinary anomaly' created in 1923.

In blunt terms, the situation that can arise if the settlers start shooting, and Britain fails to intervene, is that the exiled Z.A.P.U.

leaders under Mr Sithole and Mr Enoch Dumbutshena will set up their government in exile and demand and get recognition from a number of Commonwealth governments. Britain's diplomacy in Africa will be effectively in ruins and the Commonwealth split beyond repair. It sounds, possibly, over-dramatic. It is, none the less, likely and possible.

After all, equally dramatic and unlikely events had already taken place in 1962. There had been the resignation of the distinguished Colonial administrator, Sir Hugh Foot, from the British team at the United Nations because he felt he could no longer defend the government's policy (or lack of it) in regard to the one specific issue of Southern Rhodesia. He stressed the point that timing and initiative were crucial in colonial issues, especially when racial differences are involved, and said there had been a point in the summer of 1962 when the Macmillan administration should have acted. Did he mean direct intervention to postpone the election (at which Whitehead was defeated) and a conference with the Africans for creating a fresh constitution ? Sir Hugh stuck to the correct protocol in these things; he would not say. But it was known he had twice made a direct appeal to Lord Home and R. A. Butler in the summer and autumn of 1962 – apparently in vain – and his resignation came directly after that. To the *Observer*, in a guarded interview afterwards, Sir Hugh referred simply to 'a terrifying prospect' in which Britain should intervene to prevent 'disaster'. In terms of purest self-interest, he said, 'our future relationship with all the countries of Africa and Asia is at stake'. His key point was that the Macmillan government had it in its power to stabilize the situation by a clear statement that it would not grant independence to Southern Rhodesia so long as it was ruled by a minority government elected on a limited franchise.

How limited this franchise still is – from the African point of view – after forty years of white rule following the Churchill–Coghlan deal of 1922, can be seen from the figures of the December 1962 election. Some 72,000 Southern Rhodesian citizens went to the polls; at most 3,000 of them were Africans. It had been claimed by Z.A.P.U. that white employers had used intimidation to force Africans to register, and the curious voting figures appeared to give some confirmation. Of some 10,632 who finally registered for the 'B' roll (despite the Z.A.P.U. call for a boycott), only 2,396 actually turned out to vote and perhaps 2,000 of them were Africans. Even so, Sir Edgar Whitehead had reason to be grateful to them. For in the 'A' roll contest for fifty seats in the new parliament, Winston Field and his right-wing Rhodesian Front had taken thirty-five to a mere fifteen for the U.F.P. The fifteen seats at stake in the 'B' roll constituencies, however, almost brought Whitehead level again with Field. They returned fourteen U.F.P. candidates (a Coloured man and thirteen Africans). The odd man out was a white South African, Dr Ahrn Palley, who had blistered the Whitehead administration during the election campaign for its draconian laws intended to repress African 'extremism'. He won the fifteenth 'B' roll seat and the doubtful distinction of becoming a focus for virulent settler abuse. As a lawyer himself, he had deplored the 'August crackdown' when the Whitehead government announced two bills amending, respectively, the Unlawful Organizations Act and the Law and Order Maintenance Act. These were supposedly non-racial measures, said Dr Palley, but under the latter act, in the first year and a half of its operation, the number of persons charged was: Africans, 1,220; Europeans, 2. As for the first of the two acts, he said, its parentage was surely dubious since it had been extracted, section after section, from the similar act already put into force by the Verwoerd government in South Africa.

Lawyers and church leaders grouped together to protest to Whitehall at the time – to no avail. George Silundika of Z.A.P.U. described the crisis as the acid test for Britain and said that if 'the slightest sincerity' remained in Whitehall then Mr Macmillan must use his legal powers to veto the measures. Sir Robert Tredgold, the former chief justice of the Federation, who had resigned in protest when the original acts were passed, declared simply: 'If anything approaching this legislation is passed into law it will remove the last vestiges of doubt about whether Southern Rhodesia is a police state. In future all political action will be conducted at the pleasure of the government of the day.'

Whitehead's amending acts, however, were passed – and without a murmur from Whitehall. Jasper Savanhu, the 'moderate' African minister who had been Sir Roy's prize exhibit for all the visitors on Voice & Vision tours, resigned his post declaring that the U.F.P. government had failed to implement partnership, that Europeans were inherently 'incapable of treating other races fairly', and that Southern Rhodesia was 'on the verge of exploding'. But for the Rhodesian Front William Harper, who was to come to ministerial office a few months later with the Field victory, called for outright apartheid and the segregation of Africans into Bantustans on the South African pattern. It was hardly reassuring, even for the most moderate African. Mr Field himself had gone on record in a speech in Bulawayo that if his party succeeded in the election he would seek to set up a defence pact and special trading agreements with South Africa and the Portuguese territories – Angola and Moçambique – so as to help keep the United Nations and all other 'outside influences' out of southern Africa.

Why did Sir Edgar act as he did ? His aim seems to have been to clear the colony of all those troublesome 'extremist' Africans which he sincerely, but wrongly, regards as 'unrepresentative'. The banning of Z.A.P.U. was part of this strategy, and so was the timing of the election for mid December, so that, with Joshua Nkomo and 126 of his principal nationalist colleagues out of the way, the U.F.P. could direct maximum pressure on to African voters. Yet the tactics, surely, were appalling. Even the London *Telegraph*, traditionally pro-settler, could hardly make the actual event sound reassuring on the day Z.A.P.U. was outlawed:

Steel-helmeted troops in battle order tonight guarded airports, radio stations, reservoirs, and power stations. Riot police are touring African townships and R.R.A.F. jet bombers and rocket-firing Vampires flying over bush where African terrorists are hiding.

Yet even these displays of force were not enough to convince the dominant white voters of Southern Rhodesia – the privileged 70,000 – that the Whitehead government was going to be 'tough enough on the Munt'. The U.F.P. was pledged to a revision of the

485

Land Apportionment Act (by its removal, and replacement with something else) but the rival Rhodesian Front of Mr Field promised to retain this bastion of white supremacy. The foretaste of this new settler line had appeared in the Salisbury *Sunday Mail* in July 1962:

A powerful . . . element wishes to see Sir Edgar Whitehead removed so that they may promote a strong-arm policy designed to retain European control. This is backed . . . by certain interests in the City of London and the House of Commons. The belief here is that a resolute minority, backed by armed force, can hold southern Africa below a line drawn from Angola to Moçambique.

Small wonder, in view of these bitter developments in the Colony, that politics in the north should also show a sharp polarization on racial lines. The *Central African Mail* of Lusaka described the voting on 30 October 1962 as 'the most racial election in our history'. The rule requiring candidates in 'National' seats to get a minimum of ten per cent of the votes of both races resulted in defeat for a white supporter of U.N.I.P., Sir Stewart Gore-Brown. For though he got nearly 12,000 African votes, only fifty-five white Rhodesians were willing to mark their ballots for him. This was Kenneth Kaunda's reward for an energetic effort to woo white support for U.N.I.P. and bridge the racial gap. Indeed, ten of the fifteen supposedly multi-racial National seats remained unfilled. The failure of U.F.P. 'partnership' was crisply shown in the grand total of African votes the party received – 180. The rest of its 22,000 votes came from white supporters.

A total of 104,000 ballots were cast and the U.F.P., with less than one fifth of these, nevertheless managed to top the poll in terms of M.P.s elected to the new parliament – a block of sixteen. Mr Kaunda's U.N.I.P., with more than sixty per cent of the votes, got only fourteen seats; but by combining with Mr Nkumbula's A.N.C., which had won seven seats, a shaky African coalition was formed and the United Federal Party was thrust into opposition.

Thus, as the Central African Federation moved into its tenth anniversary year of 1963, the ironic situation had arisen in which the U.F.P. had lost control in all three territories. The party of Lord Malvern and Sir Roy Welensky had been abandoned by all the African voters (except for two per cent in the Colony and ·6 of one per cent in N.R.) and by more than half the white voters. Sir Roy's federal administration was a rump government, lacking prestige because its 'victory' in the 1962 election had been achieved by virtue of near-total boycott by all black and white parties alike. With the long-expected announcement by R. A. Butler in December 1962 that Britain had decided to sanction the secession of Nyasaland, it was clear that the break-up of Federation was going to begin even before the nation reached its tenth birthday. On 1 February 1963 Nyasaland entered a new phase with the full internal self-government that had been negotiated in the London conference of the previous November. Dr Banda took the salute at the march-past of his ministers, escorted by the same beribboned police officers who had bundled him (in pyjamas) into the car for Chileka Airport and prison in Southern Rhodesia on the day the Emergency was declared almost exactly four years previously.

The man who had now assumed the title of Prime Minister made it clear that his country would soon take its ancestral name of Malawi. Nor would it forget its common cause with the Africans of Southern Rhodesia – 'my people' as Dr Banda referred to them. He waved his white fly-switch, a gift for Self-Government Day from Jomo Kenyatta, and the faces of the honoured guests in the stadium signified this growing sense of African solidarity: Kenneth Kaunda with his lieutenants of U.N.I.P.; Joshua Nkomo with his colleagues George Nyandoro and Robert Chikerema – these last two being the Africans with the longest prison records of all. They had been among the last six men released from Gokwe prison camp when the Field government came to power; they had been put there by Sir Edgar Whitehead and held – without *habeas corpus*, without charge, and without right of trial – for a few days less than four years. It is a disgraceful miscarriage of justice unprecedented in the history of Commonwealth law – not excepting the detentions of Gandhi, Madame Pandit, and the rest during the troubled days in India.

But for the Africans of Southern Rhodesia the release of the detainees was only a brief glimmer of light before plunging once again into political gloom. Z.A.P.U. remained an outlawed organization under the new Field régime and the tactics of the new minister of justice, Clifford Dupont, were not long in emerging. Nkomo, Nyandoro, and Chikerema were soon arrested on charges of taking part in illegal processions and lengthy legal proceedings got under way. This was to be the technique, as in South Africa: harry, harry, harry the African politicians, using all the resources of courts and police. Wear them down, financially and even physically; hobble them politically by 'tailing' them with police cars and police informers night and day. Attack their morale by churning out new legislation so that the political landscape gradually becomes one vast swamp of legalities and then watch them sink. In February 1963 Mr Field opened his first session of parliament with the announcement of still further amendments to the two notorious acts which the Whitehead government had 'tightened up' before Christmas. Thoroughly alarmed at last, the Bar Council held emergency meetings in Salisbury and Bulawayo and went to petition the justice minister, Mr Dupont. In particular they objected to the notorious Section 33A which introduced a mandatory death penalty for the throwing of petrol bombs – at people, cars, aircraft, or even uninhabited buildings. Mandatory whippings and life sentences were also included.

The Black Sash women demonstrators were still picketing the parliament building with posters such as 'Heil the Police State' when, at a later session, Mr Dupont brought in a further surprise. The Constitutional Government Bill provided penalties of up to twenty years in prison for Southern Rhodesians making statements inciting strikes or violence or publishing false news. It was specified that this included statements made outside the country, and the new legislation was clearly intended to muffle politicians like Mr Nkomo or Mr Todd and discourage them from going to lobby in London or at the United Nations. The new law also threatens to gag the Rhodesian press.

By mid 1963, then, it was evident that the bitter climax that had been so long predicted was coming into view at last. Federation had been a clever smokescreen, obscuring the battlefield for ten years, affecting none of the basic issues, and ensuring only that the eventual clash will be more bitter. In one sense the settlers had succeeded in what they set out to achieve in those Victoria Falls conferences long ago: they were able to bottle up African nationalism in the two northern territories much longer than would have been the case under straight Colonial Office rule.

And by gaining control of immigration the settlers had been able to check criticism far more effectively, and to prevent the contagious spread of the dangerous virus of liberty. It was, perhaps, predictable that Rev. Michael Scott of the Africa Bureau and Miss Rosalynde Ainslie of Ronald Segal's magazine, *Africa South*, should be expelled. The distinguished list grew with the addition of Basil Davidson, the author and Africanist, and Commander Thomas Fox Pitt of the Anti-Slavery Society who had only just retired from Colonial Office Service in Northern Rhodesia. Rhodesia's best-known novelist, Doris Lessing (*The Grass is Singing*), and Per Westberg of Sweden's leading newspaper, the Stockholm *Dagens Nyheter*, were refused re-entry. But the expulsion of a British Labour M.P., John Stonehouse, and of Rev. T. S. Colvin of the Church of Scotland mission in Nyasaland, both in 1959, were the two cases that shook the Africans. A craven Tory government in London was still working on the principle of appeasing 'our kith and kin' rather than standing up to them. 'What are you trying to do, lose me another Dominion?' asked Lord Home, when the Northern Rhodesian governor jibbed about the crushing of the African Affairs Board. In the Stonehouse affair the same governor offered the unfortunate British M.P. hospitality in Lusaka, but Sir Roy was too quick for him: Mr Stonehouse was bundled on to an aircraft and forcibly expelled; the Africans were dramatically shown who was 'boss'. After this, the disgraceful expulsion of Dr Terence Ranger, the dynamic young history don at the University College in Salisbury, seemed inevitable and duly took place in the spring of 1963. Perhaps it seemed like a brilliant diplomatic victory to R. A. Butler that he was able to make a deal behind scenes with the Field government, and get

Sir Roy's concurrence that if Dr Ranger were to apply in nine months' time he would very likely be allowed to return (though this was not guaranteed). To the Africans it was clear that the British government was still spineless in the face of settler intransigence.

Does this matter? Some students of political science regard it as crucial in seeking a way out of the present Rhodesian dilemma. In the words of Colin Leys and Cranford Pratt: 'a great deal of European intransigence in opposing African aspirations has been due to confidence that the [British] government would always give in to them'. And they conclude that a determined declaration of policy from London is a necessary preliminary to getting the settlers into the frame of mind to negotiate, rather than dig in.

But it was clear that in 1963, with the failure of the Common Market negotiations behind them and the next general election no more than a year ahead, the Macmillan Tory government was in no mood for decisive action in Central Africa. For fear of offending various interest groups within the party, a kind of political paralysis descended. It seemed unlikely to be broken until either a younger Tory team or the Opposition came to power at Westminster.

It would be expensive, certainly, and gratuitously infuriating to the Turton–Clitheroe–Biggs-Davison wing of the Conservative party, as Mr Macmillan saw it, to initiate a strong policy towards Southern Rhodesia which is, now, the heart of the problem. R. A. Butler had been put in charge of the new Central African Office in 1962 because the settlers had mastered to a fine art the technique of playing off the Colonial Secretary (in charge of the two northern territories) against the Commonwealth Secretary (the self-governing colony). In 1963 Mr Butler's task was to devise a time-consuming ballet that would stretch out to cover the months until the merciful respite of the next general election. The Africans in Nyasaland were capable of causing real physical disturbances; very well, grant them larger concessions and set a learned commission to work on the 'unscrambling' process. Potentially some chance of another sabotage wave in Northern

Rhodesia like the U.N.I.P. Master Plan that got out of hand in 1961 ? Very well; grant secession and thus concede the final stage in the process of dismantling Federation, as Mr Butler did at the London talks in March, 1963. No chance of the Africans getting out of hand in Southern Rhodesia, because of armed forces second in efficiency and firepower only to South Africa ? Very well: concede nothing, negotiate nothing, and do nothing to infuriate the settlers.

Stanley Baldwin said that 'power without responsibility' had been the privilege of the harlot through the ages. But in Southern Rhodesia, nominally a colony of Britain yet bristling with settler troops and a settler air force, we have the opposite of the Baldwin formula: responsibility without power. Britain, to carry the metaphor through logically, has been made a cuckold. The situation is shameful, slightly disgusting, and inherently unstable. African pressure, or settler pressure, is going to force the British government to act. What is going to confront a British Prime Minister at the moment of decision ?

There can be little doubt about the rich, privileged, and nervous community of some quarter of a million white people in the Colony. They will be in *laager*, to use the old Afrikaans phrase: fully prepared for last-ditch military action against any intruder, Britain included. The moves began early in 1961 when Iain Macleod at the Colonial Office began the series of conferences that would lead up to a new Northern Rhodesian constitution and African government in Lusaka – the Kaunda coalition that became reality in January 1963 and whose first act was to table a motion calling for secession from Federation.

'Give me your support,' Sir Roy demanded in the Federal parliament when the news broke. 'We will fight it out.' Carefully, he did not specify how the 'fight' would be conducted. But he had already dropped a broad hint to a Johannesburg audience, just before Christmas 1962: troops and money would save southern Africa from what he called 'evil consequences'. And he added: 'Pan-Africanism has neither budget nor army.' In another speech, largely unreported, at the end of 1962 the Federal Prime Minister had spoken about 'definite limits beyond which the white man will not be pushed'. And he asked the white voters for 'the sinews of war to fight with'.

In his policy speech at the start of the 1962 session of the Federal parliament, Sir Roy had announced the re-equipping of the Royal Rhodesian Air Force with Hunter Mark IX jet fighters and a fleet of helicopters – both excellent for 'control' of hostile ground forces, of course. Winston Field, then in Opposition, called for a final constitutional settlement with Britain 'so we can have military links with South Africa or whoever we please'. Sir Roy, in his reply, asserted that white Rhodesians were not prepared to 'run out on our very good friends and neighbours, the South Africans and Portuguese'.

That statement came in the same 1961–2 winter when the Maudling Plan for Northern Rhodesia was being hammered out in London and Sir Roy startled the British public (and the Cabinet) by arriving in fighting mood at London Airport and declaring that he would use 'force if necessary' and 'go the whole hog' – though with what, and against whom, he did not specify. In May 1962, soon after South Africa's defence minister had announced the near-doubling of his country's defence budget, Welensky announced an eleven per cent rise for Rhodesia, bringing the defence bill to a new high of £8 million. The army was being strengthened, he said, with more armoured cars, artillery, and expansion of the (all-white) parachute regiment known as the S.A.S. – Special Air Service.

In theory, at least, the Rhodesian Federal army is a formidable force. Without drawing on older reservists, it can put into the field at short notice 10,500 white soldiers, and another 4,000 Africans whose regiments are one hundred per cent white-officered. There are five active battalions and eleven (infantry and artillery) in reserve, as well as scouts in Ferret cars, the paratroopers, signals, etc. All soldiers, active and reservist, have been trained to use the semi-automatic F.N. rifle, and there are (as Sir Edgar Whitehead once told a group of us correspondents) ample supplies of this efficient weapon, greased and stored. In the air, there is the efficient R.R.A.F. with its two fighter squadrons, two Canberra bomber squadrons, transport squadron, helicopters, etc. And the settlers are taking no chances: the 200 officers and 700 airmen of the R.R.A.F. are all white.

Under a recent amendment to the Federal Defence Act all able-bodied men between eighteen and fifty-five have had to register for military service. In March 1963 these men, numbering some 50,000 in all, received 'Class X Reservists notices' assigning them, on paper at least, to 'last-ditch' units to be formed in the event of extreme emergency. It provoked some white Rhodesians, who are more interested in a political rather than military settlement with their African neighbours, to speculate on the possibility of their being pitched into some Samsonian last fling by their political masters in Salisbury.

Portuguese military officers were staying in my hotel in Salisbury during one visit to the Federation; the Federal defence minister visited Lisbon and Luanda (Angola) in 1961 and in the same year detachments from the Rhodesian Army went to South Africa and Moçambique. So far as is known, all these contacts have continued in 1962-3.

What use might the white Rhodesians make of their formidable military machine? The subject remains open to speculation, though there was a broad hint in the Tea Party plan which was drawn up by settlers in February 1961, when it began to look as if the Macleod plan of constitutional revision might too clearly hand power to the Africans of Northern Rhodesia. A year later, when the final revision of this constitution was being negotiated in London, and Welensky was there, Kenneth Kaunda held a Press conference in Lusaka and said he had received details of the Tea Party plan. He declared it had called for the arrest of the British governor, police officers, and other Colonial servants. Commenting on this, the Salisbury *Evening Standard*, an Argus paper generally supporting the U.F.P., said:

It is no longer a secret that some actions at least considered by Welensky during the 1961 crisis were anything but constitutional. If he embarks on a similar course now it is impossible to see anything but disaster emerging.

A few days after Mr Kaunda made his charges, an African who

had formerly belonged to the U.F.P. gave a Press conference in Salisbury and produced copies of a memo headed 'Appendix B to minutes of emergency congress . . . Ref. NRD/CIR/168/61'. It purported to be the report of a private conference of the United Federal Party officials, held at Broken Hill in September 1961, and was printed on the light-green paper habitually used by U.F.P. offices. According to this, the delegates were addressed by Sir Roy's law minister, Julian Greenfield, who had been a frequent federal negotiator in talks with the British government. He was quoted as saying he was 'just as bitter as anyone else' about the Macleod plan, that 'it was going to be extremely difficult to bring the British government to heel by constitutional means, and . . . he was inclined to feel that hard action by unconstitutional means will inevitably be necessary'.

I can add a few personal notes to amplify this. The Tea Party plan, as it was explained to me and three other correspondents by a senior member of the U.F.P. over luncheon in February 1961, was based on the Boston Tea Party, of course, and called for a declaration of independence, together with a pledge that Rhodesia remained loyal to the Queen and wished to remain within the Commonwealth. This was seen by Sir Roy's colleagues as the only possible defence against a threat by Iain Macleod to break the pledges given by Oliver Lyttleton and others on behalf of Britain at the 1953 London conference. (If such pledges were indeed given, in closed session under Lord Salisbury's chairmanship, they amounted to pledging that the Africans would be kept firmly in permanent political slavery; Mr Macleod may have thought the time had come to obliterate them.)

Now here, from various sources, are the preparations which were being made on the British side. The Northern Rhodesia Police, which comes under the Governor's control in Lusaka and is run by the Colonial Office, became in effect a military unit for the duration of the crisis. On a tip, on one particular night in February 1961, the Chief Commissioner posted 200 constables, fully armed, in the grounds of Government House in case the expected attempt were made that evening to seize Sir Evelyn Hone and members of the judiciary and Civil Service. The Northern Rhodesia Police intelligence uncovered strong evidence of a coherent plan for taking over the protectorate in a (perhaps bloodless) *coup*. The Federal army would block airfields with water-filled petrol drums and stand by with artillery to repel aircraft. The *Central African Mail*, edited by Richard Hall, brought out a special edition at this moment (now a collector's item) with the banner headline 'Don't Do It, Sir Roy' and a report that began: 'Today Northern Rhodesia is waiting for the sound of the engines of R.A.F. planes bringing in British troops.' And some senior officers of the Federal Army were said to be wrestling with their consciences. According to Dick Hall, one major he knows appeared at the desk of the startled Provincial Commissioner at Ndola and said, inexplicably: 'I just want you to know, sir, my first loyalty is to the Queen.'

On the British side, the Colonial Secretary, Mr Macleod, was fully alerted and had ordered the preparation (on paper) of a complete plan of counter-action. The 16th Parachute Brigade of the strategic reserve was alerted, as were the R.A.F. transport units at Lyneham in Wiltshire and the R.A.F. at Nairobi and the British Army units at the Kahawa base in Kenya. Welensky dispatched a Canberra of the R.R.A.F. to Nairobi, where it rolled innocently on to the tarmac and sat for several days. R.A.F. officers plotted the routes and navigational problems Lyneham–Lusaka, via Nairobi and via Benghazi, with refuelling arrangements, etc. And in Lusaka the Northern Rhodesia Police continued on twenty-four-hour standby for a week, until the tension was over. At the height of the crisis a reservist asked a Rhodesian Army officer what he should do if airborne British troops started arriving, and was told that he should shoot. The reservist felt obliged to pass this on to the colonial authorities in Lusaka and the officer in question was abruptly transferred to Southern Rhodesia; he has never returned.

One final footnote is necessary. In 1962 I was one of five correspondents who lunched informally with someone I suppose I must refer to simply as 'a senior minister in Salisbury'. It was not an occasion for pulling out notepads, but one thing our guest said was so astonishing – and alarming – that I slid an envelope on to my knee and scribbled the words as he spoke them. He had pointed out how well girded Southern Rhodesia is for a 'fortress' operation against any outsider – 'at Kariba the power station is on our side, the south bank' – and so on. But if it came to the crunch, Rhodesians would fight, he said: 'And that includes my Africans ... many I know and trust. I wouldn't hesitate to arm them either; we'd give them F.N. rifles like the rest of us. And we'd have our own underground in London and there's not one Cabinet Minister whose life would be safe.'

Lord Malvern put it plainly enough at a dinner in London in 1962 when he told how white Rhodesians feel:

They have no intention of meekly allowing themselves to be eliminated as a community. . . . They have at their disposal defence forces which are relatively powerful for that part of the world.

Which way can we possibly look for a solution? The London *Financial Times* has noted that 'the example of South Africa suggests that a white government, if it is prepared to be sufficiently ruthless, can impose its will on a much larger black population without undue difficulty'. And this most sober of journals goes on to make this remarkable recommendation:

The British Government's best chance of finding a tolerable solution to an extraordinarily difficult problem is to be equally intransigent.

It is a formula, indeed, as old as Shakespeare: to grasp the nettle, danger, and from it pluck the flower of peace. It is a straight choice; for a British Prime Minister might alternatively let things drift, or simply wash his hands like Pontius Pilate. In either case, three million Africans in Southern Rhodesia will pass into permanent slavery. This is not melodramatic; the *Concise Oxford Dictionary* says a slave is 'the legal property of others ... bound to absolute obedience'. That is dangerously close to a definition of the black Southern Rhodesian today.

The late leader of the Labour Party, Hugh Gaitskell, told me that it had been his plan, had he won the 1959 election, to move British troops into the two northern territories before negotiating a political *détente* with Southern Rhodesia. I wonder if the soundest step towards a solution does not require one step more. Britain has never yet solved a colonial problem without troops on the spot; that was especially true of Jamaica in 1944 and Kenya in 1960, the two most acute cases of determined white-settler resistance previously encountered.

For me, this military aspect is not peripheral in the Rhodesian problem, but integral. Far too many of the worthy books already extant – indeed, all of them – make the fatal error of saying the settlers must do this and Britain must do that, without taking a plain hard look at the heart of the problem, which is *how*. So long as there is that unbalanced military factor of 10,500 tough (white) fighting men, plus a paramilitary force like the British South Africa Police (1,500 white officers plus 17,800 white reservists and special constables, all with firearms, plus 10,000 African constables) then there is a power vacuum in an explosive part of Africa. No settler government in Salisbury *dare* surrender political power to the black majority, today or ten years from now, so long as there is no sign of a military counterweight to the Rhodesian Army and R.R.A.F. It is just not realistic to expect it. Even were a group of settler politicians to contemplate it, it seems probable that the military men themselves would then step in to prevent it.

The crux of the matter, then, is getting land and air forces into Southern Rhodesia. And for this, Britain, astonishingly, holds the political key. She still holds sovereignty over the Colony, as evidenced at the United Nations, where the British delegation conducts the Rhodesian case. Thus, Britain has the right to invite the U.N. to dispatch forces to Southern Rhodesia, if events there appear to constitute a threat to the peace. And it is possible – indeed, it might be preferable – that the British army and the R.A.F. might not be assigned to carry out the task alone. Surely those Commonwealth countries – white, Asian, and African – which profess the greatest concern about the Rhodesian problem, might wish to share this burden, of both finance and personnel?

Why this emphasis on the need for outside military intervention? Because it is the *only* instrument that will make outside political intervention practical. If done on a massive scale, as a police action, there would be no need for a shot to be fired. But let it not be supposed that reason or logic could be marshalled, instead of troops, to persuade the white Rhodesians to sit down at the conference table, because hounding the thoughts of every settler is the traumatic fear of what might happen on D-Day Plus One – the day after the Africans take over. It is a nightmare summed up in a single phrase, to be found in a pamphlet by S.A.B.R.A., the Afrikaner institute in Stellenbosch: 'There is no reason to suppose They would be any fairer to Us then We have been to Them.' In other words, the terror of a night of long knives.

We may look at two real examples: first Algeria, where it took all the weight of the De Gaulle government plus the weight of French army guns to force the settlers to yield political power. Incredibly, within a year, four-fifths of the one million *colons* had uprooted themselves and gone. And the southern states of the U.S.A., where race relations drew Lincoln into a great and bitter war. President Kennedy has been able to use a better method: troops without the shooting. Yet the affair at Oxford, Mississippi, over the admission of one Negro student to university required 3,000 men of the National Guard, a U.S. Army infantry battle-group, parts of two Airborne Divisions, and air transport squadrons of the U.S. Navy and Marines. The Defence Department later tabulated the bill at $3,850,000. And this was to deal with white settlers *without* an army of their own! It is well to remember that Rhodesia goes one stage farther even than Algeria; besides an army the settlers in Central Africa have their own air force as well, with all that this implies tactically.

After the Mississippi affair the U.S. Attorney General, Robert Kennedy, said the follow-up would be 'court actions to enforce voting rights', which he called 'the key to evolution in the South'. And, indeed, the formula for Rhodesia need be no more complex than that: a gradual extension of the franchise, with a coherent programme of training African civil servants for a state that, until two years ago, had precisely none – the formula, in fact, that Britain has used in other predominantly African states, from Sierra Leone to Kenya. And, in all those cases, Britain has held sovereign military and police power during the period of tutoring and handover.

Britain today faces the dilemma that confronted Cassio after the break with Othello: 'O my reputation – I have lost the immortal part and what remains is bestial.' So in Central Africa: the shining reputation Britain won in the post-war era, when she brought 600 million non-white people forward to nationhood, may well be stained or blotted out by a blood-bath. Only massive, calculated intervention to restore the military balance can open the way to a political settlement. The question resolves itself to a single point: to save her reputation in Rhodesia, Britain must have a Lincoln in Downing Street – or at the very least a Kennedy.

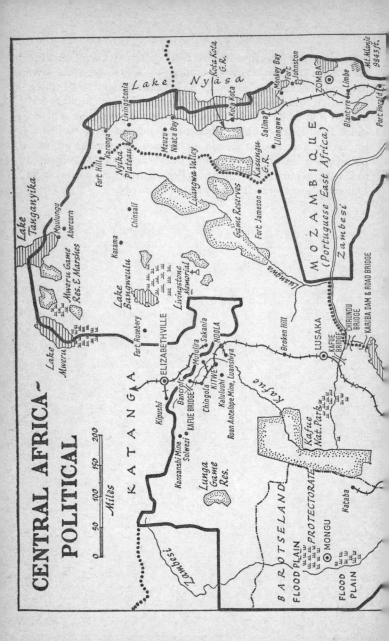

CENTRAL AFRICA—
POLITICAL

0   50   100   150   200
Miles

KATANGA

BAROTSELAND PROTECTORATE

MOZAMBIQUE
(Portuguese East Africa)

Lake Tanganyika

Lake Nyasa

Lake Mweru

Lake Bangweulu

Mpulungu
Abercorn
Mweru Game Res. E. Marshes
Fort Rosebery
Kasama
Chinsali
Fort Hill
Karonga
Nyika Plateau
Livingstonia
Mzuzu
Nkata Bay
Luangwa Valley
Kota Kota G.R.
Koca Koca
Monkey Bay
Fort Johnston
ZOMBA
Mt. Mlanje 9843 ft.
Blantyre Limbe
Port Herald
Salima
Lilongwe
Kasungu G.R.
Fort Jameson
Game Reserves
Livingstone Memorial
ELIZABETHVILLE
Kipushi
Bancroft
KAFUE BRIDGE
Chingola
Mufulira
Sakania
KITWE
NDOLA
Kalulushi
Roan Antelope Mine, Luanshya
Kansanshi Mine
Solwezi
Lunga Game Res.
Broken Hill
Kafue
LUSAKA
KAFUE BRIDGE
CHIRUNDU BRIDGE
KARIBA DAM & ROAD BRIDGE
Kafue Nat. Park
MONGU
Kataba
FLOOD PLAIN
FLOOD PLAIN
Zambesi
Luangwa
Zambesi

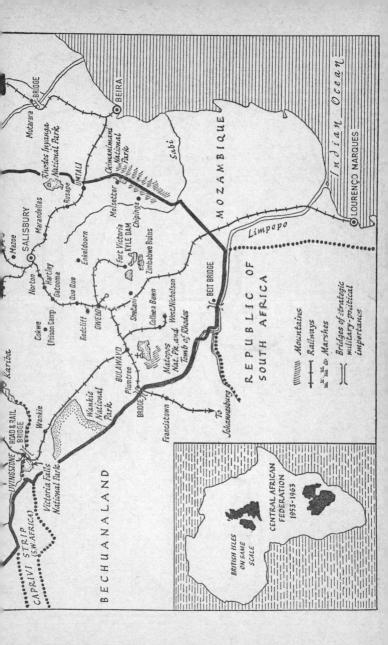

BRIDGE

● BEIRA

Mutarara

Rhodes Inyanga National Park

Indian Ocean

● LOURENÇO MARQUES

SALISBURY

Mazoe

Marandellas

Rusape

UMTALI

Melsetter

Chimanimani National Park

Chipinga

MOZAMBIQUE

Sabi

Norton

Hartley

Gatooma

Que Que

Enkeldoorn

Fort Victoria

KYLE DAM

Zimbabwe Ruins

Cokwe

Redcliff

Shabani

Collen Bawn

WestNicholson

GWELO

Limpopo

Redcliff (Prison Kamp)

Plumtree

BULAWAYO

Matopos Nat. Pk. and Tomb of Rhodes

Beit Bridge

REPUBLIC OF SOUTH AFRICA

Wankie National Park

Wankie

LIVINGSTONE ● ROAD & RAIL BRIDGE

Kariba

Victoria Falls National Park

CAPRIVI STRIP (S.W.AFRICA)

BECHUANALAND

Francistown

BRIDGE

To Johannesburg

Mountains

Railways

Marshes

Bridges of strategic military-political importance

CENTRAL AFRICAN FEDERATION 1953-1963

BRITISH ISLES ON SAME SCALE

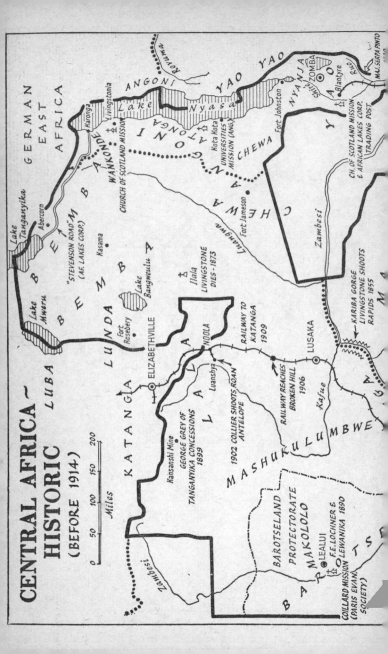

CENTRAL AFRICA ~ HISTORIC
(BEFORE 1914)

GERMAN EAST AFRICA

Ruvuma

ANGONI

YAO

YAO

NYANJA

ZOMBA

Blantyre

Lake Nyasa

Livingstonia

Karonga

CHURCH OF SCOTLAND MISSION

UNIVERSITIES MISSION (ANG.)

Kota Kota

ATONGA

Fort Johnston

CH. OF SCOTLAND MISSION & AFRICAN LAKES CORP. TRADING POST

NYA

O

ONI

WANKONDE

CHEWA

CHEWA

C

Fort Jameson

Zambesi

Lake Tanganyika

Abercorn

"STEVENSON ROAD" (AF. LAKES CORP.)

Kasama

Lake Bangweulu

Ilala LIVINGSTONE DIES - 1873

Luangwa

Lake Mweru

BEMBA

BEMBA

Fort Rosebery

LUNDA

KARIBA GORGE LIVINGSTONE SHOOTS RAPIDS 1855

LUBA

A

Zambesi

Luanshya

ELIZABETHVILLE

Kansanshi Mine

GEORGE GREY OF TANGANYIKA CONCESSIONS 1899

NDOLA

RAILWAY TO KATANGA 1909

1902 COLLIER SHOOTS ROAN ANTELOPE

RAILWAY REACHES BROKEN HILL 1906

LUSAKA

Kafue

KATANGA

L

MASHUKULUMBWE

BAROTSELAND PROTECTORATE

MAKOLOLO

B

TSE

LEALUI F.E.LOCHNER & LEWANIKA 1890

COILLARD MISSION (PARIS EVAN. SOCIETY)

MAJ. SERPA PINTO

Shire

Miles

0   50   100   150   200

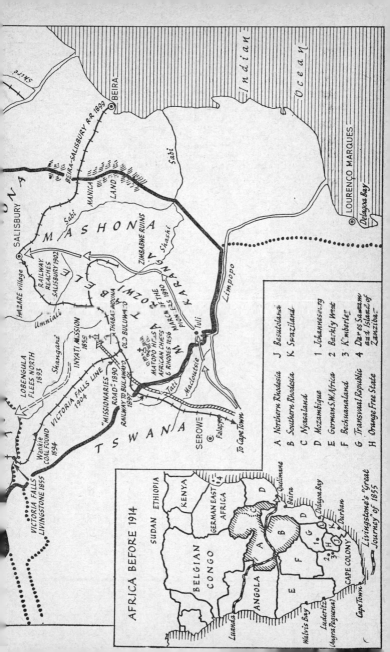

Indian Ocean

BEIRA

BEIRA–SALISBURY RR 1899

LOURENÇO MARQUES

Delagoa Bay

Sabi

MANICA LAND

Sabi

MASHONA LAND

SALISBURY

HAZARE village

RAILWAY REACHES SALISBURY 1902

Umniati

ZIMBABWE RUINS

Shashi

Shangani

INYATI MISSION 1859

THABE INDUNA

MATOPO HILLS
African Chiefs
& Rhodes 1896
OLD BULUWAYO

MARCH OF THE
PIONEERS 1890

M'ZILIKAZI

Limpopo

MANKARANGA

Tuli

LOBENGULA FLEES NORTH 1893

Wankie COAL FOUND 1894

VICTORIA FALLS LINE 1904

"MISSIONARIES ROAD" 1890

RAILWAY TO BULUWAYO 1897

Macloutsie

Shashi

Tati

VICTORIA FALLS
LIVINGSTONE 1855

TSWANA

SEROWE

Palapye

To Cape Town

A Northern Rhodesia
B Southern Rhodesia
C Nyasaland
D Mozambique
E German S.W. Africa
F Bechuanaland
G Transvaal Republic
H Orange Free State

J Basutoland
K Swaziland

1 Johannesburg
2 Barkly West
3 Kimberley
4 Dar es Salaam
   and Island of Zanzibar

AFRICA BEFORE 1914

SUDAN   ETHIOPIA

KENYA

GERMAN EAST AFRICA

4

BELGIAN CONGO

A

D Quilimane

Beira

D Delagoa Bay

B

ANGOLA

E

F

G
1
3 H K
2   J

CAPE COLONY

Durban

Luanda

Walvis Bay

Lüderitz
(Angra Pequena)

Cape Town

Livingstone's "Great
Journey" of 1855

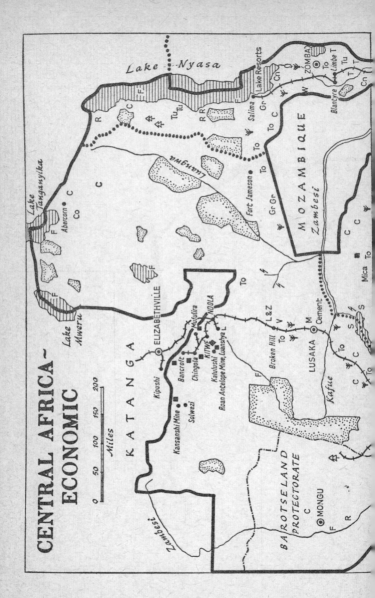

CENTRAL AFRICA—
ECONOMIC

Miles

0   50   100   150   200

Lake Nyasa

Lake Resorts

ZOMBA

Limbe T

Blantyre

MOZAMBIQUE

Zambesi

Salima

Fort Jameson

Luangwa

Lake Tanganyika

Abercorn

Lake Mweru

ELIZABETHVILLE

Mufulira

NDOLA

Mica

Cement

L & Z

KATANGA

Kipushi

Bancroft

Chingola

KITWE

Kalulushi

Roan Antelope Mine, Luanshya

Broken Hill

LUSAKA

Kafue

Kansanshi Mine

Solwezi

BAROTSELAND
PROTECTORATE

MONGU

Zambesi

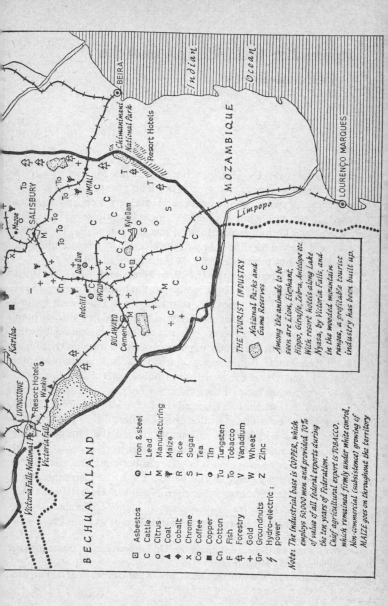

BECHUANALAND

☐ Asbestos
C Cattle
O Citrus
▲ Coal
◆ Cobalt
× Chrome
Co Coffee
■ Copper
Cn Cotton
F Fish
⚘ Forestry
+ Gold
Gr Groundnuts
∮ Hydro-electric
   power

⊙ Iron & steel
L Lead
M Manufacturing
✈ Maize
R Rice
S Sugar
T Tea
⊙ Tin
Tu Tungsten
To Tobacco
V Vanadium
W Wheat
Z Zinc

THE TOURIST INDUSTRY

▨ National Parks and
   Game Reserves

Among the animals to be
seen are Lion, Elephant,
Hippo, Giraffe, Zebra, Antelope etc.
With resort hotels along Lake
Nyasa, by Victoria Falls, and
in the wooded mountain
ranges, a profitable tourist
industry has been built up.

Note: The industrial base is COPPER, which
employs 50,000 men and provided 70%
of value of all federal exports during
the ten years of Federation.
Chief agricultural export is TOBACCO,
which remained firmly under white control.
Non-commercial (subsistence) growing of
MAIZE goes on throughout the territory

Appendix: Intimidation and the Federal Party

In August 1961 Dr Hastings Banda and his Malawi Congress Party won a sweeping victory in Nyasaland's first national general election. All twenty of the lower roll seats were won by Congress and all the opposing candidates, including those of Sir Roy Welensky's United Federal Party, lost their deposits. Dr Banda had said the voters should regard the election as a referendum on whether or not to secede from 'Welensky's Federation'.

The deputy leader of the U.F.P. in Nyasaland, Mathews Phiri (who received a total of twenty-six votes in his constituency), was one of many U.F.P. speakers who charged Malawi with 'widespread intimidation'. Election day went off quietly and without incident, the 106,000 voters evidently taking their responsibilities seriously. But in the preceding weeks of the campaign there had been frequent U.F.P. charges of arson and intimidation against Malawi, and visitors from Britain (including M.P.s) were taken to see burnt-out huts. These visitors were guests of the Federal Government, which had engaged the firm of Voice & Vision Ltd as its public relations consultants in London.

Dr Banda and Malawi repeatedly denied the charges. Four men were arrested and charged; the cases were brought to trial after the election was over. On 7 December 1961 the matter was raised at question time in the British House of Commons by a leading Conservative back-bencher, Nigel Fisher. (In the cabinet reshuffle of 1962 he was appointed junior Minister at the Colonial Office.) The report in Hansard reads as follows:

NIGEL FISHER (Surbiton) asked the Under-secretary of State for the Colonies, Mr Hugh Fraser:

Whether he is aware that members of the United Federal Party in

Nyasaland have been found guilty of conspiracy to defraud, of arson of their own houses, of fabricating charges of the arson of these houses against members of the Malawi Party, and of giving false evidence against the latter; and what action has been taken by the Nyasaland Government following these verdicts.

MR FRASER: Yes, sir. Three members of the Mbobo Branch of the U.F.P., including the chairman, Victor Chijalo, were convicted of arson and attempting to defraud by false pretences, and have been sentenced to 18 months' hard labour. One further case involving the U.F.P. is still *sub judice*.

MR FISHER: In the light of the fairly widespread charges of arson and intimidation which were made against the Malawi Party prior to the elections in Nyasaland, is it not rather scandalous that the U.F.P. supporters should themselves have committed these crimes and falsified the facts in order to discredit their political opponents ? Can my Hon. friend say that these houses are no longer included in the itinerary of the Voice & Vision tours of Hon. members ?

MR FRASER: It is not for me to comment except to see that the law takes its full and due course in Nyasaland, and this we are ensuring.

DENIS HEALEY (Leeds East): In view of the very wide publicity which was given to the falsehoods by the Voice & Vision organization, and by the Federal Government, can the Hon. gentleman say what steps Her Majesty's Government are taking, through their information officers in the Federation, to correct this false propaganda ?

MR FRASER: It is not for Her Majesty's Government to enter into matters of propaganda. It is far more effective for the facts to speak for themselves, and these facts speak outstandingly.

*

(Mr Healey, a Labour M.P., was at that time a member of the late Mr Gaitskell's shadow cabinet responsible for Commonwealth and Colonial Affairs.)

Suggestions for Further Reading

Perhaps the best service an author can render his readers, under this heading, is to suppress his own bias (as best he can) and direct them to the sources which will be of greatest practical use.

Accordingly, I am listing here some books at least with which I profoundly disagree, such as those by L. H. Gann, Richard Haw, and Nora Kane; both the timetable and the solution they propose for the Rhodesian problem seem to me impracticable. But they are valuable as expositions of the white Rhodesian point of view.

In case, like myself, you are inclined to take a ball-point pen and start marking, underlining, and annotating, I have listed the books so that author and title stand out from these notes. The really serious student of the Central African problem would be well advised to join the Institute of Race Relations in London; and thus to be able to consult its excellent library, receive the *I.R.R. News Letter*, and attend the lectures. The Rhodesian trilogy, produced by the Institute with the help of the Rockefeller Foundation and Oxford University Press, must be counted the basic reading on the subject and is listed in the section below.

A. ORIGINS

To appreciate the whole panorama of the Central African story, in terms of history, race relations, economic development, settler politics, and constitutional development up to 1960, the reader can do no better than to turn to the trilogy produced by Oxford University Press for the Institute of Race Relations:

PHILIP MASON: *The Birth of a Dilemma*
RICHARD GRAY: *The Two Nations*
PHILIP MASON: *Year of Decision*

Mr Mason, the Director of the Institute, takes the story from earliest times through to 1918 in the first volume. Dr Gray, who is now with the Institute of Commonwealth Studies in London, carries it on to the start of Federation in 1953. The third volume deals with politics and race relations in the Malvern–Welensky era through to 1960 when, according to the original plan, there should have been a final London Conference to decide the pattern for the future.

The chronic fault of all of us when trying to study any particular part of Africa is failing to see the wood for the trees. To get Rhodesia into perspective there are three standard works which will put its problems in the wider setting:

LORD HAILEY: *An African Survey* (revised 1956)

A. E. WALKER: *A History of Southern Africa* (revised 1957)

ROLAND OLIVER and J. D. FAGE: *A Short History of Africa* (1962)

The last of these (which is in the Penguin African Library) has the merit of presenting, in 280 pages, the 'continental' view of all the main events, in terms of space and time, so as to give coherence to what is all too often a patchy picture. The co-author, has written another definitive work:

ROLAND OLIVER: *Sir Harry Johnston and the Scramble for Africa* (1957)

Which deals of course mainly with Nyasaland. For an analysis of the other great political architect in Central Africa, the definitive volume is generally reckoned to be:

BASIL WILLIAMS: *Cecil Rhodes* (revised 1938)

There is also the very readable biography of Rhodes by Sarah Gertrude Millin (1933) and the Edwardian view of the great imperialist, written soon after his death by Sir Lewis Michell, who had been his financial manager and a trustee of his estate.

On Livingstone the list of books is endless; the simplest, shortest (83 pp.), and cheapest account is:

CECIL NORTHCOTT: *Livingstone in Africa* (1957)

can be picked up for half a crown at the Lutterworth Press just off Fleet Street, London EC4. The author has trekked over part of Livingstone's trails on foot and, like him, was in the service of the London Missionary Society. There is another good study by J. Simmons (1955) who is also co-author of the standard anthology of British explorers:

MARGERY PERHAM and J. SIMMONS: *African Discovery*

First came out in 1942 and is being continually reprinted.

An oddity about a nation which came into being in 1953, only to end by cracking up ten years later, was that no one in the academic field felt inclined to take on the writing of a definitive history of British Central Africa as such. Perhaps it is the swift pace of events that discourages the political scientists, or perhaps the uneasy feeling that one would be caught in the act of stalking a dodo. A British don produced in 1960 the first and, till now, only attempt to survey the history of the three territories in a single book:

A. J. HANNA: *The Story of the Rhodesias and Nyasaland*

goes into much more historical detail than I have done, but necessarily skims lightly over such things as settler psychology and current politics. Finally, another academic work which has all the attraction of a good 'whodunit' in its brilliant analysis of Victorian imperialism. These two young Cambridge dons have unearthed a mass of new clues and motivations which, to me at least, explain why the High Churchman at No. 10 Downing Street turned a blind eye while Cecil Rhodes attempted the rape of Central Africa.

ROBINSON and GALLAGHER: *Africa and the Victorians* (1961)

shows, in remorseless detail, fully documented, how the process of moral abdication began, long before the sell-out in 1953.

B. REMINISCENCE

For the reader who wants to by-pass the commentators and historians, and go direct to source, here are the twelve books I have found the clearest and most helpful. Starting with the first Rhodesian of them all:

DAVID LIVINGSTONE: *Missionary Travels* (1857)
    The Last Journals (1874)

Both are published by John Murray and can be found in most good libraries. His son-in-law, the missionary-administrator, set down his first-hand account of the early days in a book published in 1886:

JOHN MOFFAT: *The Lives of Robert and Mary Moffat*

His old friend, the French Protestant missionary in Barotseland, has given us (1897):

FRANÇOIS COILLARD: *On the Threshold of Central Africa*

Three men whose lives were, in large measure, devoted to the creation and building up of the British South Africa Company have left behind them journals which are – in all three cases – remarkable. It is the English tradition of the soldier-poet-adventurer, coming down through Raleigh and Sydney to Rupert Brooke. I suspect that Marshall Hole, Colonel Colin Harding, and Frederick Selous would, if they returned to this earth tomorrow, vote the straight U.F.P. ticket; as conservative paternalists they are Sir Roy's spiritual ancestors. Yet in their writings are the flashes of genuine poetic insight that suddenly illuminate a dimly seen Zambesia of decades ago.

H. M. HOLE: *The Making of Rhodesia* (1926)
COLIN HARDING: *Far Bugles* (1933)

F. C. SELOUS *A Hunter's Wanderings in Africa* (1811)
Sunshine and Storm in Rhodesia (1896)

Lastly, in this section, three writers who convey with real affection the flavour of pioneer days like the three above, but differ in one important respect. These are people who moved from admiration of Cecil Rhodes to a critical detachment or even outright hostility:

SIR HARRY JOHNSTON: *British Central Africa*
History of the Colonization of Africa
PETER GIBBS: *A Flag for the Matabele*
OLIVE SCHREINER: *Trooper Peter Halket of Mashonaland*

Johnston's two books are standard works, infused with the 'guardian' or trustee attitude of the Victorian Civil Servant, serving his Queen in India or Africa. The Gibbs book is a gossipy, selective account of the Rhodes–Lobengula period, as readable as a novel and digestible in one sitting. But enormously rich in atmosphere and flavour, thus conveying the 'feel' of the Pioneer Column era better than any of the academic works. Further enriched by magnificent old photos which parade the whole fantastic cast of characters – Rhodes, Lobengula and his Indunas, the traders at the royal kraal, Shippard in sun helmet and frock-coat. The Schreiner book is the celebrated novel which caused a sensation in its day, and nearly caused Rhodes to sue. It is written by one who had been an admirer of Rhodes and become his shrewdest critic. And although in the form of a novel, it undoubtedly conveys the truth as well as any history book could do.

C. RACE RELATIONS

No one can hope to comprehend the present Rhodesian dilemma without attempting to brief himself on the settler outlook. There are six books which I have found most useful. First:

E. TAWSE JOLLIE: *The Real Rhodesia*

came out in 1924. Its author not only reports the great era of settler domination at first hand, but was herself a powerful force politically in those days. In the post-war period we have another well-connected woman, an 'old Rhodesian':

NORA S. KANE: *The World's View*

She argues – forcefully – in favour of her idols: Rhodes, Coghlan, Malvern, Welensky, and others.

Less intensely partisan is

ARTHUR LEONARD: *How We Made Rhodesia*

Published in 1896, it conveys, like the first two, the origins of the settler attitude towards the African.

SUGGESTIONS FOR FURTHER READING

For cool, hard paternalism in its purest form:

RICHARD C. HAW: *No Other Home*

conveys the unyielding toughness of the white Rhodesian. Obtainable from Stuart Manning Ltd, Box 1305, Bulawayo.

More academic, and more balanced, is:

L. H. GANN: *The Birth of a Plural Society*

now obtainable only from its publishers, the Manchester University Press. The author, an Oxford scholar who emigrated to Central Africa, dedicates his book to Sir Roy Welensky. He is co-author of the Penguin book:

L. H. GANN and PETER DUIGNAN: *White Settlers in Tropical Africa*

But what of the African view? Except for Kenneth Kaunda's recent autobiography, the best sources so far are not the writings of black Rhodesians (which are scanty) but works of white authors having sympathy, empathy, or both.

BARONESS RUKAVINA: *Jungle Pathfinder*

The biography of John 'Chirupula' Stephenson, a British South Africa Company official under Rhodes and Codrington, who took two African wives during a lifetime in the Zambia bushland. Here is the tribal family life which today's African leaders half love and half reject, and which conditions so much of their thoughts and actions.

J. E. STEPHENSON: *Chirupula's Tale*

The autobiography of this same pioneer. A straight examination of race relations in southern Africa is the standard work:

W. M. MACMILLAN: *Bantu, Boer and Briton*

A much more partisan account, warm towards the black man and increasingly cold to the settler, comes from one who is of Rhodesian settler stock herself:

DORIS LESSING: *Going Home*
    The Grass is Singing

p. 489

The first book is reportage; the second, in fiction form, tellingly conveys the encompassed world of frustration which faces the black Rhodesian every day of his life (and which few white Rhodesians ever see). For a topical view in terms of anecdote and humour – yet conveying the overall bitter taste of sadness – there is a book of reminiscences by one who worked closely with Africans at Radio Lusaka:

PETER FRAENKEL: *Wayaleshi*

(The title is simply the African way of saying 'wireless'.)

My friend, Rev. Colin Morris, deals trenchantly with race relations in three books:

512

COLIN MORRIS: *Anything But This*
  Out of Africa's Crucible
  The Hour After Midnight

He arrived on the Copperbelt in the 1950s, jogged along with partnership and paternalism for a time, then broke with it, and, in the process, took part directly in Anglo-Rhodesian politics.

Three books I would recommend for dispassionate analysis of the Rhodesian dilemma:

PHILIP MASON: *Race Relations in Africa*

A twenty-four-page booklet printed by the S.C.M. Press in 1960.

EDWARD CLEGG: *Race and Politics*

The work of a scientist who went out under Colonial Office auspices for a tour of duty but kept his eyes open and took notes. It is severely practical and factual.

BERNARD SHAW: *John Bull's Other Island*

May be many years old, and concerned with quite a different colonial problem, yet the message is apt for Rhodesia today. The preface, which is the part I recommend, contains perhaps the best analysis in the language of the course of the nationalist struggle as we have since seen it in India, Cyprus, and the rest.

D. ECONOMICS

The obvious work in this field is curiously inadequate. With its 803 pages, maps, and photos, the

Handbook to the Federation of Rhodesia and Nyasaland

first published in 1960, is handled in Britain by Cassell & Co. and sells for £3 3s. It is a storehouse, but a storehouse in which the occasional room is boarded up and other bits are missing. The explanation, of course, is that the volume was prepared at Sir Roy Welenky's orders by his Federal Information division.

Report of the Urban Affairs Commission (Plewman Report)

a full survey published by the Southern Rhodesian government in 1958 as the result of a commission appointed by Todd before his political assassination. The standard work, printed in 1938 (O.U.P.) but still valid, is:

S. H. FRANKEL: *Capital Investment in Africa*

A newer work in the field is:

WILLIAM J. BARBER: *The Economy of British Central Africa*

Professor Barber contrasts the cash (white-run) economy with the subsistence (African) economy in what he sees as a dualistic society. A useful pamphlet on land apportionment as it works in practice is

KEN BROWN: *Land in Southern Rhodesia*

SUGGESTIONS FOR FURTHER READING

Obtainable from the Africa Bureau, Vauxhall Bridge Road, London SW1. The author is an agriculture specialist who went out from Britain.

SHIRLEY WILLIAMS: *The Economics of Inequality*

A pamphlet in the same series. A fuller work also severely critical of Welenskian economics as they impinge on the African, is

HAZELWOOD and HENDERSON: *Nyasaland: The Economics of Federation* (1960)

E. POLITICS TODAY

Perhaps the two most essential sources are:

The DEVLIN and MONCKTON Reports

Available as Blue Books from H.M. Stationery Offices as the *Report of the Nyasaland Commission of Inquiry* (Cmnd 814) 1959 and the *Report of the Advisory Commission on the Review of the Constitution of Rhodesia and Nyasaland* (11 October 1960).

For an overall, 'continental' view of the problem in Central Africa one might usefully dip into:

COLIN LEGUM: *Pan-Africanism* (1962)

(Ed.) *Africa: A Handbook to the Continent* (1961)

The first is invaluable for putting the history of 'Pan-Africa' into logical order, with all the relevant declarations, charters, etc. Again, to relate Rhodesian events to Africa as a whole:

RONALD SEGAL: *Political Africa* (1961)

African Profiles (1962)

Take the reader in turn through each region, with the biographical material keyed into the pattern of political developments.

African Profiles was the first volume in the Penguin African Library, of which this book is part. The reader is also directed to:

The Fourth Pafmeca Conference, 1962

A Blue Book published by the Pan-African Freedom Movement at its headquarters in Dar es Salaam; also available from the Ethiopian Foreign Office, Addis Ababa.

Five recent books combine political history with first-hand observation of the Rhodesian scene. These 'eye-witness' accounts are:

GUY CLUTTON-BROCK: *Dawn in Nyasaland*

KENNETH KAUNDA: *Zambia Shall Be Free*

MORRIS and KAUNDA: *Black Government?*

CLYDE SANGER: *Central African Emergency*

NDABANINGI SITHOLE: *African Nationalism*

Five other recent books, which might be described as academic

FORCEFUL

works in the best, most trenchant, sense, are:

T. R. M. CREIGHTON: *The Anatomy of Partnership*
THOMAS FRANCK: *Race and Nationalism*
COLIN LEYS: *European Politics in Southern Rhodesia*
LEYS and PRATT: *A New Deal in Central Africa*
PHILIP MASON: *Year of Decision*

All five books are concerned with immediate issues confronting Britain in Central Africa, and all are organized sectionally so that one can make quick reference to topics: Schools, Land, etc.

F. PERIODICALS

The serious student of the Central African problem will want to keep up with a rapidly changing situation through the broadsheets and magazines now available. First, the party publications:

SOUTHERN RHODESIA: *The Spear*
NORTHERN RHODESIA: *Voice of Zambia*
MALAWI (NYASALAND): *Malawi News*

There is no problem about the last two; one writes to Mr Kaunda's U.N.I.P. organization in Lusaka and to Dr Banda's M.C.P. office in Blantyre-Limbe. With the banning of Z.A.P.U. in the Colony in 1962, Mr Nkomo's colleague, Rev. N. Sithole, established exile headquarters in Dar es Salaam. *The Spear* is also obtainable from the Z.A.P.U. office, 131 Golders Green Road, London NW11.

Two useful magazines are:

Central African Examiner: Box 2597, Salisbury, Rhodesia.
Africa Report: Suite 505, Dupont Circle Building, Washington 6, U.S.A.

Two journals of record will provide, if filed, an exact calendar of political events in Africa, month by month, with large sections in each issue on Central Africa:

I.R.R. News Letter: Institute of Race Relations, 36 Jermyn Street, London SW1.
Africa Digest: Africa Bureau, Denison House, Vauxhall Bridge Road, London SW1.

The reader is also advised to consider getting United Nations committee papers, such as the series A /AC 109 /PV which takes one through the evidence of Kaunda, Todd, and other Rhodesian petitioners at the U.N. from March to May 1962. And three local journals in Central Africa are *Tsopano* in Blantyre, *Dissent* at the university college in Salisbury, and the *Central African Mail* in Lusaka; all of them independent and critical.

Index

517